Au Sénateur Daniel Moynihan

avec les hommages de

l'auteur

Armand de Mestral

12-12-91

EXTRATERRITORIAL APPLICATION OF EXPORT CONTROL LEGISLATION: CANADA AND THE U.S.A.

CANADIAN COUNCIL ON INTERNATIONAL LAW: RESEARCH STUDY No. 1

Extraterritorial Application of Export Control Legislation: Canada and the U.S.A.

A. L. C. de MESTRAL

Professor of Law, McGill University

and

T. GRUCHALLA-WESIERSKI

Member of the Bars of the Provinces of Quebec and Ontario

MARTINUS NIJHOFF PUBLISHERS

DORDRECHT / BOSTON / LONDON

Library of Congress Cataloging-in-Publication Data

De Mestral, Armand L. C.
Extraterritorial application of export control legislation : Canada & the U.S.A. / by A.L.C. de Mestral and T. Gruchalla-Wesierski.
p. cm.
"Commissioned by the Canadian Council on International Law"--Pref.
Includes bibliographical references.
ISBN 0-7923-0526-4 (U.S.)
1. Export controls--Canada. 2. Export controls--United States. 3. Export controls. 4. Exterritoriality. I. Gruchalla-Wesierski, T. II. Canadian Council on International Law. III. Title.
KDZ844.D4 1990
343.71'0878--dc20
[347.103878] 89-23187

ISBN 0-7923-0526-4

Published by Kluwer Academic Publishers,
P.O. Box 17, 3300 AA Dordrecht, The Netherlands

Kluwer Academic Publishers incorporates the publishing programmes of D. Reidel, Martinus Nijhoff, Dr W. Junk and MTP Press.

Sold and distributed in the U.S.A. and Canada
by Kluwer Academic Publishers,
101 Philip Drive, Norwell, MA 02061, U.S.A.

In all other countries, sold and distributed
by Kluwer Academic Publishers Group,
P.O. Box 322, 3300 AH Dordrecht, The Netherlands

Printed on acid-free paper.

Printed in the Netherlands.

CONTENTS

PREFACE

This work was originally commissioned by the Canadian Council on International Law, as part of a review of the general question of the extraterritorial application of laws. This in turn forms part of the general research project of the C.C.I.L. into the law governing international business transactions and economic relations. A second such study, dealing with the extraterritorial application of securities laws has been undertaken by the Council. Funding for the original study was provided by the Canadian Department of External Affairs. The authors wish to express their deep appreciation to the Department of External Affairs for its financial assistance, for access to departmental files and for the generous and invariably helpful attitude of many officers of that Department. In particular the authors wish to express their appreciation to Mr. Jon Fried, the officer responsible for these questions in 1984–86 whose enthusiasm, understanding of the issues and guidance were invaluable, as well as those of his successor Mr. Jim Wall who proved to be equally helpful.

Our sincere thanks are also due to the officers of the Department of External Affairs in Washington, Paris, Brussels, the Hague, Bonn, Bern and London, who were most helpful in arranging meetings with officials of the Departments of Foreign Affairs and International Trade in those capitals. We also wish to address our sincere thanks to the many officials in those capitals and in the European Economic Commission who generously gave their time and advice, as well as to Mr. Douglas Rosenthal and his colleagues in Washington D.C. Professors W.C. Graham and Jean-Gabriel Castel kindly read the manuscript and gave their comments. Thanks to grants from the Faculty of Law of McGill University Ms. Kathryn Sabo, Mr. Randall Hoffley, Ms. Susan Steffen and Mlle Suzanne Mercure provided invaluable assistance in the final stages of preparation of the manuscript.

The authors wish to thank Ms. Helen Hamilton for having typed the complete final version of the manuscript. Our sincere thanks are also extended to Mr. Alan Stephens and his staff of Kluwer Academic Publishers B.V. for their help and encouragement.

At the inception of the original C.C.I.L. research project only one of the authors, A.L.C. de Mestral, had been committed to undertake the study. When funding became available later, a number of prior commitments would have made it impossible to undertake this study alone. The authors therefore assume joint and several responsibility for whatever measure of blame or praise they merit for this study. The original study was completed in 1988 and presented to the C.C.I.L. in that year. During the course of putting the original study into book form, every attempt was made to bring it up to date to 1989. The material concerning the policies of Western European Governments was prepared in 1987.

A.L.C. de Mestral
McGill University, June 1989

ACKNOWLEDGEMENTS

A number of documents drawn from the archives of the Canadian Department of External Affairs are reproduced with the permission of that Department.

Restatement of the Law Third, The Foreign Relations Law of the United States, § 403. Copyright 1987 by the American Law Institute. Reprinted with the permission of the American Law Institute.

CHAPTER I

INTRODUCTION

A. Focus of the Book

Principles of international law seldom become in themselves the focus of a major foreign policy debate. One exception is the question of the legality of the extraterritorial application of export controls. The problem is not a new one. It has existed in one form or another since the Second World War, but few diplomats, except perhaps those of Canada, were prepared for the debate provoked in 1982 by the U.S. extension of its export controls to products manufactured abroad under U.S. license and destined for the Euro-Siberian Gas Pipeline. The U.S. measures put a long-standing but largely latent disagreement on a legal principle into very sharp focus and provoked a political crisis among close allies. The process of renewal of the *Export Administration Act* in the United States kept the issue very much alive from 1983 to 1985. Since 1985 criticism, some change of heart within the U.S. Administration as to the utility of export controls and the introduction of a number of legislative and regulatory compromises have helped to diffuse the issue.

However, if the debate has died down, it has yet to go away. The bilateral and multilateral dialogue has been vigorous, much has been said, actions have met their responses and many expressions of principle have been made. We appear in the latter part of this decade to be moving towards a new *modus vivendi* with a greater awareness of concerns, susceptibilities and perhaps limits, within a wide spectrum of debate. But as yet it cannot be said that the international community has reached a consensus on limits to state action, still less agreement on a binding rule of international law. The publication of the *Restatement of Law, Third, Foreign Relations Law of the United States*[1] in 1987 by the American Law Institute has made an innovative and significant contribution to the development of the law governing jurisdiction. However, it is as yet unclear that this Third Restatement reflects a consensus in the United States. It does not reflect an international consensus.

This book has been prepared with a view to contributing to the process of agreement upon a rule of international law. The general focus is upon the phenomenon of the extraterritorial application of laws. This phenomenon provides the fundamental issues of law and policy which are discussed. The specific focus is narrower. It is restricted to the extraterritorial application of export controls. The restriction of the focus allows for a more detailed examination of the legal and factual issues involved and an assessment of the legitimacy of the justifications which are offered for the extraterritorial extension of export controls in a wide variety of factual contexts. But in the final analysis the issues discussed in this book cannot be divorced from the broader context. It is hard if not impossible to discuss the extraterritorial application of export controls in abstraction from the similar debate taking place with respect to competition law, securities regulation and bankruptcy law, to name but three.

This Introduction is designed to block out and clarify the issues raised in the succeeding chapters of this book. The answers to many of the questions raised here should be found in the review of state practice, which is the essence of the study. The views of the authors and a number of proposals for the clarification of the applicable rules of international law are to be found in a final chapter entitled Conclusions and Solutions.

B. Purpose of the Book

The fundamental purpose of this book is to review the uniquely interesting and complex state practice of Canada and the U.S. with respect to the extraterritorial application of export controls. Of necessity the emphasis is upon Canada, given that the authors were able to review the relevant files of the Department of External Affairs in Ottawa. But, by a review of U.S. state practice and an exposition of official views of a number of European Governments, an attempt has been made to ground Canadian practice in the broader context in order to make an informed assessment of the validity of the Canadian position.

Given the very disparate views, between the U.S. and other countries on a number of fundamental issues, and to a lesser extent, the disparity of views between many of these other countries on a variety of issues, state practice, in the form of legislative and administrative action and the expression of official views as to the law, seems to provide the soundest basis for the determination of the applicable rules of international law. A fundamental concern, with respect at least to Canada and the U.S., is an assessment of the coherence of their respective practice in relation to the rules of public international law which they consider to be applicable, as well as a classification of these rules.

Finally, the information in this study is designed to allow the reader to make an assessment of the impact of the extension of U.S. export controls upon Canadian sovereignty.

C. Research Method

The primary method of study has been to review the relevant files of the Department of External Affairs. Through this method it has been possible to build up the historical record of Canadian actions and views with respect to the extraterritorial application of U.S. export controls. The basic approach is thus historical. Given that no such access was available to U.S. government files, the U.S. position has been viewed partly through a Canadian prism. Every attempt has been made to rectify this by interviewing U.S. officials in four departments, and by reviewing the published legislative and regulatory record as well as the abundant legal literature available in the U.S. Study of the Canadian record was also completed by interviewing the officials of the Department of External Affairs, including those responsible for the administration of the *Export and Import Permits Act*. The Canadian legislative and regulatory record has been fully reviewed as well as the legal literature in Canada.

The assessment of the position of the E.C. and the Governments of France, the Federal Republic of Germany, the Netherlands, Belgium and Switzerland is based essentially upon interviews with the officials and information supplied by them subsequently. Some attempt has been made to assess European writing on the subject, but this could not be as complete as that pertaining to the U.S. for reasons of time and partly of language.

One very serious issue affecting all the countries considered is that of the legitimacy of characterising export controls as a matter of private rather than public international law. This arises in a general context with respect to export controls and most particularly with respect to submission clauses required by U.S. export authorities in private export contracts between U.S. exporters and foreign importers. These submission clauses require the foreign party to agree to be bound by existing and future U.S. export control laws and orders from U.S. export control authorities concerning future disposition of the goods.

Another issue with many private law aspects and analogues is the implication to be found in U.S. laws that goods can remain subject to the laws of their country of origin or of the country under whose license they are manufactured abroad – a form of nationality of moveable property.

These questions are touched upon in this study but a complete examination of all private law issues would require detailed consideration of many questions of private international law for which there was unfortunately neither space nor time.

D. Analytical Difficulties

Few questions of international law are more complex than those posed by extraterritoriality. This is compounded with respect to export controls where the uncertainty of determining the applicable rules and principles of international law is complicated by the wide variety of factual situations which must be considered.

The factual issues have a profound impact upon the justification for varying forms of extraterritorial extension of laws. The justifications which can be advanced for arms controls may be different when an economic embargo is proclaimed, or may raise different issues from widely traded civilian commodities; arguably some technologies raise matters of national security, while others are less strategic. Extraterritorial export controls which are instituted for reasons of foreign policy arguably must be justified in terms different from matters going to military and economic security, if they can be justified at all. Extraterritorial controls of "know-how" raise issues different from the rest. Each of the methods of extension of laws via nationals, companies, subsidiaries, controlled corporations, contracts, the threat of sanctions in the home market, or the requirement for persons to provide information or to submit to inspection abroad raises other issues.

The law raises equally complex problems. The ambiguity begins with the first and only great general case on point, the *Lotus*[2] case, where a 7–7 split among the judges of the P.C.I.J. was broken by the vote of the President of the Court. The decision and dissenting opinions are open to a variety of interpretations. To some states and commentators everything turns upon the basic distinction between prescription and enforcement, the former justifying rule-making but the latter absolutely precluding extraterritorial enforcement which does not enjoy prior agreement of the states affected. But the differences are even more fundamental – with some states and commentators beginning from the premise that in international law all forms of legislative and executive action are permitted which are not expressly prohibited, while most of the others start from the opposite premise that no extraterritorial extension of laws is justified unless specifically permitted. This second view is buttressed by the argument, adopted by a number of states and commentators, that the fundamental legal premise with respect to extraterritoriality is that of a state's control of its territory. Still others insist in the same vein that one must take into account such principles as the duty of non-intervention or the abuse of rights.

Many states and commentators consider the degree of prior bilateral or multilateral agreement between states to be fundamental to the justification of any form of extraterritorial extension of export controls.

Two other factors complicate the analysis of relevant questions of fact and law. The first is the problem of secrecy which inevitably shrouds decision-making in an area widely viewed as one of national security. Secrecy and the reflex of invoking national security to justify decisions are inimical to the emergence of genuine rules. The justification of national security is too easy and fails to provide sufficient grounding to base a solid rule. The result is often intellectual confusion. How does one determine the relevant factors if they are kept from scrutiny?

A second major problem is that of determining whether, as is often alleged, the real dispute with respect to the extraterritorial extension of export controls is not one of legal principle but one of commercial interest. At worst this implies sordid and immoral standards, a willingness to do anything to make money. At best this invokes the debate between those who view security as best protected by a full and open trading relationship where all parties have too much to lose by interruption, and those who maintain that in an imperfect world some types of weapons and related technologies must be kept from the hands of real or potential enemies.

The strands of argument can therefore be seen as either infinitely complex or radically simple, depending upon one's major premise or upon the factual context with which one has to deal.

E. Significance of the Historical Record

A major premise of this study is the importance of the historical record. Given the great divergence of views on the fundamental legal rules and principles applicable, the record displayed by state practice appears to be even more important in this field than in many other areas of international law where the degree of agreement and codification of rules is greater. If there is a rule of international law here, it is to be found in customary law where the historical record is of critical importance.

Export controls are nothing new in history. They have existed since the Middle Ages when Kings and Guilds sought to prohibit the export of raw materials necessary for manufacturing processes, or the age of mercantilism, where economic philosophy implied the need to restrict the flow of international trade, to the present day when governments seek to protect military or economic security, to make foreign policy or to reinforce certain regulatory regimes by means of export controls. Today, export controls are the counterpart of the liberalization and expansion of international trade – the exception that inevitably follows the rule.

The extraterritorial application of export controls, whether by prescription or enforcement, in the eyes of many states and commentators does not partake of the same degree of inevitability as do the controls themselves. Controversy surrounds the wisdom of imposing export controls wherever they exist; the controversy is heightened by their extraterritorial extension. The historical record does reveal however that most states have had recourse to some form of extraterritorial extension in different contexts and for different purposes. The First and Second World Wars witnessed export controls with extraterritorial impact. The economic sanctions against Italy adopted by the League of Nations were given a measure of extraterritorial reach by certain states. The oldest example of extraterritoriality is probably the jurisdiction to repress piracy according to the law of nations; the most complex example is penal law in civilian jurisdictions. Other examples can be cited such as citizenship and immigration legislation, offences against currency legislation and in recent years drug smuggling, money laundering, bribery, attacks against aircraft and diplomats and other forms of terrorism. Finally, human rights violations have given rise to the adoption of laws having extraterritorial reach.

The Cold War provided the impetus for the U.S. not only to maintain many wartime export controls but also to give them extraterritorial effect. All the states closely associated with the U.S. have maintained export controls since that time, either through the CoCom forum or through parallel action for those who did not participate in CoCom. To deal with the problem of diversion from third countries Cocom and related states developed a complex system of documentation designed to allow regulation of imported commodities subject to the CoCom controls. This did not satisfy the U.S. which, in addition to CoCom controls of which it is the prime but not sole protagonist, has maintained an increasingly complex network of extraterritorial controls, applicable to CoCom and non-Cocom states alike. These extraterritorial controls, as well as the coverage of export controls and the vigour of their enforcement, were greatly expanded during the first term of the Reagan Presidency. The second term saw some scaling down of the process, but no retreat on matters of principle.

Other export controls have been adopted internationally since 1945 in relation to nuclear energy through the International Atomic Energy Agency and the *Nuclear Non-Proliferation Treaty*. But again, with the exception of the U.S., few states have given these controls extraterritorial reach. Finally, there have been a number of occasions when boycotts and trade sanctions have been implemented unilaterally, regionally and multilaterally in the wake of action, regimes or policies, against which states wished to express their disapproval. In these circumstances, particularly following the imposition of mandatory sanctions by the Security Council of the U.N. or the emergence of a broad international consensus, some states have been prepared to give extraterritorial reach to particular measures.

The existence of a multilateral process in the CoCom has done much to alleviate potential friction between the U.S. and its allies. However this has not stopped serious differences of opinion on the status of products once exported and incorporated into a new product, or used as spare parts. Nor has it completely alleviated tensions with respect to the most appropriate means of enforcement of export controls and verification of compliance.

The bulk of this book is devoted to analysis of the historical record between Canada and the U.S. In the final chapter an attempt is made to draw certain conclusions as to the legal implications of this record.

F. Why Exercise Extraterritorial Jurisdiction?

Export controls are designed to keep a military or commercial advantage or more generally to further particular domestic or foreign policies. Why are they applied by some states beyond their territory? The basic answer appears to be efficiency. With the internationalization of communications, transportation and commercial relationships, much happens abroad which has an impact within national territory. Unscrupulous persons seeking to violate domestic export controls can certainly exploit this situation and once they have goods out of the country of origin the opportunities to divert them to a destination, other than that allowed in the export permit, are certainly increased. The fear of re-export to unauthorised destinations, the knowledge that there are always individuals of countries interested in military or commercial secrets and willing to pay handsomely for them constitutes a strong incentive to resort to extraterritorial measures.

One can argue the pros and cons of the efficacy of such measures, but the fact that the mandatory sanctions against Rhodesia had extraterritorial reach and that even states strongly opposed to extraterritoriality have recourse to such techniques in times of war or extreme emergencies attests to a perception of their utility at least for powerful states.

One can also ask why in this case all states do not give extraterritorial reach to their export controls and why the U.S. tends to be the odd man out in most cases. The answer here is complex, depending on a range of factors, including the legal and regulatory culture of the U.S. In the final analysis the answer must lie in the intensity with which the regulatory policy is pursued and a vision of the U.S. as leader of the non-communist world. Other reasons are the dissatisfaction with the results reached by multilateral consultation through CoCom, uncertainty as to the efficacy of enforcement by CoCom allies and a perception that the world outside the U.S. is a very "leaky ship".

G. Techniques of Extraterritorial Extension of Export Controls

A variety of techniques is adopted to apply export controls to individuals, companies or goods abroad. One major issue which must be addressed is whether some techniques are legitimate while others are not, or whether there is a hierarchy of techniques, some of which clearly violate international law and others of which can be justified? If nothing else it is clear that certain techniques are cited by the advocates of extraterritoriality as reflecting categories of jurisdiction.

The principal forms of extraterritorial jurisdiction in respect of export controls are those applying to:

a) nationals and permanent residents;
b) corporate nationals on the basis of incorporation or business done in the jurisdiction;
c) subsidiaries of corporate nationals incorporated abroad;
d) foreign but controlled corporations doing business abroad;
e) companies producing goods abroad pursuant to a licensing agreement;
f) goods produced abroad pursuant to (e);
g) goods exported from the jurisdiction;
h) "know-how" and other forms of knowledge leaving the jurisdiction;
i) contracts for the export of goods from the jurisdiction in which commitments are made by the parties with respect to the disposition of the goods or "know-how" subsequent to their export;
j) certain forms of verification of performance of export licensing commitments to be made by officials of the exporting state abroad.

Some commentators consider that the mere threat of drastic sanctions within the U.S. against those who violate U.S. export permits abroad constitutes a form of extraterritoriality even if the sanctions are applied wholly within the U.S. This goes to the problem of defining extraterritoriality raised above.

Controls are aimed at persons, companies, goods and "know-how", transactions, especially financial transactions and other categories of services.

One issue which this study highlights is that not all extraterritorial extensions employ the same range of techniques. Whether these variations reveal different regulatory purposes and judgments as to the most effective measures in particular contexts, or whether they are based upon a judgment as to what is permissible under international law in any given context, is virtually impossible to determine. What is revealed by the study is that the most draconian measures are reserved for areas where the regulatory policy is the most intense, such as arms control. There also appear to be cases, such as the U.S. Nicaragua Regulations of 1985, where the U.S. refrained from adopting many extraterritorial techniques used elsewhere, due to the knowledge that its closest allies did not approve and would not support the actions adopted against Nicaragua. Another explanation is that certain techniques are preferred by different departments of the U.S. government charged with adopting and administering their respective regulations.

H. Justifications Given for Extraterritorial Export Controls

It is not always easy to separate the analysis of purposes and the justifications given for certain extraterritorial export controls, given that some purposes such as the protection of national security are seen as justifications in themselves. This study attempts to set out the justifications which have been given for the different forms of extraterritoriality. The basic issue here is to determine whether the justifications increase in legal value as the intensity of the governmental interest which they seek to protect increases. To give an example, does the protection of the security and the vital interests of the state justify certain forms of extraterritorial jurisdiction where questions of economic interest or foreign policy would not?

A range of justifications are given. They include:

a) The pursuit of internationally agreed policies of a humanitarian character such as the prevention of genocide and apartheid; the repression of certain universally condemned crimes such as piracy, and today reaching as far as the proscription of different forms of terrorism;
b) the pursuit of a war;
c) the protection of vital state secrets, national security and military technology;
d) the pursuit of a global cold war;
e) the protection of long-term economic security including the prohibition of industrial espionage and the retention of leading technologies and "know-how" from hostile powers;
f) effects of violations of export controls upon security and the economy;
g) other economic objectives including short supply controls, agricultural stabilisation, and domestic processing (although these seldom are covered by extraterritorial measures);
h) foreign policy objectives including the pursuit of trade embargoes against countries taking measures at home or abroad hostile to the acting state or failing to meet internationally defined standards of conduct; and
i) the characterisation of certain measures as matters of private rather public law.

How are such justifications to be measured with respect to export controls? The general arguments and categories justifying extraterritorial measures, and the fundamental disagreement between the U.S. and its allies on this topic, have already been reviewed and are clearly illustrated in different sections of this study. Analysis must clearly begin with these issues. The difference between prescription and enforcement or the importance of prior bilateral or multilateral agreement remains fundamental. It is not clear that the categories of nationality (with respect to individuals, corporations and goods) apply in quite the same fashion as they do with respect to competition policy or securities regulation. Can the various manifestations of the effects doctrine be invoked with respect to export controls as they are asserted in the context of criminal law or economic regulation? Is the dominant principle here that of protection of vital interests or territory?

These questions cannot be answered without an analysis of the factual situations to which extraterritorial export controls apply. Arguably the export of certain commodities or their export to hostile powers raise issues of national security far greater than those posed by the violation of securities or competition law. But is this true of all commodities which a state chooses to control? Does the argument not finally turn upon the significance of individual commodities, making their legal significance turn upon their value to national security? If this is so, there is arguably a gradation of justifications according to the nature of the commodities involved.

The U.S. Government maintains that the fundamental rule of international law applicable to the extraterritorial extension of export controls is that of the freedom of a state to act, in the absence of specific prohibitions. The other major argument of U.S. commentators in favour of the extraterritorial extension of export controls is based upon their congruence with a number of categories used to justify extraterritorial jurisdiction (protective principle, nationality, active and passive personality, effects within the territory, etc.). Perhaps the fundamental question to be resolved by this study is whether the record of state practice justifies either of these positions, or whether some more specific justification at international law must be provided in respect of export controls.

I. Assessment of the Canadian Record in Light of the Rules of Public International Law

A major purpose of this book is to allow the reader to assess the record of Canada's position on the extraterritorial extension of export controls. It is hoped that the information on Canadian state practice will allow an assessment of Canada's position and an opportunity to compare the stated position with the record of practice.

The Canadian economy is integrated with that of the U.S. to a degree equalled only by that of Belgium or The Netherlands within the European Economic Community. This integration has occurred almost naturally over a long period of time rather than as the result of a treaty. The *Canada-U.S. Free Trade Agreement*, which entered into force on January 1, 1989,[3] is designed to build upon and consolidate the high degree of integration of the two economies. It has produced a situation for Canada and the U.S. which involves great mutual benefit but which is not without its costs and tensions. An evaluation of the economic costs is beyond the scope of this study, but no review of the issues would be complete without an attempt to determine the impact of this situation upon Canadian sovereignty. The issues are starkly put by the extraterritorial extension of export controls. If Europe was surprised by the U.S. Euro-Siberian Pipeline measures in 1982, Canada was not. Diplomatic incidents concerning the extraterritorial extension of U.S. export controls began for Canada in the 1950s and have recurred regularly.

Since the 1950s Canada has on the one hand had to manage a fruitful and ever more complex economic relationship with the U.S., while on the other hand keeping a watchful eye open to protect its sovereignty. Canada has been on the front line of the extraterritorial extension of U.S. export controls and has thus had to defend itself more often and more strongly than any other state. But the defence of principle must be done in a way which does not jeopardise a fundamental economic and political relationship or upset a myriad of private commercial relations across the Canada-U.S. border. The defence of sovereignty must aim at the essentials, it cannot be undertaken in a manner which makes it a daily irritant between two friendly governments and their peoples. In short, the issue becomes a very pragmatic one of where to draw the line. What cooperation is acceptable, what incursions are tolerable? How does one justify the demands of a powerful and sometimes difficult neighbour, how does one retain its trust while still ensuring its respect? This has been a crucial problem for Canada, nowhere better reflected than by the extraterritorial extension of export controls.

Canada has not been alone. All the officials interviewed in Europe have had to make similar assessments of their own national interests and have adopted positions designed to protect them.

The Canadian response to the extraterritorial application of U.S. export controls as it is related in succeeding chapters of this book involves responses to major public incidents at the highest levels of government, monitoring U.S. policy, legislation and administrative action since the inception of export controls. In recent years it has involved not only responses to specific acts affecting Canada (at the public and private levels), but representations to various arms of the U.S. government on points of principle. In recent years it has even been deemed necessary in the Bureau of Legal Affairs of the Department of External Affairs to have a legal officer devote all of his time to the issue of extraterritoriality. At the same time there has been close cooperation with the U.S. and the CoCom participants to maintain a workable and effective system of multilateral controls designed to prohibit illegal diversion of strategic goods. Beyond this, there has always been close bilateral cooperation at the level of export control officials in both countries. Finally, since 1963, Canada has incorporated into its Commodity Control List a catch-all provision, requiring an export permit for the re-export from Canada of U.S. origin goods – not only those agreed by CoCom but all goods coming from the U.S. The continuity and coherence of the Canadian position is thus a major concern of this study.

Apart from monitoring the Canadian position vis-à-vis the U.S. by diplomatic contacts, protests at the working official level, as well as other public statements, such as Parliamentary declarations, Canada has also taken part in a variety of international discussions on the extraterritorial extension of laws in general and export controls in particular. Of necessity some of these discussions have taken place in secret, but where it is possible the study seeks to describe and analyse the international debate and assess whatever rules may be emerging as part of the corpus of public international law.

The final chapter contains an assessment of the Canada-U.S. experience and attempts to draw lessons from this state practice as to the rules of public international law governing the extraterritorial application of export controls. The chapter also contains a number of suggestions for the pursuit of the effort to clarify international rules in this field.

Notes

1. *Restatement of the Law, Third, Foreign Relations Law of the United States*, (St-Paul Minn: American Law Institute, 1987). In 1987 the International Law Association formed a Committee on the Extraterritorial Extension of Laws. The first major area of study of this committee is the extraterritorial extension of export control legislation. A report by this committee is expected in 1990.
2. "The Case of the S.S. Lotus" (*France* v. *Turkey*), (1927) P.C.I.J. Ser. A., No 10.
3. *Canada-United States Free Trade Agreement Implementation Act*, S.C. 1988, c. 65, Schedule – Part A, Vol. 11, no 13A, Can. Gaz. Pt III 2110.

CHAPTER II

GENERAL RULES OF PUBLIC INTERNATIONAL LAW

A. General Rules or Principles of International Law that Permit or Limit Export Controls with Extraterritorial Effect

1. Introduction

What rules of public international law speak to the extraterritorial application of export controls? The answer to this question is at once simple and complex. Simple because a ready answer is at hand in the form of the rules governing the jurisdiction of states over persons and property and events within their territory. Complex, because this answer is subject to a host of qualifications reflecting legal exceptions, a few generally accepted rules as to universal jurisdiction, the context within which the question must be answered, variations in national legal culture, differing views as to the source of authority under international law, and because at least one major world power does not accept the simple answer and acts upon other assumptions.

This book attempts to contribute to the definition of the appropriate rules by a sustained analysis of the practice of Canada which is so intertwined with that of the United States that an analysis of the practice of the latter is also necessary. The bulk of this work is taken up by the description and analysis of this practice. The final chapter attempts to draw conclusions from this practice.

In this chapter the authors seek to place the definition of appropriate rules of international law governing the extraterritorial application of export control legislation in their broader context. This chapter does not seek to restate yet again all the arguments made by public international lawyers, by governments and their legal advisors concerning the existence or non-existence of applicable rules in this area, but simply seeks to point out those elements of a very extensive debate which are most closely directed to the problems posed by export controls.

A number of general observations can be made by way of introduction to this chapter.

In the first place it is clear that there is a body of public international law which speaks to the issue of the extraterritorial application of laws. However, the detail of these rules is profoundly influenced by the basic assumptions which are made as to the source of obligation in international law. At extreme poles are the following views of international law. If public international law is seen as the creation of states and is deemed to be dependent upon their prior consent for its very existence, only those limitations which have been agreed upon in advance can restrict the capacity of states to extend the reach of their laws beyond national boundaries. On the other hand, if international law is deemed to exist independently of the will of individual states and is deemed to shape and to define the international community, then it is much easier to posit the existence of international rules which place restraints upon state action in this area and which determine the state having jurisdiction in the face of conflicting claims. These two examples are given to illustrate the point that the rules governing extraterritoriality are uniquely dependent upon the view adopted as to the nature of international law itself. It is acknowledged that many other views fall within these two poles.

In the second place it is clear that the rules developed to govern the extraterritorial extension of laws in other contexts such as competition law, securities regulation, criminal law and bankruptcy are relevant to the definition of rules respecting export controls. However, while cross-fertilisation is always valuable, wholesale transposition is extremely hazardous. A number of special factors are present with export controls which are not necessarily as significant when other branches of the law are considered. In particular, national security is often the paramount consideration with respect to export controls. States are prepared to take measures to protect their security which they might not envisage in other contexts. The survival and protection of the integrity of a state is a value recognized by international law and states are allowed considerable latitude in determining the measures which they can adopt. Context is therefore of considerable importance in attempting to define the appropriate rule.

A third general consideration which runs through analysis of extraterritoriality questions is that which may be termed legal culture. Attitudes and traditions relating to law differ considerably from one country to another even with the western European family of legal systems. The common law and the civil law differ greatly on a number of important issues. The Scandinavian approach often differs from both. Even within the same legal system there exist major differences: one need only contemplate the English and the American common law or the French or German civil law traditions to understand this fact. This can lead to very different attitudes in the field of jurisdiction to such questions as jurisdiction over criminal matters, the application of domestic law to nationals abroad and more generally to the legitimacy of submitting persons to a variety of laws at the same time. A related question is that of differing attitudes to the allegiance which physical and moral persons owe to their state of origin.

A further general consideration is that of the need to develop legal rules for a highly interdependent world. Modern systems of transportation and communications make it increasingly easy to move physical and immaterial property across boundaries: the international commercial community works in a global context which makes it exceedingly difficult for individual states to control events solely in function of their own boundaries. There is an almost inevitable tendency to seek to reach out to control certain types of events. No change in this situation is in sight; indeed it is almost certain that the phenomenon will become more pronounced. Does this justify all extraterritorial extensions of law? This is the central policy issue. Some argue that it must in the final analysis do so. Others suggest that interdependence cuts exactly the other way. Instead of concluding that interdependence inevitably must lead to a greater degree of unilateral extensions of domestic law, they suggest that interdependence forces states to be even more diligent in the search for principled solutions based on internationally agreed rules or upon customary international law.

Attitudes towards commercial relations also profoundly influence this debate. It is possible to view international commercial relations as an extension of state power and of foreign relations. In such a view commercial interests must inevitably be subordinated to the political interests of the state. This view is particularly evident in time of war or grave emergency. There is another view of commercial relations however. It is possible to view international commercial relations as the prime motor of peaceful relations between states and peoples. Modern international economic theory is posited on the premise that trade will increase the welfare of all. States which trade peacefully together are much less apt to go to war against each other and are much more likely to resolve their differences by peaceful means. Unilateral extensions of domestic law, especially with respect to export controls, have usually been associated in the latter part of the Twentieth Century with the maintenance of the Cold War or the imposition of embargoes and other trade restrictions.

Is the debate over the propriety of the extraterritorial application of export controls a debate over law or commercial policy? It is often suggested that the objections raised to extraterritorial export controls have little or nothing to do with law or sovereignty and much to do with a desire to trade and scepticism as to the effectiveness of embargoes and trade restrictions. In response, it is pointed out that the principal proponent of extraterritorial export controls, the United States, has voiced strong objections to the extraterritorial aspects of the Arab boycotts of Israel. In the final analysis, this debate cannot resolve the question. Any attempt to unravel the strands of law and policy is doomed to failure – the two are so closely interrelated. States do have firm views as to the limits of their sovereign powers under international law and as to the wisdom of extraterritorial export controls based on an expansive view of economic security or foreign policy considerations. But the views of states on these two issues do not always coincide, and the practice of states often involves exceptions to their general approach on questions of law and policy, thus making generalization on this matter extremely difficult.

A final general consideration is that of the role of advocacy. Since 1927, when the issue of the extraterritorial extension of laws was first considered by an international tribunal in the *Case of the "S.S. Lotus"*, governments and their legal advisers have been seeking to formulate rules in this area. The number of contentious disputes has often forced advocacy to creative heights. Categories of legal analysis have been proposed to assist in the resolution of a particular dispute and then subsequently invoked as rules of jurisdiction. Whether jurisdiction to prescribe, to enforce or to adjudicate constitute fundamental categories of law is posited by some and denied by others. Territory, nationality, effects, passive or active personality are held by some to be separate or coordinate bases of jurisdiction. Others suggest that most of these categories are merely a means of defining a state interest but that state interest alone cannot found jurisdiction at international law. Given the obvious inability of states to agree on general principles, as witnessed by the fact that such a topic is far too contentious to be submitted to the International Law Commission of the United Nations for codification, great scope remains for creative advocacy. As a result, students of extraterritoriality have to be especially careful to delineate rules and arguments, unless they are prepared to espouse the view that the essence of rule-making here lies in the very process of advocacy.

2. The Modern Debate, its Origins and Manifestations

The complexity of the modern debate over the rules governing the extraterritorial extension of laws was forecast by the 1927 decision of the Permanent Court of International Justice in the *Case of the "S.S. Lotus"*.[1]

The facts of the *Lotus* case were that a collision between a French and Turkish ship in the high seas resulted in the loss of the lives of eight Turkish nationals. Turkey laid a criminal charge against a French officer on board the French ship, detaining him in Turkey after requesting him to come off the ship which had put into a Turkish port. The Court followed its reasoning to the conclusion that international law required that France bear the burden of proof that the Turkish prosecution had violated international law. Turkey did not need to cite a permissive rule of international law which permitted it to prosecute.

The result that the Court reached on the burden of proof is not surprising because of the way the Court had characterised the dispute. It saw its decision as a choice between:

> ... the principle of freedom, in virtue of which each State may regulate its legislation at its discretion, provided that in so doing it does not come in conflict with a restriction imposed by international law ...

as the position of Turkey, and the French position, which was that criminal law was exclusively territorial in character:

> ... which, except as otherwise expressly provided, would, *ipso facto*, prevent States from extending the criminal jurisdiction of their courts beyond their frontiers; the exceptions in question, which include for instance extraterritorial jurisdiction over nationals and crimes directed against public safety, would rest on special permissive rules forming part of international law.[2]

The Court saw these two alternatives as boiling down to the same question – whether international law prevented Turkey from prosecuting as it did? It saw that, regardless of which way it characterised the situation, France had to establish a custom which either provided that international law restricts a state's freedom to legislate in this type of case, or a custom that does not allow a state to apply its criminal law beyond its territory unless there is a permissive rule of international law that the state may invoke.

The dispute did not involve the application of criminal laws of one state inside the state territory of another. However, the decision of the Court in the *Lotus* case, one rendered by 8 votes to 7, described ships of a state as being no different from the national territory of that state.[3]

> If ... a guilty act committed on the high seas produces its effects on a vessel flying another flag or in foreign territory, the same principles must be applied as if the territories of two different States were concerned, and the conclusion must therefore be drawn that there is no rule of international law prohibiting the State to which the ship on which the effects of the offence have taken place belongs, from regarding the offence as having been committed in its territory and prosecuting, accordingly, the delinquent.[4]

One can only surmise that the majority of the Court would have decided the same way were the dispute with respect to the application of one state's law to the land territory of the other.

It is as though the complexities of the modern debate on the law governing extraterritoriality had been framed in 1927. The battle lines were drawn then, and despite much refinement and much wisdom displayed by judges and authors since, the fundamental question remains the same. Do states enjoy general freedom to act beyond their territory in the absence of a specific prohibition, or is jurisdiction, with certain defined exceptions, an essentially territorial phenomenon?

3. Doctrinal Analysis

Given the difficulties faced by governments in agreeing upon the applicable international rules and in light of the variety of complex disputes which have arisen, particularly with respect to the extraterritorial extension of competition laws, criminal law, securities regulation, documentary and oral discovery, as well as export controls, doctrinal writers have been called upon to define the issues and to propose solutions. There is now a rich if somewhat repetitive body of writing dealing with both general and particular issues.

Major treatises address the issue of extraterritoriality.[5] In recent years a number of monographs have been devoted to the general issue of extraterritoriality.[6] Attempts have been made to summarise the increasingly complex body of statements of governmental policy flowing from recent exchanges of diplomatic correspondence.[7] Some of the most important writing is to be found in major articles,[8] or in a number of influential courses of lectures given at the Hague Academy of International Law.[9] The writing on specialized topics, particularly on problems relating to competition law and export controls is vast,[10] although there is a considerable element of duplication in a great many of these articles.

The purpose of this Chapter is not to rehearse this voluminous body of writing. Readers are invited to consult the references listed here and in the Bibliography.

What emerges from this body of writing is something close to a consensus on the categories of analysis[11] in terms of jurisdiction to prescribe, to enforce and adjudicate, and analysis of the phenomenon of extraterritoriality in function of the principles of territory, active nationality, passive nationality, protection or state interest and universality. However, while these principles are widely discussed for purposes of analysis of the varying degrees of state interest in the extraterritorial extension of laws, there is no agreement that they all constitute sources of jurisdiction. Territory is accepted by all as a source of jurisdiction, as is nationality in certain contexts and for certain limited purposes. But many claims to jurisdiction based upon nationality (both physical and corporate), the protective principle (frequently articulated in function of effects within the territory), and claims to jurisdiction over property leaving the territory or goods produced abroad under license are strongly denied by authors and governments alike. There is no consensus here. Universal jurisdiction is accepted in principle as a source of jurisdiction, but there is much dispute as to the exact categories to which it attaches.

4. Legitimate State Objects or Interests

It is the thesis of this Chapter that principles and rules of international law dealing with jurisdiction are always concerned with the question of which persons a state may command. When international law defines what a state is, it also determines the objects or interests a state may have in exercising jurisdiction. The legitimacy of the object in international law is a precondition to exercise of state jurisdiction. To use the *Lotus* case as an example, the Court decided that Turkey could take sanctions against a French officer for his conduct on a French ship on the high seas. The object of the Turkish state action, which the court approved was to punish an action which resulted in the loss of life to Turkish nationals on a Turkish ship.

The object of state jurisdiction formed an important part of the *Lotus* decision. France argued that because its object was criminal punishment, Turkey was restrained by international law from applying its jurisdiction beyond its territory, meaning that Turkey could not punish a foreigner for acts committed outside Turkish territory. But the Court decided that Turkey had a legitimate object in legislating with respect to effects that occurred within its territory and touched its nationals. The Court specifically declined to consider the question whether Turkey had a legitimate object only on the basis that Turkish lives were lost. The result of the reasoning of the Court is that it found that a state had a legitimate object in applying its laws beyond its territory to acts which produced the effect of loss of lives of nationals of the state within its territory.

For what other objects may a state exercise prescriptive jurisdiction, in the sense that it may command persons to act in a prescribed manner? The answer is that they are encompassed by the principles which function as the bases of jurisdiction allowed by international law: territory, nationality, protective and universality principles. It is submitted that these principles emanate from the definition of statehood. A state has a territory, a population, a government which are independent, and thus may exercise its personality in international law. Not surprisingly, therefore, a state's legitimate objects include the protection and control of its territory, nationals, and government. It is also not surprising that a state has a legitimate object in upholding the international legal system in which it is a person.

(a) State Territory and the Territoriality Principle

A constituent element of statehood is that a government have a territory. In order to meet this requirement a government must exercise sufficient control over the territory to exclude any other government, from laying claim to the territory as its own. It is also only natural that a state be allowed by international law to exclude all others from exercising control in that territory. The important feature of a state's territory for the purpose of international law is not its mere physical existence, but the control exercised over it. This must be kept in mind when the territoriality principle is examined.

The territorial principle flows from the importance of territory as a constituent element of a state.[12] It applies to prescriptive jurisdiction. It means that a state has jurisdiction over all events occurring within its territory.[13] It also means that a state has jurisdiction over all persons resident in its territory.

The territoriality principle has been extended to deal with events which transcend state borders.[14] Two concepts have been included within the territorial principle to deal with these situations. They are known as the subjective territorial and objective territorial principles.

(b) The Subjective Territoriality Principle

The subjective territoriality principle and the objective territoriality principle, each distinguish the place where the person subject to a state's jurisdiction is found, from where he engages in an act or omission constituting an offence. The subjective territoriality principle gives jurisdiction to the state in whose territory a person is found when he commits an act which is an offence under the law of that state.[15] It may be said that it gives jurisdiction to the state in which the act comprising the offence is initiated. This description is most often used by the authors with respect to a case in which there is a physical act, such as a shooting, across a border. It is a description which is used to distinguish the physical component of an act from its effects.

In part, the subjective territoriality principle is a logical correlative of state responsibility. It allows a state to prescribe actions which would engage its responsibility in international law. It is only logical to allow a state to control individuals in order to prevent it being responsible to another state. However, there is no agreement as to the extent of state responsibility and thus the logical connection between the subjective territorial principle and state responsibility does not fully explain the subjective territorial principle.

(c) The Objective Territoriality Principle

The objective territoriality principle allows a state prescriptive jurisdiction over a person for acts which were committed by him, although he was not in that state's territory at any material time. This gives a state, in whose territory some or all of the effects of an act were suffered, prescriptive jurisdiction over acts done by persons beyond the state's borders.[16] The effect is an essential element of the offence.[17]

The "effects doctrine", upon which the United States bases prescriptive jurisdiction over persons abroad for economic offences having "effects" in its territory, at least partly falls within the objective territoriality principle.[18] However, the U.S. position that economic effects alone suffice is not one that is fully accepted by other states. The *Lotus* case did endorse the objective territoriality principle. There the "effect" within Turkish "territory" was the death of Turkish nationals. A Turkish ship was said to be a part of Turkish territory.[19] It is likely that state practice accepts that states have prescriptive jurisdiction based on the physical effects within a state's territory. On the other hand, there is little state practice outside the United States, and possibly the European Community,[20] which would suggest that economic effects within a territory are sufficient to invoke the objective territoriality principle.

The objective territoriality principle is quite different from the subjective territoriality principle. The objective territoriality principle recognizes that a state has prescriptive jurisdiction to control certain effects in its territory caused from without. Because the prescriptive jurisdiction which results is jurisdiction over persons in another state's territory, clearly the state in which the persons are, or were, may be concerned by the other state exercising prescriptive jurisdiction. As well, if the persons are the nationals of a third state, that third state may also be concerned by the jurisdiction taken over its nationals. The result is that the international nature of the event over which a state would take jurisdiction under the objective territorial principle is undeniable. It thus can hardly be the case that a state is allowed to characterise anything it pleases as an "effect" which gives it prescriptive jurisdiction. Were that the case, a state could have prescriptive jurisdiction whenever it wished. Rather, a state may only have jurisdiction where it has an object or interest recognized as legitimate by international law.[21]

Both the subjective and objective principles of territoriality are permissive rules of international law. The subjective principle permits a state to exercise prescriptive jurisdiction over persons with respect to effects within another state. The objective principle permits a state prescriptive jurisdiction with respect to persons and acts in another state. This is permitted in each case because international law characterises the prescriptive jurisdiction as having a legitimate interest. Otherwise the other state would have a right to an international claim to exclude the other state from its territory. It is to be noted that the legitimate interest is related to territory. But, it is the nature of the occurrence within the territory which must be classified by international law as giving a legitimate state interest to prescribe in the territory of another.

(d) State Population and the Nationality Principle

The territoriality principle of prescriptive jurisdiction is that persons may be subject to a state's jurisdiction based only on their relation to the territory of a state at a material time. Whether they are nationals of that state or not, they do not always (e.g. diplomats) fall under its prescriptive jurisdiction. The nationality principle recognizes that a state has prescriptive jurisdiction with respect to the acts of certain persons without regard to the fact that the acts and their effects have no relation to the territory of that state. In other words, the territoriality principle is based on what is intraterritorial. But, the nationality principle is mostly used with respect to persons who are outside the territory, and thus is by its nature potentially extraterritorial. The reason is that there is no need to have recourse to the nationality principle where a state may rely on the territoriality principle. However, it is certainly true that the prescriptive jurisdiction of a state over its own nationals in its territory may be based on either principle.

(i) *Individual nationality.* When a government is recognized by international law to represent a state, it then has the power to protect its population in international law, regardless of where any national may be.

A national enjoys rights and is subject to the duties imposed upon him by the state. Thus, even abroad the national will be subject to duties the state imposes upon him. Such duties may be seen as the correlative of benefits. Thus prescriptive jurisdiction over a national is the consequence of the fact that population is a constituent element of a state.[22] In the *Nottebohm* case the I.C.J. described it as follows:

> Nationality is a legal bond having as its basis a social fact of attachment, a genuine connection of existence, interests and sentiments, together with the existence of reciprocal rights and duties. It may be said to constitute the juridical expression of the fact that the individual upon whom it is conferred, either directly by the law or as a result of an act of the authorities, is in fact more closely connected with the population of the State conferring nationality than with that of any other State.[23]

In the *Nottebohm* case the Court held that the nationality of an individual must correspond to the factual situation. The Court explained this to mean that there must be a genuine link between the individual and the population of only one state.[24] It is the genuine link criterion that is used to make nationality of an individual an exclusive concept in international law.

It is legitimate where the individual is indeed a national of the state which considers him a citizen and is made subject to its laws abroad. However, since the individual is also subject to the laws of the state in which he finds himself, the individual will potentially be subject to the prescriptive jurisdiction of two or more states. The simple solution might seem to be that the state having enforcement jurisdiction has the paramount jurisdiction. However, because enforcement jurisdiction is not only over the person but also over property, it too may be divided among two or more states. For example, a state having prescriptive jurisdiction on the basis of territory, may be able to throw the individual in prison to enforce it, while a state having prescriptive jurisdiction on the basis of nationality may be able to enforce by seizing the same individual's property.

(ii) *Corporate nationality*. The nationality of corporations, partnerships and other forms of enterprise is an issue that is complex and has important consequences. The complexity of the issue stems in part from the fact that the legitimate interest of states to prescribe with respect to corporations is called the corporation's "nationality". While nationality may be just as apt a term as any other it certainly suggests an analogy, if not a great similarity with the link which is described by the nationality of an individual. There is a difference. International law recognizes the link between an individual and a state. That link is based on the fact that the individual forms part of the population of the state, which is a constituent element of statehood in international law. On the other hand, legal persons such as corporations are in no way a constituent element of a state for the purposes of international law. It is the state which creates corporations.

The abstract nature of the corporation is reflected in the two ways in which it is recognized that a state has a legitimate interest upon which to base prescriptive jurisdiction. A state has a legitimate interest in corporations which are: (a) incorporated by its law, or (b) which have their head office in their territory.[25] These legitimate interests also give rise to a state's right to prescribe with respect to these corporations' activities abroad, where the state has a legitimate interest.

In the *Barcelona Traction* case[26] a corporation, incorporated in Canada but doing business in Spain, was wound up by a Spanish court for failure to pay interest on debt instruments. Belgium took up the claim of its nationals, who had a significant shareholdings in the Canadian company, against Spain. The Court found that international law recognized a corporation's personality separate from that of its shareholders, and determining the "nationality" of the corporation would decide which state had the right to protect it.[27] The nationality of the corporation was said by the Court to be either the state of incorporation or the state in whose territory a registered office exists. These states may exercise the right to protect the corporation.[28] Clearly the nationality of a corporation is not an exclusive concept. Nationality was rather found to be a link to the states whose laws give the corporation status in their domestic laws.

States have legitimate interests in corporations, which international law recognizes, apart from what is known as the corporation's "nationality". For example, by carrying on business within a state's territory a corporation is subject to its prescriptive jurisdiction on the territoriality principle. Another example is where corporation A is the owner of the shares of corporation B, and corporation A is an economic tool of an enemy state or its citizens. In this example, a state may exercise prescriptive jurisdiction over corporation A or B on the basis of the protective principle, or exercise enforcement jurisdiction and seize the corporation's property within its territory.

The result of the different types of jurisdiction that states may have over the same corporation creates problems for it which are similar to those suffered by individuals abroad. It is possible that the state of which a corporation is a national will require the corporation to act differently than does the state in whose territory the corporation carries on business. However, it is also possible that a state may require its nationals who are shareholders in the corporation to exercise their rights in such a way as to attempt to have the foreign corporation act in a way contrary to that which the host state wishes. A similar requirement might be made by the state of which the directors of the corporation are nationals. The result is that a panoply of states may be legislating various requirements which affect the corporation.

The purpose of the concept of the nationality of a corporation is to delimit which state has a legitimate interest in a corporation, *inter alia* upon which prescriptive jurisdiction may be applied outside a state's territory to that corporation. It is the corporation's nationality that is the dividing line, not the nationality of the corporation's shareholders. Thus where the territoriality and nationality principles do not apply, only the protective principle may be invoked as a basis of a state's prescriptive jurisdiction over a corporation. As will be demonstrated below, the protective principle is not based on the status of the person over whom jurisdiction is asserted, but rather on the basis of his behaviour.

(e) Passive Personality

Put simply, the concept of passive personality is that prescriptive jurisdiction may be exercised where the nationals of a state are injured, regardless where they may be.[29] While it may seem to be related to the nationality principle, in fact it is not. The nationality principle allows prescriptive jurisdiction over a person on the basis of that person's nationality, or in other words his connection to the state apart from his behaviour.[30] The passive personality concept is that prescriptive jurisdiction is exercised only on the basis of the fact of the person's behaviour: that it happens to affect the state's nationals.

Passive personality does not represent any recognized legitimate state interest upon which a state may take prescriptive jurisdiction. It is only where the protective principle applies that a legitimate state interest arises to protect its nationals.

(f) State Government and the Protective Principle

The *Third Restatement* succinctly states the protective principle. A state is said to have prescriptive jurisdiction over persons who are not its nationals, for conduct outside its territory

> which is directed against the security of the state or a limited class of other state interests.[31]

The 1935 "Harvard Draft Convention on Jurisdiction with Respect to Crime" described the protective principle as allowing prescriptive jurisdiction over aliens for:

> any crime committed outside its territory by an alien against the security, territorial integrity or political independence of that State ...[32]

Some of the state interests which may be protected under this principle are the subject of agreement, and certain opinions would add others. There seems to be widespread agreement that the state may take prescriptive jurisdiction over persons with respect to attacks on the security of the state, including espionage and counterfeiting of a state's seal or currency.[33] These are agreed to be offences in which states have legitimate interests.

The independence of a state depends upon the integrity of its government. This independence is a criterion of international law for the recognition of a government as possessing personality, or statehood. It is only logical that a state should be allowed to defend its independence. If any other state were to interfere with another state's independence, it would be intervening in that state's affairs and thus breaching international law.[34] Where a person interferes with the working of a government that is not his own, even beyond its territory, he will be subject to its jurisdiction when international law classifies the offence as sufficiently serious as having the result of bringing into operation the protective principle.[35]

The protective principle also deals with the existence and integrity of the government itself. Thus high treason, such as the murder of the head of state, would come under this principle.[36]

The principle has been stretched to account for various other offences over which states assert jurisdiction, such as the conspiracy to violate immigration or custom laws.[37]

The protective principle is descriptive of its content. It applies to cases in which the state's independence or government is threatened. Regard should be had to specific categories of acts, or possibly omissions too. General categories of domestic law do not fit well into the focus of the protective principle. For instance specific categories of export control laws must be looked at, not the genre. Many types of exports are controlled by such laws for various purposes. However it is difficult to see how extraterritorial prescriptive jurisdiction based on the protective principle can be justified where the essence of export control laws is to deal with the exit from a state's territory of what are, for the most part, physical things. If the security of a state may be threatened by these things leaving the territory of the state then surely they are to be kept there, and jurisdiction limited to the state's territory should suffice for that purpose. It is only where it is to a state's advantage to have the things be exported that jurisdiction limited to territory does not in fact suffice.

If an exported object will pose a threat to a state's security or independence, this ought to be foreseen and provided for by international agreement or arrangements with the state of destination as a condition of export. If importing states want certain goods badly enough, the exporting state should be able to receive sufficient guarantees by way of international agreement. If sufficient arrangements are not made to protect the exporting state's interest, then arguably it can be concluded that the state chose other interests over that of its security. In the result, the protective principle in general should have no application to the exportation of physical things. The one exception might be to justify measures of self-help where the state to which they have gone has breached the arrangements that have been concluded.

The situation is more difficult with respect to the exportation of information. Information in tangible form may largely be controlled in the same manner as are physical things. However the instantaneous and inter-active nature of present day telecommunications and the inseparability of much information from the individual who has it in his mind, creates problems for territorial control of information which may well threaten the security or government of a state. Only on a careful analysis can this problem be dealt with. Suffice it to say here that there are no authorities on point. It may be that the only way for states to protect their independence and government is by use of the protective principle in addition to territorial and nationality principles. The necessity may result in state practice which will support this application of the protective principle. At present, a state is allowed to exercise prescriptive jurisdiction with respect to some information exports on the basis of the protective principle where there is espionage. It remains to be seen whether state practice will support a wider control of information exports. It can also be argued that it ill befits a state to invoke the protective principle when it allows the export of information, with the possible exception of the case where arrangements made with importing governments are not respected.

The protective principle is not the only basis upon which states may protect their interests. However, unlike the usual exercise of jurisdiction under other principles, it serves as a basis for extraterritorial jurisdiction over aliens. Thus the relative rigidity of international law with respect to the instances in which it may be used does not pose a problem. States may act on the basis of self-defence, reprisal and retortion against other states. As well, they may exercise prescriptive jurisdiction under the territoriality and nationality principles. It is only rarely the case that a state will be threatened by an alien person beyond its territory. It is only in the situations where this is so, and where other states do not assist it, that such measures will be necessary. Small wonder then that the categories under this principle are so few, and that it is to be conservatively appraised.[38]

(g) State Implementation of Internationally Agreed Rules and the Universality Principle

We have seen the relation of the constituent elements of a state to the principles of jurisdiction. There is another principle which has a direct relation to statehood. To be a state in international law is to have personality in international law, or to have certain rights and duties in it. Among them is the power to create law. States are the only actors which can create international law, thus it is only natural they would have an interest in preserving the law which they create. Where international law addresses the actions of persons directly, it is in the interest of all states which have created such law to apply it. This is known as the universal jurisdiction of states. Universal jurisdiction allows states to have prescriptive jurisdiction over persons who are not its nationals, nor in its territory, nor posing an immediate threat to the integrity of the state or its government. Universal jurisdiction is prescriptive jurisdiction over persons breaching international law. By this principle, states are recognized as having a legitimate interest in upholding the law they create. They can even go to the extent of controlling the conduct of aliens abroad, with respect to other aliens, where the acts are prohibited by international law.[39]

It has been accepted for some time that piracy is among the crimes caught by the universality principle.[40] However, other crimes have become accepted as also being included. They are transport of slaves,[41] war crimes,[42] with other crimes of less general acceptance, sometimes because of their relative novelty. The *Third Restatement* lists the offences as being:

> piracy, slave trade, attacks on or hijacking of aircraft, genocide, war crimes, and perhaps certain acts of terrorism ...[43]

No author suggests that any type of export or any economic offences, by individuals, are contrary to customary international law.[44] Therefore, no state can apply its law to aliens not within its territory on the basis of the universality principle. The result is that the universality principle will not be relevant to justify the export control laws of any state. The extraterritorial aspects of export control laws of any state must be enacted pursuant to a legitimate state interest to have any extraterritorial application. We have seen that the legitimate state interests upon which a state can base prescriptive jurisdiction are tied to its personality in international law. Thus with respect to export control laws the state would have to have a legitimate interest which would fall within one of the territorial, nationality, or protective principles.

(h) Interests, Jurisdiction and Advocacy

As can readily be understood from the foregoing review of the principles of jurisdiction many of them can be invoked in justification of the extraterritorial application of laws. One can view these principles of jurisdiction merely as the expression of state interests which can be invoked in support of an argument that extraterritorial jurisdiction is justified in a particular case. At the other end of the spectrum one can view these principles as heads of jurisdiction which justify extraterritorial extensions of laws whenever they are present. Clearly they are neither and both. What is essential is context, the degree of interest of the state seeking to extend its laws, balanced against the interests of the other state. Given these variables it is not surprising that advocacy plays such an important role in this area and that it is so difficult to reach consensus on general principles of international law.

At the present time it is hard to escape the conclusion that the territorial principle and hence the interests of the state into whose territory another state proposes to extend its laws must be paramount in normal circumstances. To justify extraterritorial extensions of laws only a rule based on universal jurisdiction or the prior agreement of all states concerned will suffice to avoid conflict. In any other circumstance extraterritorial extensions of laws will raise controversy and allegations of violation of the sovereignty of the affected state. Treaties, state practice international and domestic judicial decisions and doctrinal writing assist in defining those other circumstances in which extraterritorial extensions of laws are justified.

5. Resolution of Conflicts – The Third Restatement

Reliance on the territorial principle as the basic rule of public international law speaking to the phenomenon of extraterritoriality poses two problems. Firstly, there are a number of recognized exceptions, and practice in these areas varies considerably from one state to another. Secondly, as advocates of the necessity of greater flexibility never cease to point out, economic and commercial relations between states have become so complex and the degree of interdependence is so great that strict adherence to the territoriality principle can become an obstacle to open commercial relations. To restrict a state to regulating conduct on its territory alone is to grant a license to those who would violate or commit frauds upon domestic law outside the territory. To a certain degree the European Economic Community has followed an analogous course in the enforcement of the relevant provisions of the *Treaty of Rome*. Examples of limited extraterritoriality are to be found in the legislation of other European states[45] and of Canada.[46] Another area where the U.S. refuses to refrain from acting extraterritorially is that of export controls. Strict adherence to the territoriality principle appears too restricting, while reliance on comity appears too uncertain to guarantee willing recognition of U.S. interests in extending its laws abroad.

This being the case it is not surprising that very considerable efforts have been made in the U.S. to articulate more flexible rules upon which to base extraterritorial jurisdiction. In the field of competition law in particular, U.S. courts have shown great creativity in seeking to develop rules of jurisdiction sensitive to strong legislative policies in the direction of extraterritoriality.[47] Despite some recent caution shown by the Supreme Court of the United States on questions of discovery[48] the policy in favour of the extraterritorial reach of law is strong and firmly entrenched both in the cases and in legislation. In the wake of this case law, a distinguished group of scholars and practitioners working within the American Law Institute have sought to articulate rules of public international law on a wide range jurisdictional questions in the *Third Restatement of the Foreign Relations Law of the United States*.[49] The *Third Restatement* is even more broad in scope than its predecessor.[50] The *Second Restatement* already placed considerable reliance upon the effects principle to justify the exercise of jurisdiction extraterritorially.[51] The *Third Restatement* maintains this orientation[52] and contains more extensive provisions on the resolution of conflicts in Section 403, which is entitled "Limitations on Jurisdiction to Prescribe."

Section 403(1) states:

> Limitations on Jurisdiction of Prescribe
>
> (1) Even when one of the bases for jurisdiction under § 402 is present, a state may not exercise jurisdiction to prescribe law with respect to a person or activity having connections with another state when the exercise of such jurisdiction is unreasonable.

The criterion of reasonability implies a judgment on the part of the state seeking to extend its jurisdiction abroad of the degree of its own interests in the matter as weighed against the interests of other states. The process of analysis draws heavily upon the U.S. cases cited above, which in turn rely heavily upon modern techniques of interest analysis, which have been widely current in private international law thinking in the U.S. for the last thirty years, and which are understood, if not as widely accepted, in several European States. Section 403(2) sets out a lengthy but non-exhaustive list of factors to be considered in making this decision.[53] In the event of a conflict and when it would not be reasonable for both states to exercise jurisdiction the state with the lesser interest should defer to the other.[54] The Comment to Section 403 states that while some courts of the U.S. have treated the principle of reasonableness as a matter of comity "[t]his section states the principle of reasonableness as a rule of international law."[55]

The *Third Restatement* is an impressive and ambitious document; for this reason alone but also due to its standing in the eyes of the U.S. judiciary it will doubtless influence the course of the law in the U.S. The principle of reasonableness is seen by the drafters as both an exercise of justification and of self-restraint, capable of guiding legislators and judges. Whether they have succeeded in formulating such a rule is as yet open to doubt. The initial reaction from within the U.S. government suggested that the rule implied too much self-restraint.[56] Reaction from at least one member of the U.S. Federal judiciary suggested that weighing the factors listed in Section 403(2) might not necessarily yield a clear result.[57]

The international reaction has been one of great interest, but commentators seem unconvinced that the *Third Restatement* has succeeded in formulating a broadly acceptable rule. Of particular concern is the fear that such a rule will virtually always lead to the result that U.S. courts will deem the extraterritorial extension of their laws to be acceptable. A leading Canadian commentator, Professor J.-G.Castel, has written that "[a]t the present it cannot be said that #403 states a customary rule of international law ...."[58] Castel is also concerned that such a test will fail to take into account the diplomatic and policy aspects of conflicts of jurisdiction. A distinguished European commentator, who played a consultative role in the drafting of the *Third Restatement*, is rather more positive in his appraisal. Professor Karl Meessen considers that international law must speak to the problem of overlapping and conflicting state claims to jurisdiction. In his view "[s]trict territorial limitation does not work. Transterritorial conduct would otherwise often be outside the reach of any regulation. Frequent cases of concurrent jurisdiction must be accepted as a necessary element of economic interdependence."[59] Without accepting all claims of jurisdiction made in U.S. legislation and administrative practice, Professor Meessen considers that genuine conflicts, such as the Pipeline controversy, are in fact resolved upon a calculus of reasonable claims to state interest. He points out to the *Aerospatiale*[60] decision of the U.S. Supreme Court as evidence that U.S. courts are capable of taking a balanced view of the interests of other states.

As indicated above, the approach of the *Third Restatement* has elicited considerable interest among international lawyers concerned with problems of extraterritoriality. The approach is a long step away from the territorial principle, but it is also a step back from the argument that no rule of international law limits the extraterritorial extension of laws and that the existence of a legislative or administrative policy automatically creates an interest and hence a valid claim to jurisdiction.

6. Classification of Export Control Laws in International Law

A major consideration in analyzing export controls is to determine whether they raise special issues with respect to their extraterritorial extension. This and the following section are devoted to this question. It is arguable that the extraterritorial extension of export controls is subject to the same general rules as competition law, securities regulation, criminal law, etc., but if export controls raise special issues, it is equally arguable that not all these rules apply or that certain extraterritorial extensions are more easy to justify.

If it is true that a state can only legislate over persons in international law where it has a legitimate state interest, or object,[61] it is imperative to define the legitimate state interests which would allow for extraterritorial application of export control of laws.

Export controls differ in purpose, means used, or items that are controlled. It must be emphasized that the way in which exports are controlled is not to be confused with the subject of the prescriptive jurisdiction. Prescriptive jurisdiction is always over persons (individuals and corporations). It is never over other things, corporeal, or incorporeal. Export controls are often expressed in terms of things controlled. But, in international law terms they are based on the state's legitimate interest in either the person or the person's behaviour (he has done or omitted to do something).

The principles of jurisdiction define which persons are subject to a state's prescriptive jurisdiction. However, only the nationality principle pre-determines a class of persons. The territoriality, protective and universality principles do not pre-determine the persons subject to jurisdiction. These principles determine the class of persons to which jurisdiction applies based upon each person's behaviour. This is sometimes called the application of law to a thing, or event. In other words, whereas the nationality principle directly identifies which persons will be subject to state jurisdiction if it chooses, the other principles only identify the means by which persons may be made subject to a state's jurisdiction. Only once persons meet the conditions are they identified. For example, once an alien has entered upon the territory of a state, he is identified as being subject to its territorial jurisdiction.

There are export controls on endangered species and various flora and fauna. There are also economic policy export controls, introduced largely for balance of payments reasons. There are export controls on various types of information and documents, or currency. This section concentrates upon the two types that have caused the most controversy. First is the control of militarily sensitive equipment and technology, which we shall call strategic goods. The second are embargoes.

(a) Strategic Goods

Export controls on strategic goods have as their basis the notion that strategic goods in the hands of enemies of the state will endanger its security, or at least make it more expensive to protect. The paradox with which a state has to deal is that its security may also be enhanced by the export of strategic goods, where the export is to allies. Thus the state may export to protect itself. Where this is the case, the recipient of the strategic goods will be the government of another state which will use them in the common defence. Where the government of another state will use them, the states may deal with each other on a state to state level and conclude their agreements in international law. There is no question of one state having prescriptive jurisdiction over another. As a general rule, states are immune from the prescriptive or enforcement jurisdiction of other states.[62] There are some exceptions made by a growing number of states with respect to the commercial activities of states. However it would be very difficult to characterize the purchase by a state of strategic goods for its own use as a commercial activity as this is currently defined.

The result is that prescriptive jurisdiction with respect to the export of strategic goods is over persons, in cases where they deal with the goods. It does not arise where states deal with the goods on a state to state basis. Where persons in one state export strategic goods to persons in another, the goods have already changed in nature; they may be described as commercial property. The state which allows their export has already determined they are not so vital that they may not be exported at all. It has also determined that they are not goods that have been exported to enhance its security, because they would then have been exported to the government of another state. It is true that the other state may wish the export to be made directly to one of its private firms, but here it will be the ultimate beneficiary of the goods. If such is the case, the transaction may be protected in a manner no different than a state to state transaction.

Where state to state transactions are to be legally binding, they are governed by international law. They are not governed by the law of any one state. Thus any guarantees a state may seek in a transaction with another state should be sought in international law. In all cases in which strategic goods are to be exported for the enhanced security of the exporting state, the appropriate law to govern the transaction is international law. Where national law governs the transaction it is a clear indication that the exporting state does not have its security as the foremost consideration. Rather, in almost all such cases the foremost consideration would be economic benefit.

The preceding discussion serves to demonstrate that prescriptive jurisdiction over persons with respect to even strategic goods cannot be said to be based on the protective principle, in all save the most extraordinary circumstances.[63] If it cannot be said to apply to strategic goods, *a fortiori* it cannot be said to apply to other goods.

(b) Embargoes

The second type of export control this study will examine is the "embargo". This term will be used in the sense of a prohibition to export some or all goods and information to a target state or states. A boycott is a wider term which would include an embargo, as well as an import prohibition.[64] In this study only the embargo will be discussed although it often is part of a boycott which is imposed.

Although the reasons states impose embargoes are many and complicated, they may be divided into two general groups. States impose embargoes against other states either in response to breaches of international law, or for their own political reasons. This is not to say that in any case where an embargo has been imposed, a state's reason is exclusively one or the other. Often it is a mixture of both. At least states imposing an embargo will justify their actions with a claim of breach of international law on the part of the target state. Where there is a breach of international law, a state may respond by using measures of reprisal or retortion. Reprisals are acts contrary to international law *per se*, whose illegality cannot be invoked by the state against which they are directed because of its prior breach of international law.[65] Retortions are acts which are not contrary to international law, taken in reaction to the behaviour of another state.

Where there is a breach of international law by the target of the embargo, the target will not be able to assert that another state's excess of prescriptive jurisdiction is *per se* illegal, although the normal legitimate state interests do not exist. In other words, international law acknowledges a legitimate state interest to take measures of reprisal against a delinquent state, although the measures are required to be proportional to the harm done.[66] It is a matter of debate whether such measures are opposable only to the delinquent state. On the one hand, it can be argued that no state's rights should be affected by the actions of another, but only by its own actions. On the other hand, it may be argued that a state which suffers the breach of international law has a legitimate interest in enforcing international law against the delinquent state and thus may prescribe in excess of its normal prescriptive jurisdiction. Any conflict with another state's rights would then be resolved in the normal way.

The best example of a case in which the reprisal argument could be made in recent times was the taking of U.S. hostages in Iran. The I.C.J. found that Iran breached an international law obligation it owed to the U.S.[67] On the basis of a reprisal, the U.S. could take proportionate measures, even if the measures were contrary to international law. Among the measures taken was a freeze of Iranian state assets in foreign branches of U.S. banks. If this kind of prescriptive jurisdiction could not be supported on the basis of nationality of the banks, it might be argued to have been valid as a reprisal against a delinquent state's assets. Of course, other key issues which remain are the measures' proportionality and opposability to states other than Iran. It remains to be decided to what extent states other than Iran could protest. Iran, however, could only argue that the U.S. excess of jurisdiction was disproportionate, not that it exceeded international law. Reprisals are measures *per se* illegal made legal because of another state's prior breach.

Where there is no prior breach of international law, a reprisal cannot be argued; the reason for the embargo is irrelevant with respect to determining the extent of prescriptive jurisdiction of the state imposing the embargo. It is then a question of applying the normal rules of prescriptive jurisdiction in international law.

To have a successful embargo of a target state is to deny it the items included in the embargo, while continuing the export of those items to other states. If it had such a goal, any state engaging in an embargo would be happy to know that all other states were also imposing a similar embargo on the target. Then the embargo would be as effective as possible. However, where all other states do not cooperate, there is a possibility that goods the state has exported to other countries will find their way to the target state. In other words, there is a problem with the efficiency of the embargo, even with respect to goods exported from the state applying the embargo itself, let alone that the target may be able to substitute sources of supply. In the interests of making the embargo as effective as possible, a state may wish to attempt to control the export of goods from other countries to the greatest extent allowed by international law. It may not do so by the use of its enforcement jurisdiction in other countries.[68] However, it may do so to the extent international law permits it to apply its prescriptive jurisdiction abroad.

7. Extraterritorial Jurisdiction of States and Conflicts of Prescriptive Jurisdiction as a Result of Export Control Laws

(a) General Considerations

The essence of a state's prescriptive jurisdiction is that it be a command to persons to act in a prescribed way. Although law may deal with facts or things, this work focuses on its application to persons. Where the persons are beyond the territory of the state, the prescriptive jurisdiction applied to them is extraterritorial. It is in this sense that extraterritoriality has been used in this study.

The discussion in Section 3 categorized four main principles of international law which deal with prescriptive jurisdiction. Each may be extraterritorial. Even the territorial principle allows for extraterritoriality. It does so where the objective territorial principle is applied. The nationality, protective, and universality principles are by their very definition extraterritorial. Thus the objective territoriality principle and the other three principles sum up the potential legal extraterritorial jurisdiction of a state. Exceeding those principles is illegal. However some of these illegal excesses are unobjectionable if they constitute a valid reprisal in international law.

It has been submitted that international law determines when a state may resort to a principle of jurisdiction. The state must have a legitimate interest, and classification of this interest determines which element of a state is involved. Then the principle of jurisdiction related to such an element may be applied, to the extent the state requires. Thus the extent to which export control laws are required to be extraterritorial can be determined by examining the legitimate state interests involved, and classifying their relationship to state personality.

Two distinctions are made in classifying laws for the purpose of examining the state's jurisdiction to prescribe. Some authors have classified rules of international law based on the public or private nature of the laws.[69] Some have distinguished between laws that are civil or criminal in nature.[70] These two distinctions may not be too different, other than the fact that public laws encompass a wider array than merely criminal laws. Others have argued that there is essentially no difference between civil and criminal law jurisdiction.[71]

The distinctions between public and private law, or civil and criminal law tend to isolate one type of offence from another. However, these categories are distinctions made by national laws in order to differentiate between consequences or procedure in national law. Thus, they cannot be determinative of the availability of prescriptive jurisdiction in international law, otherwise states could unilaterally determine when they did or did not have jurisdiction.

It is international practice which forms the customary law distinguishing the cases in which states may have prescriptive jurisdiction extraterritorially with respect to export controls. The ambit of state practice with respect to various cases will be examined separately. However, the legitimate objects for which a state may have extraterritorial prescriptive jurisdiction with respect to export controls must be justified on the basis of the principles of prescriptive jurisdiction. This section is devoted to the examination of two types of extraterritorial jurisdiction: the objective territoriality principle and the nationality principle. It has been shown above that the other types generally do not apply to extraterritorial export control laws, because a state will lack the required legitimate interest to apply them.

(b) The Objective Territoriality Principle

The objective territoriality principle allows a state prescriptive jurisdiction over persons outside its territory, and thus is inherently extraterritorial. It allows such jurisdiction when the person causes an effect within the territory of a state which international law recognizes to be one which a state may legitimately prevent or punish. Under the principle, it is quite clear that with respect to some physical effects within the territory, the state has a legitimate interest to prescribe. Examples would include physical injury to its residents or territory.

Extraterritorial prescriptive jurisdiction with respect to export controls may be exercised in order to keep certain goods within the territory of the prescribing state. Where this is the case, it may be that the objective territoriality principle will apply. For example, where foreign nationals abroad conspire to remove items which a state does not wish to export, it may be said that there is a legitimate interest to prevent them from doing so. Such action is with respect to a physical effect within the state's territory and thus falls under the territoriality principle.

However, the usual reason to prescribe extraterritorially is in order to keep goods from going to a certain target, although they are goods which are already exported. Here there is no physical effect within the state's territory caused by the acts of the persons abroad. Any physical effect was caused by the export itself.

One commentator argues that the effect caused within the state, in this case the U.S., by the failure of foreign subsidiaries to comply with an embargo, is that it is less effective.[72] In the first place, this is not a physical effect. It is an effect on the laws of a state. It may be argued that the territorial principle deals with the control over physical things, and thus implicitly a state's law. Such an argument might be tenable where the effect was to make ineffective the state's laws with respect to things within its territory. But this is not the case here. The effect is to make the state's laws less effective with respect to the control of things outside of its territory. Thus it can hardly be argued that the objective territorial principle covers such an effect, because the effect is not within the territory of the state.

The argument is really an assertion that it is a legitimate state object to prescribe extraterritorially with respect to any person dealing in goods or technology that were once within the territory of a state.[73] An analysis of this notion shows that it is none too different from the idea of Permanent Sovereignty over Natural Resources,[74] except that it is even wider in scope. It is wider in scope because it asserts prescriptive jurisdiction even with respect to exports that did not originate within the territory, but originally came from elsewhere and merely passed through the territory. Such an idea seems to be singularly restricted to the U.S., and not supported by the practice of states. The territorial principle cannot be contorted in this way to gain strictly extraterritorial jurisdiction.[75]

The objective territorial principle would seem to have little variance in its application to strategic goods as compared to embargoes. The objective territorial principle allows a state to prevent the export of goods from its territory, whatever their nature. It does not apply to control of the use of goods already exported.

It is difficult to see how the nature of the goods can change the entitlement of a state to extraterritorial prescriptive jurisdiction based on the objective territorial principle. Different goods have different uses. But if the use of the goods may threaten the state's integrity or control over its territory, then that is a question distinct from that of the export of the goods. The right to prescriptive jurisdiction over persons would then be for their conduct. The origin of goods used could give no greater or lesser right to prescribe. The state would have to have a legitimate interest in prescribing with respect to such conduct.

The objective territorial principle is an exception to the territorial principle; it provides a basis for legislation over transnational offences where a strict application of the territorial principle would permit no state to have prescriptive jurisdiction on the basis of territory. It is complementary to the subjective territorial principle which does the same.[76]

The objective territorial principle does not, however, serve to give prescriptive jurisdiction for a transnational offence where a state would wish to prevent certain uses of goods. It is the conduct which the state seeks to prevent: the localization required by the territorial principle has no necessary relationship to the location or origin of goods used. Thus, to be legitimate, prescriptive jurisdiction over persons must be with respect to the conduct. Otherwise, instead of localizing a transnational offence, all that would be accomplished would be the multiplication of states claiming legitimate interests.

(c) The Nationality Principle

The nationality principle is by its nature extraterritorial. It is also the principle upon which the strongest argument may be made that export control laws may be prescribed extraterritorially. Where states use the principle, their argument may be stated as follows. The nationals are subject to the rights and duties of the law of the state of which they are a national. The national cannot escape his duties by leaving the state's territory, while keeping the benefit of his rights, unless the state is content to let him do so, or international law requires it to do so. Export control laws are said to be duties of the national which a state may choose to require him to fulfil, even abroad.

The nationality principle is quite different for corporations than it is for individuals. With respect to individuals, it is based on the individual being part of the population of the state. With respect to corporations, it is a certain status given to an investment by the law of a state. But in both cases nationality defines which persons are subject to the prescriptive jurisdiction of a state merely because of their status. If the nationality of a corporation has any meaning for prescriptive jurisdiction, it is that it defines the outer limit of states' (extraterritorial) jurisdiction over it on the basis of status. It is untenable that a state require the owners of a corporation to exercise their voting rights in it to make the corporation comply with that state's prescriptions, unless the state has prescriptive jurisdiction over the corporation as well as its owners.

Before a state has a legitimate interest in prescribing extraterritorially within the nationality principle, it is, of course, an essential pre-condition that prescriptive jurisdiction be taken over a national. This is most often the point of contention. This may be restated in another way. State practice does not support the proposition that a state has a legitimate object in prescribing that its residents or nationals exercise their control of a foreign corporation in a specified manner. In fact, there have been numerous protests to claims of such jurisdiction, and examples of positive practice to the contrary.[77]

(d) Conflicts of Jurisdiction

Conceivably, a state has a legitimate interest in placing a duty on its nationals wherever they may be, to refrain from trading with a country which it has decided to embargo. It will be said that to do otherwise would encourage nationals to avoid state imposed obligations by residing abroad. Were it the case that the state in which the national found himself suffered no effect as a result of the other state's prescriptive jurisdiction, the host state would have no conflicting interest. However it is usually the case that the host state will suffer the loss of employment, or the loss of potential economic gain or perhaps even the loss of concluded contracts, as well as the loss of reputation as a reliable supplier. Any or all of these consequences might be acceptable, depending on the reason for the embargo. But, the host state will understandably want to make the decision for itself.

What is involved is the host state's right to control its territory and residents. This basic right, recognized as part of its personality by international law, comes into conflict with the right of the other state to control its nationals wherever they may be. A key issue with respect to extraterritorial jurisdiction is to determine how to resolve this conflict, if it is one which can be resolved.

With respect to export control laws, the conflict requires further analysis. The state which requires its nationals abroad to comply with an embargo has clearly imposed an economic burden on other states as well as itself. Where State A imposes the burden of an embargo upon a state by denying State B the benefit of its trade so that B will not re-export to C, there would seem to be no recourse by State B under international law, unless states were obliged by international law to trade with one another. But the situation is different if State A does indeed trade with State B. It would seem State A is then hoping to pursue its own policies with the resources of another state. In other words it is not willing to pay for the full amount of economic influence that it wishes to exercise. It uses prescriptive jurisdiction over nationals abroad as the means to avoid bearing the burden of its policies. In fact, what it is doing is controlling the relationship between persons and things, where neither are within its territory; this involves exercising territorial jurisdiction in another state under the guise of the nationality principle. The result is that against State C, State A brings to bear the economic power of State B without State B's consent. In other words, by unilateral action one state uses the resources of another state without international agreement. If this analysis is accurate, such a use of prescriptive jurisdiction cannot be said to be based upon the nationality principle of international law, in as much as it is contrary to the principle of sovereign equality and is not compatible with the independence of State B.

Beyond a rather abstract analysis of the international law principles of prescriptive jurisdiction, there is considerable state practice dealing with the apparent conflict of nationality and territoriality principles of prescriptive jurisdiction. International organizations have addressed the problem in the context of the multinational enterprise. States have protested and asserted claims to one of the two types of jurisdiction although this conflicted with another state's view that its jurisdiction was either paramount or perhaps exclusive.[78] Finally, states have agreed on a bilateral basis, on mechanisms to prevent such conflicts where possible. It remains to be noted that certain general principles of international law limit the actual conflict between nationality and territoriality principles, even assuming they have concurrent application. First this section examines the types of state practice mentioned and then turns to the general principles of international law.

(i) *State practice in international organizations*. The Annex to the OECD *Declaration on International Investment and Multinational Enterprises*[79] sets out guidelines for multinational enterprises which are stated not to be "legally enforceable". In the preamble to the guidelines, the agreed text states:

> Every State has the right to prescribe the conditions under which multinational enterprises operate within its national jurisdiction, subject to international law and to the international agreements to which it has subscribed. The entities of a multinational enterprise located in various countries are subject to the laws of these countries.[80]

The guidelines thus emphasize the primacy of the host state's jurisdiction. These guidelines themselves may not be indicative of international custom, but declaratory texts agreed to in an international organization, such as the OECD, must bear some serious weight as descriptive of the state practice of developed countries. More general state practice is found within the United Nations (U.N.). An example is the U.N. *Set of Multilaterally Agreed Equitable Principles and Rules for the Control of Restrictive Business Practices*[81] wherein enterprises are told they should conform to the laws of the countries in which they operate:

> Enterprises should conform to the restrictive business practices laws, and the provisions concerning restrictive business practised in other laws, of the countries in which they operate, and in the event of proceedings under these laws should be subject to the competence of the courts and relevant administrative bodies therein.[82]

Similar provisions can be found in the *Draft United Nations Code of Conduct on Transnational Corporations.*[83]

These types of state practice are most relevant because they address the control of persons by states on a cooperative, and not unilateral basis. It is significant that the instruments mentioned refer to general policies as well as the laws of the host state. The conclusion that can be drawn is that the importance of the host state's territorial jurisdiction is emphasized in this state practice.

One instrument which goes far to clearly set out the relative primacy of state prescriptive jurisdictions is the *Basel Concordat*,[84] an agreement between 12 developed countries concerning the supervision of banks with respect to their solvency, liquidity, and foreign exchange positions. Different corporate structures are treated differently in the Concordat. Its aim is to attribute responsibility among states for supervision, or prescriptive jurisdiction over banks. Two basic principles are established: the first is that no bank is to escape supervision, and second, that supervision is to be adequate. For each type of supervision the question of primacy of the nationality and territoriality principles is dealt with.

Generally the prime responsibility for supervision of a bank subsidiary rests with the host country. It is assumed that the host state is also the state of incorporation of subsidiaries. It is thus clear that this is a choice of the territorial principle to the extent the subsidiary only does business within that territory. If the subsidiary does business in another territory then it would be a "foreign branch" in that other territory. Foreign branches are assumed to be incorporated abroad and merely carrying on business in the host country. For solvency matters the nationality principle is chosen over the territoriality principle, but for liquidity the opposite is true.

The general rule that would seem to have been followed is that where the entity does business in the state of its incorporation, that state has prescriptive jurisdiction with respect to supervision. The state, interested only by reason of the shareholding in that entity, is to assist in making the supervision complete and efficient, or in other words to prevent shareholders shielding themselves against foreign supervision by hiding behind the corporate veil. This is in keeping with the rules of international law with respect to prescriptive jurisdiction set out above.

The rule concerning treatment of branches of a foreign bank carrying on business within a territory is of special interest. It deals with the problem that the state of incorporation may have prescriptive jurisdiction using the nationality principle while the other would have it on the basis of territoriality. Solvency, or the overall financial status of the corporation, is the primary concern of the state having jurisdiction on the basis of its status, under the nationality principle. This makes sense because the host state generally cannot have prescriptive jurisdiction outside its territory and thus is in no position to supervise the overall performance of the corporation, while the national state is in a position to do so. But with respect to liquidity, or the ability to repay the investment made in the territory, it is the territorial state which has the primary supervisory interest. This would seem to follow from the fact that liquidity is in fact a territorial matter.

The *Basel Concordat* is exceptional among rules emanating from international organizations in that the type of person dealt with is defined with enough precision that one is able to identify when the nationality principle is in fact being considered. Other international instruments blur the distinction between a separate corporate entity doing business in the host country and a branch of a foreign corporation doing business there. But, the *Basel Concordat* is a fine example of classification in international law terms by the nature of the task to be performed. On the basis of this classification, primacy of interest is determined. It is submitted that this is the proper application of international law rules and principles of prescriptive jurisdiction. It puts the resolution of the dispute on the basis of international law and not within the unilateral determination of one state.[85]

(ii) *Bilateral state practice in agreements and arrangements in other areas.* Where states have cooperated with respect to potential conflicts of jurisdiction, they have preferred bilateral agreements. Taxation treaties, for example, usually create rules upon which states are given exclusive prescriptive jurisdiction to tax a person.[86] In the antitrust field a number of arrangements have been entered into between states, to deal with potential conflicts between national and territorial jurisdiction. Some arrangements avoid treaty obligations[87] and some are in treaty form.[88] The antitrust treaties and arrangements do not choose between the territorial and national principles, but merely seem to serve to prevent conflicts from escalating due to a lack of cooperation between the parties.[89] Other treaties also deal with prescriptive jurisdiction of states.[90]

Bilateral state practice is perhaps best summarized by stating that it is diverse. Often it does not deal with the resolution of conflicts between the territoriality and nationality principles of prescriptive jurisdiction, even by implication. In cases where it does, states provide for notification or consultation in an attempt to provide a cooperative mechanism to avoid conflicts. The same goals may then be achieved by cooperation rather than unilateralism. In other cases, states provide, as they do in taxation treaties, for exclusive prescriptive jurisdiction of one state.

There do not seem to be any treaties which deal specifically with the matter of the conflict of territoriality and nationality principles in the case of export control laws. However, general types of treaties may have specific application to the export control context. One such agreement is the *Treaty Between the United States of America and the Government of Canada on Mutual Legal Assistance in Criminal Matters.*[91] It provides for a scheme by which either of the states party to the agreement may request that the other investigate, take evidence, and communicate the results to the other, where it relates to an offence. An offence is defined in terms which would include export control offences in both countries. The treaty provides for cooperation between the two states in the exercise of their enforcement jurisdiction. The enforcement jurisdiction assistance is provided upon criteria which are wholly within the control of the other state. It applies to U.S. offences which are punishable by one year of imprisonment or more, and to Canadian offences which may be prosecuted by indictment.

The Canada-U.S. treaty on Mutual Legal Assistance provides that requests for assistance may be denied where a "substantial interest related to national security or other essential public policy" is involved for the state requested to provide assistance. It seems this will not allow a state to invoke the lack of the other's prescriptive jurisdiction as such a substantial interest. It would seem to admit the other state's own interpretation of its prescriptive jurisdiction. However, a "substantial interest" might be invoked where the state whose assistance is requested has prescriptive jurisdiction.

The *Canada-U.S. Free Trade Agreement*[92] which entered into force on January 1, 1989 contains an interesting provision covering export controls and embargoes. This provision does not deal explicitly with conflicts of jurisdiction. However, it is possible that such conflict will be covered by the general arbitration of disputes provisions of Chapter 18 of the Agreement.

(iii) *State practice in domestic legislation.* State practice has asserted the primacy of the territoriality principle over the nationality principle in a growing number of cases. Practice in the form of blocking legislation is exploiting the fact that the territorial state has the enforcement jurisdiction over the person, as well as prescriptive jurisdiction under the territoriality principle, while the state relying upon the nationality principle has only prescriptive jurisdiction. This in itself may be reason to suggest that blocking legislation only makes express the legitimate state interests that were tacit before. It also suggests that the state with enforcement jurisdiction has reason to consider that its jurisdiction ought to be paramount, if not exclusive, in the cases in which it is a territorial state with a legitimate state interest.

There are some 18 states resorting to blocking legislation, and it is a growing practice. Some states' legislation is quite vague, giving a large discretion to the government to intervene on a case by case basis.[93] Others are much more specific. They set out the interests the state wishes to protect[94] and then provide for action in specific cases. The best example of the application of blocking legislation is a U.K. order under its *Protection of Trading Interests Act, 1980*.[95] In 1982, the U.K. invoked its blocking legislation against several extraterritorial provisions of the U.S. export controls dealing with the Siberian Pipeline. Even if one assumes that the U.S. had not exceeded the nationality principle,[96] this is an example of state practice choosing the territoriality principle over the nationality principle.

(iv) *Prior consultation.* If the lowest threshold of state practice in treaties and international arrangements is taken it would seem that treaties, arrangements and instruments of international organizations constantly repeat that there is to be consultation prior to recourse to extraterritorial prescriptive jurisdiction which may involve a conflict with the interests of another state having prescriptive jurisdiction as well. This is true for other fields as well as for export controls. However the type of consultation varies. For example, when antitrust laws are concerned, treaty and other state practices provide for, or encourage prior consultation. Here the state proposing to take extraterritorial prescriptive jurisdiction is to consult the state in whose territory persons affected will find themselves. If all such territorial states are consulted, conceivably all interested states have had an input. However with respect to strategic export controls or embargoes, the target state or states would still have an interest in the prescriptive jurisdiction being taken. Yet they are never consulted, because the very purpose of export controls is to deny the target benefits and not to cooperate with them.

Prior consultation would then seem to be a phenomenon that exists among states which are vulnerable to another's actions because of previous cooperation between them. With respect to such states, prior cooperation may be seen as an obligation correlative to the good faith of the other state. It may be that an obligation in international law is being formed. At present it is, at best, *de lege ferenda*. As an author who has extensively surveyed state practice with respect to prior consultation in general has written:

> State practice establishes that prior consultation is a widely utilized, but certainly not universal, procedural mechanism serving to inject into national decision-making processes the extra-national effects of proposed decisions .... Despite the growth of prior consultation norms, it is unlikely that there will be any all-encompassing prior consultation duty in the foreseeable future.[97]

However, a regional custom is more likely to develop in this regard than is a general custom. For example, some states have formed an international forum specifically for prior consultation and harmonization of export controls on strategic goods. This is the Coordinating Committee of the Consultative Group (CoCom). CoCom is a forum which devolved from NATO, but includes a non-member Japan, and does not include two NATO members. In CoCom, a system of consultation has been highly refined and works to facilitate cooperation between trading partners in goods in which there is a common interest to control. It is arguable that an export of goods agreed by CoCom members to be prohibited to certain destinations, without consulting as required in the forum would be the breach of an international legal obligation. The legal obligation may be argued to be either a regional custom, or perhaps an oral treaty. In either case, the state asserting such an argument would have the burden of proof and in this case the onus may decide the dispute.

Certain bilateral relationships may have an even clearer pattern of cooperation and prior consultation. Perhaps the closest such relationship in the world is that between Canada and the U.S. In that relationship various types of consultation have been arranged in differing fields of laws. Among them is a pattern of consultation on export controls since the Second World War. The study of this bilateral relationship is undertaken separately below. The consultation on export controls was undertaken in part within CoCom, but on a major level outside that forum as well. Both states cooperate and consult in the export control field in their treaties, in joint communiqués, in the close cooperation which exists between the export control bureaucracies of both governments[98] and have also referred to the cooperation in unilateral statements. It would seem that there is ample evidence here of a binding regional custom between the two states to consult on export controls.

(v) *Abuse of rights.* Some argue that the notion of retortion in international law suggests there is no rule of international law that prohibits a state from abusing its rights.[99] However, others argue that there is such a rule of international law and that it applies to prevent abuse of state prescriptive jurisdiction.[100]

It is said that where State A attempts to repress an activity in the territory of State B that is both allowed and protected by State B, and is not contrary to international law, State A's repression is an abuse of its rights.[101] If "repression" is to mean that an act or omission is prescribed extraterritorially as being criminal by one state, this would be another way of stating that the express laws of the territorial state are to be chosen over those which are extraterritorial.[102]

Another view is that it is an abuse of rights for a state to exercise prescriptive jurisdiction where it has no connection with the person over which or event upon which it takes the jurisdiction.[103] Certainly it is correct to say that it is contrary to international law for a state to take prescriptive jurisdiction in such cases. However, it is submitted that the principles of prescriptive jurisdiction in international law will generally determine when the state has rights, and where a state has no connection with the person or event it has no prescriptive jurisdiction and therefore no rights to prescribe. This is not an example of the abuse of rights, nor is it a semantic argument. It demonstrates that the notion of abuse of rights is a restriction beyond the requirements inherent in a state's prescriptive jurisdiction to conform to the principles of international law. But, that is only arguable if the abuse of rights is contrary to international law, which itself is arguable.

The notion of abuse of rights is at least conceptually linked to the principles of international jurisdiction. It remains for state practice to determine whether it describes a method for choosing one principle of jurisdiction over another. It is submitted that in the most blatant cases of malicious intervention in the affairs of another state it could be said to be illegal as an abuse of rights. Support for this could be found in the Charter of Economic Rights and Duties of States,[104] Article 2 of which has engendered much controversy with respect to provisions dealing with the duty to compensate for nationalization. But even amendments to it proposed by those states disagreeing with its compensation provisions, agreed that the territorial state has the right to regulate foreign investment within its territory with a view to its own national objectives and priorities.[105] The territorial state therefore always has jurisdiction although the same is not provided for the state from which the investment comes. The implication is that precedence is given to the territoriality principle in some, if not all, cases.

Tied in with the notion of abuse of rights is the idea of *sic utere tuo ut alienum non laedas*, or that a state is not to use its territory to harm the territory of another. This is a notion which seems to have implications for the physical effects caused by the use of one state's territory. This principle of international law helps explain the physical nature of the objective territorial principle.

(vi) *Reciprocity.* One of the most basic principles of international law is the sovereign equality of states.[106] One aspect of the sovereign equality of states is that of reciprocity, in the sense that what is permitted in international law for one state is permitted for another.[107] Reciprocity thus requires that unilateral acts of prescriptive jurisdiction of one state be legal only where it is legal for all other states to have prescriptive jurisdiction in the same circumstances.[108] Thus where a state claims a type of prescriptive jurisdiction, it also acknowledges that all other states have the right to exercise it in similar circumstances. While this may not limit state practice by any legal constraint, it constitutes a practical constraint upon states which do not wish to have certain types of jurisdiction exercised in their territory from exercising extraterritorial prescriptive jurisdiction of that type in other states. In that way state practice is indicative as much for what prescriptive jurisdiction is not claimed, as for the prescriptive jurisdiction which is claimed.

(vii) *Comity and private international law.* Some authorities treat the concept of comity as a rule of international law.[109] Others say that it is not a rule of international law but is a unilateral decision of a state which takes into account the interests of another.[110] An historical analysis of the genesis of comity shows it to have developed in the last quarter of the seventeenth century in the Netherlands.[111] It was tied to the issue of the recognition of the laws of one state in another. It is said by some authors that this was a matter of courtesy, or discretion, in the state recognizing the law.[112] Others maintained that a state's laws might be applied everywhere as a matter of right, unless prejudicial to the forum.[113] The first view is that it is a decision to apply another state's law out of comity, while the second was the right of a state to have its law apply as a result of comity.[114] In either case the reasoning, however different, was to explain the application of foreign laws in the territory of a state without diminishing the state's territorial sovereignty.[115]

An interesting point in the analysis of comity is that it was necessary to have an explanation to justify the application of one state's law within the territory of another. The very concept of extraterritorial prescriptive jurisdiction may be said to have required an explanation. Since the beginning of the eighteenth century, it has been assumed that the extent to which foreign judgements and laws were to be given effect within the territory of a state is for the territorial state to decide as a matter of domestic law. Clearly this deals with the choice of a state to apply the law of another rather than its own. This is the notion of exclusivity that permeates the private international law of states. The domestic law chooses to apply only one law rather than two or more.

When the law that is chosen is that of another state, it is said that this is comity at work. In other words, comity is at the basis of the application of only one law, to the exclusion of all other laws. But it is only the application of one law by each state that is contemplated. This is not to say that comity requires that all states choose the same law: what may be punishable by the criminal law of Brazil may also be subject to the tort law of England,[116] without the breach of the notion of comity.

The notion of comity is an added restriction on the state's application of its own law, when exercising prescriptive jurisdiction. It would seem to be a question which is not really relevant to the substance of international rules of prescriptive jurisdiction. However, this is not true. An example will serve to illustrate the importance of the choice of law to prescriptive jurisdiction. If State A prescribes extraterritorially the law of State B, then to the extent of the prescription there is no actual conflicting prescription of laws within State B. Despite the exercise of the extraterritorial prescriptive jurisdiction of State A in State B, no issue of conflicting jurisdictions would arise.

It is on the level of choice of law that the doctrine of comity will apply. It is essentially a private international law concept. However, if there is generality and uniformity of state practice in their private international law rules, this practice will likewise form a rule of public international law. The source of the rule would be either customary international law or perhaps general principles of law. Thus, the enquiry with respect to the legitimate state objects in prescribing extraterritorially may continue to the law which the state is prescribing.

If one subscribes to the theory that comity is a rule of public international law then its implication will be that it will require that states in certain cases prescribe a law other than their own, extraterritorially, just as they are required to do territorially. It is only here that the distinction between criminal and civil laws becomes relevant. State practice treats the civil laws of other states differently from their criminal laws. Civil laws of other states may be applied by a state but criminal laws of those states are not.

If one subscribes to the theory that comity is only an exercise of the state's discretion, then public international law only requires that it choose the law prescribed by its domestic law. This is, of course, tautological. The state chooses the law which international law requires it to apply.

It must be emphasized that there may be practice of states, other than what may be described as comity, which requires the choice of any law. In all cases where law other than that of the prescribing state is applied extraterritorially, what is occurring is that the prescribing state is gaining a basis upon which it may enforce its laws within its territory against persons who were not within it at the material time. This is a common occurrence in private international law cases.

It must be considered that, when a state has a legitimate object to prescribe a law, public international law may be just as interested in which law is applied, as it is in the fact of prescription of a law. Perhaps the best example of such a case is where a state requires that a clause in an export contract submit the recipient to the domestic law including administrative action of the exporting state, *in futuram*. This means that any post-contractual change in the exporting state's law is to bind the recipient. This may well be a case in which the prescription of the exporting state's law extraterritorially is not a legitimate state object and thus not within the international law principles of prescriptive jurisdiction. On the other hand, were the state to require the recipient to abide by the laws of the territory in which he was present such a requirement would likely be unobjectionable, even where it required such compliance *in futuram*.

It is difficult to conceive that states will prescribe extraterritorially the laws of another state in the field of export controls because of the general unwillingness of many domestic legal systems to apply the public laws of another state. However, clearly this would be one measure which would go towards resolving the friction caused by extraterritorial prescriptive jurisdiction in the area of export controls. It would have the advantage of giving states with legitimate interests the ability to enforce within their territory against persons who have breached another state's export control laws. It would at the same time eliminate the attack on the plenitude of state control in its territory that extraterritorial prescriptive jurisdiction may represent. It would also put other states' standards of control of exports from those states on the international negotiating table. The international law of prescriptive jurisdiction with respect to export controls in some cases would recognize that more than one state had a legitimate interest, and would tend to avoid unilateralism which leads, in most cases, to a possibility of serious disagreement.

B. International Agreements, Arrangements and Understandings

1. The General Agreement on Tariffs and Trade (GATT)

The *General Agreement on Tariffs and Trade*, commonly known as the *GATT*, was concluded in the period immediately after the Second World War.[117] The *GATT*, together with the various international instruments which have subsequently interpreted it, is principally thought of as a tool for doing away with import restrictions, yet it also provides for the control of export restrictions.

The *GATT* does not expressly deal with extraterritorial export controls. Yet it does restrict the purposes for which export controls may be imposed. The result is that the *GATT* restricts the bases of international law upon which a state may impose extraterritorial export controls. The *GATT* also requires that a state demonstrate the purpose of its export controls and thus justify any extraterritorial export controls.

In general, the *GATT* export control provisions have been summarized as follows:

> Export duties and taxes may be raised when they are not bound. In principle, export prohibitions and restrictions of any other kind are prohibited by Article XI, save for a number of exceptions ...[118]

In other words, unless there is an agreement fixing the amount of an export charge, a state may vary it at any time. However, the state may not prevent any export outright unless it falls within an exception.

As a general rule of interpretation it would seem that the exceptional case is to be restrictively construed. Thus the exceptions to the general rule that export restrictions are prohibited should be interpreted restrictively.

The general rule is that export controls are only to be in the form of duties or taxes. But the *GATT* requires that export controls in any form are not to discriminate between states.[119] A provision requires that any export prohibition or restriction be applied to a contracting party of the *GATT* only where it is also applied to all third countries. Another provision requires that any favorable treatment given to one country be given to all other *GATT* members; this is most-favoured nation (MFN) treatment.[120] These provisions, on their face, would prevent strategic or foreign policy export controls (which are inherently discriminatory) were it not for some of the exceptions provided to the rule.

Export controls are also required to be transparent. Article X of the GATT requires that they be published before they can be enforced. Implicitly, Article X may be interpreted to require disclosure of motivations also.

The two general limits placed on export controls by the *GATT* are that they be transparent, and that they be non-discriminatory. Quantitative restrictions are also prohibited, but are subject to exceptions.[121] Two exceptions to quantitative restrictions are where the goods are in short supply,[122] or where restrictions are imposed to maintain standards for commodities.[123] These exceptions specify the purpose of the restriction. The transparency requirement implies that such a purpose is to be claimed in the publication of the legal measures to apply any restrictions. Thus where one of these exceptions is to be relied upon, the state should make it clear in its publication that such is the case. In fact, these exceptions to quantitative restrictions have not been invoked in strategic or foreign policy export controls. Those kinds of export controls are by their very nature and purpose discriminatory. Thus the state imposing them must rely on an exception to the non-discriminatory and MFN requirements of the *GATT*, and not an exception only to the prohibition on quantitative restrictions. However, the overall exceptions to the *GATT* are applicable as exceptions to the prohibition against discrimination as well as the one against quantitative restrictions. Thus the general exceptions to the *GATT* are those most directly impinging upon extraterritorial export controls.

The *GATT* has two articles which provide exceptions to its general rules. The first, Article XX, is titled General Exceptions; and the second, Article XXI, is titled Security Exceptions. Their effect is to allow states to discriminate in imposing export controls. The General Exceptions do not all apply to export controls, and even fewer apply to strategic or foreign policy controls. In reality, only one has some impact on those types of extraterritorial export controls. The Article XX(d) exception to the rule of non-discrimination provides that the *GATT* does not prevent states' export controls "necessary to secure compliance with laws or regulations not inconsistent with the *GATT* ... ", including enforcement of customs laws. On the basis of this exception, the *GATT* is not breached when export restrictions are imposed as sanctions for non-compliance with export control laws, where those laws themselves are not contrary to the *GATT*. The sanctions against specific persons or states may be imposed by restricting exports to them. This type of sanction must, however, be "necessary". In other words, without such a sanction the laws could be flaunted.

While this *GATT* provision allows for the use of export controls as sanctions, and thus opens up their potential use against foreign persons, such a sanction is only allowed where the law being enforced is not inconsistent with the *GATT*. The primary question is whether the export control law being enforced conforms or not.

The security exceptions of Article XXI are thus the basis upon which discriminatory export controls such as strategic and foreign policy controls are justified. The transparency requirement of Article X read in conjunction with Article XXI implies that the precise basis of discrimination in export controls is to be provided in each case. However, Article XXI provides an exception to such a transparency requirement as well. It provides that a state is not required to provide any information "the disclosure of which it considers would be contrary to its essential security interests".[124] This provision allows the state to auto-interpret the applicability of the exception because it is where the state "considers" disclosure to be prejudicial that it is not required to disclose the information. Thus there may be a problem in ascertaining on what basis a state imposes export controls. However, in practice, political reality has usually made a state imposing export controls justify them and thus the reliance upon *GATT* exceptions can usually be evaluated.

Two discrete types of security exceptions are defined by Article XXI. State action under the *U.N. Charter* is the first. State action for the protection of its essential security interests is the second.

Article XXI(c) states that nothing in the *GATT* is:

> to prevent any contracting party from taking any action in pursuance of its obligations under the *United Nations Charter* for the maintenance of international peace and security.

This provision is more restrictive than it may seem at first glance. It is arguable that the phrase "for the maintenance of international peace and security" modifies "action" and not "obligations". However, this would mean that the action could be pursuant to any obligation under the *U.N. Charter*. The preferable interpretation would be to read the exception restrictively. This would mean that of all state actions which could be allowed as an exception to the general rule of nondiscrimination, only those which a state takes to discharge its "obligations" under the *U.N. Charter* are to be excepted. This latter interpretation also leaves the interpretation of "the maintenance of international peace and security" with either the United Nations, or an international tribunal, rather than with the acting state itself. To take away the interpretation of the state's obligation from the state itself is the preferable interpretation because a supposedly objective obligation should be susceptible of objective and accurate interpretation by a third party. The case is arguably different for the interpretation of a state's own "essential security interests".

The problem remains of determining the extent to which a state action is pursuant to an "obligation" under the Charter. What is an "obligation"? When is a state action "in pursuance" of the obligation?

A restrictive interpretation of the provision would extend the meaning of the word "obligation" only to those requirements under the Charter to which a state is bound by international law. Under this interpretation, reference would only be made to the Charter itself, and possibly to the Security Council, to determine whether it had decided there was a threat to international peace. But the use of the plural in the word "obligations" suggests that reference is made not only to the general principle of maintaining international peace and security, but, moreover, to the rules forming part of the general principles of law. The result is that state action pursuant to U.N. organ decisions would also be looked at.

Examination of which U.N. organs' decisions form part of a state's "obligations" once again raises the question whether only those decisions by which states are bound in international law are to comprise "obligations". Under a fairly restrictive interpretation, mandatory Security Council sanctions would be "obligations", but "recommendatory" Security Council sanctions, or any type of General Assembly sanction would not be "obligations" under the Charter. It is difficult to reconcile such an interpretation with state practice pursuant to U.N. recommendations, which, under the *Vienna Convention on the Law of Treaties*, are said to assist in interpreting treaties.[125] States have frequently imposed discriminatory sanctions against other states, following U.N. recommendations, without being legally obliged by international law to do so. Such state action is sometimes even prior to the U.N. making recommendations and may thus be an aid in interpreting the words "in pursuance" as allowing for retroactive approbation of state action once there is U.N. action. Clearly, however, state practice does not conform to a restrictive interpretation of the meaning of "obligation".

State practice also poses significant problems in interpreting what is "in pursuance" of an obligation. At times states clearly impose greater sanctions than they are required to. Arguably this would be within the *GATT* exception because the state action is to be "in pursuance" of a general obligation under the Charter to maintain international peace and security rather than conforming to the modalities of U.N. action interpreting the obligation. We have seen that a preferred interpretation of the obligations to which Article XXI(c) refers is that they comprise Security Council decisions and perhaps even some U.N. recommendations where there is a legal obligation in international law to comply with them. But the preferred interpretation does not limit state action to only U.N. instigated sanctions. It allows sanctions "in pursuance" of the general obligations of U.N. members to preserve international peace and security, on their own. However, such actions can be objectively reviewed by the standards provided by the Charter or the U.N. organizations.

It is much more difficult to provide an objective standard by which a state's "essential security interests" are to be judged. Article XXI(b) of the *GATT* manages to effectively limit the ambit of the concept, and thus restrict the exception which allows states to protect their "essential security interests" without breaching the *GATT*. Thus a state's export controls may discriminate between states where they fall within this security exception as well.

Article XXI(b) allows a state to protect its essential security interests, but makes the state's action objectively reviewable. It does so, not by defining the term "essential security interests", but rather by requiring that the action taken by a state be action the state "considers necessary" and that it be:

(i) relating to fissionable materials or the materials from which they are derived;
(ii) relating to the traffic in arms, ammunition and implements of war and to such traffic in other goods and materials as is carried on directly or indirectly for the purpose of supplying a military establishment; (or)
(iii) taken in time of war or other emergency in international relations.

All these criteria are objectively ascertainable. Whether a state's action has fallen within the exception is also ascertainable. Thus, a state may not claim the benefit of an exception from the discrimination or quantitative restriction prohibition of MFN treatment requirement of the *GATT* by merely claiming that its "essential security interests" required it to act in the manner in which it did. The objective criteria are all matters which could be the subject of evidence and ascertained by an international tribunal to exist, or not. The weakness of this formulation, as pointed out recently by the International Court of Justice,[126] lies in the fact that the state has a broad measure of discretion as a result of the fact that Article XXI(b) permits the state to make a judgment as to which action it "considers necessary" to protect its essential security interests.

In fact, the security exceptions of Article XXI(b) were twice the subject of panel proceedings, both times the complaint being made by a member to a panel of the *GATT*. A third complaint involved but did not lead to further analysis of the same issues.

The first such complaint was made by Czechoslovakia in 1949 against U.S. export restrictions. The contracting parties of the *GATT* rejected the complaint without reasons nine days later.[127] The Czechoslovakian complaint asserted that U.S. export restrictions on trade with Eastern Europe breached the MFN requirement of the *GATT* and did not fall within the Security Exceptions of Article XXI(b). Its summary dismissal was explained in the following terms by one commentator:

> Although the Czech complaint was not frivolous, the infant *GATT* had neither the capacity nor the prestige to undertake a serious examination of U.S. cold war measures.[128]

The second complaint came more than 30 years later. Argentina complained of measures taken against it by the E.E.C., Australia and Canada on the occasion of the U.K.-Argentine war in the Falklands in 1982.[129] Although that case involved a complaint against imposing import measures, not export measures, the complaint alleged that the Article XXI(b) exception did not even apply to England because its "metropolitan territory" had not been affected or threatened. Apparently no direct response to the complaint was ever made.

The Contracting Parties did go some way to clarifying the extent of Article XXI. The decision of the Contracting Parties was more concerned with the effect on third parties by actions taken by members where they use an Article XXI exception.[130] The decision was that information to the fullest possible extent was to be given other contracting parties. In other words the transparency implications of Article X were confirmed with respect to the use of the Article XXI exceptions. However, other contracting parties affected were said to "retain their full rights under the *GATT*". Thus they could still complain. Article XXI was not to be interpreted unilaterally by the state relying upon it.

In 1985 Nicaragua complained to the Council of the CONTRACTING PARTIES alleging that the U.S. trade embargo violated Articles I, II, V, XI, XIII, XXXVI, XXXVII, and XXXVIII of the GATT. The U.S. responded by invoking Article XXI(b)(iii).[131] Subsequently the Council gave its Chairman a mandate to strike a Panel to assist in the resolution of the dispute.[132] The Panel report has not been adopted or issued.

The *GATT* can thus be seen as providing the first objective hurdle for export controls to be passed by a *GATT* member. Because the security exceptions are the only real way in which discriminatory export controls may be justified, the *GATT* forces member states to take prescriptive jurisdiction extraterritoriality on the protective principle. Only the protective principle meets both the requirements of the *GATT* and provides a basis for extraterritorial jurisdiction.

2. CoCom

CoCom was established as the working committee of the Consultative Group, by a "gentlemen's agreement" in November 1949[133] between seven members. It was the result of consultations between the U.S. and its principal Western European allies in which the U.S. urged its allies to adopt parallel controls to those it had already adopted on strategic trade with the Soviet bloc.[134] The U.S. consultations were on a bilateral basis with Western European countries.[135] The controls discussed were on military and atomic energy items.[136] The U.K. and France adopted their own, Anglo-French list, which was somewhat less comprehensive than the U.S. one.[137] The original members of the Consultative Group[138] were joined by others in 1952 and 1953[139] bringing the total to 15 countries, being all NATO countries, save Portugal, Iceland and Japan.[140] Clearly the action was an adjunct to NATO policy[141] although NATO was thought not to be the appropriate agency for systematically coordinating the relevant policies of member nations.[142] This resulted from the fact that coordination, to be effective, had to include non-NATO members, such as Japan.

These restrictions were not eagerly adopted by the Western European nations.[143] Rather the U.S. used its aid legislation as a lever to pressure the European governments to cooperate in anti-communist trade policy.[144] The Consultative Group coordination took on the name of its coordinating committee (CoCom). It served to coordinate the lists of items subject to control and measures to regulate them.[145] Two of the international measures that resulted from CoCom were the Import Certificate – Delivery Verification and the Transit Authorization Certificate systems.[146]

The Import Certificate-Delivery Verification (IC/DV) mechanism is one which requires the importer of controlled items under the CoCom list to certify to its own government its intention to import such items. It is then certified by the government and returned to the exporter's government, which will license the export. The importer's government is then to verify the delivery of the items at the option of the exporter's government.[147]

The IC/DV system went into full effect in 1952.[148] However, Canada did not have a specific regulatory scheme for the IC/DV system until June 1954.[149]

The Transit Authorization Certificates (TAC) are certificates provided by the exporter's government and given to any participating transit country. Without it controlled items would not be permitted to be shipped through a participating member's country.[150] Canada implemented this system through its *Transshipment Regulations*.[151] The *Transshipment Regulations* prohibited shipment through Canada of goods to an Area Control country and complemented then Group 9 in the Export Control List which required goods originating outside Canada to be licensed for export except when in transit in bond.[152]

These two systems were to guarantee that the controls of items on the CoCom lists were effective. There were three sub-lists. List I items were subject to a prohibition on export. List II items were subject to quantitative controls. List III items were subject to surveillance but could be exported.[153] Lists II and III were abolished in 1958 and replaced by a watch list known as List IV.[154]

An additional list was introduced under the aegis of another working group set up to control the export of materials to China. This list of items was of those prohibited to China and North Korea under a working group known as ChinaCom. It was established in 1952 and discontinued in 1957.[155]

In practice, U.S. officials are reported to have tended to err on the side of caution and thus apply IC/DV treatment to goods that were not in fact prohibited exports.[156] However it would seem that the IC/DV and TAC mechanisms were designed only to support the Consultative Group prohibited exports list. They are now applied to some non-members of CoCom which cooperate with the application of the systems for the likely reason they wish to continue the flow of CoCom countries' exports which might otherwise be denied them.

During the 1950s, as well as eliminating certain lists, CoCom also pared down the items listed.[157] In 1965-66 an exception procedure was instituted which allowed for exceptions to be made for specific cases of proposed exports of prohibited items.[158] An exception could be requested by any CoCom member but was subject to the concurrence of all other members. The practice was that CoCom would be notified of the proposed export and any country objecting would state its objection and then enter into bilateral consultations with the country proposing the export.[159]

The number of exceptions approved each year increased from 11 approvals in 1967 to 214 in 1977.[160] There were about 1,000 requests a year in the mid 1970s.[161] Computers are the largest value items that reappear in recent exceptions cases.[162] There were 981 requests for exceptions made to CoCom in 1977 to which the U.S. objected in 30 cases. Objections were made for reasons such as fears the end-user intended to use the export for military purposes, the performance of the equipment was much more sophisticated than required for the stated end use, the computer export involved integrated circuit data, or that it was dual use technology susceptible of military uses.

The discretion remains in the country proposing the export to go ahead with it. This appears to have seldom occurred.[163]

The organization of the CoCom lists changed from time to time.[164] Their focus, however, remained on military items and those items and data that would enable their production, as well as atomic energy items and data.[165]

The more restrictive attitude of the U.S. has put strain on the CoCom system during the decade of the 1980s.[166] The U.S. has been instrumental in pressing for the inclusion of computer and high technology items on the CoCom lists. Nevertheless, this results in the number of exceptions requested by and granted to the U.S. exceeding those of all other CoCom members combined.[167] However, CoCom agreement on a new listing of small computers and sophisticated telephone equipment was reached in Paris in July 1984.[168] This updated the computer embargo list first drawn up in CoCom in 1976.[169] In return, the U.S. agreed to the liberalization of some less advanced computers to Soviet Bloc countries.[170]

CoCom has also become a coordinating forum for the administration and enforcement of export controls.[171] Its Export Control Subcommittee meets on an annual or semi-annual basis to perform this function.[172]

CoCom has developed three functions. The first is to develop lists of items to be controlled. The second is to provide a forum for exceptions to the prohibitions agreed. The third is the coordination of administration and enforcement of the controls. In this way it can be seen that CoCom has embraced an administrative function which goes much beyond the mere agreement on the items its members will control themselves. A second tier of control on listed items has grown up. First they are subject to national export controls. Second they are subject to the objection of other governments. This has diluted the member state's exclusive sovereign right to control its exports and "internationalized" export controls within the Consultative Group. The result is a second level of control which is politically binding. If it is deemed that the CoCom agreement is made by representatives of governments accredited to bind the states legally it may be an oral treaty and thus provide even a legally binding commitment.[173]

3. *The O.E.C.D.*

The Organization for Economic Cooperation and Development ("O.E.C.D.") is not primarily a vehicle for the resolution of legal disputes or even for the development of rules of law. Nevertheless, the economic impact of the extraterritorial extension of U.S. export control legislation has been too great to escape comment in the O.E.C.D. Some delegations in recent years have sought to stimulate a debate on this issue within the O.E.C.D. This debate potentially goes beyond the limits of the various Council Recommendations on restrictive business practices which urge the view for respect for national legislation by multinational corporations and call for notification and consultation in the event of investigations involving important interests of another O.E.C.D. country, and conciliation by the O.E.C.D. if such consultations fail.[174] The interest of this new debate is that its focus is more general and potentially embraces all forms of extraterritorial legislation, including that respecting export controls. It purports to be seeking a principle of international law or national behaviour which might be universally applicable.

The forum of this debate is the O.E.C.D. Committee on International Investment and Multinational Enterprises, Working Group on International Investment Policies. This debate flows from the May 1984 Review Report and Ministerial Communiqué on the Declaration on International Investment and Multinational Enterprises[175] which contains the statement that in legislating potentially conflicting requirements respecting the activities of multinational companies, states should follow an approach of "moderation and restraint".

It is unfortunate that, to date, these debates, working papers and O.E.C.D. sectorial studies should remain restricted for they contain many useful ideas both as to state conduct and the formulation of a rule of law governing state action in the face of conflicting requirements.[176] It is interesting that all the parties to the Discussions in the Working Group appear to be agreed that moderation and restraint constitute the soundest base for free ordonnance of conflicts. There is, however, disagreement as to which factors states should take into account in defining the parameters of moderation and restraint. Some states are believed to consider the principle to imply a duty to avoid conflicts by refraining from taking prescriptive and enforcement action reaching out beyond national boundaries. Others are concerned that the principle should not act as a "one-way street" and consider that it implies the need to recognize the exigencies of efficient law enforcement and the accommodation of the broad national interests of different states.

There appear to be even sharper differences over the basis of the principle of moderation and restraint. Some states, reportedly including Canada, consider the principle to be a rule of international law flowing from jurisdiction over territory and the duty of non-interference in the domestic affairs of other states. On the other end of the spectrum, a few states apparently regard the principle as based only on comity and further maintain that no rule of international law compels the consideration of particular factors on the choices resulting from the principle. Surprisingly, for a group of states whose fundamental position is largely territorialist, there is a broad range of opinion as to the source of the principle. Many delegations have reportedly expressed the view that the principle is based upon comity and is not grounded in law at all. Some insist on the importance of nationality. Among those considering that the principle is legally based, are those delegations which feel that considerations of comity also enter into its application.

There has reportedly been an interesting discussion on whether the legislative, judicial and executive branches of government have acted in recent years in a manner consistent with the principle of moderation and restraint. But again there is apparently no broad agreement as to the precise manner in which each branch of government should act.

This debate, coupled with the concept of the obligation to notify and consult in such cases, constitutes a most interesting attempt to formulate the basis for state action and possibly a rule of international law directly applicable to the extraterritorial extension of export controls. The future of this debate is, however, in considerable doubt. It is no secret that many participating delegations, including that of Canada, would like to see the debate continue, while a few doubt the wisdom of such a legally oriented debate within the context of the O.E.C.D.

4. Other Multilateral Conventions

Only one multilateral treaty deals with export control laws. It is the 1980 *Convention on the Physical Protection of Nuclear Material.*[177] States are required to punish by their national law:

The intentional commission of:

(a) an act without lawful authority which constitutes the receipt, possession, use, transfer, alteration, disposal or dispersal of nuclear material and which causes or is likely to cause death or serious injury to any person of substantial damage to property;
(b) a theft or robbery of nuclear material;
(c) an embezzlement or fraudulent obtaining of nuclear material;
(d) an act constituting a demand for nuclear material by threat or use of force or by any other form of intimidation;
(e) a threat:
 (i) to use nuclear material to cause death or serious injury to any person or substantial property damage, or
 (ii) to commit an offence described in subparagraph (b) in order to compel a natural or legal person, international organization or State to do or to refrain from doing any act;
(f) an attempt to commit any offence described in paragraphs (a), (b) or (c); and
(g) an act which constitutes participation in any offence described in paragraphs (a) to (f).[178]

Clearly subparagraph (a) contemplates exports without lawful authority. Thus nuclear material export controls are placed on a different footing from other export controls by this treaty. States have managed to agree to provisions because, while the potential of very serious consequences from inappropriate use of nuclear materials is obvious, states have also a common interest in commerce in nuclear materials. This will be an important factor to consider in conjunction with the *GATT* exception which frees member states to control exports of nuclear materials.[179]

The extent to which national laws may be extraterritorial is also dealt with by the 1980 *Nuclear Material Convention.* States are to have their national laws, in this respect, extend to offences committed in their territory, by one of their nationals and by a person it has in its territory after the commission of the offence.[180] The Convention specifies that it does not prevent any state from taking any jurisdiction in conformity with its own national law.[181] In other words, the Convention treats offences with nuclear material as being universal crimes. Nevertheless it includes a curious provision allowing parties to take prescriptive jurisdiction on the basis of their status as an exporting or importing state:

> In addition to the States Parties mentioned in paragraphs 1 and 2, each State Party may, consistent with international law, establish its jurisdiction over the offences set forth in article 7 when it is involved in international nuclear transport as an exporting or importing State.[182]

The provision is interesting for two reasons. First it implies that a state has a legitimate interest in prescribing with respect to nuclear material merely on the basis that it is the country of import or export. Second, prescriptive jurisdiction is allowed only where it is "consistent with international law". This provision should be interpreted as adding something to the previous types of prescriptive jurisdiction, otherwise it would have no meaning at all. Thus "consistent with international law" cannot be interpreted as meaning the state may have prescriptive jurisdiction on the territorial or nationality principles, as these were specifically covered earlier in that article. On the other hand, it cannot be said that the mere export or import of the nuclear materials can be the basis of prescriptive jurisdiction, because such a claim would not be "consistent with international law". International law does not recognize that exporting or importing alone creates a basis for prescriptive jurisdiction. It would seem that the conclusion to which one is driven is that the provision defines a legitimate interest, not recognized by custom or general principles of law, for a state to have recourse to prescriptive jurisdiction based on the protective principle, or the universality principle.

The provision requires that two criteria be met. One is that there be a basis for the prescriptive jurisdiction in international law, or that it be "consistent with international law". The other is that the state be the importing or exporting state. This latter criterion seems to derive from the fact that importing and exporting states have international obligations under the same treaty not to export or import nuclear materials without appropriate safeguards. The special provision merely states that states have a legitimate interest in ensuring the fulfilment of their international obligations, by prescribing under an appropriate principle of international law.[183]

C. Conclusions

International law is the law that governs the relations between states and governs the actions of states with respect to persons in contexts not dealt with solely in domestic laws. Statehood, in international law, is accorded upon there being certain constituent elements and confers certain attributes as a consequence of according personality in international law. If a state prescribes where neither a constituent element nor an attribute of its personality is concerned it has no legitimate state interest, unless international law supplies the legitimacy as for example with the *Nuclear Materials Convention.*

Legitimate state interests are determined by reference to rules of international law. With respect to extraterritoriality these rules are encompassed by the four principles of prescriptive jurisdiction in international law. This Chapter has examined the four principles, along with the ways in which they have been stretched to describe rules allowing states prescriptive jurisdiction in cases which are not literally described by the formulation of the principles themselves. The extraterritorial nature of these principles can be appreciated by analyzing which ones deal with prescriptive jurisdiction over persons who are not within the territory at the material time. The principles which are extraterritorial in this sense are the objective territorial principles, the nationality principle, the protective principle and the universality principle.

In this Chapter it is submitted that it is only the objective territorial and nationality principles which may generally give rise to extraterritorial prescriptive jurisdiction for the purposes of export control laws. That is not to say that the claim to be using these principles will confer upon a state the prescriptive jurisdiction it seeks. The state must have a legitimate state interest according to the objective classification of international law. That classification is determined by state practice creating a custom and by general principles of laws.

The classification of state interests in international law is one way in which conflicts of jurisdiction are avoided. Precision of when a legitimate state interest is involved will prevent contradictory assertions of apparent prescriptive jurisdiction. Another way in which conflicts of jurisdiction may be avoided is by recourse to the comity principle. The *Third Restatement* would take an approach which is somewhat akin to that of an application of comity. It would have states consider the interests of other states in making their own decisions whether to exercise prescriptive jurisdiction, where it is assumed they have a legitimate state object to take it.[184] Unfortunately, in relying upon this criterion, which may be called the "reasonableness" of taking prescriptive jurisdiction, the *Third Restatement* suggests that it is the only limit to taking prescriptive jurisdiction where any minimum connection with the person may be established by the state.[185] In sum the *Third Restatement* takes a very expansive view of the principles of a prescriptive jurisdiction and hopes that this self-interpreted criterion can be seen to cut down the scope of those principles. However, it is submitted in this Chapter that, as in any system of law, interpretation of the rules and principles of the system is to be made by recourse to that same law. Thus, international rules of prescriptive jurisdiction are to be interpreted by classification with the assistance of other rules and principles of international law on the subject. They are not to be interpreted by recourse to the domestic law of any state.

This Chapter has also pointed out that not only is the fact that a state prescribes important, but it is also important what law the state is prescribing. This is something which has been recognized in private international law for some time. Because it may lead to, or avoid conflicts of jurisdiction, it must also be seen to be vital in international law.

International law has a paucity of state practice which is detailed enough to be able to resolve the potential conflicts of jurisdiction. However a proper classification of legitimate state objects will eliminate the incidence of actual conflicts of jurisdiction. To a large extent the *Basel Concordat* is an example of just such a classification according to the legitimate state interests which fall under the four principles of prescriptive jurisdiction in international law. Certainly a rigorous examination of the reality of state interests and state practice, with respect to similar cases, is preferable to the sweeping interpretation of the principles of international law dealing with prescriptive jurisdiction as some sort of minimum contact and then having each state use its discretion, although presuming itself to have a right to prescribe.

Where it is recognized that states having prescriptive jurisdiction do not always have the jurisdiction to require all information to adjudicate a matter, conflicts will be avoided. International law defines when, and which states may act to adjudicate by separately considering the question of jurisdiction over persons in order to resolve an adjudication. When a state does not have access to sufficient information to resolve a dispute, it should resort to international cooperation, not unilateralism.[186]

Notes

1. *France* v. *Turkey* (1927) P.C.I.J. Ser. A, No. 10, [hereinafter the *Lotus* case].
2. *Ibid.* at 20.
3. This aspect of the holding has been criticised. Contrary opinions can be seen in L. Oppenheim, *International Law, A Treatise*, 8th ed. by H. Lauterpacht, vol. I (London: Longmans, 1955) [Peace] at 597–98 [hereinafter *Lauterpacht*]; D.P. O'Connell, *International Law*, vol. II (London: Stevens, 1965) at 662–63, [hereinafter *O'Connell*] and the dissent in the *Lotus* case itself, *supra*, note 1 at 52–53, (Judge Finlay); Law Reform Commission of Canada, *Extraterritorial Jurisdiction*, Working Paper 37, (1984) at 36–37.
4. *Lotus* case, *supra*, note 1 at 25.
5. *O'Connell*, *supra*, note 3; *Lauterpacht*, *supra*, note 3; I. Brownlie, *Principles of Public International Law*, 3rd ed., (Oxford: O.U.P., 1979) at 298–320 [hereinafter *Brownlie*]; D.W. Grieg, *International Law*, 2nd ed. (London: Butterworths, 1976) at 210–14; M.N. Shaw, *International Law*, 2nd ed. (Cambridge: Grotius, 1987) at

342–71; C. Rousseau, *Droit international public*, vol. II (Paris: Dalloz, 1977) at 15 [hereinafter *Rousseau*]; D. Carreau, *Droit international* (Paris: Pedone, 1986) at 311–40; M. Virally, "Panorama du droit international contemporain" 1983 Recueil des cours 13 at 92 [hereinafter *Virally*].
6. J.-G. Castel, *Extraterritoriality in International Trade* (Toronto: Butterworths, 1988); A.D. Neale & M.L. Stephens, *International Business and International Jurisdiction* (Oxford: Clarendon Press, 1988) [hereinafter *Neale & Stephens*]; D.E. Rosenthal and Knighton, *National Laws and International Commerce: The Problem of Extraterritoriality*, Royal Institute of International Affairs, Chatham House Paper No. 17, (1982); B. Stern, *L'application extraterritoriale des lois* (Paris: Economica, 1987).
7. The most comprehensive is by A.V. Lowe, *Extraterrritorial Jurisdiction* (Cambridge: Grotius, 1983) [hereinafter *Lowe*].
8. M. Akehurst, "Jurisdiction in International Law" (1972–73) 46 Brit. Y.B.I.L. 145; D.W. Bowett, "Jurisdiction: Changing Problems of Authority over Activities and Resources", (1982) 53 Brit. Y.B.I.L. 1; G. Kegel & I. Seidl-Hohenveldern, "On the Territoriality Principle in Public International Law", trans. J. Danby (1982) 5 Hastings Int'l and Comp. L.R. 245 at 311 [hereinafter *Kegel & Seidl-Hohenveldern*].
9. Bourquin, "Crimes et délits contre la sûreté des états étrangers" (1927) 16 Recueil des cours 117 at 178; F.A. Mann, "The Doctrine of Jurisdiction in International Law" (1964) 111 Recueil des cours 1 [hereinafter *Mann*]; F.A. Mann, "The Doctrine of Jurisdiction in International Law Revisited After Twenty Years" (1984) 186 Recueil des cours 9; A.F. Lowenfeld, "Public Law in the International Arena; Conflict of Laws, International Law and Some Suggestions for their Interaction" (1979) 163 Recueil des cours 311.
10. See generally works listed *supra*, note 5.
11. Even this is not always assured. See K.M. Meessen, "Conflicts of Jurisdiction under the New Restatement" (1987) 50 Law and Contemp. Problems 47.
12. J.-G. Castel & S. A. Williams, *Canadian Criminal Law: International and Transnational Aspects* (Toronto: Butterworths, 1981) at 3 [hereinafter *Castel & Williams*].
13. *Rousseau, supra*, note 5, vol. III at 8; *Bourquin, supra*, note 9 at 136–37. Bourquin explains that historically this was not always the case. Rather, prescriptive jurisdiction over the person used to be based on personal links with a sovereign, apart from residence, and even earlier, in feudal times, jurisdiction was based on allegiance. The establishment of states on a territorial basis put those resident there under the state's jurisdiction.
14. *Mann, supra*, note 9 at 36.
15. *Castel & Williams, supra*, note 12 at 29. *Lauterpacht, supra*, note 3, vol. I at 325 states that each state has jurisdiction over all persons and things which are within its territory.
16. *Castel & Williams, ibid.*
17. *Mann, supra*, note 9 at 86.
18. *Restatement of the Law, Third, The Foreign Relations of the United States*, (St. Paul Minn.: American Law Institute, 1987) at 239 [hereinafter *Third Restatement*]; D. Wallace, Jr. "Extraterritorial Jurisdiction" (1983) 15 L. & Pol. Int'l Bus. 1099 at 1102.
19. *Lotus* case, *supra*, note 1 at 22.
20. With respect to violations of competition law under Articles 85, 86 of the *Treaty of Rome*. See *I.C.I.* v. *E.E.C. Commission* [1972] E.C.R. 619; *MacMillan Bloedel Ltd* v. *E.C. Commission, Re Wood Pulp Cartel: A. Anlström OY and Others* v. *E.C. Commission*, [1988] 4 C.M.L.R. 901.
21. *Mann, supra*, note 9 at 95, states a "close connection" is needed. At 104 he states any effect is insufficient to be such a "close connection".
22. *Virally, supra*, note 5 at 92.
23. *Nottebohm* case (*Liechtenstein* v. *Guatemala*) 2d phase, I.C.J. Rep. 1955, 1 at 23.
24. *Ibid.* at 22–23.

25. *Virally, supra*, note 5 at 94; *Brownlie, supra*, note 5 at 421–22; *Rousseau, supra*, note 5, vol. III at 134 merely states that the nationality principle also applies to corporations; *O'Connell, supra*, note 3, vol. II at 1124–26; *Third Restatement, supra*, note 18 does not seem to recognize the head office test *per se*. It states in s. 402, comment e) at 239, "the nationality of a corporation or comparable juridical entity is that of the state under whose law it is organized." R.Y. Jennings, "Extraterritorial Jurisdiction and the United States Antitrust Law" (1957) 33 Brit. Y.B.I.L. 146 at 154 states the two tests as being domicile and corporate registration.
26. *Barcelona Traction, Light and Power Company, Limited* (*Belgium* v. *Spain*), I.C.J. Rep. 1970, 3 [hereinafter *Barcelona Traction*].
27. *Ibid.* at 33–34. See also *Panevezyts Saludutiskis Railway* (1939) P.C.I.J. Ser. A/B No. 76.
28. *Barcelona Traction, ibid.*
29. *Brownlie, supra*, note 5 at 303.
30. See *Castel & Williams, supra*, note 40 at 8.
31. *Third Restatement, supra*, note 18, s.402(3) at 238.
32. (1935) 29 Am. J. Int'l L. Supp. I, 435, art. 7 at 439 [hereinafter *Harvard Draft*].
33. *Third Restatement, supra*, note 18, s. 402, Comment f) at 240; *Virally, supra*, note 5 at 95; Mann, *supra*, note 19 at 94; *Lauterpacht, supra*, note 3 at 331; G. Schwarzenberger, *A Manual of International Law*, 5th ed. (U.S.A.: Professional Books, 1967) at 97 [hereinafter *Schwarzenberger*]; *Harvard Draft, ibid.* at arts. 7 and 8.
34. *Mann, supra*, note 9 at 94 states: "... the independence standard is supplied solely by international law, i.e. by the general practice of civilized states."
35. *Lauterpacht, supra*, note 3, vol. I at 331.
36. This is not to be confused with the passive personality concept. It is the fact that the victim forms an integral part of the government that invokes the protective principle, not the fact that he is a national of the state.
37. *Third Restatement, supra*, note 18, s. 402, Comment f) at 240.
38. *O'Connell, supra*, note 3, vol. II at 905.
39. *Mann, supra*, note 9 at 39, 95; *Brownlie, supra*, note 5 at 304; *Castel & Williams, supra*, note 12 at 137; *Eichmann* case (1962–62) 36 I.L.R. 26 at 289.
40. *Harvard Draft, supra*, note 32, art. 9.
41. *Mann, supra*, note 9 at 95; *Brownlie, supra*, note 5 at 304; *Castel & Williams, supra*, note 12 at 137; *Virally, supra*, note 5 at 96; *Third Restatement, supra*, note 18 s. 404 at 254.
42. *Virally, supra*, note 5 at 96 says that only some states accept this; but see *Third Restatement, supra*, note 18 s. 404 at 254.
43. *Third Restatement, ibid.*
44. It is true that some authors do lump in counterfeiting of currency as a universal crime. See *Mann, supra*, note 19 at 395; and *Brownlie, supra*, note 5 at 304 who calls this contrary to "international public policy," and thus giving rise to any state's jurisdiction. The protective principle allows the state jurisdiction over counterfeiting only of its own currency; there is a risk of confusion between this and other principles.

    It may be that in the future international law will recognize some economic offences as contrary to international law because of the increasing interdependence of states. *The Set of Multilaterally Agreed Equitable Principles and Rules for the Control of Restrictive Business Practices*, UN Doc. TD/RBP/Conf./10 (1980) [hereinafter *The Set*] may be indicative of the fact there is a trend to recognize some form of restrictive business practices as contrary to international law. As of now, no prescriptive jurisdiction over persons breaching *The Set* has been recognized on the universality principle.
45. See *infra* Chapter VII.
46. See *infra*, note 94.
47. *United States* v. *Aluminum Co. of America*, 148 F.2d 416 (2nd Cir., 1974); *Timken*

Roller Bearing Co. v. *United States*, 341 U.S. 593, 71 S. Ct. 971, 95 L. Ed. 1199 (1951); *United States* v. *National Lead Co.*, 332 U.S. 319, 67 S. Ct. 1634, 91 L. Ed. 2077 (1947); *United States* v. *Sisal Sales Corpn.*, 274 U.S. 268, 47 S. Ct. 592, 71 L. Ed. 1042 (1927); *Thomsen* v. *Cayser*, 243 U.S. 66, 37 S. Ct. 353, 61 L. Ed. 497 (1917); *United States* v. *Pacific and Arctic Ry. and Navigation Co.*, 228 U.S. 87, 33 S. Ct. 443, 57 L. Ed. 742 (1913); *United States* v. *General Elec.*, 82 F. Supp. 753 (D.N.J., 1949); *Continental Ore Co.* v. *Union Carbide and Carbon Corpn.*, 370 U.S. 690, 705, 82 S. Ct. 1404, 1413, 8 L. Ed. 2d 777 (1962); *Mannington Mills Inc.* v. *Congoleum Corpn.*, 595 F.2d 1287 at 1291 (3d Cir., 1979); *United States* v. *The Watchmakers of Switzerland Information Centre, Inc.* (the *Swiss Watch* case), 1963 Trade Cases para. 70,600, at 77, 456–57 (S.D.N.Y., 1962); *The Fleishmann Distilling Corpn.* v. *Distillers Co. Ltd.*, 295 F. Supp. 221, at 226–227 (S.D.N.Y., 1975); *Re Uranium Antitrust Litigation*, 617 F. 2d 1248 (7th Cir., 1980); *Laker Airways Ltd.* v. *Sabena Belgian World Airlines*, 731 F.2d 909 (D.C. Cir., 1984). For a review of some of the cases, see *Timberlane Lumber Co.* v. *Bank of America, N.T. and S.A.*, 549 F.2d 597, at 610–611 (9th Cir., 1976); *Timberlane Co.* v. *Bank of America*, 574 F. Supp. 1453 (N.D. Cal., 1983); *Industrial Development Corp.* v. *Mitsui & Co.*, 617 F.2d 876 (5th Cir., 1982). For a recent general review of these cases see *Neale & Stephens supra*, note 6.

48. *Société Nationale Industrielle Aérospatiale* and *Société de Construction d'Avions de Tourisme* v. *U.S. District Court for the Southern District of Iowa*, (1987) 482 US , 96 L Ed 2d 461, 107 S. Ct 2542.
49. *Supra*, note 18.
50. *Restatement of the Law, Second, Foreign Relations Law of the United States*, (Washington D.C.: American Law Institute, 1965) [hereinafter *Second Restatement*].
51. *Ibid.* § 18.30.33.
52. *Third Restatement*, *supra*, note 18 at §§ 401, 402 and 404. See in particular 402(1)(c) and 402(3).
53. *Third Restatement*, *ibid.* at § 403 (2) Whether exercise of jurisdiction over a person or activity is unreasonable is determined by evaluating all relevant factors, including, where appropriate:

    (a) the link of the activity to the territory of the regulating state, i.e., the extent to which the activity takes place within the territory, or has substantial, direct, and foreseeable effect upon or in the territory;

    (b) the connections, such as nationality, residence, or economic activity, between the regulating state and the person principally responsible for the activity to be regulated, or between that state and those whom the regulation is designed to protect;

    (c) the character of the activity to be regulated, the importance of regulation to the regulating state, the extent to which other states regulate such activities, and the degree to which the desirability of such regulation is generally accepted;

    (d) the existence of justified expectations that might be protected or hurt by the regulation;

    (e) the importance of the regulation to the international political, legal, or economic system;

    (f) the extent to which the regulation is consistent with the traditions of the international system;

    (g) the extent to which another state may have an interest in regulating the activity; and

    (h) the likelihood of conflict with regulation by another state.
54. *Ibid.* at § 403 (3) When it would not be unreasonable for each of two states to exercise jurisdiction over a person or activity, but the prescriptions by the two states are in conflict, each state has an obligation to evaluate its own as well as the other state's interest in exercising jurisdiction, in light of all the relevant factors, Subsection (2); a state should defer to the other state if that state's interest is clearly greater.

55. *Ibid.* at 245.
56. D.R. Robinson, "Conflicts of Jurisdiction and the Draft Restatement" (1983) 15 L. & Pol. Int'l Bus. 1147 at 1153; D.R. Robinson, "Conflicting Assertions of National Jurisdiction over Multinational Enterprises" in *Proceedings of the 1983 Conference of the Canadian Council on International Law* (Ottawa: C.C.I.L., 1984) at 23.
57. Letter from Judge Malcolm Wilkey to Professor L. Henkin, (April 24, 1984), in (1984) 25 Va. J. Int'l L. 43.
58. J.-G. Castel, *Extraterritoriality in International Trade* (Toronto: Butterworths, 1988) at 269.
59. See *supra*, note 11 at 63
60. *Supra*, note 48.
61. See also W.L.M. Reese, "Limitations on the Extraterritorial Application of Law" (1977–78) 4 Dalhousie L.J. 589 at 600. Although most of his article deals with the laws of constituent parts of federal states, he argues that in this respect, there is no difference between international and constitutional laws of the states examined. (U.S., Australia and Canada.)
62. *O'Connell*, *supra*, note 3, vol. II at 913; *Lauterpacht*, *supra*, note 3, vol. I at 264–66; *Virally*, *supra*, note 5 at 98–99; *Third Restatement*, *supra*, note 18, § 441 at 341, and § 463 at 452–53.
63. An example may be where an export of strategic goods to the government of another country is intercepted by aliens abroad.
64. There is less than homogeneous use of the terms in the literature on the subject. The distinctions are well made in P.A. Shneyer & V. Barta, "The Legality of the U.S. Economic Blockade of Cuba Under International Law" (1981) 13 Case W. Res. J. Int'l L. 451 at 452, and those distinctions have been adopted here. See also C. Lebon, "Les contre-mesures inter-étatiques et les réactions à l'illicéité dans la société internationale" [1982] A.F.D.I. 1. In the *Military and Paramilitary Activities in and Against Nicaragua (Nicaragua* v. *United States of America*), *Merits*, I.C.J. Reports 1986, 14, para 276 at 138 [hereinafter *Nicaragua* v. *U.S.A.*], the I.C.J. implicitly accepts the legitimacy of certain forms of boycotts and the trade embargoes, unless they violate a treaty obligation.
65. For a brief and clear description of reprisals and retorsion, see *Virally*, *supra*, note 5 at 217–20.
66. *Ibid.* at 220.
67. *Case Concerning United States Diplomatic and Consular Staff in Teheran* (*United States* v. *Iran*) I.C.J. Rep. 1980, 3.
68. *Supra*, notes 119, 120.
69. *Kegel & Seidl-Hohenveldern*, *supra*, note 8 at 289, [hereinafter *Kegel and Seidl-Hohenveldern*] state that acts that seek to promote the welfare of the state are effective only within the territory of a state. *Bourquin*, *supra*, note 9 at 188 writes that a state would have a well founded complaint against another trying to enforce its political laws extraterritorially.
70. F. Matscher, "Études des règles de compétence judiciaire dans certaines conventions internationales" (1978) 161 Recueil des cours 127 at 141–57 [hereinafter *Matscher*], distinguishes between civil and repressive powers of the state. *Mann*, *supra*, note 9, makes this distinction by considering each a separate type of jurisdiction.
71. *Brownlie*, *supra*, note 5 at 299 and 309.
72. R.B. Thompson, "United States Jurisdiction over Foreign Subsidiaries: Corporate and International Law Aspects" (1983) 15 L. & Pol. Int'l Bus. 319 at 364 [hereinafter *Thompson*], states that the U.S. is the prime exponent of such action.
73. The U.S. Siberian Pipeline sanctions were of this nature. They were imposed on foreign corporations without regard to even their ownership or control, on the mere basis that U.S. technology was used. See *Third Restatement*, *supra*, note 18, § 414, Reporters' Note 8 at 281 and R. Ergec, *La compétence extraterritoriale à la lumière*

du contentieux sur le gazoduc euro-sibérien (Bruxelles: Bruylant, 1984). See also the very valuable collection of articles on this issue in (1984) 27 German Y.I.B.L.

74. UNGA Res. 1803, 17 UN GAOR Supp. (No. 17), UN Doc. A/5127 (1962) 15.
75. *Virally, supra*, note 5 at 96–98.
76. The difference is the state having prescriptive jurisdiction on the basis of the objective territorial principle will, by definition, not have enforcement jurisdiction over the person at the time of the offence.
77. See *Lowe, supra*, note 7 at 79–129, for examples of protests and blocking legislation.
78. See particularly *Lowe, ibid.* whose book lists examples of both claims and responses to conflicting claims of jurisdiction. It then lists examples of cooperative efforts to resolve potential disputes, especially in the anti-trust law area.
79. June 21, 1976, reprinted in (1976), 15 Int'l Leg. Mat. 967 [hereinafter *OECD Declaration*]. See also OECD International Investment and Multinational Enterprises (1984).
80. *OECD Declaration, ibid.* par. 7.
81. Unanimously adopted by the U.N. General Assembly. See UN Doc. TD/RBP/Conf./10 (1980), reprinted in (1980) 19 Int'l Leg. Mat. 813 [hereinafter *UN Doc. TD/RBP/Conf./10*]. See also W. Fikentscher, "United Nations Code of Conduct: New Paths in International Law" (1982) 30 Am. J. Comp. L. 577.
82. *UN Doc. TD/RBP/Conf./10 ibid.* s. D, para. 1.
83. UN Doc. E/C.10/1982/6, paras 6–10. These paragraphs have not all been agreed to. However, the formulations being considered state that transnational corporations are to respect not only the laws but the policies, objectives and priorities of the countries in which they operate.
84. 12 I.M.F. Survey 201 (July 11, 1983), reprinted in (1983) 22 Int'l Leg. Mat. 901. Its importance is recognized in *Third Restatement, supra*, note 18, § 414, Reporters' Note 6 at 279.
85. This argument was made about the *Basel Concordat* by Canada in the U.S. Supreme Court in *Re Grand Jury Proceedings The Bank of Nova Scotia*; *United States* v. *The Bank of Nova Scotia* 740 F.2d 817 (11th Cir., 1984) after remand 722 F.2d 657 (11th Cir., 1983), *cert denied* 105 S. Ct. 778 (1988) although it was apparently rejected. See "Brief of the Government of Canada as Amicus Curiae in Support of Petition for Writ of Certiorari" No. 84–329 at 13–14.
86. See *Third Restatement, supra*, note 18, s. 413, Reporters' Note 3 at 269, wherein is listed a number of model tax conventions dealing with the avoidance of double taxation.
87. See, for example, the "Antitrust Notification and Consultation Procedure" between Canada and the United States. Exchange of letters between W.P. Rogers, Attorney General, U.S. Department of Justice and E.D. Fulton, Minister of Justice and Attorney General of Canada, of Jan. 31, Feb. 5, Feb. 12, and March 11, 1959, H. C. Debates 1959, vol. I p. 617–19, Feb. 3, 1959. Renewed by a Joint Statement concerning Cooperation in Anti-trust Matters, Nov. 3, 1969 reprinted in *Lowe, supra*, note 7 at 226–28. Superseded by the "Memorandum of Understanding Between the Government of Canada and the Government of the United States of America as to Notification, Consultation and Cooperation with Respect to the Application of National Antitrust Laws", March 1, 1984 appended to Government of Canada News Release NR–84–6, March 9, 1984. Article 2 provides for notification of investigations or proceedings involving the national interests of the other. Article 4 provides that either party may request consultations. Article 6 provides that each will give careful consideration to the significant national interests of the other. Article 8 recognizes the territorial state's right to obtain relevant information from any resident, regardless of nationality. Article 12 states that the Understanding does not constitute an "international agreement".
88. *Australia-United States Agreement Relating to Cooperation on Antitrust Matters*,

June 29, 1982, reprinted in *Lowe*, *supra*, note 7 at 233. Like the Canada-U.S. understanding, it provides for notification and consultation in order to avoid conflicts of jurisdiction.

89. See *Lowe*, *supra*, note 7 at 228 for the Federal Republic of Germany-U.S. Treaty on Anti-trust cooperation as well.
90. See generally *Matscher*, *supra*, note 70 especially at pages 162–74; see also references in (1981) 19 C.Y.B.I.L. 407.
91. Concluded at Quebec City, March 18, 1985, reprinted at (1985) 24 Int'l Leg. Mat. 1092.
92. *Canada-United States Free Trade Implementation Act*, S.C. 1988 c. 65, Schedule A, Part A, Article 407.3. Reprinted (1988) 27 Int'l Leg. Mat. 281. For further comment see *infra*, Chapter IV, Section F.
93. An example is the *Australian Foreign Antitrust Judgements (Restriction of Enforcement) Act l979*, Act No. 13, 1979, assented to March 15, 1979, reprinted in *Lowe*, *supra*, note 7 at 83. Lowe reproduces some good examples of the range of statutes in force.
94. Canadian *Combines Investigation Act*, R.S.C. 1970, c. C–23, as amended by S.C. 1974–75, c. 76, ss. 31.5, 31.6, and 32.1, reprinted in *Lowe*, *supra*, note 7 at 104, S.C. 1986 c. 26; Canadian *Foreign Extraterritorial Measures Act*, S.C. 1984, S.C. 1984, c. 49, proclaimed in force Feb. 14, 1985; *U.K. Protection of Trading Interests Act* (U.K.) 1980, c. 11.
95. *Ibid.* The order is S.I. 1982, No. 885, made pursuant to the statute cited in note 94.
96. It may be argued that the U.S. application of the nationality principle is illegal. It would seem that the U.S. constantly is stretching the principles out of shape in order to have a way to justify any extraterritorial legislation it wishes to adopt.
97. F.L. Kirgis, Jr., *Prior Consultation in International Law: A Study of State Practice* (Charlottesville: University Press of Virginia, 1983) at 241 [hereinafter *Kirgis*].
98. *Ibid.* at 374–75. See also *infra*, Chapter IV, Sections H and I.
99. *Schwarzenberger*, *supra*, note 33 at 106; *Harvard Draft*, *supra*, note 32, arts. 7 and 8.
100. *Brownlie*, *supra*, note 5 at 444, note 2 collects many of the authorities on the subject.
101. *Bourquin*, *supra*, note 9 at 188.
102. If, on the other hand, "repression" is to mean use of a state's enforcement jurisdiction, then this view adds nothing to the general rule that enforcement jurisdiction is territorial, and thus the other meaning of repression is to be preferred.
103. *Mann*, *supra*, note 9 at 44; *Matscher*, *supra*, note 70 at 157.
104. UNGA Res. 3281 (XXIX), Dec. 12, 1974, 29 UN GAOR Supp. (No. 31), U.N. Doc. A/9631, specifically with respect to non-intervention, political independence, and sovereign equality of states.
105. Compare UN Doc. A/9946, Dec. 9, 1974, for the proposed amendment by countries voting against the *Charter* formulation.
106. *Virally*, *supra*, note 5 at 76.
107. C. De Visscher, *Théories et réalités en droit international public*, 4th ed. (Paris: Pedone, 1970) at 27 [hereinafter *De Visscher*].
108. L.H. Legault, "Draft Notes for a Speech" Canadian Council on International Law Annual Conference, Ottawa, October 22, 1983; H.G. Maier, "Extraterritorial Jurisdiction at a Crossroads: An Intersection between Public and Private International Law" (1982) 76 Am J. Int'l L. 280 [hereinafter *Maier*] at 307; see *Mann*, *supra*, note 9 at 30, 105, 153; *Kegel & Seidl-Hohenveldern*, *supra*, note 8 at 249–50; *De Visscher*, *ibid.* at 272.
109. *Mann*, *ibid.* at 22.
110. *Maier*, *supra*, note 108 at 281; *Brownlie*, *supra*, note 5 at 31; D. Wallace, Jr., "Extraterritorial Jurisdiction" (1983) 15 L. & Pol. Int'l Bus. 1099 at 1106.
111. H.E. Yntema, "The Comity Doctrine" (1966–67) 65 Mich. L. Rev. 9 at 9.
112. *Ibid.* at 24, summarizes some of these views.

113. *Ibid.* at 25–26, and 30, summarizes some of these views.
114. *Ibid.* at 30.
115. *Maier*, *supra*, note 108 at 281.
116. *Machado* v. *Fontes* (1897) 2 Q.B. 321. Of course, the facts of any case may give rise to an international complaint if either state has exceeded its prescriptive jurisdiction. *Mann*, *supra*, note 9 at 59 suggests that England, in *Machado* v. *Fontes*, did in fact exceed its jurisdiction.
117. *Protocol of the Provisional Application of the General Agreement on Tariffs and Trade*, signed October 30, 1947; 55 U.N.T.S., 308; Can. T.S. 1948 No 31.
118. M. Rom, "Export Controls in *GATT*" (1984) 18 J. World Trade L. 125 at 125.
119. *GATT*, *supra*, note 117 article XIII(1), and article XVII provide a similar non-discrimination provision for state trading enterprises.
120. *Ibid.* art. 1.
121. *Ibid.* art. XI.
122. *Ibid.* art. XI(2)(a).
123. *Ibid.* art. XI(2)(b).
124. *Ibid.* art. XXI(a).
125. Article 31(3) of the *Vienna Convention on the Law of Treaties*, concluded May 23, 1969, UN Doc. A/Conf. 39/27.
126. *Nicaragua* v. *U.S.A.*, *supra*, note 64 at 116, para 222, where the Court contrasted the wording of the GATT, article XXI(b), and article XXI of the Nicaragua-U.S.A. ICN Treaty which deals with similar questions, but does not include the word "considers" and is thus considerably more restrictive than the GATT.
127. Complaint - *GATT* Doc. CP. 3/33 (May 30, 1949); Decision - *GATT* Doc. CP. 3/SR. 22 (June 8, 1949); II B.I.S.D. 28 (1952).
128. R.E. Hudec, *The GATT Legal System and World Trade Diplomacy* (New York: Praeger, 1975) at 68.
129. *GATT* Doc. L/5317.
130. *GATT* Doc. L/5426 (Nov. 30, 1982); B.I.S.D. 29th Supp. 1981–82 (March 1983) at 23.
131. GATT/C/M/188, (June 28, 1985)
132. GATT/C/M/191, (September 11, 1985). Throughout the discussion the U.S. Representative maintained that the U.S. decision as to its security interests, pursuant to Article XXI, could not be the subject of dispute settlement or debate. Analysis of the published records of the Council does not reveal complete sympathy for this proposition on the part of all representatives.
133. A.F. Lowenfeld, *International Economic Law*, 2nd ed., vol. IV (U.S.A.: Matthew Bender, 1983) [*Trade Policy for Political Ends*] at 12 [hereinafter *Lowenfeld*]. See also R. Côté, "Les *Gentlemen's Agreements* à l'ère technologique", (1989) 34 McGill L.J. 336.
134. "East-West Trade", Statement of Secretary Dean Rusk to the Senate Committee on Foreign Relations, Mar. 13, 1964, 50 Dep't State Bull. 474, Mar. 30 1964 at 475.
135. 17th Battle Act Report, 1964, reprinted in part in 52 U.S. Dep't State Bull. 148, Feb. 1, 1965 at 148.
136. *Ibid.*
137. *Ibid.*
138. *Ibid.* at 149, lists the U.K., France, Italy, the Netherlands, Belgium, Luxembourg and the U.S.
139. 25th Quarterly Report under the *Export Control Act*, U.S. Department of Commerce, Dec. 1, 1953 at 8; and M.P. Doxey, *Economic Sanctions and International Enforcement* (Oxford: Oxford University Press, 1971) at 22 [hereinafter *Doxey*].
140. *Supra*, note 135 at 149.
141. *Doxey*, *supra*, note 139 at 23.
142. "Report of the Committee of Three on Non-Military Cooperation in NATO", Dec. 14,

1956, reprinted in 36 Dep't State Bull. 18, 7 Jan. 1957 at 24.

143. G. Adler-Karlsson, "International Economic Power: The U.S. Strategic Embargo" (1972) 6 J. World Trade L. 501 at 511.
144. *Ibid.* at 503 and 511.
145. *Supra*, note 135 at 149.
146. *Ibid.*
147. 18th Quarterly Report required under the *Export Control Act*, U.S. Dep't of Commerce, Feb. 25, 1952 at 2.
148. 22nd Quarterly Report required under the *Export Control Act*, U.S. Dep't of Commerce, Mar. 20, 1953 at 4; also see the 34th Quarterly Report required under the *Export Control Act*, U.S. Dep't of Commerce, Feb. 15, 1956 at 12.
149. P.C. 1954–790, May 27, 1954, in force June 1, 1954, SOR/54–202, 88 Can. Gaz. Pt II 552; see also H.C. Debates 1953–54, vol. III, p. 3965, Mar. 16, 1954, Mr. J.H. Dickey at 3066.
150. 30th Quarterly Report required under the *Export Control Act*, U.S. Dep't of Commerce, April 1, 1955 at 10.
151. P.C. 1955–17, Jan. 4, 1955, SOR/55–3, 89 Can. Gaz. Pt II 990.
152. P.C. 1953–1213, Aug. 5, 1953, SOR/53–329, 87 Can. Gaz. Pt II 750 (1954) which amended similar provisions in force since 1949, P.C. 6561, SOR/49–552, 84 Can. Gaz. Pt II 224 (1950).
153. *Doxey, supra*, note 139 at 23; H.J. Berman and J.R. Garson, "United States Export Controls - Past, Present and Future" (1967) 67 Colum L. Rev. 791 at 835 [hereinafter *Berman & Garson*].
154. *Berman & Garson, ibid.* at 835–36.
155. *Ibid.* at 835.
156. *Ibid.* at 839.
157. *Doxey, supra*, note 139 at 24–25.
158. *Ibid.* at 25.
159. Details are given of the system in 1978 in "Special Report on Multilateral Export Controls" sent to Congress July 10, 1978, by President Carter.
160. *Ibid.*
161. *Ibid.*
162. *Ibid.*
163. "The Activities of the Department of Export Control" Mar. 22, 1976, 74 U.S. Dep't State Bull. 520, 19 Arr. 1976 at 521–22.
164. *Ibid.* gives an example at 521.
165. *Ibid.*
166. See Maxwell Glen, "Exporting Technology - Can Trade and National Security Coexist?" (18 Aug. 1979) National Journal 1370, particularly at 1374.
167. "Export Policy Seen Harmful to CoCom" (10 Sept. 1979) Aviation Week & Space Technology.
168. P. Lewis, "Computers Pact 2 1/2 Years in Making", *International Herald Tribune* (18 July 1984) 9.
169. *Ibid.*
170. *Ibid.*
171. "East-West Relations and Technology Transfer" (Address by M.B. Marks to the Federal Bar Association 29 March 1984) 84 U.S. Dep't State Bull. 68, Aug. 1984 at 70.
172. *Ibid.*
173. The legally binding nature of CoCom agreements was not accepted in a court decision in Japan. In *The Association of the 1969 Peking-Shanghai Japanese Industrial Exhibition* v. *Minister of International Trade and Industry*, Case No. A30 of July 8, 1969, Tokyo District Court, as described in Chin Kim, "The 'Cocom' Case" (1970) 4 J. World Trade L. 604. In that case the court stated CoCom is an "unofficial interna-

tional organ directly aimed at slowing down of strength of potential war power of the Communist bloc countries. Agreement entered through this body does not have the effect of a treaty domestically or internationally." However it would seem the binding nature of the institution itself, that is to consult about one's export controls, is not directly addressed by the decision.

Accounts of the CoCom generally describe it as a non-binding agreement in the sense of international law by referring to it as having no treaty. See *Doxey*, *supra*, note 139 at 23; *Lowenfeld*, *supra*, note 133 at 13; the U.S. Dep't of Commerce Reports cited above; 74 U.S. Dep't State Bull. 520, 19 April 1976 at 521; M. Boyer, "Le Cocon de Cocom" *Le Monde* (5 May 1981) 21–23. There seems to have been agreement that the items on the CoCom lists are to be controlled as to the lists content, however, while it may be that no state is bound to apply the lists the state is certainly politically obliged to control the item.

The degree to which European Governments consider CoCom to be non-binding and informal varies from country to country. Officials of some governments speak of a CoCom "list", while officials of others insist that there is no such thing as a formally agreed list.

A widely circulated version of the List appeared in British Business, June 1985, Supplement entitled "Security Export Control", issued by the U.K. Minister of Trade.

174. See in particular O.E.C.D., Extracts from the Guidelines for Multinational Enterprises, 21 June 1976, and the Council Recommendation concerning Restrictive Business Practices Affecting International Trade including those involving Multinational Enterprises, 20 July 1978. Reprinted in *Lowe*, *supra*, note 7 at 246, and O.E.C.D. Council Recommendation concerning Cooperation between Member Countries on Restrictive Business Practices Affecting International Trade, 25 Sept. 1979. Reprinted in *Lowe*, *ibid.* at 251.

175. *O.E.C.D., International Investment and Multinational Enterprises* (Revised Edition 1984). See pp. 23–24: Section on Conflicting Requirements, Endorsed by Ministers on May 17, 1984, para. 5.

5. In contemplating new legislation, action under existing legislation or other exercise of jurisdiction which may conflict with the legal requirements or established policies of another Member country and lead to conflicting requirements being imposed on multinational enterprises, the Member countries concerned should:

i) Have regard to relevant principles of international law;

ii) Endeavour to avoid or minimise such conflicts and the problems to which they give rise by following an approach of moderation and restraint, respecting and accommodating the interests of other Member countries;

iii) Take fully into account the sovereignty and legitimate economic, law enforcement and other interests of other Member countries;

iv) Bear in mind the importance of permitting the observance of contractual obligations and the possible adverse impact of measures having a retroactive effect.

176. Information obtained from interviews with officials of a number of participating delegations.

177. Concluded in New York, March 3, 1980, signed by Canada in 1980.

178. *Ibid.* art. 7.

179. See *supra*, Chapter II Section B.1: "The GATT".

180. *Supra*, note 177.

181. *Ibid.* art. 8(3).

182. *Ibid.* art. 8(4).

183. See also The *Convention on the Prevention and Punishment of Crimes against Internationally Protected Persons including Diplomatic Agents*, reprinted at (1974) 13 Int'l Leg. Mat. 41, provides in article 3 that states prescribe on the basis of territory, nationality and protective principles with respect to violent crimes against representatives of a state. It also provides that states are to establish their jurisdiction over

persons committing such offences who merely happen to be within the state's territory, article 3(2). Article 3 also states that no criminal jurisdiction exercised in accordance with internal law is excluded by the convention. The result is that prescriptive jurisdiction over the offences contemplated is very wide.

The *International Convention against the Taking of Hostages*, concluded at New York, December 18, 1979, article 5, covers the same types of jurisdiction as the Protected Persons Treaty. In addition, it allows jurisdiction on the basis of passive personality, in article 5. This fact shows that the convention treats hostage-taking almost as if it were an offence allowing for universal jurisdiction. If hostage-taking is indeed an universal offence then the passive personality jurisdiction provision becomes unimportant. Otherwise, it is a rare example of states agreeing to each other's jurisdiction on the passive personality basis.

184. *Third Restatement*, *supra*, note 18, § 403 at 244.

185. *Ibid.* Comment (a) at 245–46.

186. See, e.g., Agreement on Implementation of Article VII of the *General Agreement on Tariffs and Trade*, in *GATT*, B.I.S.D. 26th Supp. 116 (1978–79). By way of example, article 6, paragraph 2 of the Tokyo Round GATT *Customs Valuation Code*. The Code stipulates that states are to resort to a computed value of imports for duty where other methods cannot be applied. The computed method requires information about the costs of production of the goods, or in other words information obtained from persons in another state. Nevertheless it is specifically stated that states are not to require that those persons abroad provide the information required for the computation. This is a prohibition of the use of prescriptive jurisdiction to gather the information, although it is clear the importing state has jurisdiction to decide, or adjudicate the question of customs value. Here is an example of the distinction between having prescriptive and enforcement jurisdiction over persons importing, yet not having the jurisdiction to require information with respect to it.

CHAPTER III

DOMESTIC LEGISLATION

A. Canada

1. Federal Legislative Action: Export and Import Permits Acts *and Predecessors*

The question of the extraterritorial application of Canadian laws can be broached from the vantage of the Constitution of Canada. Despite the fact that the power to apply laws extraterritorially was only given in the *Statute of Westminster*, 1931,[1] by virtue of the *Extraterritorial Act*[2] all acts of the Parliament of Canada that by necessary or reasonable implication are intended to have such operation, are to be so construed. In principle the provincial legislatures cannot validly legislate with extraterritorial effect.[3]

Until World War II Canadian export controls were not of a general nature. *The Export Act*[4] was a statute that imposed controls on certain products such as wood but seems to have had no strategic or military significance. Other export controls were even more specific. For example section 8 of *The Customs Tariff*, 1897,[5] prohibited the exports of game carcasses or parts.[6]

Controls over strategic goods were exercised during the First World War. This was accomplished by Order in Council.[7] The Preamble of the Order in Council relied on the *Customs Act*:

> Whereas by section 291 of *The Customs Act*, it is enacted that "the Governor in Council may, from time to time, prohibit the exportation or the carrying coastwise or by inland navigation of arms, ammunition and gunpowder, military and naval stores, and any articles which the Governor in Council deems capable of being converted into or made useful in increasing the quantity of military or naval stores, provisions or any sort of victual which may be used as food by man" ... ... and under and in virtue of section 6 of the *War Measures Act*, 1914, ... it is hereby declared as follows: - (A) That the exportation of the following goods be prohibited to all destinations other than the United Kingdom, British Possessions and Protectorates, France, Russia (except Baltic Ports), Japan, United States when for consumption in the United States only, or shipped to specified consignees in United Kingdom via United States, or exported via United States under license or dispensation from Canada ...

There followed a list of mostly agricultural goods and coal and mica. Further in the Order in Council there was a list of goods that could only be exported to the United Kingdom, Possessions and Protectorates.[8] There were also lists of goods whose export was prohibited to all foreign ports in Europe and on the Mediterranean and Black Seas other than those of France, Russia (except Baltic ports), Belgium, Spain and Portugal. Finally, there was the export prohibition for tin plates to ports in Denmark, The Netherlands, and Sweden.

The two bases of export controls enacted during World War I were *The Customs Act* and the *War Measures Act*. This was true again in World War II. The *Regulations respecting Trading with the Enemy*, 1939 were enacted by Order in Council on September 5, 1939.[9] The amendments made to the Regulations were consolidated in the *Consolidated Regulations Respecting Trading with the Enemy* (1919)[10] which prohibited trading with "enemy"[11] subjects as well as "specified persons".[12] "Specified persons" were listed in regulations published periodically. The first list was in force February 7, 1940[13] and was revised seven times by September 26, 1940. However, it was stated that any transaction permitted "by proclamation or otherwise by the Secretary of State ... shall not be deemed to be trading with the enemy".[14]

Under the *Regulations respecting Trading with the Enemy*, "persons" were liable to criminal sanctions for the "offence of trading with the enemy".[15] A "person" was defined to include corporations "wherever incorporated".[16] It was also provided that "every director, manager, secretary, or other officer of" a company committing an offence who "is knowingly a party to the offence or default", was deemed also to be guilty of the offence.[17] These provisions might suggest the regulations were to be applied even to aliens abroad. However, interpretation of the regulations as a whole tempers this conclusion. Part of the offence of trading with the enemy included aiding or abetting:

> ... any other person, whether or not such person is in Canada to enter into, negotiate, or complete any transaction or to do any act which, *if effected or done in Canada* by such other person would constitute an offence of trading with the enemy. (emphasis added)[18]

The clear suggestion is that to be an offence "trading with the enemy" must have been "effected or done in Canada". This is further supported in as much as there was specific provision for appointment of inspectors and supervisors for a "business carried on by any person within Canada".[19] This provision would have been unnecessary were the regulations to apply to all aliens anywhere. What it does do is make clear that powers under the regulations extended to foreign companies doing business within Canadian territory. The conclusion that seems to result from this interpretation of the regulations as a whole is that the offence of trading with the enemy was strictly limited to Canadian territory with respect at least to aliens or alien companies.

Canadian export controls under the *War Measures Act* during World War II had a greater ambit than merely prohibiting trade with belligerents. An Order in Council Establishing Regulations re: Permits to Export to Neutral Countries was made on January 23, 1940.[20] These regulations prohibited exports of any goods to "any neutral country contiguous to the territories under enemy occupation or control ..." without having been issued a permit by the Minister of National Revenue.

As well as the measures passed under the *War Measures Act* were those that were passed under section 290 of the *Customs Act*.[21] Like those in World War I, they prohibited the export from Canada of arms, ammunition and implements of war. They first came into force by Order in Council on July 30, 1937.[22] Shortly after the war was declared by Canada[23] permits were required for yet more items before they might be exported.[24] There were various additions to the items controlled from time to time.[25]

Due to the confusion of traders resulting from having various ministries responsible for issuing permits for different exports, and in order to be able to usefully collect information to monitor diversions of goods, or to encourage trade, on April 8, 1941, a single body was established to issue export permits for most controls.[26] The Export Permit Branch in the Department of Trade and Commerce was thus established.

With periodic changes to the lists, the situation remained the same for the duration of the war. Since the *War Measures Act* applied only in times of "real or apprehended" war, at the end of the war the regulations thereunder would have lapsed were it not for exceptional authority given the Governor in Council. This was accomplished by The *National Emergency Transitional Powers Act, 1945*,[27] which continued the authority of the Export Permit Branch by virtue of an Order in Council issued thereunder.[28] The Act was to expire within a year[29] but had provision to continue longer if Parliament was not sitting when it was about to expire.[30] Thus the regulations issued under it were continued until the coming into force of the *Export and Import Permits Act*[31] which itself was to expire in 1948.[32]

The Regulations under the *National Emergency Transitional Powers Act* listed items under ten groups.[33] The items were not restricted; rather the Act set out basic goals that were to be the purpose of the regulations.[34] They included facilitating the readjustment of industry and commerce,[35] ensuring economic stability and transition to peace conditions,[36] distributing essential supplies and services to countries in distress as the result of the war[37] as well as generally continuing measures adopted during and by reason of the war.[38]

The Act also served as the legislative basis for the amendment of the *Trading with the Enemy Regulations* (1943)[39] in 1947. By April of that year a significant number of non-strategic items were deleted from the export control list.[40] Trade with Germany was resumed days later.[41]

On May 14, 1947 the *Export and Import Permits Act*[42] was assented to and *Export Permit Regulations* passed thereunder.[43] The Regulations exempted goods of small value and other minor cases, but were mainly designed to outline procedures under the new Act. The same day a list of commodities placed under export control was passed,[44] again following the ten groups used in the 1946 regulations.

The Act authorised regulations to extend only to items that were (a) arms and munitions; (b) to ensure adequate supply in Canada; or (c) to implement an intergovernmental arrangement or commitment.[45] Because the Act did not extend to the field covered by the *Trading With The Enemy Regulations*, on the expiry of *The National Emergency Transitional Powers Act*, special legislation was enacted to continue these regulations.[46] However, export controls were largely subsumed under the *Export and Import Permits Act*, and the special act can be seen to have had no effect on exports from this time on.

In 1948 the *Export and Import Permits Act* was amended to allow regulation of any goods to countries listed.[47] It was also extended until March 31, 1950.

The first list of countries to which exports required a permit was established June 29, 1948.[48] The Soviet Bloc countries were listed, as well as Germany and many others. In total 45 states were listed. Japan however was not listed.

The regulations listing items under control were revised from time to time, and the miscellaneous group was eliminated leaving only the nine others.[49]

On July 20, 1949 the *Export Permit Regulations* were amended to allow the Export Permit Branch to issue General Permits which entitled classes of persons to export goods specified on the terms and conditions also specified.[50]

Another important amendment was that the country of ultimate destination, the consignee and end user were to be provided in the application for the permit as well as a description of the goods of sufficient detail to allow proper classification.[51]

The *Export and Import Permits Act* was again extended until July 31, 1951.[52] In 1951 the Act was further extended until July 31, 1954[53] but otherwise had no relevant changes until the amendments adopted on June 1, 1954.[54]

On December 29, 1949 the list of countries under area control was amended to add eighteen more bringing the total to 63.[55] New additions included China, Korea (both North and South), Japan, Hong Kong, and other far eastern countries. Some middle eastern countries were also added.[56]

The same day a vital change was made to the commodity control list. With a revision of items under control was added a new group 9 "Goods originating outside Canada":[57]

> All goods originating outside Canada when tendered for export in the same condition as when imported, without further processing or manufacturing in Canada, with the exception of:
>
> a) goods in transit in bond on a through journey on a bill originating outside Canada, clearly indicating the ultimate destination of the goods to be a third country;
>
> b) goods consigned to the United States of America as the country of ultimate destination and not specifically listed in this Schedule.

In the result, Group 9 would bring under export control goods originating outside Canada which were being re-exported from Canada. One exception would allow for the shipment to the U.S. of any goods not found on the commodity control list, but would otherwise control them to all other destinations. The other exception would allow goods not listed specifically to be shipped through Canada to any other country. This was necessary in order to fulfil Canada's obligations under *GATT* Article V,[58] where export controls could not be justified under the exceptions in Articles XX and XXI.

This is the first example of special treatment of the U.S. in the Canadian export control regulations. This preferential treatment with respect to the U.S. could be seen as contrary to the *GATT* Article I. The article provides that all rules and formalities in connection with exportation granted by a contracting party to any product destined for any other country shall be "accorded immediately and unconditionally to the like product originating in or destined for the territories of all other contracting parties".[59] The regulation could also be seen as contrary to Article XI (1) or Article XIII. Article XI allows only tariff restrictions. Article XIII prohibits discriminatory export restrictions or prohibitions. However the exception to these latter two provisions found in Article XIV(4) may be said to apply. This exception allows a country applying import restrictions under the *GATT* rules to direct exports in such a manner as to increase its earnings or foreign currency holdings. Canada had to curtail its imports in 1947 due to gold and U.S. dollar shortages.[60]

On September 25, 1950 three changes were made to the regulatory structure under the *Export and Import Permits Act*. First, certain exceptions to the regulations, such as small-value shipments, were abolished.[61] Second, certain countries bordering on the U.S.S.R. and China were added to the area control list.[62] The third change split the list of goods into two: Schedule 1 listing goods which could only be exported with a permit; and Schedule 2 listing goods for which an export permit was required for all countries save the U.S.[63] The list of goods followed the same basic categories as were created in the amendments of December 29, 1949. However, due to the creation of the two schedules, Group 9 was amended to drop the sub-paragraph regarding goods consigned to the U.S. The result was that a much greater number of items could now be exported to the U.S. without export permits. In addition to goods originating outside Canada described in Group 9, the schedule listed a very large number of items for which a permit was not required to the U.S. This same format was continued for the items listed through the next two revisions.[64]

In May 1951, the export list provisions of the *Export and Import Permits Acts* were amended, but only in form.[65] The only relevant substantive change was to continue the Act until July 31, 1954.[66] Under the continued Act changes were made to the lists of both goods and countries.[67] But more significant was the change that was made to the Regulations for export permits. The ultimate destination of the goods was required previously.[68] Now the applicant had an added responsibility to satisfy himself of the destination, and to keep documentary evidence of it.[69] The "country of ultimate destination" was also defined to be the one in which the goods were to be consumed or to finally remain.[70] This defined the exception of items under Schedule 2 of the item control lists which exempted items whose "ultimate destination" was the U.S. In addition, information about the consignee became a mandatory part of the application in all cases.[71] Hitherto the information had been necessary only when the Export Permit Branch so required.[72]

The list of goods was amended in respect of Group 9, on July 4, 1952.[73] Shipments from the U.S. were required to be accompanied by a copy of the U.S. export declaration. However Group 9 was amended again shortly thereafter,[74] to read:

All goods originating outside Canada, except the following:

a) any such goods that have been further processed or manufactured in

Canada, by combining them with other goods or otherwise, so as to result in a substantial change in the value, form and use of the goods or in the production of new goods, or

b) any such goods that are in transit in bond on a through journey on a billing originating outside Canada which billing

(I) clearly indicates that the ultimate destination of the goods is a country other than Canada of the country of origin, and

(II) in the case of goods shipped from the United States, is accompanied by a copy of the United States export declaration which does not contain terms conflicting with those of the billing and is presented to the Collector of Customs at Canadian sea-port.

The changes had the following two results. First, they defined to a greater extent when goods had undergone a change significant enough in Canada to be excluded from application as goods originating outside Canada. The second result was to clarify that the U.S. export declaration was to be provided for the purpose of comparing it with the bill of lading. In this way it would be possible at least to monitor the consistency between the Canadian and U.S. controls.

On June 1, 1954 a new *Export and Import Permits Act*[75] was proclaimed[76] in force, and the previous Act and its amendments repealed. It made arms and munitions export controls subject to the requirement that their use might be "detrimental to the security of Canada".[77] Also included in this section was the provision that in addition to arms and munitions "articles deemed capable of being converted thereinto or made useful in the production thereof, or otherwise having a strategic nature" were to be treated alike. The other change to the purposes for which export controls might be instituted was minor. It was merely the specification that controls to ensure adequate supplies in Canada could be for "defence or other needs".[78] The combination of these provisions allowed export controls on nuclear materials to be instituted effective on the day the Act came into force.[79]

The *EIPA* made clear that permits could be issued only to a person who is a "resident of Canada".[80] The term is defined as individuals ordinarily resident in Canada, and corporations having their "head office in Canada or operating a branch office in Canada".[81] Previously the Act had stated that permits ought to be issued to "any person".[82] However Regulations required applicants be resident in Canada[83] and then permanently resident there.[84]

The new Act also made provision[85] for the incorporation of the import certificate scheme into the legislative framework.[86] Regulations were also issued for the Import Certificates.[87] Their purpose was explained in section 2 of the Regulations. These certificates would be issued where a certificate was required by the exporting country before it would allow an export to Canada.[88] Only residents of Canada could apply. Canadian residents were defined in the same way as in the *EIPA*.[89] The regulations also provided for delivery verification certificates to be issued "to any person" upon the arrival of the goods in Canada.[90]

The offences under the Act were brought into it in eight sections dealing with the subject and one section dealing with the penalties for the breach.[91] Under the previous legislation there had merely been an offence to breach the Act.[92] The 1952 Act prohibited exporting and attempts to export.[93] Now, intending to cause or assisting, or in fact making a shipment to countries on the Area Control List,[94] transferring a permit,[95] furnishing false information[96] and aiding or abetting[97] were added as statutory offences. As well, resident applicants were made responsible for the offences of non-residents,[98] and officers or corporations and directors were made responsible for the offences of the corporation.[99]

The Act was to be enforced by customs officers.[100] In this respect it was no different from its predecessors.[101]

This new Act was basically the same as the one in force in 1989, although it has been subject to some additions[102] and minor amendments. It was proclaimed two months prior to the expiry of the previous Act but also provided a three year life span. It was subsequently continued at three year intervals until 1969, then for five years to 1974, after which point there has been no expiry provision.[103]

The regulations that controlled export permits were effective June 1, 1954,[104] or on the coming into force of the 1954 *Export and Import Permits Act.* Among them was the provision that the applicant was no longer required to have documentary evidence of the ultimate destination of the goods, but to satisfy himself of it "as far as is reasonably possible".[105] The obligation however extended not only to the ultimate destination but also to the fact there would not be transshipment or diversion.[106]

On June 1, 1954 the list of items, the export of which was to be controlled, was re-issued as the newly defined Export Control List under the new statute.[107] The Export Control List placed the items into ten groups but many of the groups were new. The most important changes included the abolition of the two schedules, one for all countries, the other for all save the U.S. In its place, the whole list excepted the U.S. save where the item mentions otherwise. Another significant change was the inclusion for the first time of nuclear and radioactive materials, for which a permit was required even for export to the U.S. Group 10 was added to assist in the enforcement of the Area Control List. It required export permits for all goods where their ultimate destination was not declared. Apart from some minor clarifications, however, Group 9 dealing with goods originating outside Canada was not changed.

Coinciding with the changes to the Export Control List were changes to the Area Control List.[108] From the previous high number of seventy countries listed, the list was reduced to 18. The countries left on the list were the Soviet Bloc, China and bordering countries.

There was also a new feature introduced into the regulatory scheme of export controls. Three General Export Permits were issued pursuant to the *Export Permit Regulations.*[109] General Export Permit 1 allowed for exports of small value and personal effects. General Export Permit 2 allowed for export of some listed items included in the Export Control List. The effect was to substitute a case by case approval for permits concerning these items and allow merely the filling out of a customs forms endorsed with the general permit number authorizing the export. However, neither General Export Permits 1 or 2 allowed any export to the 18 countries listed on the Area Control List.[110] General Export Permit 3 allowed export of items normally taken on board ships or aircraft for consumption thereon, if they were to be so used. The only exception to Ex. 3 was that bunkering fuel destined for China or North Korea was not included, but there was no exception made for Area Control countries.

Subsequent changes to the Export List gave greater space and importance to the description of "Atomic Energy and Materials".[111] In other respects the List remained more or less the same, however Group 9 items were more strictly controlled. The control was effected by the establishment of the *Transshipment Regulations*.[112]

The *Transshipment Regulations* expanded upon the notion contained in Group 9 of the Export Control List which exempts items transported through Canada in bond to and from points outside Canada. Section 4 prohibits shipment through Canada of goods to an Area Control country by any means other than by which they arrived in Canada without authorization.[113] Section 5 allowed for a transit authorization to be issued for exports from Canada that were to be shipped through a country other than their ultimate destination. On December 31, 1954 the Area Control List was amended to all Indo-China as the nineteenth country.[114] The name of Indo-China was changed to North Viet-Nam at the end of 1958, and Hong Kong and Macao dropped from the list.[115] The same changes were then made to General Export Permit 2 which excepted exports to Area Control destinations from the permit.[116]

From time to time new General Export Permits were put into place and revoked.[117] It was in the General Export Permits that Canadian measures against Cuba appeared in December 1960.[118] But when sanctions against Rhodesia were put into place not only were the General Export Permits amended so as not to apply to Rhodesia[119] but the Area Control List was also changed to include Rhodesia.[120]

The General Export Permit was used to differentiate between Area Control Countries. It was also used to further specify the countries to which Export Control List Group 9 was to apply. Thus in 1956 General Export Permit 2, a list of goods which could be exported even to Area Control Countries, was created.[121] It distinguished between Area Control Countries. It allowed export of listed goods to Macao and Indo-China irrespective of their origin [122] but exports to the other Area Control countries could only be of Canadian goods.[123]

The Export Control List underwent numerous changes in the years following the introduction of the 1954 *Export and Import Permits Act*, but only a few were of general significance. Most were additions or subtractions of items. The List increased dramatically in length over the years. It was 12 pages long at the beginning of 1957, [124] but had swollen to 45 pages by 1967.[125] The added length was due largely to the length of Group 4, General Purpose Industrial Machinery and Electronic Devices.

Changes to the Export Control List were largely to the number of items rather than the general categories. However, one change to the categories was to form a new Group 8, Atomic Energy Materials and Equipment.[126] This change showed the increased importance of nuclear items and created the groups that are in use today.[127]

A major change in 1973 to the items on the list was the inclusion in the miscellaneous items of technical data in material form.[128] This item only included tangible forms of data but it was the recognition that data was to be controlled if related to other items in the List, specifically Groups 3 to 9 thereof.[129] These changes also involved the rewording of Group 9, goods originating outside Canada,[130] and then splitting it into two separate items, 9001 and 9002.[131] The new item 9001 had the effect of highlighting the fact that exports of goods of U.S. origin required a Canadian export permit. By this redrafting of Group 9 the Government of Canada sought to send a signal to the U.S. Administration that it was conscientiously controlling the export of U.S. origin goods from Canada. The wording also coincided with changes in U.S. export documentation.[132]

The working of the List was also amended.[133] The result was that the List was to apply to all countries save the U.S. Where the U.S. was also to be included, it would be expressly stated, as had been the practice for some time. The new wrinkle was that where there were to be controls on products to only certain specific countries, those countries' names would be listed after the item.[134]

A new type of controlled item was added in 1975. This involved export controls on wild fauna and flora.[135] Some eighteen pages of items were listed. Within one year the number of pages had swollen to 50 pages in length.[136] The items were made subject to certain General Export Permits.[137]

The Area Control List was amended in 1970.[138] In 1978, thirteen countries were on the Area Control List.[139] It was pared down to only eleven countries when China was deleted July 2, 1981.[140] In 1989 a major step was taken. All countries of the East-Bloc, including Viet-Nam and North Korea, were removed from the Area Control List.[141]

The 1978 consolidation of Canadian federal regulations did not change either the *Import Certificate Regulations*[142] or the *Transshipment Regulations*.[143] The only change made to the *Export Permit Regulations* was that the words "ultimate destination" were no longer used but the same provisions with respect to it applied.[144]

Another change to the *Export and Import Permits Act* scheme was to change the Minister responsible for the Act from the Minister of Trade and Commerce[145] to the Secretary of State for External Affairs.[146] At the same time, the Export Permits Branch became part of the Department of External Affairs.

Pursuant to this power the Secretary of State for External Affairs had entered into a Memorandum of Understanding with the Royal Canadian Mounted Police (R.C.M.P.) respecting investigations, prosecutions, and enforcement related to the *Export and Import Permits Act*.[147] The cooperation between the two parties to the understanding was set out as well as the extent to which the R.C.M.P. could rely on External Affairs assistance. The upshot of the understanding is that it is clear that the R.C.M.P., as well as the Customs officials specifically mentioned in the Act,[148] are to enforce the Act.

A major change in the form of the Export Control List occurred in 1989 when a new and extensively revised and modernized list was issued.[149] The declared purpose of this amended Export Control List was to modernize many of the definitions of controlled technology in the light of the latest developments in military and strategic technology and to respect Canada's CoCom commitments.[150] The list is extensively rewritten and a new coding system is implemented to give effect to the new definitions.

The situation with respect to goods of U.S. origin is unchanged. The new section 5400 reads as follows:

> 5400. All goods that originate in the United States, unless they are included elsewhere in this List, whether in bond or cleared by Canadian Customs, other than goods that have been further processed or manufactured outside the United States so as to result in a substantial change in value, form or use of the goods or in the production of new goods. (*All destinations other than the United States*)[151]

B. U.S.

1. Brief History of Laws, Regulations and Administration of Export Controls

The United States restricted exports as long ago as the Napoleonic Wars of 1803–1815. At that time the U.S. boycotted the United Kingdom.[152] Although there have been a number of pieces of legislation dealing with export controls since then it was only after the Second World War that an integrated scheme of controls developed. That scheme, however, evolved from the previous controls and cannot be divorced from them.

Prior to the Second World War U.S. export controls were limited to war materials or to countries which were at war.[153] Such controls on exports were instituted in 1898, three days prior to the declaration of war against Spain.[154] The powers given to the President under this legislation to prohibit exports were amended in 1912 to prohibit certain exports of arms except when allowed by the President.[155]

On the U.S. entry into World War I, presidential powers were expanded to restrict any articles to named destinations for the duration of the war.[156] As well, the *Trading with the Enemy Act of 1917*[157] prohibited trade with designated enemies subject to Presidential permission. This power was limited to war-time until the *Emergency Banking Relief Act* of 1933 amended section 5b of the *TWEA* by adding the words "or during any other period of national emergency declared by the President".[158]

After World War I, the 1898 and 1912 legislation was replaced[159] and the President was given the power to licence arms exports. This power included any country in which the United States exercises extraterritorial jurisdiction.[160] In 1934 the President was authorized to prohibit the sale of arms to Bolivia and Paraguay, which were engaged in a war.[161]

Realizing that a general power needed to be given to the President, Congress adopted the *Neutrality Act* of 1935 empowering the President to prohibit arms exports to belligerent nations.[162] In 1937 the *Neutrality Act* was amended to allow the President to prohibit other exports to belligerent nations, where the controls promoted the security or peace of the U.S. or protected the lives of U.S. nationals.[163] These powers were continued in the *Neutrality Act* of 1939.[164]

Previous pieces of legislation purported to affect "persons" who could be either individuals or legal entities.[165] However, there was no express extraterritorial effect until the *Neutrality Act* of 1939. In it certain obligations were placed on "citizens" who were to be subject to certain consequences resulting from a Presidential declaration under the Act. Because the definition of "citizen" in section 16(f) included a "partnership, company or association composed in whole or in part of citizens of the United States", certain foreign persons could be affected by the provision. But the more important provision was that "citizen" only included corporations "organized and existing under the laws of the United States".[166] Thus, *Neutrality Act* controls expressly affected persons in the United States and potentially only the foreign partners of an unincorporated body.

This was the situation at the commencement of the Second World War. Prior to the entry of the U.S. into the War, an *Act to Expedite the Strengthening of the National Defense* was passed on July 2, 1940.[167] Section 6 of the Act allowed the President to control the export of arms or industrial machinery. In 1941, this was extended to include all U.S. territories.[168]

On the day the 1940 Act was to expire, it was extended and broadened to include "technical data" as well as articles, and it dropped the requirement that the control be in the interest of national defence.[169] With other extensions[170] the Act continued in its amended state until the coming into force of the *Export Control Act*, on February 28, 1949.[171] Challenges to the wartime delegation of export control powers to the President were upheld by the U.S. Courts.[172] These cases relied primarily on *United States* v. *Curtiss-Wright Export Corp.*[173] However, after World War II many of the controls over domestic distribution were eliminated by the *First*[174] and *Second*[175] *Decontrol Act of 1947.*[176]

The *Export Control Regulations* enacted under the 1940 Act[177] merely set out the forms to be used and listed the terms which were placed under licensing requirements. This was also true of the regulations made under the *Neutrality Act* of 1939 for the control of exports of arms.[178]

The Export Control Act of 1949[179] set out two findings of Congress and Senate. They were that short supply of certain items in the U.S. and abroad affect the welfare and the foreign policy of the U.S., and that national security could be affected by the unrestricted export of materials of military significance.[180] On the basis of these findings, it was declared that it was the policy to control exports where necessary.[181]

The *ECA* of 1949 applied to technical data as well as goods. For enforcement of controls, rules and regulations could apply to the financing, transporting and other servicing of exports and the participation therein by any person.[182] The definition of "person" included legal entities as well as natural persons.[183]

The Act gave the power to the President to prohibit or curtail exports, and allowed this power to be delegated.[184] The power was delegated to the Secretary of Commerce.[185]

The scheme adopted in the regulations was to place under control all exports from the U.S. save those to Canada for consumption there.[186] General licenses were issued for some classes of goods, for others case by case approval was required by way of a validated license.[187]

The regulations outlined the extraterritorial scope of the *ECA* of 1949. The main extraterritorial provisions were those prohibiting the re-export of items from foreign countries where their export was based on documentation or representations to the contrary.[188] Similar provisions were made for the control of technical data.[189]

Despite the potential to create a comprehensive scheme for the control of exports under one act, this has not occurred to the present day. The *ECA* of 1949 and the Commerce Department regulations were merely one type of export control. The *TWEA* continued as the other major type of export control on strategic materials because, unlike the *ECA* of 1949, it was not limited to the control of exports from the U.S. The *TWEA* allowed application of controls to all persons subject to the jurisdiction of the U.S. Since 1941, it had been clear that the *TWEA* would be applied to foreign corporations owned or controlled by U.S. persons.[190] Thus the bulk of extraterritorial application of export control laws was found under the *TWEA* in the *Treasury Department Regulations*.[191] The regulations under the *TWEA* include the *Foreign Asset Control Regulations*;[192] the *Transaction Control Regulations*;[193] the *Cuban Assets Control Regulations*.[194]

Although the *ECA* of 1949 had two main interests, short supply and militarily significant items, it was also applied to items of economic significance. The licensing practice of considering the economic significance of items with respect to national security was recognized in an amendment to the language setting out the scope of the Act, in 1962.[195] This amendment recognized the strategic nature of controls, and not only their military nature.[196]

The 1962 amendments also stated that the economic resources of the U.S. were to be used to further foreign policy objectives as well as national security.[197] By 1965 the Act was amended to state that the policy of the U.S. was to oppose restrictive practices or boycotts of foreign countries.[198] As mentioned previously, on April 1, 1964 the Department of Commerce actually began to exercise control over exports of technical data as well as goods.

The *ECA* of 1949 was replaced by the *Export Administration Act of 1969*.[199] It did not alter the scope of the export controls in place under the *ECA* of 1949, nor their extraterritorial application. Re-exports continued to be the prime area in which the Act was applied extraterritorially. Administrative techniques were also used to affect persons outside the U.S. however, and persons not complying with U.S. law were subject to denial of exports from the U.S.[200]

A procedure was used to maintain a list of firms to whom exports should be scrutinized, the Economic Defence List.[201] More recently another list, "Atlas", is used to list persons subject to even greater scrutiny than those on the Economic Defence List.[202]

These three lists are a key part of the U.S. enforcement scheme and are practical ways to avoid much potential jurisdictional conflict with other nations. The lists control the exit of exports from the U.S. using the list as consideration for the issuance of export permits. The denial list forbids any "person" from doing business with them.[203] The definition of "person" includes citizens and nationals of foreign countries.[204] Thus denial orders apply in fact to any person, anywhere, who is subject to U.S. jurisdiction.

The other main administrative procedure used is the consent order. Consent orders were also made against foreign persons.[205] The advantage of consent orders is that the party waives the question of jurisdiction.[206] Although most states will argue that as a matter of international law an individual cannot waive the jurisdiction of a state without its express consent, the practical result of such an agreement to U.S. jurisdiction is not to seek the protection of one's own state and avoid the issue.

In 1977 a restructuring of the legislation dealing with the control of exports increased the scope of *EAA* of 1969 to give the President the power to regulate the conduct of foreign companies.[207] The *EAA* of 1969 was amended to give the Secretary of Commerce the power over goods and technical data and any other information "subject to the jurisdiction of the United States".[208] This amendment was retained in the 1979 revision of the *EAA*.[209] It was clear from the legislative history of the *EAA* of 1979 that this was an express provision to control foreign companies abroad.[210]

The 1977 amendments were passed as part of a reorganization of the U.S. export control laws. A new act, the *International Emergency Economic Powers Act* was adopted.[211] It was to be used for all non-wartime export controls and the *TWEA* was to be regulated to war-time use only.[212] The *IEEPA* required that the President declare a national emergency with respect to an "unusual and extraordinary threat... to the national security, foreign policy, or economy of the United States".[213]

The *EAA* of 1979[214] made a sharp distinction between national security controls[215] and foreign policy controls.[216] Foreign policy controls were to expire at the calendar year end following their imposition unless extended by the President.[217] Before imposing or extending the foreign policy controls, the specific subject matter was to be considered by the President[218] and a report made to Congress on those criteria and any alternatives that had been attempted first.[219]

Since the *EAA* of 1979, there has been reconsideration of the *EAA*, once again on the occasion of its renewal. During a lengthy debate many bills were laid before both the House and the Senate before a final version was adopted in 1985.[220] Passage did not occur until the middle of that year.[221] Issues which had to be resolved were whether contract sanctity provisions (periods in which pre-existing contracts might be completed) were to be included and what time period they were to specify, if any and whether violators of U.S. export controls were to be denied the right to export into the U.S.[222] To a lesser extent the extraterritorial reach of the *EAA* was also debated, largely due to European Community pressure[223] and to some extent due to Canadian protest.

Despite the presence of some balancing language, the *EAA* of 1985 maintains the full panoply of potential extraterritorial controls and strengthens the hand of the Administration with respect to national security controls,[224] militarily critical technologies[225] and foreign policy controls.[226]

In 1985, practice under the Department of Commerce regulations gave a greater role to the Department of Defence to ensure "an appropriate balance between national security and export interests."[227] A Memorandum of Understanding between the Department of Defence and the Commerce Department provided for Defence Department review of case by case licences (validated licences).[228] This is a recent addition to the system of inter-agency review for licence applications. The review scheme calls for consultation with the other agencies interested either on an informal basis, or through the Operating Committee of the Advisory Committee for Export Policy.[229] Consultations of one type or another are used in approximately 10% of all applications.[230] The consultations can work their way up through five levels for the ultimate decision of the President if there are inter-agency disputes.[231]

The enforcement of the *EAA* is undertaken by the Department of Commerce in the first place by the review of licence applications.[232] Pursuant to a Commerce/Customs Memorandum of Understanding, the enforcement of the *EAA* outside of the U.S. is to be the sole responsibility of the Customs Department, which is to be the liaison with foreign law enforcement agencies unless the foreign country uses its equivalent of the Commerce Department to conduct investigations.[233]

Along with the export controls administered under the *TWEA*, the *ECA* of 1949 and its successors, the *EAA*s of 1969, 1979 and 1985 and the *IEEPA*, there are also export controls on arms. The present system originated with the *Mutual Security Act of 1954*.[234] Section 414 of that Act was known as the *Munitions Control Act*,[235] and was the basis for presidential power to control, in furtherance of world peace and the security and foreign policy of the United States, the export and import of arms, ammunition, and implements of war, including technical data relating thereto, other than by a United States Government Agency.[236] These controls were limited to specific goods and data relating to them. When involved in private sales[237] the President had the power to designate which articles were to be considered such.[238] The purposes for which control of these items was authorized include foreign policy as well as national security.[239]

Presidential powers under the *MCA* were delegated to the Secretary of State,[240] who issued regulations to govern arms controls known as the *International Traffic in Arms Regulations*.[241] The lists of items were agreed upon with the Secretary of Defence.[242] The Office of Munitions Control reviewed export licensing requests with the consultation of the Department of Defence which arrived at a committee view of the various forces involved, and with regard to defence policy as a whole.[243]

The statutory basis of the *ITAR*s has changed but the general description of the working of the Office of Munitions Control and the consultations with the Department of Defence in creating the lists and considering export licensing requests, remains the same. The statutory basis is now the *Arms Export Control Act*.[244]

Under the *Arms Export Control Act* prohibitions were authorised on all military sales to certain countries such as Argentina and Chile.[245] These embargoes were based on human rights violations, but despite statutory amendments to lift these embargoes on Presidential certification of improvement of the conditions there,[246] subsequent events prevented such certification from following upon the amendment.[247]

The U.S. export controls on military items involve a licensing requirement for listed items which include technical data.[248] Manufacturing licensing and technical assistance agreements require prior approval of the Department of State before coming into effect.[249] In practice it appears that the State Department's Office of Munitions Control will deny approval of re-exports of military items to any destination to which they could not have been directly exported regardless of the percentage the items may form in a foreign product.[250]

The State Department's controls extend to the prior approval of manufacturing licensing and technical assistance agreements involving listed items.[251] The State Department administers these controls through its Office of Munitions Control. The licensing policies are at times guided by Presidential directives.[252]

The controls distinguish between classified and unclassified equipment and data. An exemption for unclassified items is granted for their shipment to Canada, so that a license is not required if they are to be used in Canada.[253] The Canadian exemption was amended effective January 1, 1985 along with other changes to the *ITAR*s to make it clear that even where the original export was not subject to licensing requirements, its re-export required prior approval.[254]

Apart from the licensing scheme, the *ITAR*s also require manufacturers and exporters in the U.S. to register.[255] They are to maintain records for six years,[256] and these are subject to inspection.

2. *Contractual Stipulations and other Methods to Effect Export Controls*

The U.S. requires foreign persons abroad to agree to the control of re-exports of U.S. controlled exports in order to allow them access to the items. Under the *Export Administration Regulations* and their predecessors, re-exports require prior authorization of the Office of Export Control.[257] The *EAR*s require the statement from the ultimate consignee or purchaser that foreign consignees and purchasers are fully aware of their responsibilities for the representations made to the Office of Export Control and for the disposition of the licensed commodities only in those foreign countries where the Office of Export Control has specifically authorized disposition.[258]

The responsibilities of exporters and foreign consignees include potential liability for misrepresentations.[259] These are said to be of continuing effect and the persons must report any change of facts,[260] because the statements are made in support of an export licence application.[261] In similar fashion the ultimate consignee and purchaser become subject to other types of enforcement measures under the enforcement provisions of the *EAR*s.[262]

A similar requirement is found in the *ITAR*s. Re-exports are not allowed without prior approval of the State Department. The ultimate consignee and purchaser is required to fill out a form (the DSP-83) stating he will not re-export without prior authorization.[263] Only unclassified technical data does not seem to require the DSP-83. The certification of the foreign end-user on form DSP-83 reads, in part:

> Except as specifically authorized by prior written approval of the U.S. State Department, we will not re-export, resell or otherwise dispose of any of those articles, data (1) outside the country…, or (2) to any other person.

Manufacturing and technical assistance agreements have additional requirements. The *ITAR*s require the agreements to contain certain clauses.[264] Both manufacturing licensing and technical assistance agreements require a non-transfer clause,[265] and a submission clause which reads:

> This agreement is subject to all United States laws and regulations relating to exports and to all administrative acts of the U.S. government pursuant to such laws and regulations.[266]

Manufacturing licensing agreements also require another non-transfer clause,[267] a clause which requires an annual report of sales or other transfers of licensed articles,[268] and a clause which affirms prior U.S. Government approval must be obtained for a transfer of licensed articles outside the approved sales territory.[269]

The effect of the forms and contractual clauses is to give the U.S. a basis upon which to claim jurisdiction over the foreign recipient of controlled items. The form has the effect of requiring a foreign person to agree to U.S. control over transfers of the items involved. The U.S. position is that it subjects the person to the provisions of the regulations which punish violations of the requirements. The submission clause bases the jurisdiction of the U.S. over the foreign contracting party on a contract with a U.S. person. This requirement in the *ITAR*s rounds out the measures that are used to gain jurisdiction over foreign persons in export transactions. Because there is no license required in manufacturing license and technical assistance agreements, no submission by the foreign person is possible as part of the license application procedure. Instead the submission is sought in the contractual document.

While such a submission will almost surely be enforced in a U.S. court, there is serious doubt that a clause of submission to the legislative power of another state would be enforced routinely by foreign courts.

A further method of controlling the re-exportation of U.S. origin goods from foreign countries is the establishment of an internal auditing system within foreign firms abroad, which import such goods from the U.S.A. A foreign firm which establishes internal auditing procedures designed to keep track of the use of U.S. origin goods may submit these procedures to the scrutiny of the Office of Export Control. Should these procedures meet the requirements of the O.E.C. and provided that they continue to do so, such firms receive validated licenses authorizing multiple exports much more rapidly and readily than others. The verification of such auditing procedures may be conducted directly by officers of the O.E.C. or by independent auditors named by the O.E.C. These provisions were expanded greatly in the 1985 amendments.[270]

The primary purpose of this auditing process is to speed up the granting of the U.S. export license. But the process can also be seen as a means of extending U.S. export controls in a less obtrusive manner than others authorized by various laws and regulations reviewed above. Such audits are voluntary, they place the burden of compliance squarely upon the U.S. exporter and the foreign importer, and reduce extraterritorial scrutiny to a minimum by allowing for verification by non-official private auditors. Whether the U.S. has succeeded in producing a non-contentious form of extraterritorial enforcement jurisdiction can be judged by the reaction of other states. This reaction has not been uniformly favorable.[271]

The application of extraterritorial controls to U.S. origin parts, components and materials built into foreign products outside the U.S. had long been a source of contention with Canada and other allies. An important step was taken in 1987 to ease this tension with the adoption of new *Export Administration Regulations* dealing with this issue. The new rule allowed re-export of such U.S. origin parts, components and materials incorporated abroad into a foreign manufactured product without prior approval if a) the ultimate destination is a Supplement 2 or 3 country and b) if the U.S. content value is 25% or less or both less than 10% and $10,000.[272]

The measure helped to remove a long-standing irritant between the U.S. and its allies. It can also be interpreted as something of a change of heart with respect to extraterritoriality as well as recognition that the rigid and uncertain measures prevailing before did much damage to U.S. exporters. One must note however that this step does not apply to the export of military equipment and only applies to the goods and countries covered by the *Export Administration Regulations*.

The long-awaited *Omnibus Trade and Competitiveness Act of 1988*[273] contains a chapter devoted to export controls.[274] As with other parts of this controversial statute, the provisions of the *Omnibus Trade Act* dealing with export controls caused both relief and dismay to foreign governments. The dismay, albeit somewhat muted in comparison to earlier years, flows from the fact that there is no returning from the positions of principle in favour of the extraterritorial extension of the *Export Administration Act* and regulations made under that Act, and that these provisions continue to be justified not only on grounds of national security, but also on the basis of foreign policy as well as being based on CoCom commitments. Even those new provisions designed to strengthen the enforcement of multilateral controls[275] raise the spectre of extraterritorial extensions of mandatory sanctions for violations of CoCom rules out of the U.S.[276] On the other hand, the stress laid upon the enforcement of multilaterally agreed rules is evidence of a greater willingness to work through multilateral channels. Even more important is the reconfirmation and strengthening of the threshold of 25% put upon the application of the *Export Administration Act* to "controlled technology" exported abroad and incorporated there into another product. This provision will do much to avoid controversy between Canada and the U.S. and in all likelihood with other CoCom partners also. Several provisions instituting various forms of internal review mechanisms[277] may also have the effect of alleviating the effect of U.S. export controls.

Notes

1. (U.K.), 1931, c. 4.
2. S.C. 1932–33, c. 39.
3. Although it is not always easy to distinguish *intra* from *extra*-provincial activity. See generally P. Hogg, *Constitutional Laws of Canada*, 2nd ed. (Toronto: Carswell, 1985) at 272–75.
4. S.C. 1897, 60–61 Vict., c. 17, assented to June 29, 1897.
5. S.C. 1897, 60–61 Vict. c. 16.
6. An *Act Further to amend the Customs Act*, 1899, 62–63 Vict., c. 22, assented to August 11, 1899, s. 2 provided for regulations to control the quantity of deer carcasses and parts that would be exported.
7. Consolidating Orders respecting the Export of Commodities No. 200, Extra Can. Gaz. April 28, 1915.
8. Mainly airplanes, airplane parts, chemicals, pharmaceuticals, and specific manufactured goods.
9. P.C. 2512, Extra Can. Gaz. 1, September 11, 1939, which recited the *War Measures Act*, R.S.C. 1927, c. 206.
10. Established by Order in Council P.C. 3959, 21 Aug. 1940, 74 Can. Gaz. 757, Sept. 7, 1940.
11. *Ibid.* s. 1(6).
12. *Ibid.* s. 3.
13. 73 Can. Gaz. 2523, Feb. 8, 1940.
14. *Ibid.* s. 3.
15. *Ibid.* s. 63.
16. *Ibid.* s. 1(a).
17. *Ibid.* s. 65.
18. *Ibid.* s. 3(4).
19. *Ibid.* s. 17.
20. P.C. 1940–286, 73 Can. Gaz. 2393, Feb. 3, 1940.
21. S.C. 1927, c. 24, s. 10.
22. P.C. 1937–1838, Extra Can. Gaz. 1, July 31, 1937.
23. Sept. 10, 1939, Extra Can. Gaz., Sept. 10, 1939.
24. Order in Council restricting exportation of certain articles, P.C. 1939–2785, Sept. 20, 1939, 23 Can. Gaz. 931, Sept. 23, 1939.
25. P.C. 1940–5994, 26 Oct. 1940, 74 Can. Gaz. 1589, Nov. 9, 1940; and P.C. 1941–7674, 4 Oct. 1941, Extra 75 Can. Gaz. 1, Oct. 8, 1941.
26. Order in Council establishing Export Permit Branch in Department of Trade and Commerce, P.C. 1941–2448, 74 Can. Gaz. 3781, April 21, 1941.
27. In force Jan. 1, 1946, S.C. 1945, 9–10 Geo. VI, c. 25, s. 5.
28. *Export Permit Regulations, 1946*, P.C. 1946–3398, in force Aug. 13, 1946, SOR/46, 276, s. 2.
29. *Ibid.* s. 6.
30. *Ibid.* s. 6, amended S.C. 1946, 10 Geo. VI, c. 60.
31. Assented to May 14, 1947, S.C. 1947, 11 Geo. VI, c. 17, s. 14.
32. *Ibid.* s. 14.
33. *Export Permit Regulations*, *supra*, note 31, 1) Agricultural; 2) Animal Products; 3)

Fibres and Textiles; 4) Wood Products; 5) Iron and Steel; 6) Non-Ferrous Metal products; 7) Other Meral Products; 8) Chemicals; 9) Miscellaneous; 10) Arms, etc.

34. *Supra*, note 31 at s. 2.
35. *Ibid.* s. 2(1)(b).
36. *Ibid.* s. 2(1)(c).
37. *Ibid.* s. 2(1)(b).
38. *Ibid.* s. 2(1)(e).
39. Jan. 14, 1947 P.C. 1947–156, SOR/47–42, 81 Can. Gaz. Pt. II 124 recites the Act as authority to amend the Regulations.
40. Export Permit Branch Order No. 18, SOR/47–418, 81 Can. Gaz. Pt II 972 (1947).
41. Notice Re: Germany, April 23, 1947, SOR/47–433, 81 Can. Gaz. Pt II 994, after limited trade with Germany had been allowed since June 25, 1946.
42. *Supra*, note 31.
43. P.C. 1947–1891, May 14, 1947, SOR/47–480, 81 Can. Gaz. Pt II 1111.
44. P.C. 1947–1893, May 14, 1947, SOR/47–482 81 Can. Gaz. Pt II 1119.
45. *Supra*, note 31 at s. 3.
46. S.C. 1947, 11 Geo. VI, c. 24, and the accompanying Schedule.
47. S.C. 1948, 11–12 Geo. VI, c. 16, amending s. 3 and 5 of the 1947 statute in this respect.
48. P.C. 1948–2984, SOR/48–311, 82 Can. Gaz. Pt II 1688.
49. P.C. 1949–570, Feb. 8, 1949, SOR/49–47, 83 Can. Gaz. Pt II 446. The groups of items minerals and chemicals were listed together thus reducing the number of groups to eight; P.C. 1949–3595, July 20, 1949, 83 Can. Gaz. 1534.
50. P.C. 1940–3594, SOR/40–283, 83 Can. Gaz. 1539.
51. *Ibid.* s. 3(1).
52. Assented to December 10, 1949, S.C. 1949 (2nd Sess.), 13 Geo. VI, c. 22.
53. S.C. 1951, 15 Geo. VI, c. 15, s. 5.
54. *Export and Import Permits Act*, S.C. 1953–54, c. 27, repealing R.S.C. 1952, c. 104 as amended by R.S.C. 1952, c. 321.
55. P.C. 1950–6562, SOR/50–549, 84 Can. Gaz. Pt II 211.
56. This was done to account for the formation of Israel and the war conditions created in the region.
57. P.C. 1950–6561, SOR/50–552, 84 Can. Gaz. Pt II 224.
58. Can. T.S. 1948 No. 31.
59. *Ibid.* art. I (1).
60. See Exchange of aide-mémoires at Washington, Nov. 14, 1947, in force Nov. 15, 1947, 6 Bevans 454, 18 Dept. State Bull. 1054, Nov. 30, 1947 which terminated Jan. 1, 1948 with the coming into force of the *GATT*.
61. P.C. 1950–4636, SOR/50–440, 84 Can. Gaz. Pt II 1301.
62. P.C. 1950–4637, SOR/50–441, 84 Can. Gaz. Pt II 1302.
63. P.C. 1950–4638, SOR/50–442, 84 Can. Gaz. Pt II 1302.
64. P.C. 1951–458, Jan. 27, 1951, SOR/51–27, 85 Can. Gaz. Pt II 154; P.C. 1951–4141, Aug. 22, 1951, 85 Can. Gaz. Pt II 941.
65. S.C. 1950–1951, c. 15, assented to May 31, 1951.
66. *Ibid.* s. 5.
67. For goods see P.C. 1951–4141, *supra*, note 64; for countries see P.C. 1951–4142, SOR/51–392, Aug. 22, 1951, 85 Can. Gaz. Pt II 951. No countries were added to the Area Control list in August 1951, but the list was consolidated.
68. P.C. 1951–6560, 84 Can. Gaz. Pt II 46.
69. P.C. 1951–4320, Aug. 22, 1951, SOR/51–396, 85 Can. Gaz. Pt II 959 s. 2(2). As well the exporter needed to state in his application if he did not know the ultimate destination of the goods: s. 2(2)(b).
70. *Ibid.* s. 2(1).
71. *Ibid.* s. 4(1).

72. P.C. 1951–6560, *supra*, note 68 at s. 3(1).
73. P.C. 1952–3458, SOR/52–275, 86 Can. Gaz. Pt II 588.
74. P.C. 1953–1213, Aug. 5, 1953, SOR/53–329, 87 Can. Gaz. Pt II 750.
75. S.C. 1953–54, c. 27, assented to May 31, 1954 [hereinafter *EIPA*].
76. 88 Can. Gaz. Pt II 1740.
77. *EIPA*, *supra*, note 75 at s. 3(a).
78. *EIPA*, *ibid.* at s. 3(c).
79. P.C. 1954–791, May 27, 1954, SOR/54–203, 88 Can. Gaz. Pt II 480, in group 8.
80. *EIPA*, *supra*, note 75 at s. 7 for export permits and s. 8 for import permits.
81. *EIPA*, *ibid.* at s. 2(e).
82. R.S.C. 1952, c. 104, s. 8 for export permits and s. 9 for import permits.
83. P.C. 1947–1891, *supra*, note 43 at s. 6.
84. P.C. 1940–3594, *supra*, note 50 at s. 2(2) and a corporation with either head office or branch in Canada.
85. *EIPA*, *supra*, note 75 at s. 9.
86. The Import Certificate and Delivery Verification schemes had previously been established by the Consultative Group.
87. P.C. 1954–790, May 27, 1954, in force June 1, 1954, SOR/54–202, 88 Can. Gaz. Pt II 471.
88. *Ibid.*
89. *Ibid.* at s. 3(1).
90. *Ibid.* at s. 9.
91. *EIPA*, *supra*, note 75 at ss. 13–21.
92. R.S.C. 1952, c. 104, s. 14.
93. *Ibid.*
94. *EIPA*, *supra*, note 75 at s. 15.
95. *Ibid.* at s. 16.
96. *Ibid.* at s. 17.
97. *Ibid.* at s. 18.
98. *Ibid.* at s. 21 requires the knowledge or consent of the resident or a failure to use due diligence to prevent the offence. The last obligation is certainly quite onerous for the resident.
99. *Ibid.* at s. 20. In addition to this requirement holding residents responsible for non-residents' offences there was also a requirement that the position be held at the time the corporation committed the offence.
100. *EIPA*, *supra*, note 75 at ss. 24–25.
101. S.C. 1947, c. 17, s. 12, granting customs officers powers over imports and exports under the Act, and S.C. 1951, c. 15, s. 4, for the duty of customs officers to enforce the Permits Act.
102. S.C. 1974, c. 9, ss. 1–2; S.C. 1980–81–82–83, c. 167; Schedule I, Item 8, S.C. 1984, c. 26, ss. 104-05, amending ss. 5(2), 8, 10; S.C. 1986, c. 1, Schedule I, Item 4, amending s. 5(1); S.C. 1987, c. 15, s. 26, amending s. 3a; S.C. 1987, c. 16, amending ss. 5–1, 8.1, 10(2), 10(3).
103. S.C. 1953–54, c. 27, s. 27, as amended by S.C. 1956–57, c. 7, s. 1; S.C. 1960, c. 12, s. 2; S.C. 1963, c. 4, s. 1; S.C. 1966–67, c. 16, s. 1; S.C. 1968–69, c. 19, s. 2; provides for the continuation and s. 27 was repealed by S.C. 1974, c. 9, s. 3, thus making the Act one which need be terminated as it will no longer expire.
104. P.C. 1954–788, May 27, 1954, SOR/54–200, 88 Can. Gaz. 1952 Pt II 421.
105. *Ibid.* at s. 4(2)(c).
106. *Ibid.*
107. S.C. 1953–54, c. 27, s. 2(b).
108. P.C. 1954–792, May 27, 1954, SOR/54–204, 88 Can. Gaz. Pt II 491.
109. May 25, 1954, SOR/54–207, 88 Can. Gaz. Pt II 493, General Export Permit No. Ex. 1; SOR/54–208, 88 Can. Gaz. Pt II 494, General Export Permit No. Ex. 2;

SOR/54–209, 88 Can. Gaz. Pt II 497, General Export Permit No. Ex. 3.

110. As of May 27, 1954.
111. P.C. 1954–1226, Aug. 18, 1954, SOR/54–375, 88 Can. Gaz. Pt II 1146.
112. P.C. 1955–17, Jan. 4, 1955, SOR/55–3, 89 Can. Gaz. Pt II 927.
113. *Ibid.* see s. 3 for definitions and s. 4 for the prohibition and types of authorization possible.
114. P.C. 1954–2072, SOR/54–738, 89 Can. Gaz. Pt II 811.
115. P.C. 1958–1769, Dec. 31, 1958, effective Jan. 1, 1959, SOR/59–12, 93 Can. Gaz. Pt II 16, Jan. 14, 1959.
116. SOR/59–13, Dec. 18, 1958, effective Jan. 1, 1959, 93 Can. Gaz. Pt II 17, Jan. 14, 1959.
117. As examples see: General Export Permit No. Ex. 4, SOR/60–34, Jan. 13, 1960, effective Jan. 18, 1960, 94 Can. Gaz. Pt II 104, Jan. 27, 1960; General Export Permit No. Ex. 5, SOR/60–183, April 19, 1960, effective April 19, 1960, 94 Can. Gaz. Pt II 538, May 11, 1960; Ex. 5 revoked by SOR/60–510, October 31, 1960 effective Nov. 14, 1960, 94 Can. Gaz. Pt II 1432; General Export Permit No. Ex. 5, SOR/62–332, Aug. 23, 1962, effective Sept. 17, 1962, 96 Can. Gaz. Pt II 958, Sept. 12, 1962; General Export Permit No. Ex. 9, SOR/73–544, 107 Can. Gaz. Pt II 2370, Sept. 26, 1973; General Export Permit No. Ex. 10, Sept. 14, 1973, SOR/73–545, 107 Can. Gaz. Pt II 2371, Sept. 26, 1973; General Export Permits No. Ex. 6 and Ex. 7 revoked Dec. 5, 1971, SOR/71–6653, 105 Can. Gaz. Pt II 2133, Dec. 22, 1971; General Export Permit No. Ex. 6, SOR/65–5124, Nov. 22, 1965, 99 Can. Gaz. Pt II, 1797, Dec. 8, 1965.
118. General Export Permit No. Ex. 2 amended, SOR/60–562, Dec. 16, 1960 94 Can. Gaz. Pt II 1532.
119. General Export and Import Permits partially suspended, SOR/66–89, Feb. 4, 1966, effective Feb. 24, 1966, 100 Can. Gaz. Pt II 237, Feb. 23, 1966.
120. P.C. 1965–2252, Dec. 20, 1965, SOR/66–4, 100 Can. Gaz. Pt II 6.
121. June 11, 1956, in force July 16, 1956, SOR/56–237, 90 Can. Gaz. Pt II 681 at s. 3.
122. *Ibid.* at s. 2.
123. *Ibid.* at s. 3.
124. P.C. 1956–1930, Dec. 28, 1956, in force Jan. 1, 1957 SOR/57–6, 91 Can. Gaz. Pt II 25.
125. P.C. 1967–35, Jan. 12, 1967, SOR/67–49, 101 Can. Gaz. Pt II 111.
126. P.C. 1970–2000, Nov. 17, 1970, effective Dec. 9, 1970 SOR/70–502, 104 Can. Gaz. Pt II 1344.
127. Group 1: Animals and Agricultural Products; Group 2: Wood Products; Group 3: General Purpose Industrial Machinery and Electronic Devices; Group 4: Transportation Equipment; Group 5: Metal, Minerals, and their Products; Group 6: Chemicals, Metaloids and Petroleum; Group 7: Arms and Munitions: Group 8: Atomic Energy Materials and Equipment; Group 9: Goods originating outside Canada; Group 10: Miscellaneous.
128. P.C. 1973–1105, May 8, 1973, effective May 23, 1973, SOR/73–253, 107 Can. Gaz. Pt II 1100, May 23, 1973.
129. The specificity was added by P.C. 1974–1431, June 20, 1974, SOR/74–383, 108 Can. Gaz. Pt II 1935, July 10, 1974.
130. P.C. 1972–1531, July 11, 1972, SOR/72–254, 106 Can. Gaz. Pt II 1038, July 26, 1972.
131. P.C. 1973–1105, *supra*, note 128.
132. Again changed by P.C. 1974–1050, May 7, 1954, SOR/54–296, 108 Can. Gaz. Pt II 1624, May 22, 1974 (to coincide with U.S. export documentation).
133. P.C. 1974–2763, Dec. 13, 1974, SOR/74–673, 108 Can. Gaz. Pt II 3046, Dec. 26, 1974.
134. *Ibid.* at s. 1.

135. P.C. 1975–1531, July 3, 1975, SOR/75–395, 109 Can. Gaz. Pt II 1681.
136. P.C. 1976–2336, Sept. 21, 1976, SOR/76–630, 110 Can. Gaz. Pt II 2676, Oct. 13, 1976 although the manner of setting out the list would account for some of the added length.
137. Ex. 14, SOR/75–397, July 4, 1975, 109 Can. Gaz. Pt II 1701, July 23, 1975; Ex. 15, SOR/75–398, July 4, 1975, 109 Can. Gaz. Pt II 1702, July 23, 1975.
138. P.C. 1970–1999, Nov. 17, 1970, SOR/70–501, 104 Can. Gaz. Pt II, 1343, Dec. 9, 1970.
139. C.R.C. 1978, c. 600, p. 4027; Rhodesia was deleted from the list December 28, 1979: P.C. 1979–3511, Dec. 19, 1979, effective Dec. 28, 1979, SOR/80–32, 114 Can. Gaz. Pt II 105, Jan. 9, 1980; Iran was added to the list May 22, 1980: P.C. 1980–1397, May 22, 1980, SOR/80–374, 114 Can. Gaz. Pt II 1928, Extra, May 22, 1980; and was deleted: March 3 1981, P.C. 1981–560, March 1, 1981, SOR/81–210, 115 Can. Gaz. Pt II 820, March 25, 1981.
140. P.C. 1981–1793, July 2, 1981, SOR/81–543, 115 Can. Gaz. Pt II 1059, July 22, 1981.
141. P.C. 1989–613, April 13, 1989, SOR/89–201, 123 Can. Gaz. Pt II 2098, April 13, 1989.
142. C.R.C. 1978, c. 603, p. 4115.
143. C.R.C. 1978, c. 606, p. 4145.
144. C.R.C. 1978, c. 602, p. 4109.
145. *EIPA*, *supra*, note 75 at s. 2(d).
146. P.C. 1983–3832, Dec. 7, 1983, S.I./83–225, 117 Can. Gaz. Pt II 4436.
147. Memorandum of Understanding between the R.C.M.P. and the Department of External Affairs, concluded June 11, 1984.
148. R.S.C. 1970, c. E–17, s. 24–25 repealed and replaced by the *Customs Act*, S.C. 1986, c. 1.
149. 123 Can. Gaz. Pt II 2101, 13 April, 1989.
150. *Ibid.* at 2264.
151. *Ibid.* at 2262.
152. April 14, 1812, 2 Stat. 707, see L.T. Lee & J.B. McCobb, "United States Trade Embargo on China, 1949–1970: Legal Status and Future Prospects" (1971) 4 N.Y.U.J. Int'l L. & Pol. 1 at 16.
153. An excellent resumé of the U.S. controls is found in H.J. Berman & J.R. Garson, "United States Export Controls – Past, Present and Future" (1967) 67 Colum. L. Rev. 791 at 791, note 1 [hereinafter *Berman & Garson*].
154. Joint Resolution of April 22, 1898, c. 187, 30 Stat. 742.
155. S.J. Res. 89, 37 Stat. 630 (1912).
156. Act of June 15, 1917, c. 30, title VII, s. 1, 40 Stat. 225.
157. October 6, 1917, c. 106, 40 Stat. 411 [hereinafter *TWEA*].
158. March 9, 1933, H.R. 1491, c. 1, Pub. L. 73–1, 48 Stat. 1; codified 12 U.S.C. s. 95 (1978).
159. S.J. Res. 124, c. 44, 42 Stat. 361 (1922).
160. *Berman & Garson*, *supra*, note 153, at note 1.
161. *Joint Resolution to Prohibit the Sale of Arms or Munitions of War in the United States under Certain Conditions*, May 28, 1934 H.J. Res. 347, c. 365, 48 Stat. 811.
162. *Inter alia*, August 31, 1935, S.J. Res. 173, c. 837, 49 Stat. 1081.
163. May 1, 1937, S.J. Res. 51, c. 146, s. 2(a), 50 Stat. 121 at 122.
164. November 4, 1939, H.J. Res. 306, c. 2, 54 Stat. 4.
165. See for example *Neutrality Act* of 1939, *ibid.* at 12, s. 16(b) which defined "person".
166. *Ibid.* at 12, s. 16(f).
167. R. 9850, c. 508, 54 Stat. 712.
168. May 28, 1941, S.J. Res. 76, c. 134, 55 Stat. 206.
169. *An Act to Further Expedite the Prosecution of the War by Authorizing the Control of the Exportation of Certain Commodities*, June 30, 1942, S. 2558, c. 461, 56 Stat. 463

(1942) extended the 1940 Act until June 30, 1944.

170. July 1, 1944, S. 1826, c. 360, 58 Stat. 671; June 30, 1945, H.R. 2944, c. 205, 59 Stat. 270; May 23, 1946, S. 1980 c. 269, 60 Stat. 215; June 30, 1947, S.J. Res. 139, c. 84, 61 Stat. 214; July 15, 1947, H.R. 3647, c. 248, 61 Stat. 321; December 30, 1947, S.J. Res. 167, c. 526, 61 Stat. 945.
171. Feb. 26, 1949, S. 548, 63 Stat. 7 [hereinafter *ECA* of 1949.
172. *United States* v. *Rosenberg* 150 F. 2d 788 (2d Cir. 1945) aff'd. 47 F. Supp. 406 (E.D.N.Y. 1942), cert. denied, 326 U.S. 752 (1945); *United States* v. *Bareno* 50 F. Supp. 520 (D. Md. 1943).
173. 299 U.S. 304 (1936).
174. March 31, 1947, S. 931, c. 29, 61 Stat. 34.
175. July 15, 1947, H.R. 3647, c. 248, 61 Stat. 321.
176. See in this regard Comment, "Export Controls" (1949) 58 Yale L.J. 1325 at 1328, note 11.
177. Title 32, C. VIII, 32 C.F.R. Supp. 4489 (1940).
178. 32 C.F.R. Supp. 4403 (1940).
179. *Supra*, *ECA* of 1949, note 171.
180. *Ibid.* s. (a) and (b).
181. *Ibid.* s. 2.
182. *Ibid.* s. 3(a).
183. *Ibid.* s. 9. The enforcement section of the *ECA* of 1949 seemed to imply enforcement was only to be within the territory of the U.S. S. 6(a) allowed for the investigation or taking of testimony from "any person" and it could be enforced by "the district court of the United States for any district in which such person is found or resides or transacts business".
184. *Ibid.* s. 3(a), and (b).
185. J.T. Haight, "United States Controls over Strategic Transactions" (1965) U. Illinois L. Forum 337 at 338 [hereinafter *Haight*] cites Exec. Order No. 10945, 26 Fed. Reg. 4487 (1961) and Exec. Order No. 11038, 27 Fed. Reg. 7003 (1962). See also P.H. Silverstone, "The Export Control Act of 1949: Extraterritorial Enforcement" (1959) 107 U. Pa. L. Rev. 331 at 332 [hereinafter *Silverstone*].
186. 15 C.F.R. 370.2 (1957).
187. 15 C.F.R. 372.1 (1957).
188. 15 C.F.R. 381.6 (1957).
189. Technical Data was controlled by the Treasury Department under the *Trading with the Enemy Act*, until April 1, 1964, when the power reverted to the Secretary of Commerce. *Haight*, *supra*, note 185 at 343.
190. December 18, 1941, H.R. 6233, c. 593, 55 Stat. 840 (1941) amended the *TWEA* to apply to "persons subject to the jurisdiction of the U.S." and presidential powers under the *TWEA* were delegated to the Secretary of the Treasury by Exec. Order 8389, C.F.R. 645 (Cum. Supp. 1938–45) and Exec. Order No. 193, 3 C.F.R. 1174 (Cum. Supp. 1938–45). The definition of persons subject to the jurisdiction of the U.S. under the *TWEA* was regulated by 7 Fed. Reg. 2503-04 (1942).
191. These have been discussed in conjunction with the U.S. international practice relating to specific cases described in part III of this study.
192. 31 C.F.R. 500 [hereinafter the *FACR*s].
193. 31 C.F.R. 505 [hereinafter the *TCR*s].
194. 31 C.F.R. 515 [hereinafter the *CACR*s].
195. *Berman & Garson*, *supra*, note 153 at 800, cite the codified version at 50 U.S.C. App. s. 2021(b)(1964).
196. *Berman & Garson*, *supra*, note 153 at 801.
197. *Berman & Garson*, *supra*, note 153 at 802 cite the codified version 50 U.S.C. App. s. 2022 (1964).
198. 50 U.S.C. App. s. 2022(4) (Supp. I 1965), as cited in *Berman & Garson*, *supra*, note

153 at 804.

199. December 30, 1969, H.R. 4293, Pub. L. 91–184, 83 Stat. 841 (1969) [hereinafter *EAA* of 1969].
200. 15 C.F.R. 387.10 (1970). See also *Berman & Garson*, *supra*, note 153 at 854.
201. *Berman & Garson*, *supra*, note 153 at 810–11 call it a "gray list".
202. Also known as the "black list". See Lowenfeld, A.F., *International Economic Law*, 2nd ed., vol. III (U.S.A.: Matthew Bender, 1983) [*Trade Controls for Political Ends*] at 22.
203. 15 C.F.R. 387.10 (1970).
204. 15 C.F.R. 370.2 (1970), "person or firm".
205. Pursuant to 15 C.F.R. 382.10 (1966). See *Raytheon Manufacturing Co. et al.* 24 Fed. Reg. 2626 (1959) and the discussion in *Berman & Garson*, *supra*, note 153 at 854–66, and J.F. Davison, "Exports of Technical Data and the *Export Control Act*: Hearing Examiners and Consent Decrees" (1964) 33 Geo. Wash. L. Rev. 209 at 235–39 for their use and value as administrative precedents.
206. In some cases there is only agreement not to question jurisdiction in the specific case, while in other cases the consent order has more general language.
207. Dec. 28, 1977, H.R. 7738, Pub. L. 95–223, Title III, 91 Stat. 1625 at s. 301(a).
208. See R.B. Thompson, "United States Jurisdiction over Foreign Subsidiaries: Corporate and International Law Aspects" (1983) 15 L. & Pol. Int'l Bus. 319 at 344–47 for the legislative history of the amendment [hereinafter *Thompson*]; also Note, "Extraterritorial Application of the Export Administration Act of 1979 Under International and American Law" (1983) 81 Mich. L. Rev. 1308 at 1313.
209. Sept. 9, 1989, S. 737, Pub. L. 96–72, 93 Stat. 503 s. 6(a)(1).
210. Note, *supra*, note 208 at 1313–14.
211. Dec. 28, 1977, H.R. 7738, Pub. L. 95–223, Title II, 91 Stat. 1625 [hereinafter the *IEEPA*].
212. *Ibid.* s. 101(a) removed the Presidential power to use the *TWEA* "during any other period of national emergency declared by the President" that had been added in 1933 by Pub. L. 73–1, *supra*, note 158.
213. *Supra*, note 211 at s. 202(a).
214. Sept. 29, 1979, S. 737, Pub. L. 96–72, 93 Stat. 503.
215. *Ibid.* s. 5.
216. *Ibid.* s. 6.
217. *Ibid.* s. 6(a)(2).
218. *Ibid.* s. 6(b).
219. Alternatives are first to be tried, s. 6(d), then the report made on imposition, s. 6(e).
220. *Export Administration Amendments Act of 1985*, July 12, 1985, S. 883, Pub. L. 99–64, 99 Stat. 120; (1985) Int'l Leg. Mat. 1370 [hereinafter *EAA 1985*].
221. July 12, 1985.
222. See, for example, testimony of Honorable Richard Perle, before the House Armed Services Committee, Technology Transfer Panel, June 9, 1983 at pp. 11 and 13; Paige Sullivan, "Renewal of the Export Administration Act: the Legislature Picture" (May 30, 1983) Bus. America 7, and Statement of the Honorable Kenneth W. Dam before the Senate Committee on Foreign Relations, June 27, 1983 and James M. Bierman, "The 1983 Export Administration Act Legislation: The Extraterritoriality Issue" (1983) 15 J. L. Pol. & Int'l Bus. 1181 [hereinafter *Bierman*].
223. *Bierman*, *ibid.* at 1182.
224. See *EAA 1985*, *supra*, note 220 at s. 105.
225. *Ibid.* at s. 106.
226. *Ibid.* at s. 108.
227. White House Press Release, March 23, 1984; authority is in s. 10(g) of the *EAA*.
228. *Ibid.*
229. A.P. Olschwang, "Current Status of United States Export Controls" unpublished

speech given at the meeting of the International and Foreign Law Committee of the Chicago Bar Association, Nov. 23, 1983 at 15–16.

230. *Ibid.* at 16.
231. "Overview of the Export Administration Program" U.S. Dep't of Commerce at 8.
232. *Ibid.* at 14.
233. In the latter case U.S. Commerce Department is the liaison. "Commerce/Customs Memorandum of Understanding Overseas Enforcement of the Export Administration Act", Jan. 16, 1984.
234. Aug. 26, 1954, H.R. 9678, c. 937, Pub. L. 665, 68 Stat. 832, codified at 22 U.S.C. s. 1934 (1958). See P.J. Monahan, "The Regulation of Technical Data under the *Arms Export Control Act* of 1976 and the *Export Administration Act* of 1979: A Matter of Executive Discretion" (1983) 6 Int'l & Corp. L. Rev. 169 at 172–73 [hereinafter *Monahan*]. He points out that this Act, unlike the *Neutrality Acts* first included technical data control at 173.
235. *Haight, supra*, note 185 at 346 [hereinafter the *MCA*].
236. *Supra*, note 234 at s. 414(1).
237. Government to Government Sales are controlled under 22 U.S.C. 2751–77.
238. *Ibid.*
239. *Ibid.*
240. Exec. Order No. 10,893, 25 Fed. Reg. 10731 (1960) and Exec. Order 10,973, 26 Fed. Reg. 10,469 (1961).
241. 22 C.F.R. 121 (1983) [hereinafter the *ITAR*s].
242. *Supra*, note 234 at s. 105, and Exec. Order No. 10, 937, 26 Fed. Reg. 10,469 (1961).
243. *Haight, supra*, note 185 at 347.
244. 22 U.S.C. s. 2751 (1976 & Supp. IV 1980) as amended by Dec. 29, 1981, S. 1196, Pub. L. 97–113, 95 Stat. 1519 [hereinafter *Pub. L. 97–113*].
245. 22 U.S.C. 2372 (Supp. IV 1980) for Argentina and 22 U.S.C. 2370 (1976 & Supp. IV 1980) for Chile.
246. *Pub. L. 97–113, supra*, note 244 at s. 725 and 726.
247. J.L. Ellicott, "Trends in Export Regulations" (1983) 38 Bus. Law. 533 at 548.
248. 22 C.F.R. 123.1 (1984) as amended by 49 Fed. Reg. 47,682 (Dec. 6, 1984), for equipment; 22 C.F.R. 125.3 (1984) as amended by 49 Fed. Reg. 47,682 (1984) for classified equipment and classified technical data; 22 C.F.R. 125.2 (1984) as amended by 4 Fed. Reg. 47,682 (1984) for unclassified technical data. Data and equipment are classified if specified in Executive Order 12,356.
249. 22 C.F.R. 124.1 (1984) as amended by 49 Fed. Reg. 47,682 (1984). Prior approval for their re-export from abroad is also needed. 22 C.F.R. 123.9 (1984) as amended by 49 Fed. Reg. 47,682 (1984) for equipment, 22 C.F.R. 125.1 (1984) as amended by 49 Fed. Reg. 47,682 (1984) for technical data, and 22 C.F.R. 123.9 (1984) as amended by 49 Fed. Reg. 47,682 (1984) for other items. The requirement pertains regardless of the fact that the item may form a tiny part of another item manufactured abroad. 22 C.F.R. 123.9(b) (1984) as amended by 49 Fed. Reg. 47,682 (1984) makes this clear by requiring a statement in the shipper's export declaration to that effect.
250. Interview with Mr. C. Hamilton of the Office of Munitions Control (May 1985). In this respect there is much less flexibility in the administration of the export controls of the Department of State than is the case for the Commerce Department export controls. Given that they pertain to military items, this fact is not surprising.
251. 22 C.F.R. 124.1 (1984) as amended by 49 Fed. Reg. 47,682 (1984).
252. See for example 17 Weekly Comp. Pres. Docs. 749 reproduced in part in *Monahan, supra*, note 234 at 183–84.
253. 22 C.F.R. 126.5 (1984) as amended by 49 Fed. Reg. 47,682 (1984) although there are exceptions for which licenses are required even though the items are not classified.
254. 22 C.F.R. 123.9 (1984) as amended by 49 Fed. Reg. 47,682 (1984).
255. 22 C.F.R. 122.1 (1984) as amended by 49 Fed. Reg. 47,682 (1984).

256. *Ibid.* part 122.5
257. 15 C.F.R. 375.2 (1983) [hereinafter the *EAR*s] requires form DIB–629P or Form ITA–629, depending on the destination, of the ultimate consignee and purchaser unless an exemption is available. Where there is another end-use statement such as an International Import Certificate that is required of the consignee under 15 C.F.R. 375.3 (1983), the other form is not needed. 15 C.F.R. 375.121(b)(1). This system has been in effect from the early days of the *ECA* of 1949. See *Berman & Garson, supra*, note 153 at 826–27.
258. 15 C.F.R. 375.2(a) (1983). See Special Report: Export Control, U.S. Dep't of Commerce, May 29, 1973 at 59–60 for a good description of the use of the Ultimate Consignee/ Purchaser statement form. It is said to provide "a legal basis for pinpointing the persons responsible for any misrepresentations that may be found ...", *ibid.* at 59.
259. 15 C.F.R. 387.5(a) (1983).
260. 15 C.F.R. 387.5(c) (1983).
261. They are thus brought within the definition of 15 C.F.R. 370.2 (1983) "Export Control Document".
262. 15 C.F.R. 387 (1983) provides criminal sanctions in 15 C.F.R. 387.1(a)(2), denial of export privileges in 15 C.F.R. 387.1(b)(1), and a civil penalty in 15 C.F.R. 387.1(3).
263. 22 C.F.R. 123.10 and 123.22(e)(3) (1984) requires a form DSP–83 for equipment exports, 22 C.F.R. 124.11 (1984) requires the DSP–83 for manufacturing licensing and technical assistance agreements, and 22 C.F.R. 125.3 (1984) requires the form DSP–83 for exports of classified equipment and technical data. All sections as amended by 49 Fed. Reg. 47, 682 (1984).
264. 22 C.F.R. 124.9 and 124.10 (1984) as amended by 49 Fed. Reg. 47, 682 (1984).
265. 22 C.F.R. 124.9(e) as amended by 49 Fed. Reg. 47, 682 (1984).
266. 22 C.F.R. 124.9(b) (1984) as amended by 49 Fed. Reg. 47, 682 (1984).
267. 22 C.F.R. 124.10(a)(1)(1984) as amended by 49 Fed. Reg. 47, 682 (1984).
268. *Ibid.* part 124.10(a)(5).
269. *Ibid.* part 124.10(b)(2).
270. *Export Administration Amendments Act of 1985*, July 12, 1985, S. 883, Pub. L. 99–64, 99 Stat. 120, 50 USC App. 2401, s. 104; s. 104(a)(2)
    A "The Secretary shall grant the distribution license primarily on the basis of the reliability of the applicant and foreign consignees..."
    B "The Secretary shall grant the license [comprehensive operations license] to manufacturing, laboratory, or related operations on the basis of approval of the exporter's systems of control...."
271. See Chapter VII, *infra.*
272. *Revision of Controls on Foreign Products Incorporating U.S. Origin Parts, Component, and Materials*, 52 Fed. Reg. 9147- 9151 (1987); 15 C.F.R. 373, 376, 385. Ethiopia and Lebanon are also excluded and the limit for Nicaragua is 10%. Supercomputers are explicitly excluded.
273. Aug. 23, 1988, Pub. L. 100–418, 102 Stat. 1107, 19 USC 2901, reprinted in (1989) 28 Int'l Leg. Mat. at 15 & 399 [hereinafter the *Omnibus Trade Act*].
274. *Ibid.* Title II Export Enhancement, Subtitle D - Export Controls, s.. 2401–33.
275. *Ibid.* s. 2441–47.
276. *Ibid.* s. 2443–44.
277. *Ibid.* s. 2419, 2425, 2428, 2433.

CHAPTER IV

CANADA/U.S. BILATERAL AGREEMENTS, ARRANGEMENTS AND UNDERSTANDINGS

A. 1940–1947

The Canada-U.S. bilateral relationship that has developed since the beginning of the Second World War has greatly affected each country's domestic measures in the field of export controls. The two countries developed a close cooperation in both the defence and economic fields. As a matter of fact, they recognized that for them the two fields were interdependent, so that the adequate consideration of one necessitated the consideration of the other. This relationship began with two treaties. First was the 1940 *Ogdensburg Agreement* that set up the Permanent Joint Board on Defence.[1] The other foundation stone of the bilateral relationship was the 1941 *Hyde Park Declaration.*[2]

This is not to say that Canada-U.S. bilateral economic relations did not exist prior to this. Indeed Canada and the U.S. had had a Trade Agreement since 1936.[3] It was suspended on the entry of the two countries into the *General Agreement on Tariffs and Trade* (the *GATT*).[4] As well as trade agreements, the two countries had agreements that each would accept the certificate of the other to attest to certain standards for exported items.[5]

Perhaps the first time the U.S. received special treatment in a Canadian export control measure was in 1940. It predated the *Ogdensburg Agreement* even if only by a month. It was the *Exchange of Notes (June 18, 1940) Regarding Exemptions from Exchange Control Measures Between Canada and the United States of America.*[6] The agreement exempted U.S. nationals from Canadian foreign exchange controls if they were resident in Canada. It was to lapse if and to the extent that the U.S. imposed controls of the kind from which U.S. nationals resident in Canada were exempted.[7] The agreement exempted U.S. nationals from Canadian foreign exchange controls imposed at the beginning of World War II on the foreign currency or securities they held prior to the controls coming into force, and with respect to some foreign currency and securities acquired after institution of the controls.[8]

The *Hyde Park Declaration*[9] was made on April 20, 1941. It was not at first apparent that it had any export control implications, as it concentrated on the production of defence articles by the two states and their provision to one another. However, the question of export controls surfaced shortly afterwards from the two states' Joint Committees on Economic Cooperation. The Joint Committees were established when Canada suggested on March 17, 1941 that some arrangement be made for the coordination of the industries of the two countries. The Canadian "aide-mémoire" was accepted by the U.S. on June 6, 1941, and the Committees' personnel largely appointed by June 17, 1941.[10] The Joint Committees' powers were limited to making recommendations, but were allowed to include in their inquiry "such other topics as may appear to fall within the terms of reference..."[11]

When the Joint Committees had their first meeting they produced a resolution which dealt with export controls, although the "aide-mémoires" that constituted them had not expressly referred to controls. Specifically in its resolution, the Joint Economic Committees believed "the mutual defence interests of both countries would be promoted" by the implementation of "a more coordinated policy in the field of export control". This coordination would contribute to the defence effort of one or both countries and would require that "accurate, complete and continuous transmission of information" take place between the export control authorities of the two countries.[12]

The recommendations were sent to the Canadian Secretary of State for External Affairs in a letter which stated that the committees had considered:

> ... certain alleged discrepancies in the export control policies and procedures of Canada and the United States. It was the unanimous opinion of the members of the Committees that it was in the mutual interest of the two countries that there should be the highest degree of co-ordination in the export systems.[13]

Nevertheless, there is no direct evidence of implementation of these recommendations of the Joint Committees.

In September, 1941 the Joint Economic Committees recommended that a Joint Defence Production Committee be set up. This recommendation was acted upon.[14] The resolution of the Joint Economic Committees that was put into effect recited the essential part of the *Hyde Park Declaration* dealing with coordination of programmes to provide each other with defence articles. It then listed the joint bodies that the U.S. and Canada had established: the Permanent Joint Board on Defence (military strategy),[15] the Joint Materials Coordinating Committee (primary materials)[16] and the Economic Committees themselves.

The main task of these Joint Defence Production Committees was to effectively coordinate the capacities of Canada and the U.S. for the production of defence "material". Renamed the Joint War Production Committees,[17] they unanimously adopted a declaration of policy calling for a "combined all-out war production effort and the removal of any barriers standing in the way of such a combined effort".[18] The barriers "referred to were:

> legislative and administrative barriers, including tariffs, import duties, customs, and other regulations or restrictions of any character which prohibit, prevent, delay, or otherwise impede the free flow of necessary munitions and war supplies between the two countries for the duration of the war."[19]

Clearly the barriers contemplated that were to be "suspended or otherwise eliminated for the duration of the war"[20] included export controls.

Through this, admittedly indirect, route the export control implications of the *Hyde Park Declaration* became more clear. The removal of export control barriers between Canada and the U.S. was a logical necessity. It was the correlative of the states providing one another with the defence articles which each could best produce quickly. The export control implications of the *Hyde Park Declaration* may be seen as resulting from subsequent practice interpreting a treaty.[21] However, implementation of the resolution of the Joint War Production Committees was called a "policy" by both the President of the U.S. and the Committees themselves, which may be an indication of the intention of the states to avoid a legally binding commitment.

In practice the commitment was complete. The U.S. President stated:

> To further its implementation, I have asked the affected departments and agencies in our Government to abide by its letter and spirit so far as lies within their power.[23]

Subsequent agreements between Canada and the U.S. referred to both the *Hyde Park* and *Ogdensburg Declarations*. In one exchange of notes the U.S. called them: agreements to provide "mutual aid both in defence and in economic matters".[24] In another *Exchange of Notes (May 7 and 15, 1945) Between Canada and the United States of America Providing for the Continuation of the Principle of the Hyde Park Declaration into the Post-War Transitional Period, with Special Reference to the Problem of Reconversion of Industry*,[25] the U.S. note states that the *Hyde Park Declaration* contains "no termination date, specific or implied". The U.S. also stated that it believes that measures taken to make the most prompt and effective utilization of the productive facilities of the United States and Canada for wartime purposes "apply as a matter of course to the Pacific War". The note continued:

> Accordingly, under the instructions of my Government, I have the honor to propose that the general principles of the Hyde Park Declaration be continued on a fully reciprocal basis for the remainder of the war and that the same spirit of cooperation between the two countries should characterize their treatment of reconversion and other problems of mutual concern as the transition to peace-time economy progresses.

It also stated that the U.S. implementation of the *Hyde Park Declaration* was achieved "in large part by the equal application to Canada of [U.S.] domestic procedure in respect of priorities and allocations".[26]

In this note the U.S. treated the *Hyde Park Declaration* as a binding legal obligation. Continued U.S. cooperation was offered on the "condition of reciprocity". This caution reinforces the interpretation that the U.S. thought *Hyde Park* to be legally binding, and its language certainly leads to the same conclusion. It may be useful to note that at the time the U.S. seems to have been eager to have continued Canadian cooperation for the war in the Pacific. It was in the U.S. interest to have the *Hyde Park Declaration* binding.

There is not much doubt that the *Hyde Park Declaration* itself is an instrument binding in international law. It is the extension of the *Ogdensburg Agreement* into the economic field.[27] The *Ogdensburg Agreement* did establish the Permanent Joint Board on Defence but it was jointly denied that it created any treaty or other obligation for Canada and the U.S. to cooperate on joint security purposes.[28] This denial was made when the two governments agreed in 1947 to "collaborate for peacetime joint security purposes". Thus, this collaboration may be argued to be a political obligation, not a legal one.

Export control arrangements of the period also have to be examined in light of the 1938 Canada-United States bilateral trade agreement.[29] Article XII of the bilateral trade agreement contained measures that were exceptions to the general rule of the treaty. The general rule of the treaty was that each state was to give the other most-favored-nation (MFN) treatment[30] and non-discriminatory treatment.[31] Article XII specifically excepts, *inter alia*, export controls on gold[32] or silver[33] arms, and in "exceptional circumstances, all other military supplies",[34] measures relating to "neutrality or public security",[35] and those the country may see fit to adopt if engaged in war.[36] On the condition of no arbitrary discrimination, exceptions to the agreement were allowed provided that they were imposed on moral or humanitarian grounds,[37] to protect human, animal or plant health,[38] relating to prison-made goods and the enforcement of "police or revenue laws".[39]

B. 1947–1957

The *GATT* also has provisions which treat the same subject matter. However it treats some of these exceptions in a different manner. Thus when the 1947 agreement to suspend the Canada-U.S. trade agreement was concluded, there was a change in the conditions upon which some export controls were excepted from the general MFN and non-discriminatory treatment treaty rules binding Canada and the U.S. in international law. For example, export controls on gold and silver were now subject to a condition that they not constitute "arbitrary or unjustifiable discrimination between countries..."[40] More important is that export controls on arms and military supplies, those controls relating to public security and controls used when engaged in war were considerably restricted by the *GATT*.

In the bilateral trade agreement, it was stated that the agreement did not prevent the enforcement of such measures as the Government of either country might see fit to adopt relating to "arms or public security". It would seem then, that as long as measures dealt with arms they were beyond reproach. It would seem that where they related to public security they too were beyond reproach. If engaged in war, any measures were beyond reproach. The only restraint was that measures relating to all military supplies other than "arms, ammunition, or implements of war" were only to be taken "in exceptional circumstances".[41] Clearly a wide field of action was left to the discretion of the two states.

The *GATT* dealt with these matters in a different way. Excepted from its general provisions is state action "which it considers necessary for the protection of its essential security interests". But they are only excepted where the essential security interests relate to fissionable materials, military goods, or are taken in time of war "or other emergency in international relations".[42] Thus the scope of security interests was narrowed by relating them to certain goods, or time of war, or emergency. Likewise the scope of wartime or emergency measures is restricted to the protection of security interests. If any provision may be said to have been broadened by the *GATT* it would be that measures in cases of emergency could be related to essential security interests and not merely "other military supplies".[43]

However the width of the "public security" exception in the bilateral trade agreement would suggest that the net result is that the *GATT* significantly restricted the ability of the United States and Canada to impose export controls with respect to one another. It can be said that in the *GATT* the trade implications of export controls were given higher priority than the purposes for which they were adopted had been given before.

By 1948 the series of Canada-U.S. agreements and arrangements presented a fairly detailed picture of the policies and international legal obligations that impinged on export controls of each country. The intertwining of defence and economic cooperation during World War II was continued in instruments concluded between the two countries.

Defence and economic cooperation were linked by the establishment of the Joint Industrial Mobilization Committee "in order that the most effective use may be made of the productive facilities of the two countries".[44] The Committee was to cooperate with the Permanent Joint Board of Defence.[45] The link between defence and economic cooperation continued in the Exchange of Notes of October 26, 1950, between Canada and the United States of America giving formal effect to the "Statement of Principles for Economic Cooperation"[46] which attributes the cooperation in the field of industrial mobilization during and after the war to the "operation of the principles embodied in the *Hyde Park Declaration* of 1941".[47] The Statement of Principles was said to be an extension of the field of common action.[48] The aim was to be cooperation "to the end that the economic efforts of the two countries be coordinated for the common defence and that the production and resources of both countries be used for the best combined results".[49] One specific principle was that, where necessary, "coordinated controls over the distribution of scarce raw materials and supplies shall be instituted."[50]

Principle 3 provided details about the controls:

> Such United States and Canadian emergency controls shall be mutually consistent in their objectives, and shall be so designed and administered as to achieve comparable effects in each country. To the extent possible, there shall be consultation to this and prior to the institution of any system of controls in either country which affects the other.[51]

Not only is this a legal commitment to coordination of export controls in scarce supply situations, but it also is an international law obligation to consult to the greatest extent possible on any controls which affect the other country. Such controls would include export controls.

Principle 5 provided that:

> Barriers which impede the flow between Canada and the United States of goods essential for the common defence effort should be removed as far as possible. 5

Use of the word "should" makes the command of this legal obligation weak and allows for each state to leave some barriers that impede the flow of the goods without breach of the legal obligation. A stronger provision was made in Principle 4 for the exchange of technical knowledge and productive skills involved in essential production. They "shall, where feasible, be freely exchanged".[53] This obligation is legal in nature although conditional upon the feasibility of the exchange.

The end of the war had clearly not affected Canada-U.S. cooperation. At a two-day meeting between the U.S. President and the Canadian Prime Minister on May 8, 1953 a joint communiqué was issued.[54] The communiqué stated that both "the President and the Prime Minister emphasized the desirability and effectiveness of cooperation on the basis of the *Ogdensburg Agreement* of 1940.... Post-war arrangements for continental defence have continued in this framework".[55] By an Exchange of Notes of November 12, 1953[56] the Joint Committee on Trade and Economic Affairs was established. Among its functions was the consideration of matters affecting harmonious economic relations between Canada and the U.S.

In another joint communiqué the President and the Prime Minister alluded to the Committee on Trade and Economic Affairs as a cooperative mechanism between Canada and the U.S.[57] The communiqué again emphasized the *Ogdensburg Agreement* as the origin of defence cooperation between the two countries.[58] The 1947 joint statement[59] was also recited and the principles it contained said to be "equally valid" in 1953.

The Joint Committee on Trade and Economic Affairs, at its first meeting, considered the "need for action toward freer trade" especially since long-term effective defence programmes were required by many Western countries.[60] This theme was reiterated in the communiqué after the committee's second meeting[61] although, rather than referring to defence, the term used was "security".

By this time the Canadian view could be expressed as follows:

> We have an understanding with the United States by which we enjoy freedom on our own behalf from the operation of their export controls, but we in turn undertake to control the re-export of United States goods from Canada to overseas destinations.[62]

The understanding, however, may not have been a legal obligation.[63]

C. 1957–1967

The election which saw John Diefenbaker replace Louis St. Laurent as Prime Minister was one during which foreign investment became "a full-fledged issue."[64] Consequently, the third meeting of the Joint Committee on Trade and Economic Affairs raised the issue of U.S. investment in Canada for the first time.[65] At the meeting the Canadian delegation "clarified" concerns that had been expressed about the nature and extent of U.S. investment in Canadian natural resource and manufacturing industries.[66] The Canadian delegation stressed that Canada welcomed the inflow of capital, but expressed the hope that U.S. companies would develop closer relationships "with the people of Canada".[67]

This diplomatic language seems to reflect the Canadian desire that the U.S. recognize greater control by Canada of U.S. companies doing business in Canada.

This view is supported by the joint communiqué, released after the meeting, which stated:

> In this connection note was taken of the recent supplementary tax convention ... which was designed to facilitate greater Canadian participation in American-owned corporations operating in Canada.

At the same time it was recognized that there was a large trade imbalance between Canada and the U.S., with Canada supplying the U.S. raw materials and the U.S. supplying Canada with capital equipment and other highly fabricated products.[68] It seems that this issue was not one that was aired at the Joint Committee meeting, but is a vital one in the assessment of the effects of U.S. export controls on Canada.

On the occasion of President Eisenhower's visit to Canada in July, 1958 the two countries issued a joint statement on export controls:

> The Canadian and United States Governments have given consideration to situations where the export policies and laws of the two countries may not be in complete harmony. It has been agreed that in these cases there will be full consultation between the two governments with a view to finding through appropriate procedures satisfactory solutions to concrete problems as they arise.[69]

Again this was a clear commitment which can be compared with the wording of the Statement of Principles for Economic Cooperation.[70] In the Statement of Principles there was only the obligation to consult prior to the institution of any system of controls.[71] Nevertheless, in the joint statement of 1958 it was agreed that consultation was to be on a case by case basis. The fact that the two countries' export controls were not in harmony was to be a condition of the case by case consultation. Thus it was clear the consultation obligation was ongoing.

Defence cooperation became still closer after Canada and the United States integrated their air defences by a series of acts. Through an Exchange of Notes the Canada-United States Committee on Joint Defence was established.[72] Close on the heels of this agreement came the U.S.A.F./R.C.A.F. arrangement on the interchange of information from research and development projects.[73] The air forces arrangement was made pursuant to a 10-year-old recommendation of the old Permanent Joint Board on Defence, and was approved by Canada on Jan. 16, 1947, and the U.S. on Feb. 4, 1947. It may have been the formation of the Committee on Joint Defence that spurred conclusion of the arrangement between the air forces. Still, the arrangement did not relate to information or materials the release of which was "prohibited by legislation or national policies of the governments".[74]

The Canada-United States Committee on Joint Defence "reviews not only military questions but also the political and economic aspects of joint defence problems".[75] As part of this role the Committee reviewed defence production sharing at its July 1960 meeting. It noted that this was a "long range program".[76] There can, therefore, be seen to be an ongoing commitment to the integration of the defence economies of the two countries. One component of such integration is the export controls of each country.

The specific mention of export controls is not found in the Joint Defence Committee's communiqués.[77] The exchange of information and coordination of defence production and research was furthered by it and other[78] instruments.

The cooperative efforts of the two countries did not seem to include the specific treatment of export controls; yet the reason for harmonization, namely the integration of the economies and defences of the two countries, received constant attention. For example, the communiqués at the end of each meeting of the Joint Committee on Trade and Economic Affairs during this period were concerned with general trade and financial matters with specific attention only being given to energy and agricultural matters.[79] This was to change by the Committee's tenth meeting to include export controls and the control of U.S. subsidiaries incorporated in Canada.[80]

The 1958 Eisenhower/Diefenbaker joint statement had set out that export controls were to be treated on a case by case basis. In each case there was to be "full consultation". The necessity, desirability and modalities for consultation were made the subject of a joint U.S.-Canada study prepared by the former ambassadors for each country.[81] The report examined the working of the system of joint bodies and consultations on other levels in relation to certain subject matters. It is of more than passing interest that these subject matters included trade with Cuba, defence production sharing and the extraterritorial implications of domestic legislation, specifically the U.S. *Trading with the Enemy Act*, antitrust legislation and securities legislation.[82]

The Report noted the close cooperation between the two countries in the areas of mutual defence and economics. It also noted that problems had developed with respect to the extent of American ownership in Canadian industry,[83] and recommended that:

> each country should avoid efforts, or apparent efforts, to extend its domestic law into the territory of the other. A case in point – the administration of foreign assets controls under the United States *Trading with the Enemy Act*, as it relates to United States-owned branches and subsidiaries domiciled in Canada, occasionally comes into conflict with the laws, regulations and policies of the Canadian Government. We strongly recommend that the two governments examine promptly the means, through issuance by the United States of a general license or adoption of other appropriate measures, by which this irritant to our relationship may be removed, without encouraging the evasion of United States law by citizens of the United States.... Each country should respect scrupulously the other's exercise of its sovereign authority in legislation and the functioning of its judicial system. There are clearly identifiable areas where good fences contribute to good neighborly relations.[84]

The report recommends certain principles among which is that the U.S. be "continuously alert, throughout the entire process of policy-formulation and decision-making, to the potential impact on Canada or United States actions, especially in the economic area".[85]

The main thrust of the Report was to deal with consultation:

> The need is clear for our two governments to confirm the practice of intimate, timely and continuing consultation on all matters of common concern, at the appropriate level, employing such machinery and procedures as are most effective for this purpose.[86]

The Report concluded that there is a lack of full and timely consultations in cases which the two governments have not resolved to their mutual satisfaction. In those that they have resolved satisfactorily, an essential element was full consultation.

The Report also elaborated several fundamental rules for the implementation of consultations on a case by case basis. They were to begin as early as possible, at the planning stage in fields such as air defence arrangements, so as to cover both foreseeable problems as well as actual crises. When policies were formulated that would impinge on the other, the country formulating them should initiate consultations. Existing mechanisms should be utilized and public positions avoided where they might contribute to public division.[87]

The Joint Committee, at its meeting the next year, discussed the corporate control of U.S. subsidiaries incorporated in Canada. The U.S. Delegation emphasized that U.S. subsidiaries abroad should behave as good citizens of the country in which they are located.[88] The Committee also discussed the effects of U.S. foreign assets controls on Canadian exports. The U.S. delegates

> reaffirmed their readiness to consult promptly on any transactions of importance to Canada which are affected by United States foreign assets control ... and that ... further consideration will be given to the possibilities of additional modifications of the regulations.[89]

The Committee made specific reference to the Report on consultation between the two countries.

This theme of consultation was evident in the next meeting of the Joint Committee. Canadian delegates brought up the problem of U.S. laws affecting Canadian companies and "especially as regards securities regulation and foreign assets control" (i.e. one type of export controls).[90] Then the topic began to be treated differently.

D. 1967–1975

The problem of U.S. extension of laws into Canada was first jointly described with the term "extraterritorial application" of export controls in 1970.[91] The meeting in 1970 concluded that there should be pursuit of further steps that may be taken to avoid problems of the extraterritorial application of U.S. export control laws.[92]

However, in the early 1970s there was little public indication of such cooperation. Part of the reason certainly was the progressive relaxation of U.S. trade restrictions on China beginning in January, 1970. This was a policy introduced by U.S. President Nixon. It left intact U.S. export restrictions on Cuba, but seems to have contributed to reducing the instances in which export controls would be applied extraterritorially.

In fact, Canada and the U.S. were each going their separate ways. The Joint Committee on Defence had not met since 1964, and seemed not to be the mechanism of cooperation which had been hoped for.[93] Upon becoming Prime Minister of Canada in 1967, Pierre Trudeau had called for a reassessment of the Canadian relationship with NATO.[94] Because Trudeau thought foreign policy should dictate military policy, at first the trade relations with the U.S. dictated favouring cooperation with the U.S. over NATO. Nevertheless, by the mid 1970s, foreign policy had changed and the so-called "third option" became a governmental policy.[95] The third option called for strengthened and more extensive trade with Europe. This being the foreign policy, defence policy followed and NATO once again became a priority in Canadian defence politics and relations if not in defence spending.

At the same time Canada was not prepared to give up the economic relationship it had with the U.S.

> Canadians were anxious to maintain, at the same time, full independence and a working military alliance with the United States; they insisted on economic independence but sought the benefits of United States participation in their economic development. The pursuit of contradictory aims led to irritation between the two countries...[96]

Certainly these goals were no different than those for which Canada had been striving since the Second World War. What was different was the emphasis which was placed on asserting economic independence. The private consultations between the two countries' officials continued.[97] Unilateral legislative measures were taken by Canada however to protect its economic independence.

The Canadian measures served two purposes. Politically, they could be taken as a response to public government reports which had highlighted the issue of extraterritoriality of U.S. laws. Legally, they strengthened Canada's position in international law by allowing action which would assert a claim, rather than protest the claim of another state, and thus place the burden of proof on another state to challenge the action.

Politically, the Canadian pressures were public responses to the extraterritoriality problem. The 1968 Watkins Report[98] had suggested that a government export agency have a register of export orders from state trading agencies of communist countries. These orders would be offered to Canadian-owned or foreign-owned firms where a U.S.-owned firm refused to export. Failing such availability elsewhere in Canada, the agency would determine whether U.S. export controls were the sole reason for the inhibition of the export. If that were found to be the case then the agency would have a legislated power to require, on pain of criminal sanctions, that the U.S.-owned firm sell to it, and it would then make the export.[99] The Watkins Report also criticised the Canada-U.S. Interparliamentary Group as amounting to little more than a channel for information on U.S. actions.

In addition to this criticism there was also the report of the House of Commons Standing Committee on External Affairs and National Defence.[100] These reports at the end of the 1960s and the beginning of the 1970s focused public attention on U.S. extraterritoriality.[101]

The Canadian unilateral response was multifaceted. By the mid-1970s the Canadian government had enacted the *Foreign Investment Review Act*.[102] The *Canada Business Corporations Act* required that the Board of Directors of any corporation incorporated under that statute have a majority of Canadian residents on it,[103] and that a majority of Canadian directors generally had to be present at a meeting for it to be able to transact business.[104] The *Combines Investigation Act* was amended to provide the power to an administrative tribunal to order Canadian corporations to fulfil export orders despite any instructions from its owners.[105]

As well as these legislative responses, on July 18, 1975 the "New Principles of International Business Conduct" were publicized by the government as guidelines for "foreign-controlled firms" in Canada, exhorting them to "aggressively pursue and develop ... international markets as well as in Canada" and to:

> [g]ive appropriate support to recognized national objectives and established government programs, while resisting any direct or indirect pressure from foreign governments or associated companies to act in a contrary manner.[106]

The road to this legislation was paved by an outcry against foreign influence in Canadian corporate decision-making.[107] It would also seem, however, to have much to do with the changing direction of foreign policy in Canada and the U.S. as well as the relationship of their leaders. When the two leaders met in December 1971, Prime Minister Trudeau reported that President Nixon had assured him it was "in the clear interests of the United States to have a Canadian neighbour not only independent both politically and economically but also one which was confident that the decisions and policies in each of these sectors would be taken by Canadians in their own interests..."[108]

While extraterritorial export controls certainly were not excluded from the scope of such an assurance, a more important trade issue between Canada and the U.S. was the measures the U.S. was taking to correct balance of payments difficulties it was having.[109] The U.S. measures required certain steps to be taken by foreign corporations, where there was some degree of U.S. control. Thus it can be seen that the extraterritorial control exercised over Canadian corporations was a key issue between the two countries.

Although the heads of state did not specifically discuss the extraterritoriality of U.S. export control laws when they met again in April 1972, Prime Minister Trudeau stated this was an issue frequently discussed between Canadian and U.S. officials and ministers.[110]

By 1972 it was clear that Canada had embarked upon a pursuit of the "third option". As the Canadian Secretary of State for External Affairs described it, this meant that decisions had to be taken in Canada by Canadians.[111] Canada had to realize however that "in an age of interdependence, it would be impossible to make Canada totally invulnerable to continental pressures and unrealistic even to try to do so."[112]

Canada did in fact seem to implement such a policy. It legislated to both demonstrate and protect its economic independence. It also continued to interact with the U.S. through consultation and cooperation, as well as diplomatic communications.

Canadian cooperation with the U.S. can be seen in a change made in the Canadian Export Control List in 1973. Although it is true that export permits had been required for the export from Canada of items originating abroad, new item 9001 specifically mentioned "goods originating in the United States" for the first time.[113] It thus appears that the Canadian government was sending a clear signal to the U.S. that it was controlling the export from Canada of U.S. origin goods. The implication of this was that the U.S. did not have any justification in practice for extraterritorial export controls because, while Canada controlled only some items of its own, it required export permits for any item originating in the U.S. While this had been the case before, specifically naming the U.S. origin items made it easier to demonstrate to the U.S.

E. 1975–1981

Canada/U.S. consultation continued both on the executive level as well as the legislative level. The Interparliamentary Group meeting in early 1976 discussed the extraterritoriality of U.S. export controls on Cuba. This was one way in which Canadian concerns were directly communicated to U.S. Congress members. Canadian diplomatic correspondence also was aimed at U.S. Congress action. Protests were made about amendments to the U.S. *Export Administration Act* because of their extraterritorial application. The protest was in the following terms:

> The view that a foreign legislative body may impose obligations upon a Canadian person or corporation in respect of his or its activities in Canada or in a third country continues to be completely unacceptable to the Canadian government.[114]

Clearly Canadian action was being taken on all fronts. Still, agreement between the two countries on the issues was elusive.

In 1976 the U.S. Ambassador to Canada, Thomas Enders, stated that consultation before taking actions that affect the other country, with the corollary willingness to consider accommodation, was important. Consultation was credited as a Canadian initiative.[115] It appears that the history and agreements between the countries to consult had been temporarily forgotten, perhaps an indication of the state of Canada-U.S. relations in the 1970s. The Ambassador also suggested that multilateral fora were perhaps better suited to solving problems between Canada and the U.S. This too can be seen as an indication of the lack of agreement between the two states.

In 1977 the most important international forum for these two countries dealing with export controls, the Coordinating Committee (CoCom) of the Consultative Group, redefined the ambit of agreed types of export controls. The member states agreed to control three categories of strategic items:

(a) items whose design or principal use is for the production of or use with arms;
(b) items whose technology would assist enemy states in developing arms or defences to them;
(c) items which enemy states have in short supply and may usefully use for arming themselves.[116]

The criteria, however, were general enough to lead to significant differences of opinion between CoCom members in specific cases. Canada and the U.S. differed on the interpretation of dual use items as well as items which formed a component of a larger item. Item 9001 on the Export Control List prohibited exports of U.S. origin goods without an export permit. The practice was, and has continued to date to be, not to issue export permits in cases in which the U.S. would not allow direct shipment of the items to their eventual destination. However item 9001 specifies that it does not include:

> such goods that have been further processed or manufactured outside the United States, by combining them with other goods or otherwise, so as to result in a substantial change in value, form and use of the goods or in the production of new goods, unless the goods to be exported are listed in another Group in this List.[117]

Since 1974 Canadian policy has also been to permit export of U.S. origin goods, which fall under item 9001, as spare or replacement components for Canadian goods exported without merely applying U.S. policy to them.[118] Thus, where U.S. origin goods were combined with other goods, they would not be caught by item 9001 if new goods were produced, or the value, use or form of the goods was substantially changed. Of course a permit would be required where the Export Control List controlled the export of the type of item created; almost always this would involve a CoCom designated item.

Canadian export controls, however, assisted the U.S. in enforcing its controls in cases where Canada required an export permit. Item 9002 required all goods originating outside Canada and listed on the Export Control List to also require an export permit, unless they were in transit in bond to a foreign destination. Nevertheless, for U.S. origin goods being shipped through Canada in bond, Canadian Customs would verify that the goods were accompanied by a copy of the appropriate U.S. documentation and that the information thereon did not conflict with the bill of lading.[119]

Relations between Canada and the U.S. seemed to have become more harmonious once Jimmy Carter became the U.S. President. Vice-President Mondale noted great progress in Canada-U.S. relations in the year after Carter became President in 1977.[120] Among the matters the Vice-President discussed with Canadian officials was the extraterritoriality of U.S. discovery procedures. As a response to an incident in which U.S.-owned corporations in Canada had been required to provide information to U.S. export control authorities, Vice-President Mondale stated it had been agreed that if information was required from Canadian corporations the Canadian government would be informed first and efforts would be made to obtain it voluntarily. He made it clear, however, that the U.S. would not waive its right to pursue compulsory legal remedies if there was failure on the voluntary basis.[121] In this way the consultation between the two governments was reaffirmed. Nevertheless, the U.S. insisted that it had the right to pursue unilateral and extraterritorial remedies. Canada continued to send diplomatic notes to the U.S. protesting its claims of extraterritorial jurisdiction.

The harmony of the first year of the Carter Presidency did not last long. Canadian-initiated diplomatic correspondence on the subject of U.S. extraterritorial export controls increased greatly in the period 1977-79 over prior years. In late 1977 Canada was protesting that the U.S. was asserting extraterritorial jurisdiction to enforce its anti-boycott regulations.[122] In early 1978 Canada complained about amendments to the U.S. *Export Administration Act* which defined the ambit of the act as extending to U.S. owned or controlled corporations abroad. In one note the Canadian Embassy wrote:

> The Canadian Government wishes to reiterate its position that the USA authorities are not entitled to exercise jurisdiction over Canadian companies solely on the basis that these companies may be "controlled" by U.S. citizens, nor to exercise jurisdiction with respect to business activities of such Canadian companies carried on outside the United States.[123]

The note referred to the fact that the same concerns had been expressed to President Carter by Prime Minister Trudeau.[124] The note concluded that the Canadian government trusted that the U.S. would consult in any instances where Canadian interests might be affected.

This period marked a transition stage for Canadian-U.S. relations with respect to export controls. Canada had heretofore been content to wait for application of extraterritorial controls before it would react to them. But now Canada began to take a more aggressive posture. Canada closely monitored the U.S. legislative process and consulted with the U.S. about the extraterritorial impact it foresaw in legislation, before it was applied, and then before it was even passed, hoping to influence the course of events before problems arose. Canada had heretofore reacted to practice, often phrasing its complaints in terms of principle. Now Canada was reacting to practice and to principle.[125]

F. 1981–1988

The Reagan era marked a transition back to a U.S. oriented foreign policy, and away from the "third option". An example of the change was the orientation of Canadian defence spending. In the mid-1970s the major Canadian defence purchase was from Europe in order to strengthen economic ties between them:

> The purchase of the Leopard tanks from West Germany was undertaken in 1976 as a means of building onto an existing NATO military connection broader political and economic linkages with the European Community.[126]

Canada had also negotiated the Framework Agreement with the E.E.C.[127] setting up broad goals to be achieved in increasing trade between the two. However in 1980, the most expensive defence procurement contract in Canadian history, for the F-18A fighter aircraft, was signed, procuring the fighters from the U.S.[128]

Canada began making its position more clear in legal terms, as well as political terms. Every appropriate occasion was seized to put forward its position. Unlike the U.S. position the Canadian position was not clear. The U.S. position can be seen to be presented by its continuous assertions of extraterritorial jurisdiction based on control of foreign corporations, and even the fact that goods or technology involved had once been within U.S. jurisdiction. The Canadian position was now being clarified. It was presented to the U.S. and that position began to be made public more and more. What had been presented to the U.S. in closed meetings before was now being publicized in speeches, diplomatic notes made public, and even laws. The result of the publicity campaign by the Canadian government was to highlight the issue and to reach a closer understanding of the issues involved.

A prominent discussion of the issues putting forth the Canadian viewpoint was a speech by the Canadian Ambassador to the U.S. in April, 1982. He remarked that extraterritoriality by means of control of a corporation is not on the wane:

> This is because, increasingly a nation's trading is pursued in the context of its foreign policy objectives. Trade may even become an instrument of foreign policy.[129]

The Ambassador stated that Canada must get used to the idea that any two states as interdependent as they are will have to accept that the laws of the other will have some effect on persons and property in the other state:

> Indeed, one can accept that international law at present does not impose a general prohibition against the application of domestic law to persons, events and conduct abroad. At the same time one must also recognize that such extraterritorial regulation almost always engages the sovereign interest of another state.[130]

He continued that the absolute insistence on the exclusive legitimacy of either the territoriality or nationality principles was not helpful:

> These concepts may provide useful first premises in determining jurisdiction, but they no longer provide – if they ever did – any basis for claims of absolute exclusiveness. On the other hand I find equally unhelpful the assertion that any connection at all with a jurisdiction legitimizes the application of its laws.[131]

The Canadian Ambassador's discourse related these legal problems of jurisdiction to the structure of international investment. These questions were being addressed in the OECD, the U.N. and at high level meetings multilaterally, but as yet had not provided any solutions.[132] Either joint and complementary approaches would have to be taken or a pattern of friction and defensive legislation would be the result.[133]

The Canadian publicity campaign did not prevent it from continuing its cooperative and diplomatic communications with the U.S.

When the Siberian Pipeline controversy arose in 1982 Canada sent another diplomatic note. There did not seem to be any concrete incident which stirred the protest, although it was suggested some Canadian corporations might be affected.[134] It was strictly on principle. The Canadian note stated:

> It is not apparent under what principle of international law the USA asserts jurisdiction over the commercial and trading activities of foreign persons and entities when they have previously entered into private contractual arrangements with U.S. persons that were in accordance with U.S. law and U.S. export policy of the day.[135]

This was the first time Canada had taken a firm position in this matter, perhaps because it was the first time that U.S. export controls were at the same time retroactive and dealt purely with goods produced abroad under U.S. licence and without the support of any other country. They were of course extraterritorial, which is why the other issues had come into play. But the reason the U.S. stood alone on the Siberian Pipeline was that the measures were foreign policy motivated and other countries' foreign policy did not coincide.

The Canadian note avoided comment on the motivation of the U.S. controls and emphasized the procedural and substantive principles which it felt had been violated:

> [T]he course of action chosen by the Government of the United States is not consistent with the longstanding and close cooperation that exists between the two Governments concerning the implementation of export controls ... It is noted that the U.S. measures appear to assume that U.S. domestic law and policy can guide foreign enterprises in which there is some U.S. investment or regulate the disposition of foreign goods in which there is a U.S. element without regard to the policies of the countries under whose laws the enterprises are incorporated or where the goods are produced. The Government of Canada wishes to observe that such an assumption is incompatible with the principles of self-restraint and non-interference that underlie the international order.[136]

The note was perhaps most important as a reminder to the U.S. of the years of cooperation in the matter of export controls on the bilateral level. Canada was reaffirming the special relationship it had had with the U.S. since the Second World War. Only in the years of the Nixon Presidency had the relationship drifted apart so that, at least on the surface, it seemed that the cooperation had been discontinued.

The question of whether U.S. laws were preventing Canadian exports with respect to the Siberian Pipeline was referred to the Director under the *Combines Investigation Act*.[137] Prime Minister Trudeau stated that European countries which had complained about Canada's Foreign Investment Review Agency might now better appreciate Canada's motivations.[138]

Canada continued its campaign of diplomatic protest on matters of principle. In 1983 Canada sent another note to protest the extraterritorial aspect of the U.S. *Export Administration Act* which was awaiting Congressional review. The note was one of the most complete expositions of the Canadian government's position on the extraterritoriality of U.S. export controls since the Second World War.

It began by summarizing the significance of the cooperation between the two countries since the Second World War:

> The Government of Canada and the Government of the United States of America have long cooperated with respect to export controls, following upon the 1942 *Hyde Park Declaration.* This is manifest in the treatment that is accorded each country in the administration of the export control laws of the other. Generally speaking, pursuant to the *Hyde Park Declaration,* U.S. goods are exported to Canada without U.S. export licences, and vice versa. To prevent the circumvention of U.S. controls, Canada regulates the re-export of controlled U.S. origin goods. This system has benefited both countries. It has helped to maintain bilateral trade flows free of the impediment of export licences, while still safeguarding mutual security objectives.[139]

Noticeable by its omission is the fact that the U.S. does not regulate the re-export of controlled Canadian origin goods. Perhaps it is assumed that it is sufficient that the breadth of U.S. export controls, compared with the Canadian measures, would serve to require licenses for any such Canadian items. A key distinction remains however. Whereas Canada uses item 9001 to implement U.S. export policy with respect to what Canada considers U.S. origin goods, there is no reciprocal application of Canadian export policy.[140] Although the cases in which conflicts arise are rare, it is with respect to arms shipments, where U.S. regulations are most rigid, that Canadian policy is most likely to conflict with that of the U.S.

The *Defence Production Sharing Agreement* between the two countries basically creates an open border between the two countries for goods and information falling within its ambit. There have been complaints that during the U.S. war in Vietnam although Canadian arms were not being shipped directly, they were being shipped there by the U.S. after purchase.[141] The Canadian government was content in diffusing the issue by stating:

> Defence equipment sold by Canada to the United States is absorbed into the general inventory of the military services of that country and its ultimate disposition and destination is a matter for the authorities of the United States to decide. The same principle applies to defence equipment which Canada purchases from the United States.[142]

Nevertheless, Canadian arms export policy has been not to supply arms to countries involved in hostilities, or to countries in which there is an imminent threat of hostilities, or to regimes pursuing policies contrary to Canadian standards and practices.[143] Thus Canada may not wish to supply Israel with arms, for example, while the U.S. clearly does. Or since the 1970s Canada may not have been willing to supply arms to Taiwan, while the U.S. policy was to the contrary. Canada seems to have been content to control direct shipments, but to consider exports to the U.S. forming a component of an export to Taiwan as a strictly U.S. matter consistent with its approach under 9001 where the reciprocal case would arise.

Thus it can be seen that U.S. controls in themselves are insufficient to provide any assurance that the U.S. is not a backdoor to some countries for certain items, most notably arms sales. But, it may be that this is a convenient omission for the Canadian Government. Canada can stand firm on a policy basis as having a control of the exports of arms, but may be able not to lose the business in fact.

In its 1983 note Canada reaffirmed its view of U.S. extraterritoriality being unfounded in international law. Extraterritorial export controls were said to hamper the ability of a multinational enterprise to comply with the OECD Guidelines for Multinational Enterprises.[144] It also stated:

> The Government of Canada believes that extraterritorial problems and conflicts of jurisdiction would be greatly limited if the United States would take due account of the principle of reciprocity and assert unilaterally its jurisdiction over conduct outside its territory only in circumstances where it would be prepared to recognize and accept, in similar circumstances and on the same basis, the same unilateral assertion of jurisdiction by another state over conduct within the United States Territory.

The note also stated that cooperation was to be followed on a multilateral level within CoCom. The note stated that this type of cooperation is a permissible way to define and secure common security objectives between states:

> The parties to CoCom are, themselves, responsible for implementing multilaterally-agreed controls and imposing domestic penalties in the event of infractions of their national export control laws.[145]

In all the note was a strong presentation of the Canadian position. It protested U.S. extraterritorial controls on corporations in Canada as being contrary to international law. It also pointed out that the reciprocity principle of international law requires that any claim of extraterritoriality is one that a state opens itself up to suffer. As well as relying on principle, the note urged cooperation both bilaterally based on the *Hyde Park Declaration* and subsequent cooperation, and multilaterally within Cocom. The note was in fact passed along to appropriate Congressional committees during their deliberations of the *Export Administration Act.*

Canada continued its consultations with the U.S. on the basis that the Canada-U.S. relationship was different from other bilateral ones. The degree of U.S. investment had provided the U.S. the means by which to affect Canadian corporations. High level meetings between Canadian and U.S. officials constantly raised the problem and sought a means of finding accommodation.[146] The Canadian Secretary of State for External Affairs and the U.S. Secretary of State had the issue on their agenda when they met in early 1984.[147] Cooperative procedures with respect to extraterritoriality had been worked out between the two states with respect to antitrust laws,[148] but a similar understanding has still eluded the states on the topic of export controls. It would seem that, unlike antitrust policy, export control policy is formed of many heterogeneous factors and is thus likely to give rise to conflict. The Canadian Secretary of State for External Affairs noted this fact:

> Where Canada and the U.S.A. share policy objectives, accommodation can often be found. However, where there is disagreement over policy, as may be the case in respect of certain export controls ... our respective positions can become difficult to reconcile.[149]

The U.S. had begun to enforce its export control laws more strictly since the election of President Reagan in 1980. One means of enforcement that had been suggested by some U.S. lobbies was that the exemption from U.S. export permits that existed in favor of most items sent to Canada for consumption there, might be revoked.[150] The U.S. had been worried about leaks of high technology to the Soviet Union and was singling out Canada as potentially lax in monitoring the re-export of high technology goods.[151] However Canadian officials stated they had not seen evidence that Canada was a leak.[152] It was possible that the U.S. was seeking some more political justification for its extraterritorial export controls on the ground of efficiency if not international law.

The enforcement emphasis of the U.S. administration carried over into the bilateral discussions between officials of the two countries. The result was the *Agreement Regarding Mutual Assistance and Cooperation between Customs Administrations.*[153] "Customs laws" were defined to include export and transshipment controls of either country.[154] The Agreement provided that each was to assist the other in the prevention, investigation and repression of Customs offences.[155] However it was stated that the Agreement was to be in addition to any mutual assistance and cooperation already in effect between the two states.[156]

The Agreement provides for a mechanism by which a state would request the assistance of the other.[157] In response the Customs Administration of the other state will undertake the necessary acts.[158] The acts which it will undertake include: investigations, interviews, and allowing a representative of the requesting state to be present.[159]

The Agreement is strictly territorial in nature[160] which is most simply explained by the fact that it involves the exercise of enforcement jurisdiction of a state. Even the U.S. does not allege that enforcement jurisdiction may be exercised within the territory of another state.

The Agreement was also made subject to the standard exception in trade-related international agreements. That exception is the national security exception. However the wording of this exception was somewhat wider:

> Where the Customs Administration whose assistance is requested is of the opinion that compliance with a request is likely to be detrimental to its national sovereignty or security, public policy or other important interests of its country, it may decline to provide its assistance in whole or in part, or may stipulate that its provision of assistance shall be dependent upon the fulfilment of certain conditions or requirements.[161]

Two items mentioned clearly contemplate the legitimate interests affected by extraterritorial jurisdiction. It affects the national sovereignty or "other important interests" of other states. If Canada is not prepared to accept that these interests be affected by prescriptive jurisdiction, it certainly would not want to be obliged to allow them to be affected by its own enforcement jurisdiction. Of course, this is not a case of extraterritoriality because it involves a state acting with respect to persons in its own territory. Still the provision allows each state to avoid enforcing the other objectionable law. It allows Canada to desist from enforcing U.S. export control laws where it objects to the basis of U.S. extraterritorial export controls.[162]

Export control laws were continuously the subject of discussions between the two countries in this period. U.S. Secretary of State Schultz stated before the South Carolina Bar Association in May 1984 that, since he had been confirmed in his office, he had met with his Canadian counterpart, the Secretary of State for External Affairs, and they had agreed between them to meet at least four times a year to discuss issues:

> We have already met seven times, and issues of extraterritoriality have invariably been at the top of our list. These issues range from banking and taxation to export controls and antitrust regulations.[163]

He stated that strategic controls had not generally created problems because they are coordinated in CoCom.[164] Nevertheless, the extraterritoriality problems arise in the context of foreign policy controls because there is no consensus on them. He then even cited the Canadian Ambassador to the U.S. in support of the proposition that doing away with extraterritoriality is not practicable. He stated that the alternative, a strictly territorial approach to sovereignty, does not recognize the reality of the world in which international communications assist parties in several nations to deal with each other avoiding important national regulations. He put the issue this way:

> The question we face ... is not whether extraterritorial reach should be permissible but rather how and when it should be done.[165]

Thus there seems to have developed an understanding at the highest level of generality between Canada and the U.S., that extraterritoriality itself was not a synonym for illegality in international law, nor was it practical to hope to eliminate it. But this understanding did not imply agreement as to how and when it was permissible.

In his speech U.S. Secretary of State Schultz pointed out some of the results of U.S. export controls. The controls encourage foreign purchasers to design around U.S. origin components. He also pointed out that U.S. extraterritorial export controls lead foreign governments to shy away from giving U.S. owned corporations in their territory national treatment, a long cherished goal of the U.S. According to the Secretary of State, they also encourage foreign countries to enact blocking statutes, which forbid individuals or companies from complying with U.S. law or regulations.[166]

G. Adoption of the *Foreign Extraterritorial Measures Act*

Canada followed other countries and introduced blocking legislation in Parliament on May 28, 1984. A government news release stated its purpose was to "protect Canadian citizens and corporations from measures taken by foreign governments or foreign tribunals with unacceptable extraterritorial scope."[167] Earlier a *Foreign Proceedings and Judgements Bill* had been prepared but was not introduced into Parliament. That Bill was revised and renamed and introduced for First Reading, but it too failed to pass before a new election was called, and died on the order paper. Finally the new conservative government of Prime Minister Mulroney introduced it again in Parliament[168] in December 1984. The Bill received third reading and was proclaimed in force February 14, 1985, a surprisingly quick passage.

Upon its introduction in December 1984, a government news release stated the new legislation was to be used where diplomatic efforts to solve the problems had failed and irreconcilable policy differences remained;

> ... the Government of Canada remains fully committed to pursuing all diplomatic efforts to resolve any issues that may arise from the extraterritorial application of foreign laws. The Canada/U.S.A Antitrust Understanding, signed on March 9, 1984 is a good example of a measure which can assist in working out political problems through notification and consultation.[169]

This policy could be implemented by the executive branch of the Canadian government by reserving to the Attorney General the power to prohibit or restrict certain practices under the *Foreign Extraterritorial Measures Act.*[170]

The *FEMA* makes a distinction between foreign antitrust law and other types of law. The reason is that a "clawback" provision is included. It allows for suit to recover any amount of damages paid under an antitrust judgement declared by the Attorney General to be unenforceable in Canada[171] or the excess of any damages paid under a judgement that the Attorney General reduces. The latter provision is similar to a British one, and is aimed at recouping treble damages awarded in U.S. antitrust cases.[172] To avail itself of the provision the party involved must be a Canadian citizen, a resident of Canada, a corporation incorporated in Canada, or "a person carrying on business in Canada".[173]

The *FEMA* has two other main thrusts. It allows the Attorney General to restrict the power of foreign states to discovery or production of records in Canada or from Canadians. It also allows the Attorney General to prohibit compliance with extraterritorial measures of a foreign state.[174]

Section 5 of the *FEMA* allows the Attorney General to prohibit compliance with foreign measures only with the concurrence of the Secretary of State for External Affairs.[175] In this way consideration of Canada's international legal and political position will be assured prior to any such order being made. The order under the section is specific about the primary focus of the section – international trade – but does not restrict the power to such cases. Rather, an order may be made where:

> a foreign state or a foreign tribunal has taken or is proposing or is likely to take measures affecting international trade or commerce of a kind or in a manner that has adversely affected or is likely to adversely affect significant Canadian interests in relation to international trade or commerce involving business carried on in whole or in part in Canada, or that otherwise has infringed or is likely to infringe Canadian sovereignty....[176]

The difficulty in appreciating what are "significant Canadian interests" or "Canadian sovereignty" makes such a provision one which could cause considerable difficulty in the courts since they have traditionally given great weight to the views of the executive on such matters. It is not surprising, therefore, that the power was vested in the executive branch of the Canadian government.

The scope of the Section 5 power under the *FEMA* is indeed very wide. It applies to actual, proposed or likely measures taken or to be taken by foreign states. Whether a measure is "likely" is not explicitly said to be determinable by the Attorney General. Thus it leaves open the possibility that a person subjected to a section 5 order will challenge it on the grounds that the order was not objectively likely, but was merely speculative.

The actions of a foreign state or tribunal that may fall within the scope of section 5 are also very wide. They include:

> judgements and rulings made or to be made by the foreign state or foreign tribunal and directives, instructions, intimations of policy and other communications issued by or to be issued by the foreign state or foreign tribunal.[177]

It would seem that there needs to be a causal link between the action of a foreign state and the object of the measures in Canada. It need not however be a direct link. Orders may be made to prohibit compliance "relating to such measures" where the intimation or communication of such measures is "from a person who is in a position to direct or influence the policies of the person in Canada."[178] Thus only two criteria need be met. First there must be actual or likely measures of a foreign state. Second, these measures must be communicated to a person in Canada either directly, by the foreign state or tribunal, or by a person with influence on the Canadian person. It seems clear that there need not be any actual influence upon the Canadian person. It is also clear that the communication may be of measures themselves, and not the fact that the measures themselves require the Canadian person to comply with them. Thus in a situation where the measures do not require the Canadian person to comply with them, communications about them may bring the section into play. A foreseeable case of that would be when a Canadian corporation is told by its U.S. parent company that U.S. export control measures require the parent not to export X or Y to State A. In such a case an order could be made under section 5 to prohibit the Canadian corporation from complying with such a practice, whether the U.S. law was also aimed at foreign subsidiaries or not.

It would seem that section 5 would also cover any contractual stipulation requiring a Canadian person to refrain from exporting something to a state which is named or which may be named. It would be sufficient if there were measures of a foreign state which did affect one of the contracting parties directly, whether in fact they were express in the contract, or required to be in such a contract or not. Such measures would still be "intimations of policy or other communications relating to such measures."[179] If evidence could prove that the foreign measures were not in fact related to the contractual stipulation, but that there was some valid business reason for them, perhaps section 5 would not apply.

It is also the case that "submission clauses" would be caught by section 5. Thus where a Canadian person in a contract agrees to be bound by the laws of another state, whether as they existed at a certain date or will exist in the future, the Attorney General may prohibit export restrictions, among others. This is a useful power because the validity of such clauses has never been tested before a Canadian court.

Section 5 provides for two sorts of mechanisms. The first is that the Attorney General may require information about such foreign measures from Canadian persons.[180] It would seem that any such notice can be required from a class of persons;[181] however, there does not seem to be a defined way of publishing such a requirement. Thus where a class of persons is required to provide information, the class must be served with notice personally, or upon application to a superior court in a manner the court approves.[182] It would surely seem preferable for the government to allow for regulations which would require information with respect to foreign measures which become irritants from time to time – such as the Siberian Pipeline regulations of the U.S. The business community would surely prefer personal service of an order for information, which would avoid the burden of scanning the Canada Gazette for regulations in order to avoid breaching such an order.

The second mechanism in section 5 is the prohibition order. It allows the Attorney General to prohibit a person in Canada from complying with the foreign measures themselves, or any instructions or communications relating to them from any person with influence over the person in Canada.[183] Like the information order, it must be personally served unless a Superior Court agrees otherwise.[184]

The territorial scope of section 5 remains to be seen. The orders which may be made are only with respect to "persons in Canada". This may imply any person resident in Canada, or carrying on business in Canada if it is a corporation, as is the case for defining the scope of the "clawback" antitrust provision.[185] It is clear that the "clawback" provision is wider. It gives the right to any "Canadian citizen" to sue in Canada as well as a "resident of Canada".[186] It would seem that the words "person in Canada" would not include Canadian citizens abroad. The words "in Canada" in section 5 seem to refer to the geographical mass of Canada, with appropriate abstraction for non-physical persons.

If nothing else, the *FEMA* is a bargaining chip to take to discussions with the U.S. The U.S. seems to have been relying on an interpretation of international law that any domestic act of a state must be proved by another state to breach international law or it is presumed legal. This is based on a reading of the *Lotus* case[187] which put the burden of proof on France to allege that Turkey had breached international law by taking jurisdiction over a French national. But, by making an order under the *FEMA*, Canada can respond to a foreign assertion of jurisdiction with one of its own. Thus the burden of proof will not decide the matter. The focus will shift to a consideration of the substantive issues and interests involved.

H. Recent Developments: The Pattern of Consultation

Canada and the U.S. have concluded one treaty which indirectly seems to include export controls. The *Treaty on Mutual Legal Assistance in Criminal Matters* was concluded in March 1985.[188] It applies with respect to "offences" in each state. An "offence" is defined:

> for the United States, an offence for which the statutory penalty is a term of imprisonment of one year or more, or an offence specified in the Annex.[189]

Because the penalty for export control offences in the U.S. meets the requirement of the Treaty definition of an "offence", it is clear that U.S. export control offences are included thereunder. The same is true for Canadian export controls.

The Treaty clearly overlaps with the 1984 *Customs Agreement*.[190] The Treaty also provides for assistance in matters relating to the "investigation, prosecution and suppression of offences,"[191] and for assistance in obtaining information and discovery as well as the transferring between states of persons in custody.[192]

Unlike the *Customs Agreement*, which implies reciprocity, here:

> [a]ssistance shall be provided without regard to whether the conduct under investigation or prosecution in the Requesting State constitutes an offence or may be prosecuted by the Requested State.[193]

Thus it is clear that even where the scope of U.S. export controls exceeds that of Canada, assistance is to be provided. In the context of export controls, this may thus include extraterritorial U.S. export controls or foreign policy export controls aimed at a target with which the other state does not agree. For this reason, perhaps, the exceptions to the treaty are carefully drawn. To put together the definitions with the substantive provisions of the Treaty, the exception reads as follows:

> The Requested State may deny assistance to the extent that ... execution of the request is contrary to its substantial interest related to national security or other essential public policy, as determined by its Central Authority.[194]

Arguably, national sovereignty, or not recognizing the other state's claim to prescriptive jurisdiction in the matter, would be such an "essential public policy", especially since it is determined by the state denying assistance itself.

It would seem that, as broad as the scope of the Treaty may be, a party cannot be required to prosecute persons within its jurisdiction when a request is made. That would be a fanciful interpretation of its provisions, not in keeping with the *Vienna Convention on the Law of Treaties*. Thus the widest scope of the Treaty would seem to be that, where one party has claimed extraterritorial jurisdiction of any sort, the other is required to assist it, despite disagreement with the assertion of jurisdiction unless it invokes its essential public policy. Even so the Treaty requires that once a request is made the Requested State:

> shall consult with the Requesting State to determine whether assistance may be given subject to such terms and conditions as the Requested State deems necessary.[195]

Invocation of the exception is subject to a mandatory consultation procedure. Thus, at the very least, the Treaty provides a means by which the state taking extraterritorial export control jurisdiction may require consultations with the other state, although not vice versa.

The Treaty also has another provision for consultation:

> Where denial of a request or delay in its execution may jeopardize successful completion of an investigation or prosecution, the Parties shall promptly consult, at the instance of either Party, to consider alternative means of assistance. Unless the Parties otherwise agree, the consultations shall be considered terminated 30 days after they have been requested, and the Parties' obligations under this Article shall then be deemed to have been fulfilled.[196]

Again the requesting party may at least force the other to consult on any case. Thus the Treaty supports a principle between Canada and the U.S. that a state may require the other to consult with respect to any specific "offence" where the other will not provide it with requested assistance. Using this Treaty to initiate mandatory consultations would not seem to be of any practical importance. It has usually been the state suffering the extraterritorial jurisdiction that wanted to initiate consultations. But with the advent of the Canadian *FEMA* it may well be that the U.S. will want to initiate consultations respecting an order under section 5 of that Act, and may require Canada to do so by relating it to a request for assistance under the Treaty.

This is not to say that a request for consultations would not be respected apart from the Treaty. It is clear that practice since the Second World War has been to have continuous consultations on varying levels. The various treaties and other agreements provide a number of pieces of clear evidence of the *opinio juris* to consult at the request of the other party on the matter of export controls. The practice of actual consultation since the *Ogdensburg* and *Hyde Park* declarations provides a consistent pattern of state practice. The practice has continued virtually uninterrupted for close to 50 years. It would seem that the evidence is clear that there is a regional custom, binding in international law, that Canada and the U.S. must consult with each other at the request of the other with respect to export controls and the issues arising from their extraterritoriality. There is, however, insufficient evidence to prove that such consultation should be prior to any state action.

A recent example of such consultation is provided by the U.S. embargo on Nicaragua. The Canadian position was against the embargo, but Canada would apply U.S. policy to U.S.-origin items which were being exported from Canada, under item 9001 of the Export Control List.[197]

The *Free Trade Agreement between Canada and the U.S.A.*[198] which entered into force on January 1, 1989 contains considerable evidence of a practice of prior consultation between both countries on economic questions. Indeed, implementation of this Agreement is largely in the hands of a wide variety of standing or *ad hoc* committees as well as a permanent Commission. Given that the Agreement covers the broad spectrum of the commercial relations between Canada and the U.S.A. one might expect to find provisions dealing with extraterritoriality. This is not the case. The Agreement makes no change in the formal legal relationship of the two countries on this matter, although the breadth and complexity of the scope of the Agreement make it possible that the organic relationship of Canada and the U.S. has changed. It may well be harder for Canada to maintain its position of principle on questions of extraterritoriality in the face of increased integration of both the economic and the legal relationship.

The only Article of the Agreement which speaks to extraterritoriality is Article 407.3 and 407.4.[199] As can readily be seen this Article does little more than countenance measures takes as a condition of exit and entry of goods from the territories of either party.

The Agreement affirms and incorporates the general exceptions and the national security exceptions of the GATT but on a significantly narrower basis.[200] The wording of the general national security exception Article 2003 is close to Article XXI of the GATT, but the other Articles limit the basis on which export controls can be imposed. Does this have implications for extraterritoriality? This can be argued both ways. On the one hand one can suggest that the increased integration of both economies makes Canadian resistance to U.S. extraterritorial measures all the more difficult. On the other hand, one can argue that the restricted basis for the imposition of export controls may well limit the justifications previously given by the U.S. in justification of its extraterritorial export controls. Certainly all the considerations pertaining to the application of the GATT to export controls[201] are applicable *a fortiori* between Canada and the U.S. in the context of the Free Trade Agreement.

Since the Free Trade Agreement does not speak directly to questions of extraterritoriality, it is difficult to see how disputes concerning extraterritorial export controls between Canada and the U.S. could arise under the compulsory dispute process of Chapter 18 of the Agreement. However there is a second ground for dispute settlement under Chapter 18. Article 2011 envisages the possibility of dispute settlement in the event of "nullification or impairment of any benefit reasonably expected to accrue…" to a party under the Agreement. It is possible that disputes over the extraterritorial extension of export controls will at some point be raised in Chapter 18 proceedings, although it is by no means clear that this will be judged the most appropriate forum for the resolution of such disputes by either party.

Early in 1988, Canada and the U.S. concluded the *Memorandum of Understanding on Administration and Enforcement of Securities Law*.[202] This non-treaty Memorandum of Understanding is a document of considerable interest. It provides for a wide measure of consultation and cooperation between the Securities and Exchange Commission and the Canadian Provincial securities commissions in the enforcement of their respective legislation. Particular attention is paid to the contentious issue of obtaining information from the other jurisdiction. Of particular interest is Article 3, which provides that even where the pattern of cooperation breaks down no regulatory authority shall proceed unilaterally without utilizing "moderation and restraint" and subject to prior notification and a duty to consult. Article 11 carries the usual disclaimer that the Memorandum of Understanding does not prejudice the positions of the Governments of the regulatory authorities on the principles of international law applicable to the obtaining of information located abroad, but the Memorandum will do much to remove the potential for disagreement on these principles.

I. Conclusions

The U.S. maintains its insistence on its right to extraterritorial export controls, whether they are strategic or foreign policy based. The U.S. is willing to seek some sort of compromise where it can be assured that its domestic laws cannot be avoided by action abroad. Thus, where an identical policy and equally vigorous enforcement of it is applied abroad, its extraterritoriality has no logic.

Canada maintains that by coordinating such a policy in CoCom, with respect to strategic controls, the U.S. and Canadian policy cannot be said to differ, because it is their coordinated version, their international version which is important. Canada further maintains that its export controls under item 9001, for what are described therein as U.S.-origin goods, applies U.S. policy whether it is based on strategic or foreign policy grounds. Thus, Canada can only admit that there may be conflicting policies with respect to goods originating in the U.S. where they do not fall within item 9001 because they are components in a larger or different item, or replacement parts for a previously exported Canadian item. This is a serious but minor issue. The prime irritant between the two countries is the U.S. extraterritorial jurisdiction over U.S. controlled corporations which are incorporated in Canada. Secondary in importance is the U.S. claim of jurisdiction over persons, not Canadian nationals including corporations, wherever they were incorporated, while they are doing business or are resident in Canada. Here the U.S. is no longer controlling exports from its country. It is controlling the conduct of persons clearly subject to the jurisdiction and power of Canada. Canada finds this unacceptable where there is no principle of international law which allows the U.S. to do so. In particular, Canada finds it unacceptable where it feels that it is not just a question of principle, but that Canadian economic interests are being prejudiced.

The positions of the two states are distinct. Apart from any specific treaty provisions and the obligation to consult, there is little evidence of any other legally binding obligations between the two states in respect of export controls. There is one exception: the reciprocal practice of exempting exports from one state to the other from requiring export licenses. It may be argued that there is a binding regional customary rule of international law between the two countries to continue to do so. It is based on the longstanding practice which has been consistent and general. *Opinio juris* is difficult to piece together. One must look at the treaties between the two states, described above, as well as the implementation of the exemption in the domestic laws of the two countries. One may also look at the tenor of diplomatic notes between the two states. Certainly the argument is a good one, even though it may not be sufficiently strong to convince an international tribunal that it is a binding rule of customary law between the two states.

Despite the fact that no regional custom might be provable between the two states, other than the requirement to consult, this does not detract in any way from the series of treaties and agreements in force between the two countries. None of them has been terminated or repudiated. They all continue in force and provide a number of meaningful obligations which should do much to prevent extraterritorial export controls being used between the countries.

Notes

1. *Declaration by the Prime Minister of Canada and the President of the United States of America Regarding the Establishing of a Permanent Joint Board on Defence Made on August 18, 1940*, in Ogdensburg, N.Y., Can. T.S. 1940 No. 14 [hereinafter *Ogdensburg Agreement*].
2. *Declaration by the Prime Minister of Canada and the President of the United States of America Regarding Co-operation for War Production Made on April 20, 1941*, Can. T.S. 1941 No. 14 [hereinafter *Hyde Park Declaration*].
3. Entire agreement in force May 14, 1936, Can. T.S. 1936 No. 9, which was superseded by the *Trade Agreement Between Canada and the United States of America* signed at Washington, Nov. 17, 1938, in force June 17, 1939, Can. T.S. 1939 No. 8; E.A.S. 149; 6 Bevans 117 [hereinafter *1938 Trade Agreement*].
4. The *GATT* was in force January 1, 1948; Can. T.S. 1948, No. 31; T.I.A.S. No. 1700, 4 Bevans 639; 55 U.N.T.S. 194 in force pursuant to 55 U.N.T.S. 308. The Canada-U.S. agreement suspending their bilateral trade relation is the *Agreement Between Canada and the United States of America Supplementary to the General Agreement on Tariffs and Trade of October 30, 1947*, operative Jan. 1, 1948, Can. T.S. 1947, No. 27, Appendix A, 61 Stat. 3695, T.I.A.S No. 1702, 6 Bevans 451.
5. An example is the *Exchange of Notes (July 28, 1938) Recording an Agreement Between Canada and the United States of America Relating to Certificates of Airworthiness for Export*, in force August 1, 1938, Can. T.S. 1938 No. 10.
6. Between Canada and the United States of America, in force June 18, 1940, Can. T.S. 1940 No. 5.
7. *Ibid.* para. 4.
8. *Ibid.* para. 1.
9. *Supra*, note 2.
10. Joint Committees on Economic Cooperation, entered into force June 17, 1941, 6 Bevans 223, 55 Stat. 1444; termination announced 10 U.S. Dep't State Bull. 264, Mar. 18, 1944.
11. *Ibid.*
12. Resolution of the Joint Economic Committees dated July 16, 1941 signed by W.A. Mackintosh, Canadian Chairman and Alvin H. Hansen, United States Chairman, appended to the Letter from Acting Chairman, Canadian Section, Joint Economic Committee, W.A. Mackintosh of the Department of Finance to the Right Honourable W.L. Mackenzie King, Secretary of State for External Affairs, July 23, 1941, Ottawa.
13. Letter, *ibid.*
14. The Joint Defence Production Committee was established and a press release made

available November 5, 1941, 5 U.S. Dep't State Bull. 360, November 8, 1941.
15. *Hyde Park Declaration*, *supra*, note 2.
16. E.H. Armstrong, "Canadian-American Cooperation in War and Peace 1940–1945" 13 U.S. Dep't State Bull. 674 at 676 states it was set up in May, 1941 and was the link for Canada to the Combined Raw Materials Board (U.S./U.K).
17. D. Richardson, "Economic Cooperation with Canada" 16 U.S. Dep't State Bull. 1185 at 1186, June 22, 1947.
18. Statement by the President of the United States of America, released to the press December 23, 1941, 5 U.S. Dep't State Bull. 578, December 27, 1941.
19. *Ibid.* Resolution of the Joint War Production Committees, para. 6.
20. *Ibid.*
21. As provided for in article 31(3) of the *Vienna Convention on the Law of Treaties*, concluded on May 23, 1969, UN Doc. A/CONF. 39/27.
22. Resolution, *supra*, note 19.
23. *Supra*, note 18.
24. *Exchange of Notes (November 30, 1942) Between Canada and the United States of America Constituting an Agreement Respecting Post-War Economic Settlements*, in force November 30, 1942, Can. T.S. 1942 No. 17; 6 Bevans 292; 56 Stat. 1815.
25. Notes of May 7 and 15, 1945, Can. T.S. 1948 No. 1; 6 Bevans 397; 61 Stat. 3958.
26. *Ibid.*
27. E.H. Armstrong, "Canadian-American Cooperation in War and Peace, 1940–1945" 13 U.S. Dept State Bull. 674, October 28, 1945 at 676. However Armstrong states "... there was no question at all of any hard and fast arrangements". While this may be another way of saying there was no legally binding commitment, subsequent practice makes it clear that the agreement is in fact legally binding in international law. The question that remains is its interpretation, and for the purposes of this study, whether export controls have in some way been subsumed into the *Hyde Park Declaration*.
28. *Joint Statement by the Governments of Canada and of the United States of America Regarding Defence Cooperation Between the Two Countries, Made in Ottawa and Washington on February 12, 1947*, Can. T.S. 1947 No. 43; 6 Bevans 430.
29. *1938 Trade Agreement*, *supra*, note 3. The trade agreement was suspended on the entry into the *GATT* of the two countries, *Agreement Between Canada and the United States of America Supplementary to the General Agreement on Tariffs and Trade of Oct. 30, 1947*, *supra*, note 4.
30. *1938 Trade Agreement*, *ibid.* at art. 1(1).
31. *Ibid.* at arts I(2), and II. Article X(2) allows quantitative regulations of certain kinds where they are likewise imposed on the domestic producers.
32. *Ibid.* at art. XII(1)(a).
33. *Ibid.* at art. XII(1)(b).
34. *Ibid.* at art. XII(1)(c).
35. *Ibid.* at art. XII(1)(d).
36. *Ibid.* at art. XII(2)(a).
37. *Ibid.* at art. XII(2)(b).
38. *Ibid.* at art. XII(2)(c).
39. *Ibid.* at art. XII(2)(d).
40. *GATT*, *supra*, note 4 at art. XX. See Chapter II, Section B.1: The GATT, *supra*, for a more detailed examination of the *GATT* provisions.
41. *Supra*, note 3 at art. XII(1)(b).
42. *Ibid.* at art. XXI(b)(I), (ii), (iii).
43. *1938 Trade Agreement*, *supra*, note 3 at art. XII(1)(b) restricted measures dealing with other military supplies to "exceptional circumstances". The *GATT* seems to allow wider measures where exceptional circumstances would constitute "an emergency in international relations". However, it may be argued that the "public security" exception in the *1938 Trade Agreement* would have allowed any measures the *GATT*

allows as an exception from its general provisions. The net result must be seen as a restriction of the types of controls and circumstances in which they might be exercised. However, it must be noted that the prefatory wording "action which it considers necessary" gives back a broad range of discretion as noted by the I.C.J. in *Nicaragua* v. *U.S.A.*, *supra*, note 64 at para. 222.

44. *Exchange of Notes (April 12, 1949) Between Canada and the United States of America Constituting an Agreement Regarding the Establishment of a Joint Industrial Mobilization Committee*, at Ottawa, entered into force April 12, 1949, Can. T.S. 1949 No. 8; 63 Stat. 2331; T.I.A.S. No. 1889; 6 Bevans 486; 29 U.S. Dep't State Bull. 537.
45. *Ibid.* at Bevans 487.
46. *Exchange of Notes (October 26, 1950) Between Canada and the United States of America Giving Formal Effect to the Statement of Principles for Economic Cooperation*, Can. T.S. 1950 No. 15.
47. *Ibid.* at 4.
48. *Ibid.* at 6.
49. *Ibid.*
50. *Ibid.*
51. *Ibid.* Principle No. 2.
52. *Ibid.* at 6.
53. *Ibid.*
54. 28 U.S. Dep't State Bull. 752, May 25, 1953.
55. *Ibid.* at 753.
56. *Exchange of Notes (November 12, 1953) Between Canada and the United States of America Constituting an Agreement for the Establishment of a Joint Canada-United States Committee on Trade and Economic Affairs*, in force November 12, 1953, Can. T.S. 1953 No. 18.
57. 29 U.S. Dep't State Bull. 738, November 30, 1953.
58. *Ibid.*
59. *Supra*, note 28.
60. 30 U.S. Dep't State Bull. 511, April 5, 1954.
61. 33 U.S. Dep't State Bull. 576, October 10, 1955.
62. H.C. Debates, 1953–54, vol. III, p. 3065 at 3066, March 16, 1954, Mr. J.H. Dickey Parliamentary Asst. to Min. of Defence Protection on 2nd reading of *Export and Import Permits Act*. Also H.C. Debates 1957, vol. II, p. 1911, March 5, 1957, Mr. J.H. Dickey.
63. It was said not to be "an intergovernmental arrangement or commitment" for the purpose of s. 3(b) of the *Export and Import Permits Act*, S.C. 1947, c. 17 as amended: H.C. Debates 1953–54, vol. III, p. 3140, March 18, 1954, Mr. Dickey.
64. J. Corcoran, "The Trading With the Enemy Act and the Controlled Canadian Corporation" (1968) 14 McGill L.J. 174 at 189 [hereinafter *Corcoran*].
65. 37 U.S. Dep't State Bull. 683, October 8, 1957.
66. *Ibid.* at 684.
67. *Ibid.*
68. J.W. Jones, "Canadian-American Cooperation" 37 U.S. Dep't State Bull. 380 at 382–83.
69. Statement of July 9, 1958, 39 U.S. Dept State Bull. 209, Aug. 4, 1958. In Parliament July 11, 1958, Prime Minister Diefenbaker elaborated upon the discussions between President Eisenhower and him. H.C. Debates, 1958, vol. II, pp. 2139–45, July 11, 1958, Right Hon. J.G. Diefenbaker.

> I raised with the President the question that some Canadian subsidiaries of United States companies may have been prevented from accepting orders from communist China, or from peoples in that country, by the application of United States foreign assets control regulations, even though acceptance of such orders would be

> permitted by the policy of the Canadian government. The President expressed the view that the United States regulations should not be applied in any way to the disadvantage of the Canadian economy. If cases arose in the future where the refusal of orders by companies operating in Canada might have any effect on Canadian economic activity, the United States government would consider favourably exempting the parent company in the United States from the application of the foreign assets control regulations with respect to such orders.
>
> It was made perfectly clear, and I want to underline this fact, that there was no question at any time that, with respect to the operations of Canadian companies, Canadian law shall govern and Canadian wishes shall be respected.

However, the Leader of the Opposition, Mr. Lester B. Pearson, was still not content stating:

> Is it not an intolerable position that the United States should pass laws of extraterritorial application of the kind covered by this particular law, administered in such a way as to ignore the interests of Canada in her own trade? If in fact, as we have more or less been led to believe, the application of this law so far as Canadian exporters are concerned can be set aside by administrative action, I should hope that the United States administration would announce that they were going to adopt that policy with regard to such administration rather than merely suggest that every time there is a special Canadian case under this law consultations will take place.

70. *Supra*, note 46.
71. *Ibid.* at 6, Principle 3.
72. *Exchange of Notes Between Canada and the United States of America Concerning the Establishment of Canada-United States Committee on Joint Defence*, in force September 2, 1958, Can. T.S. 1958 No. 22.
73. *Basic Arrangement on Collaboration in Research and Development between the United States Air Force and the Defence Research Board of Canada/Royal Canadian Air Force*, in force December 31, 1958. Information obtained from officers of the Department of External Affairs.
74. Ibid. para. 5(c).
75. Communiqué, July 16, 1960, 43 U.S. Dep't State Bull 172, Aug. 1, 1960.
76. Ibid.
77. See also Press Release No. 297, June 25, 1964, 51 U.S. Dep't State Bull. 45, July 13, 1964.
78. For example, *The Basic Standardization Agreement*, 1964, Oct. 1, 1964 an agreement between the U.S., Canada, the U.K., and Australia armies on cooperation and ensuring compatibility of equipment, practices, theory and research.
79. Press Release No. 135, March 14, 1961, 44 U.S. Dept State Bull. 487, April 3, 1961; Jan. 13, 1962, 46 U.S. Dep't State Bull. 168, Jan. 29, 1962; Press Release No. 484, Sept. 21, 1963, 49 U.S. Dep't State Bull 548, Oct. 7, 1963; April 30, 1964, 50 U.S. Dep't State Bull. 774, May 18, 1964.
80. March 5, 1966, 54 U.S. Dept State Bull. 464, March 21, 1966.
81. "A Report by Livingston T. Merchant and A.D.P. Heeny", June 28, 1965, 53 U.S. Dep't State Bull. 193, Aug. 2, 1965.
82. *Ibid.* at 207, "Annex B".
83. *Ibid.* at 197.
84. *Ibid.* at 202.
85. *Ibid.* at 202-03.
86. *Ibid.* at 205.
87. *Ibid.* at 201.
88. Information obtained from offices of the Department of External Affairs.

89. Mar. 5, 1960, 54 U.S. Dep't State Bull. 464, Mar. 21, 1966 at 464.
90. Communiqué of June 22, 1967, 57 U.S. Dep't State Bull. 44, July 10, 1967 at 45.
91. Press Release No. 326, Nov. 26, 1970, 63 U.S. Dept. of State Bull. 730, Dec. 14, 1970.
92. *Ibid.* at 731.
93. M.J. Abrams, *The Canada-United States Interparliamentary Group* (Ottawa: Canadian Institute of International Affairs, 1973) at 75 [hereinafter *Abrams*].
94. F.D. Schneider, "Exploring the Third Option: Canadian Foreign Policy and Defence" (1980) Curr. Hist. 121 at 123.
95. *Ibid.* at 123–24.
96. *Ibid.* at 153.
97. H.C. Debates 1972–73, vol. II, p. 1346, April 17, 1972, The Rt. Hon. P.E. Trudeau, Prime Minister.
98. *Report on Foreign Ownership and the Structure of Canadian Ownership* (1968); see also the suggestion that the Canadian Commercial Corporation be used to fulfil this mandate: H.C. Debates, 1968, vol. III, pp. 2374–75, Nov. 4, 1968, Mr. Saltsman and Mr. Jamieson; H.C. Debates, 1968, vol. III, pp. 2764–65, Nov. 14, 1968, Mr. Saltsman. See also the more general review of the Watkins Report and Mr. Watkins personal views in H.C. Debates, 1968, vol. III, pp. 2914–15, Nov. 19, 1968, Mr. Gilbert.
99. This was pointed out in Mr. Gilbert, *ibid.*; *Abrams*, *supra*, note 93 at 77 and 118 states that, because the actions of Congress often were the reason Canada was affected, this communication function served a preventive function, alerting legislators to the problems their legislation may cause.
100. Report No. 33, 28th Parl., 2d sess., 1969–70.
101. Gray Task Force, *Foreign Direct Investment in Canada* (1972) at 253–90.
102. S.C. 1973–74, c. 46, since repealed and replaced by the *Investment Canada Act*, S.C. 1985, c. 20.
103. S.C. 1974–75–76, c. 33, s. 100(3).
104. *Ibid.* s. 108(3).
105. S.C. 1973–74–75, c. 76, adding ss. 31.1, to the *Combines Investigation Act*, R.S.C. 1970, c. C–23. Legislation before the House of Commons, Bill C–90, was proclaimed in force June 19, 1986 and renamed the *Competition Tribunal Act*, making wholesale changes to the *CIA*. See S.C. 1986 c. 26. The compliance power is now in sections 47 to 54 but remains the same. See also J.-G. Castel, A.L.C. de Mestral and W.C. Graham, *International Business Transactions and Economic Relations* (Toronto: Emond Montgomery, 1986) c. 9 [hereinafter *Castel, de Mestral, Graham*].
106. These "new" guidelines succeeded to "Some Guiding Principles of Good Corporate Behavior for Subsidiaries in Canada of Foreign Companies" in Department of Industry Trade and Commerce, *Foreign-Owned Subsidiaries in Canada* (1967), see *Castel, de Mestral, Graham*, *ibid.* at 390.
107. See H.C. Debates, 1972–73, vol. IV, pp. 3503-04, Mr. Harding June 26, 1972 or H.C. Debates, 1974–76, vol. VIII, pp. 7764–65, July 21, 1975, The Hon. Mr. Herbert and Hon. Mitchell Sharp.
108. (Dec. 1971) International Canada at 231.
109. See the President's Executive Order 11,387 "Governing Certain Capital Transfers Abroad" 33 Fed. Reg. 47 (Jan. 3, 1968) which prevented persons subject to U.S. jurisdiction from transferring capital from foreign corporations, in which they had an interest, other than to the U.S., and in fact required certain capital to be repatriated.
110. H.C. Debates 1972–73, vol. II, p. 1346, April 17, 1972, The Rt. Hon. P.E. Trudeau, Prime Minister.
111. (Oct. 1972) International Canada at 164.
112. *Ibid.*
113. SOR/73–253, P.C. 1973–1105, 107 Can. Gaz. Pt II 1100, May 8, 1973.

114. Note of the Canadian Embassy to the U.S. Department of State, May 15, 1974.
115. (March 1976) International Canada at 80–81.
116. CoCom Doc. Reg. (78) 1.
117. *Supra*, note 113 at 1101; in 1989 Item 9001 was re-numbered Item 5400 in the revised regulations 123 Can. Gaz. Pt II 2101, 13 April 1989.
118. Information obtained from officers of the Export Control Division Department of External Affairs. It is reported that this approach has from time to time led to confrontation with U.S. authorities.
119. *Ibid.* amended by SOR/74–296, P.C. 1974–1050, May 7, 1974, 108 Can Gaz. Pt II 1624.
120. (Jan. 1978) International Canada at 2.
121. *Ibid.* at 3.
122. See (June 1978) International Canada at 136.
123. Note 48 of the Canadian Embassy to the U.S. Dep't. of State, Jan. 27, 1978.
124. *Ibid.*
125. *Ibid.*
126. W.M. Dobell, "Defence Procurement Contracts and Industrial Offset Packages" (Jan./Feb. 1981) International Perspectives 14 at 15 [hereinafter *Dobell*].
127. *Framework Agreement for Commercial and Economic Co-operation Between Canada and the European Communities*, Can. T.S. 1976 No. 35, (1976) O.J. Eur. Comm. (No. L/260).
128. *Dobell*, *supra*, note 126 at 14.
129. "Canadian Ambassador Allan Gotlieb's Address to the American Society of International Law on Legal Aspects of International Investment, The Canada/U.S. Experience, April 22, 1982" (May 5, 1982) U.S. Import Weekly 137 at 140.
130. *Ibid.*
131. *Ibid.*
132. *Ibid.* at 141–42.
133. *Ibid.* at 141.
134. (Nov./Dec. 1982) International Perspectives Supp. at 2.
135. Note of the Canadian Embassy to the U.S. Dep't of State, July 7, 1982.
136. *Ibid.*
137. *Supra*, note 134 at 2–3.
138. (Sept./Oct. 1982) International Canada at 3.
139. Note No. 169 of the Canadian Embassy to the U.S. Dep't. of State of May 4, 1983.
140. Information obtained by interviews conducted in May 1985 with officials of the U.S. State Department, Commerce Department, Treasury Department and Department of Defence.
141. H.C. Debates, 1971, vol. VI, p. 5949, May 19, 1971, Mr. Rondeau and Mr. J.A. Jerome. The *Defence Production Sharing Agreement* (*Exchange of Notes Between Canada and the United States of America Concerning Improvement of the Air Defence of the Canada-United States Region of NATO; The Defence Production Sharing Programme of the Two Governments and the Provision of Assistance to Certain Other NATO Governments*) Can. T.S. 1961 No. 5 was signed June 12, 1961 but the policies date back to the agreement in 1947 (see *supra*, note 28 – extended on June 25, 1970 by the *Exchange of Notes Between the Government of Canada and the Government of the United States of America Extending the Terms of the Agreement on Air Defence and Related Co-operation Signed June 12, 1961*, Can. T.S. 1970 No. 18) and the *Hyde Park Declaration*, *supra*, note 2.
142. *Ibid.*
143. H.C. Debates, 1974–76, vol. XII, p. 1392, May 27, 1976, Miss M. Begin. See also at vol. VII, p. 6650, June 11, 1975, Hon. Mitchell Sharp.
144. Reprinted in (1976) 15 Int'l Leg. Mat. 967.
145. *Supra*, note 139.

146. An example was the meeting of the Canadian Ambassador and the U.S. Secretary of State at the end of January 1983.
147. Statement by the Honourable Allan J. MacEachen, Deputy Prime Minister and Secretary of State for External Affairs, on Extraterritoriality and the Proposed Amendments to the U.S. Export Administration Act, Standing Committee on External Affairs and National Defence, March 15, 1984.
148. *Memorandum of Understanding Between the Government of the United States of America and the Government of Canada as to Notification, Consultation and Cooperation with respect to the Application of National Antitrust Laws*, signed March 9, 1984, reprinted (1984) 23 Int'l Leg. Mat. 275.
149. *Supra*, note 147.
150. "U.S. Fears Leaks of Technology Through Canada" *Toronto Star* (Mar. 15, 1984) C3.
151. *Ibid.*
152. "Canada, U.S. to Discuss High-tech Embargoes" *Globe and Mail* (Mar. 15, 1984) B6.
153. *Agreement Between Canada and the United States of America Regarding Mutual Assistance and Co-operation Between their Customs Administrations*, concluded in Quebec June 20, 1984, in force Jan. 8, 1985, Can. T.S. 1985 No. 23.
154. *Ibid.* at art. 1(b).
155. *Ibid.* at art. 2(1)(a).
156. *Ibid.* at art. 2(3).
157. *Ibid.* at art. 5.
158. *Ibid.* at art. 7.
159. *Ibid.*
160. *Ibid.* at art. 17.
161. *Ibid.* at art. 4(1).
162. The Agreement also provides an indication that the agreement is to be reciprocal. Where an Administration requests assistance which it could not provide in its own country, this fact is to be indicated in the request. Then it is in the other state's discretion to decide whether it will comply with the request. *Ibid.* at art. 4(2).
163. "Trade, Interdependence and Conflicts of Jurisdiction" 84 U.S. Dep't State Bull. 33 at 34.
164. *Ibid.*
165. *Ibid.* at 36.
166. *Ibid.* at 35.
167. Government of Canada News Release "Government Introduces Foreign Extraterritorial Measures Bill", Ottawa, May 28, 1984.
168. Government of Canada News Release "Government Introduces Foreign Extraterritorial Measures Bill", Ottawa, December 3, 1984.
169. *Ibid.*
170. S.C. 1984, c. 49 [hereinafter *FEMA*].
171. *Ibid.* at s. 9(1)(a).
172. *Ibid.* at s. 9(1)(b).
173. *Ibid.* at s. 9(1).
174. *Ibid.* at s. 5.
175. *Ibid.* at s. 5(1).
176. *Ibid.*
177. *Ibid.* at s. 5(2).
178. *Ibid.* at s. 5(1)(b).
179. *Ibid.* at s. 5(1)(b) and 5(2).
180. *Ibid.* at s. (1)(a).
181. *Ibid.* at s. 5(3).
182. *Ibid.* at s. 6(1) and (2).
183. *Supra*, note 178.
184. *Supra*, note 182.

185. *Supra*, note 173.
186. The "clawback" anti-trust provision does not command extraterritorially that Canadian citizens do anything. Thus it is not extraterritorial. It confers rights on Canadian citizens to sue before a court in Canada to invoke the enforcement jurisdiction of Canada against the person to whom damages were paid. It may be, in a given case, that it would be contrary to international law to in fact do so in any specific case because a precondition to enforcement jurisdiction is that a state have prescriptive jurisdiction over the person. It may be that there is no basis of international law upon which to take prescriptive jurisdiction against such a person. The so-called "passive personality principle" is not a valid ground of jurisdiction, thus the mere fact of a judgement being rendered against a Canadian citizen will not give Canada jurisdiction. Jurisdiction will most often be obtainable on the basis of the territoriality principle.
187. Case of the S.S. "Lotus" (*France* v. *Turkey*), (1927) P.C.I.J. Ser. A, No. 10.
188. *Treaty Between the Government of the United States of America and the Government of Canada on Mutual Legal Assistance in Criminal Matters*, concluded in Quebec City, March 18, 1985, reprinted in (1985) 24 Int'l Leg. Mat. 1092.
189. *Ibid.* at art. 1. The Annex lists securities, wildlife, environmental and consumer protection laws as being included in any case.
190. *Supra*, note 153.
191. *Ibid.* at art. II(1).
192. *Ibid.* at art. II(2).
193. *Ibid.* at art. II(3).
194. *Ibid.* at art. V(1)(b) incorporating the definition of "public interest" given in article I.
195. *Ibid.* at art. V(3)(b).
196. *Ibid.* at art. V(2).
197. See the general policy statement in (July/Aug. 1985) International Perspectives Supp. 4 expressed by The Canadian Secretary of State for External Affairs, Hon. Joe Clark.
198. *Canada – United States Free Trade Agreement Implementation Act*, S.C. 1988, c. 65, Schedule-Part A, Vol. 11, no 13A Can. Gaz. Pt III 2110. Reprinted in (1988) 27 Int'l Leg. Mat. 281.
199. Article 407: Import and Export Restrictions.

    3. In circumstances where a Party imposes a restriction on importation from or exportation to a third country of a good, nothing in this Agreement shall be construed to prevent the Party from:

    a) limiting or prohibiting the importation from the territory of the other Party of such good of the third country; or
    b) requiring as a condition of export of such good of the Party to the territory of the other Party, that the good be consumed within the territory of the other Party.

    4. In the event that either Party imposes a restriction on imports of a good from third countries, the Parties, upon request of either Party, shall consult with a view to avoiding undue interference with or distortion of pricing, marketing and distribution arrangements in the other Party.
200. *Ibid.* see articles 907, 1201, 1301 and 2003.
201. See Chapter II, Section B.
202. Done at Washington, January 7, 1988. Reprinted (1988) 27 Int'l Leg. Mat. 410.

CHAPTER V

STATE PRACTICE – CANADA

A. Participation in International Action

1. U.N. Sanctions

(a) Mandatory Sanctions

(i) *Rhodesia.* On November 11, 1965 the government of Southern Rhodesia (Rhodesia) issued its "Unilateral Declaration of Independence" (UDI).[1] Britain announced it was assuming full authority over Rhodesia and adopted political and economic measures affecting Rhodesia and those who dealt with it.[2] Britain also called for a U.N. Security Council meeting.[3] The same day the UDI was made, the U.N. General Assembly condemned it and called the matter to the attention of the Security Council.[4] The Security Council, the following day, called upon members of the U.N. not to recognize the regime in Rhodesia. The resolutions, however, did not deal specifically with the questions of trade with Rhodesia.

Canada had earlier stated it would not recognize a UDI by Rhodesia. Upon hearing of the UDI, Canada announced the same day a number of measures including an embargo on arms and military equipment and the termination of export financing facilities.[7]

On November 20, 1965 the U.N. Security Council passed a resolution recommending that member states desist from providing Rhodesia with arms and military material and sever their economic relations through measures including an embargo on oil and petroleum products.[8] Significantly the resolution stated that continuance of the situation in Rhodesia "constitutes a threat to international peace and security".[9] This language repeats the purpose for which the Security Council may investigate a dispute.[10] It also suggests the Security Council had recognized the pre-conditions for exercising its power to make a decision binding in international law on its members although the Security Council did not then exercise the power itself.[11]

On November 26, 1965 Canada and Britain exchanged notes about the UDI in Rhodesia. The operative part of the Canadian note read:

> In these circumstances, it would seem desirable and important that our two governments arrange to cooperate closely in the application of such further measures, including economic measures with respect of Rhodesia, as either Government may deem desirable.[12]

In its note Britain confirmed that it was "desirable and important" that it and Canada "should arrange to cooperate closely in this field."[13]

A month later Canada put Rhodesia on its Area Control List, making necessary an application for an export permit before any export could be made to that country.[14] By February of 1966, 90% of trade between the two countries had been affected by the embargo.[15]

The Canadian action was part of a Commonwealth effort to support British measures. Other organizations also supported the same measures. Among them were the U.N., as has been described, and the Organization of African Unity (O.A.U.). The O.A.U. was called upon to implement sanctions by the U.N. in its November 20 resolution,[16] and in December 1965 announced a boycott of Rhodesian exports.[17]

Britain adopted a series of economic measures in the days following the UDI. Tariff preferences were removed and import restrictions on Rhodesian goods were imposed.[18] Like the Canadian measures, Britain banned the exports of arms and denied export credit facilities for other exports to Rhodesia.[19] The British controls were imposed on transactions in Great Britain, or on those outside where a British resident was participating.[20] It also took upon itself the authority to legislate for Rhodesia and in this capacity prohibited certain imports to and exports from Rhodesia.[21] These restrictions were imposed by order of January 20, 1966.[22]

The Canadian action was extended to a total embargo on all imports from and exports to Rhodesia by February 1966.[23] This was an extension of the arms and petroleum embargo and the import boycott that had restricted over 90% of imports from Rhodesia.[24] It was accomplished by a clamp-down on the issuance of permits for exports to Rhodesia. Although Rhodesia had been placed on the Area Control List in December of 1965, the General Permits found in the regulations under the *EIPA* allowed some exports without case by case consideration. This was terminated when the general permits were revoked, as far as Rhodesia was concerned, in February 1966.[25]

Canada's arms embargo had been based on the *Export and Import Permits Act*.[26] The *EIPA*, however, required these powers be exercised on the bases specified therein.[27] The arms embargo was implemented by the denial of permits required for all arms exports by Export Control Regulations. It could be justified either on the basis that use of the arms by Rhodesia might be detrimental to "the security of Canada",[28] or the embargo was to "implement an intergovernmental arrangement or commitment".[29] The government seemed unsure that it was supportable on the basis of "the security of Canada" in as much as it emphasized the exchange of notes with the U.K. as an "inter-governmental agreement".[30] The same basis would have been used for the oil embargo.[31] The exchange of notes was a tenuous basis on which to conclude there was an "intergovernmental arrangement" to support controls under the *EIPA* as was pointed out by the opposition in Parliament.[30] This was all the more true once the government decided to make the embargo a total one. Here the "security of Canada" provision could only be invoked with respect to arms and strategic items, so the only basis in Canadian internal law remaining was the "intergovernmental arrangement".

Arguably, the U.N. Security Council resolution of November 20th could have provided an "intergovernmental arrangement or commitment" to satisfy the *EIPA*. The argument was weakened by the fact the Security Council resolution was not mandatory. As well, it is difficult to argue that the resolution of an international organization *per se* is an "intergovernmental arrangement". It may be argued that the U.N. is the result of an "intergovernmental arrangement or commitment" and that its decisions are likewise the result of one. The fact, however, that the Security Council could reach a decision without the direct contribution and affirmative vote of Canada was likely enough to put its resolution beyond the pale of the definition. The probable interpretation of "intergovernmental arrangement or commitment" would require that Canada be bound voluntarily by the arrangement and not the mechanism that results in an arrangement.

The fact there were no mandatory resolutions of the Security Council until December 1966, prevented Canada from relying on its *United Nations Act* to support its measures.[33] Thus the only statutory authority for the embargo was the *EIPA* and the items not on the Export Control List for strategic reasons had to be supported on the rather tenuous base of the exchange of notes between Canada and Britain of November 26, 1965. The denial of permits for items on the list could also only be justified on the basis of the purpose for which the items could be listed under the *EIPA*. The exchange of notes was thus pivotal in justifying Canadian measures internally. The same exchange of notes could serve to demonstrate that Canadian action was part of an international effort and certainly a Commonwealth effort to support Britain's position in Rhodesia.[34]

The government, however, told Parliament that, as a member of the Commonwealth, it had not been asked to take measures other than the sanctions on arms and oil.[35] This appears difficult to understand from a comparison of the measures imposed by Canada and the U.K. and with regard to their exchange of notes. If it was true, then the Canadian measures prior to the mandatory U.N. embargo must be considered to have been unilateral.

As talks continued between the United Kingdom and the regime in Rhodesia, Canada declared that its position was to support the U.N. Security Council selective obligatory sanctions against Rhodesia if the talks broke down.[36] It was clear that the voluntary sanctions were not as successful as some had hoped.[37]

Meanwhile the U.N. Security Council had begun to impose mandatory sanctions. First on April 9, 1966 it imposed a mandatory measure on U.N. members to divert ships carrying oil for Rhodesia.[38] Then, on December 16, 1966, the Security Council imposed a mandatory embargo on arms, oil and transportation vehicle exports.[39] This latter resolution required states to prevent "any activities by their nationals or in their territories which promote or are calculated to promote" the supply to Rhodesia of arms or transportation vehicles.[40] The same control of nationals and within territory was required for the oil embargo. It also required control of vessels of the member's registration.[41]

The Security Council Resolutions now required that all U.N. members comply with the decisions contained therein, otherwise the member would be in violation of article 25 of the *U.N. Charter*.[42] This requirement allowed Canada to invoke its *U.N. Act*.[43] In February 1967 Canada issued regulations under the Act to comply with the Security Council resolution.[44] The regulations prohibited transactions, in language common to export permit regulations, which would result in the U.N.-prohibited items being exported to Rhodesia, regardless of the origin of the goods or the place of the transaction.[45]

> s.31: No person shall knowingly do anything, in Canada or any other place, that causes or assists or is intended to cause or assist any shipment, transshipment or diversion of any goods specified ... to be made, from Canada or any other place, to Rhodesia.

The language of the U.N. Security Council Resolution was repeated also:

> s.9: No person shall knowingly do any act or thing, in Canada or any other place, to promote or that is calculated to promote the sale or supply to any other person of any goods specified ... if he has reason to believe
> (a) that such goods will be sent by such other person to Rhodesia; or
> (b) that the ultimate destination of such goods is Rhodesia.[46]

The ambit of the prohibitions was restricted to the criteria required by the Security Council Resolution – nationality and territory.[47] By defining "person" to include only a Canadian citizen or a "Canadian corporation", foreign persons were not affected by the *Rhodesia Regulations.*[48] The test used in the *Rhodesia Regulations* to determine the identity of Canadian corporations was that of incorporation in Canada.[49] The regulations were therefore applied in Canadian territory, to Canadian citizens and to corporations incorporated in Canada.[50]

Section 10(1) described the penalties to which violators were liable; section 10(2) allowed for an immunity where a certificate had been obtained stating the act was not one prohibited by the Security Council Resolution, and section 10(3) required consent of the Attorney General of Canada for prosecution of persons for acts done outside of Canada.[51] It is difficult to see in what way the exception in section 2(i) could affect the nature of the jurisdiction the regulations embody. In fact the exception seemed either redundant or pointless and was dropped in the version of the *Rhodesia Regulations* that was enacted subsequently.[52]

The reason the Canadian government gave for the mandatory sanctions was:

> ... Britain and all Commonwealth countries, and most other countries in the world, have agreed to the mandatory sanctions program of the United Nations ... because they wish to bring down a government that has exercised a form of discrimination which in this day and age simply cannot be tolerated by the international community.[53]

The Canadian position was that:

> ... Rhodesia must not be granted independence before majority rule is attained, and that Canada had complied strictly with the terms of the security council's decision to apply mandatory sanctions against Rhodesia.[54]

Canada was party to two sets of internationally organized sanctions. As well as the U.N. action, Canada took part in the Commonwealth action which gave rise to a sanctions committee.[55] However the Canadian government claimed it was its understanding that the Commonwealth committee was a deliberative structure and that implementation of any action would be by U.N. Security Council resolution.[56]

Security Council Resolution 253 extended the embargo on exports to Rhodesia to all goods, transportation of goods and investment in Rhodesia on May 29, 1968.[57] Canada had already instituted a total embargo some time before.[58] Nevertheless Canada implemented the May 29 Security Council Resolution by amending its *Rhodesia Regulations* several months later.[59]

The Canadian revisions to the *Rhodesia Regulations* in December 1968 distinguished the selling and supplying of goods to Rhodesia[60] from the shipping, transshipping or diversion of goods to Rhodesia.[61] The *Rhodesia Regulations* of December 1968 incorporated the Security Council Resolution prohibitions against investment by prohibiting the sending, transfer or assignment of money to any person in Rhodesia.[62] The new *Rhodesia Regulations* also included a provision making directors and officers liable for the acts of their corporation. This liability was extraterritorial, but outside Canada was limited to the directors or officers of corporations incorporated in Canada who were Canadian citizens or ordinarily residents.[63] In other words, the vicarious liability was limited to Canadian territory and Canadian nationality.

The Canadian regulations had extraterritorial reach. This was clearly required by the Security Council Resolution 253 of May 29, 1968. That Resolution was similar to Resolution 232 of December 16, 1966 in this respect. Resolution 253, however, did more than extend the range of the embargo. It also made clear that the prohibitions on shipping goods to or from Rhodesia applied to shipments in bond, and that the prohibitions on exports were to apply to nationals of member states in respect of any goods "whether or not originating in their territories".[64]

Canada was thus a strong supporter of the U.N. action. Any delay in implementing U.N. Security Council Resolution 253 of May 1968 was with respect to its extraterritorial reach and the export of capital. In these respects Canada was not prepared to act unilaterally. The all encompassing embargo, however, seems to have been unilaterally undertaken even prior to the Security Council Resolution 253 under the already existing regulations of the *EIPA* which required permits for exports to Rhodesia.

Canada was, for the most part, relying on U.N. action to provide the basis for its measures. When it became apparent that South Africa and Portugal were violating the mandatory U.N. embargo Canada would not react unilaterally, saying it was for the Security Council to initiate action.[65] While it followed U.N. action, Canada did not follow all initiatives in the U.N. For example, it abstained from a resolution which supported the British use of force in Rhodesia.[66]

The Security Council sanctions were reaffirmed in 1970[67] and the legislation was subsequently concerned with enforcement of the sanctions.[68] The adoption by the United States of the *Byrd Amendment* in 1971 prompted the Security Council to urge compliance by U.N. members.[69] The *Byrd Amendment* prevented the President of the U.S. from prohibiting the import of certain strategic materials.[70] Although it dealt with imports from Rhodesia, the *Byrd Amendment* was significant because it put the U.S. in the same camp as South Africa and Portugal as voluntarily and publicly violating the U.N. sanctions.[71] Canada, however, did not waver on the sanctions.[72]

The Security Council called for severe penalties to be imposed on violators of the U.N. sanctions in May, 1973.[73] Resolution 333 also dealt with the problem of violations, calling for penalties for dealing with clients known to re-export to Rhodesia.[74] It also requested that states dealing with South Africa or Portugal stipulate in their contracts that re-exports to Rhodesia were prohibited.[75]

The Canadian regulations, however, were not affected. No changes were made until after final agreement was reached, at Lancaster House, on a settlement in Rhodesia which would lead to black majority rule.[76] On December 28, 1979 Rhodesia was deleted from the Area Control List under the *EIPA*. The *Rhodesia Regulations* made under the *United Nations Act* were also revoked December 28, 1979.[77]

On December 21, 1979 the Security Council, by Resolution 460, had called on all states to terminate the measures taken against Rhodesia pursuant to Chapter VII of the *U.N. Charter*.[78] Thus, in fact, the Canadian measures remained in force until terminated by the Security Council. It may be seen that the Canadian revocation was premature as it was made by Order in Council on December 19. But because it was not effective until December 28 it did not breach the *U.N. Charter*, no matter what view is taken of the continued effect of the U.N. mandatory sanctions prior to Resolution 460.

(b) Recommended Sanctions

(i) *South Africa – apartheid.* The U.N. Security Council called upon all nations to cease the export of arms to South Africa in Resolution 181 on August 7, 1963.[79] The General Assembly had done so in 1962.[80] However, as in the case of Rhodesia later, Canadian measures preceded the U.N. action.[81] The Canadian Parliament was told that Canada had not permitted the shipment of arms to South Africa "for several years" prior to the Security Council recommendation.[82] The policy was to deny exports where they "might be used against the non-white population for the enforcement of the policy of apartheid."[83] As a result of the adoption of Resolution 181, the Canadian government decided it would not accept any new orders for the export of military equipment.[84] Exports of spare parts, however, would be considered on a case by case basis.[85]

The changes in Canadian policy after Resolution 181 had two important aspects. First, they respected contracts already formed. Second, rather than having export permits for military equipment (any such exports were controlled under the *EIPA*) issued after consideration of the connection of the proposed export and the South African apartheid policy, the rule was made clear and absolute. Rather than an exercise of discretion by the Export Permit Branch of the Department of Trade and Commerce,[86] the denial of military exports was to be applied routinely.[87]

On December 4, 1963 the U.N. Security Council recommendation was extended to include the equipment and materials used for the manufacture and maintenance of arms in South Africa.[88] There seems to be no indication that the Canadian policy was at all changed by this second non-mandatory resolution.[89] Canadian exports for the years 1964 and 1965 did not contain any equipment that would fall into the class described.[90] Canada refused to allow a sale of paramilitary trucks to South

Africa by Ford Motor Company of Canada.[91] Exports did however include some steel and aluminum[92] which might have served a variety of uses.

In 1968 it became apparent that South Africa and Portugal were not complying with the mandatory U.N. economic sanctions with respect to Rhodesia. Canada had a chance to vote on a resolution in the trusteeship committee of the U.N. General Assembly on October 30, which would have encouraged the British use of force in Rhodesia as well as recommending economic sanctions against South Africa and Portugal. Canada abstained from voting on the resolution because it was opposed to the use of force in Rhodesia.[93] Canada's position on the sanctions on the non-complying states was to doubt whether they were a "practical proposition" at that time.[94]

To mark the tenth anniversary of the *Declaration of the Granting of Independence to Colonial Countries and Peoples*, the U.N. General Assembly Resolution 2621 (XXV)[95] adopted a programme of action. The programme included a call for states to heed General Assembly and Security Council resolutions relating to territories under colonial domination. Because of the presence of South Africa in Namibia,[96] the General Assembly called on the Security Council to consider the imposition of a full and internationally supervised embargo on arms to South Africa.[97] There was no immediate action from the Security Council, however.

Generally Canadian exports to South Africa, from 1963 to 1969, grew from $60.29 million to $78.51 million. Re-exports from Canada did not show a consistent trend, increasing from $.38 million in 1963 to $2.03 million in 1965, and falling to $1.66 million in 1969.[98] The Canadian policy in 1970 changed to add spare parts to the items completely embargoed.[99] Nevertheless it continued with respect to the maintenance of an embargo on military equipment, but otherwise did not treat South Africa any differently than any other country. This reflected a general policy to trade "in peaceful goods with all countries and territories regardless of political considerations."[100]

There was one incident of a Crown corporation, Polymer, divesting itself of holdings in a South African company in June 1970.[101] The Canadian position, however, was criticised by the opposition as overly cautious.[102] In the following month, however, the Canadian government announced that it had

> informally contacted those Canadian companies with holdings in South Africa and encouraged them to act, within the bounds of South African laws, as good corporate citizens in the Canadian sense in regard to payment of salaries to their Black workers.[103]

This announcement, although informal, and even if made to Canadian companies in Canada, certainly dealt with matters that were extraterritorial. It required specified conduct abroad with respect to foreigners on the basis of ownership or control of foreign companies. This was similar to the kind of situation to which Canada had always objected when the U.S. required its companies to act in a certain way abroad. The one difference was that it was made clear that South African (i.e the territorial) laws were to prevail in case of conflict. This had never been made clear by the U.S. and the contrary was sometimes indicated. The other difference was, of course, the wide international condemnation of apartheid.

The U.N. Security Council considered a resolution which would have imposed mandatory sanctions on South Africa because of its presence in Namibia.[104] The resolution would have made mandatory the embargo on arms and that on equipment used to manufacture military supplies. It specifically mentioned that it would have effect despite any existing contracts.[105] The U.S., France and the U.K. voted against the resolution so it failed. There was indication that the pressure for a mandatory embargo was mounting.

In 1976 the Special Committee on Apartheid sent a letter to U.N. Secretary General, Mr. Kurt Waldheim, alleging that several countries were assisting South Africa in developing nuclear power.[106] It invoked U.N. General Assembly Resolution 3411G (XXX) of December 10, 1975[107] and expressed grave concern over reports of states helping South Africa establish nuclear installations and technology. On this basis the Special Committee requested its letter be forwarded to the International Atomic Energy Agency which it hoped would take all possible action to prevent transfer of nuclear capacity to South Africa.[108]

Canada held to its policy of not dealing in militarily sensitive items with South Africa, including spare parts. In the U.N. General Assembly, however, Canada voted against a resolution calling for the Security Council to impose a mandatory (Chapter VII of the *Charter*) arms embargo on South Africa.[109] Canada had found itself in some difficulty voting for some of the General Assembly resolutions condemning apartheid because they also condemned economic links with South Africa.[110] The difference between the two resolutions was that Resolution 3411G (XXX) mentioned specific Western countries and accused them of economic collaboration with the South African regime. It called for strict enforcement of an arms and nuclear embargo on South Africa. Resolution 32/105K was more general, declaring collaboration with the racist South Africa regime as illegal. Canada abstained because it believed in the merit of maintaining economic ties with South Africa to encourage change.[111]

On November 4, 1977 the U.N. Security Council adopted Resolution 418 which determined that the acquisition of arms and military material by South Africa was a threat to international peace and security.[112] On that basis, it decided to implement a mandatory arms embargo including paramilitary police equipment, spare parts and all equipment and technical data for the manufacture of these items.[113] The resolution also decided that all states were to refrain from any cooperation with South Africa in the development of nuclear weapons (but not necessarily all nuclear uses).[114]

The only change the resolution implied for Canadian export controls was to consider police equipment as well. Technical data in material form which related to items on the Canadian Export Control List had been controlled since 1973.[115] Other states had had to change their regulations to control technical data.[116]

A month later the Security Council adopted Resolution 421.[117] It established a committee to study ways to implement and to make the embargo more effective in Resolution 418.[118] It also decided to seek, from all states, information in this regard.[119] Meanwhile pressure from non-governmental organizations mounted to sever economic links with South Africa.[120]

The Canadian government announced additional measures prior to the end of 1977.[121] First, the government announced it was phasing out all government sponsored commercial support activities in South Africa. These measures included denial of export credit, loan and foreign investment insurance.[122] Trade commissioners were withdrawn from South Africa.[123] It also announced that it would be publishing a code of conduct to govern "employment and similar practices" of Canadian companies in South Africa.[124] Such a code had been adopted by the European Community's foreign ministers in Brussels for European companies with South African subsidiaries on September 20, 1977.[125] It was implemented by a requirement to report on the application of the code.[126] This was one of several codes of labour conduct that were adopted in this period.[127]

A resolution initiated by three African countries at the end of January 1978, which would have prohibited loans and investment incentives, was not even brought to a vote. Canada had abstained on a similar resolution that was adopted in the U.N. General Assembly by a vote of 120 to 0 with 5 abstentions. Canada objected to the suggestion therein that the South African problem was a colonial one.[128] This was not the first time trade and investment sanctions had failed to pass in the Security Council.[129]

The Canadian policy of neither encouraging nor discouraging investment in South Africa was also coming under attack in Parliament.[130] Despite recalling its trade officers, Canada still offered technical assistance to Canadian corporations wishing to do business in South Africa.[131]

The *Code of Conduct Concerning the Employment Practices of Canadian Companies Operating in South Africa* was released by the Canadian government April 28, 1978.[132] The *Code of Conduct* required public reports detailing the extent of compliance by Canadian companies. The requirement was, however, a voluntary one. This type of inducement to change conduct in another country is clearly extraterritorial. It may seem to conflict with the stated policy of the host country, South Africa.[133] While the objectionable features normally characterising Canadian objections to U.S. laws and practices are present, there is one difference. The Canadian action was based on a policy of enforcement of international human rights. In this way taking jurisdiction to remedy what is arguably an international crime – apartheid – the Canadian government could claim to be exercising a form of universal jurisdiction, and thus justify its acts as having legislative or subject matter jurisdiction. There is state practice supporting the Canadian action in this instance notably the *Code of Conduct of the European Communities* and that of the U.S.[134]

As Canada became more involved in the affairs of persons in South Africa, it was alleged that the Space Research Corporation of Quebec had manufactured artillery shells that were used in Namibia and South Africa.[135] Ten charges were laid in Canada against the corporation, and charges were also laid against the U.S. affiliate of the corporation for violations of the export control laws.[136] The firm pleaded guilty in both U.S. and Canadian courts on charges of illegally shipping arms to South Africa.[137] Apparently the artillery shells had been shipped to

Antigua for testing and then diverted to South Africa. Allegations made on the C.B.C. television programme the Fifth Estate of Nov. 7, 1978, also alleged artillery shells were being sent to South Africa from the U.K. and the F.R.G.

The *British Code of Conduct* seemed to work quite well with respect to its reporting requirement.[138] In Canada however, six companies issued public reports in 1979, five in 1980, and only one in 1981.[139]

On June 13, 1980 the U.N. Security Council adopted Resolution 473 unanimously. The resolution condemned South Africa and requested the committee established under Resolution 421 to find ways to close all loopholes in the arms embargo.[140] The committee provided its report in September.[141] It concluded that there was strong evidence that illicit exports to South Africa continued to take place. It noted that some definitions were needed for the terms used in Resolution 418.[142] It also made 16 recommendations.[143] The Committee Report could be used as a useful aid to interpretation with respect to dual use items and other items which the report suggests are *prima facie* of a military character.[144]

Within a few years it became apparent that the Canadian government was not going to make its December 1977 *Code of Conduct* a genuinely effective tool in its announced objective of fighting apartheid in South Africa. As the reports dwindled in number, disappointment with the implementation and the extent of the government measures was made known. The Taskforce on the Churches and Corporate Responsibility presented a brief to the Secretary of State for External Affairs and Minister of Industry, Trade and Commerce in May 1981.[145] It pointed out that Canadian curtailment of export development support was limited to its government account and did not extend to its corporate account.[146] It also reported that the corporate account had been used for exports to South Africa in September 1980 and January 1981. Two corporations, owned 30% and 100% by the Crown, were given as examples of continuing Canadian investment in South Africa.[147] Of the Canadian code it was said:

> (it) is timid and lacks precision. It does not even require the accountability found in other codes, notably the British code which requires itemized annual reporting to a body appointed by the government .... The (Canadian) Code does not answer the question who receives such reports ...[148]

Further it pointed out that an export permit had been granted to Canadair for three amphibian water bombers.[149] The U.N. Security Council Committee recommendation (vi) had stated aircraft exports to South Africa should be prohibited on the basis that their purchaser was the South Africa Forest Department.[150]

This record, brought out by the Taskforce report, tends to suggest Canada was not using the U.N. Security Council Committee Report of 1980 in interpreting Security Council Resolution 418. It also pointed out the inconsistencies in the Canadian action. One Crown corporation was asked to divest its South African investments at one time but others were not. One private firm was not allowed to export vehicles to South Africa before sanctions, but another firm was allowed to export aircraft after the imposition of the sanctions. Perhaps the differences in the cases of the vehicle exports would go to some extent to explain the different treatment of the two cases. Nevertheless, it does suggest the Canadian government was prepared to interpret non-mandatory obligations wider than mandatory ones.

In January 1984 South Africa announced that it would conduct and administer its external nuclear affairs in line with the principles, goals and spirit of the *Nonproliferation Treaty*, and the nuclear supplier's group guidelines.[151] However, South Africa would not actually agree to the treaty, or place all its internal nuclear facilities under International Atomic Agency safeguards.[152] This did not change much however as the Security Council adopted Resolution 558,[153] which supported the Security Council Committees report,[154] without any change with respect to the U.N. General Assembly policy to request that states not collaborate with South Africa with respect to nuclear technology. Resolution 558 reaffirmed Resolution 418 stressing the continuing need for its strict application. It remains to be seen whether or not Canada will interpret this resolution with the result that greater emphasis will be placed on the Committee report in interpreting Resolution 418.

(ii) Namibia. The second basis for sanctions against South Africa was its continued presence in Namibia despite a judgement of the International Court of Justice (ICJ) holding it had no authority to be there.[155] Security Council Resolution 276 called upon South Africa to leave Namibia, although the resolution itself presupposed that the mandate had already been terminated by General Assembly Resolution 2145 (XXI)[156], as had been recognized by the Security Council Resolution 264.[157] The Security Council also called on all states to refrain from all dealings with South Africa purporting to act on behalf of Namibia.[158] It followed with a call to all states to ensure that

> enterprises owned by or under direct control of the State, cease all dealings with respect to commercial or industrial enterprises or concessions in Namibia.[159]

The same resolution called for withholding government financial support to facilitate such trade and to ensure all government and private investment in Namibia cease.[160] The call also extended to the discouragement of tourism and emigration to Namibia.[161]

The effect of the U.N. resolutions was to terminate the South African mandate in Namibia and to impose a trade and investment embargo on Namibia to encourage South Africa to leave. The trade sanctions were voluntary however, not mandatory.

The U.N. General Assembly established the U.N. Council for Namibia to administer the territory. The Council for Namibia adopted Decree No. 1 for the Protection of the Natural Resources of Namibia.[162] In Decree No. 1 it was declared that Council for Namibia authority was needed to exploit natural resources and any South African grant was void.[163] It also declared that any natural resource of Namibian origin found outside Namibian territory without Council for Namibia consent might be seized, along with any ship it might be on, to be held in trust for the people of Namibia.[164]

The uncommon situation of having an assertion of jurisdiction by an authority that was not in control of the territory of Namibia created special problems of enforcement. The normal rule that enforcement jurisdiction was coincident with territorial boundaries would result in the Council for Namibia having no enforcement jurisdiction for any of its measures. This helps to explain the assertion of enforcement jurisdiction beyond the territory of Namibia in Decree No. 1. The basis for this jurisdiction was reliance on General Assembly Resolution 1803 (XVII) dealing with permanent sovereignty over natural wealth and resources.[165] Thus the extraterritorial assertion of enforcement jurisdiction in Decree No. 1 was based on the origin of the goods.

The problems associated with not having control of the territory of Namibia also resulted in not having control over the actions of the enterprises within. In order to assert as much control as was possible, the Security Council Resolution 283 called for states to ensure enterprises "owned by or under direct control of the state" cease all dealings in Namibia.[166] While this Resolution stopped short of calling for states to cease the dealings of private corporations in Namibia, it did adopt the principle of control of foreign subsidiaries by government parent corporations. While the resolution was not mandatory, it nevertheless encouraged the assertion of this type of jurisdiction.

The result was that the controls asserted or encouraged with respect to Namibia went beyond those implemented or urged with respect to South Africa for its apartheid policies and other acts within its territory. Those controls were based only on each member state asserting jurisdiction over its own territory or its nationals, ships and aircraft.

In 1975 a mandatory arms embargo was proposed before the Security Council for South Africa and Namibia, but it was vetoed.[167] The resolution was specifically concerned with the situation in Namibia. It may have suffered from excess in as much as it would have affected pre-existing contracts and licenses.[168]

Canada maintained that the U.N. sanctions with respect to Namibia were not mandatory, and were not to be applied in Canada for that reason.[169] It also maintained that Decree No. 1 had some objectionable features.

> Under Canadian law the government cannot force a mode of conduct on business operations of subsidiaries of Canadian corporations in Namibia. It is furthermore, a principle of government policy not to interfere in the operations of Canadian companies abroad. The various Security Council resolutions on Namibia, and the General Assembly resolutions of 1967, are not mandatory resolutions under Chapter VII of the *U.N Charter* and do not, therefore, impose binding obligations on member states, as is the case with regard to Rhodesia.[170]

In Parliament, however, the opposition insisted it was not right to allow Canadian companies in Namibia to claim a tax credit for payments of taxes to the South African government administering Namibia.[171]

The Council for Namibia in June 1980 called for the Security Council to impose comprehensive and mandatory sanctions on South Africa under Chapter VII of the U.N. Charter.[172] No specific action of the Security Council resulted from this call.

Canada seemed to have no specific measures geared to the presence of South Africa in Namibia. Its measures against South Africa, including its *Code of Conduct*, may have had application to Namibia as well.[173] The *EIPA* permit system seems to have been applied so as to prevent the arms embargoed to South Africa from being sent to Namibia.

The Taskforce on the Churches and Corporate Responsibility[174] in its report of May 1981 also addressed Canadian performance with respect to Namibia. It criticised the lack of Canadian support for Decree No. 1, and the tax credits allowed companies operating in Namibia.[175] It did not however have specific examples of the Canadian practice.

Later in 1981 journalists reported that El Dorado Nuclear, a Crown corporation, was processing uranium ore from Namibia.[176] The import certificates made out the country of origin to be South Africa. It was the Canadian position that processing ore from South Africa on a "commercial basis", and not a military basis, was not contrary to the U.N. embargo on South Africa.[177] The problem may have been that import licenses required by the Canadian Atomic Energy Control Board (AECB) allowed the country of origin specified to be either the point from which the ore was shipped or the ultimate source of the ore. U.N. General Assembly Resolution 3399 (XXX)[178] condemned the exploitation of uranium and other natural resources in Namibia and demanded that it cease.[179] The Resolution also called for the IAEA to discourage exploitation of uranium in Namibia.[180] It seemed to be the Canadian position that even this non-mandatory resolution had not been infringed since what was involved was only processing, not exploiting the ore. This incident demonstrates the limited extent to which Canada was willing to constrain its trade in the face of a non-mandatory resolution of the General Assembly.

One view of the question of extraction of Namibian resources holds the direct or indirect commercial relations with Rossing Uranium Limited, the source of the ore, to be unlawful.[181] This report argues that Decree No. 1 is on a higher plane than merely a decree of a foreign state because many states participated in its creation. All U.N. members were addressees of U.N. resolutions requesting full application of the decree,[182] thus it had international consequences.[183] This report states that the Council for Namibia can bring a suit in any jurisdiction to recover products outside Namibia taken out without its consent. It is also contended, however, that it suffices that the Council for Namibia has the authority to make rules in Namibia such that its decrees have the force of law.[184] An overwhelming majority of states, with the exception of certain Western states and Israel, have been complying with Decree No. 1 according to a U.N. Conference report.[185] Six states were named as exceptions, but Canada was not among them. It was, however, named as the base of corporations involved in illegal exploitation of Namibia's resources.[186]

(iii) *Portugal.* In 1961 U.N. General Assembly Resolution 1699 (XVI)[187] called for states to deny support to Portugal that it may use for the suppression of peoples in its territories that were not self-governing. Canada interpreted that resolution consistently with its pre-existing policy to deny the export to Portugal or the territories under Portuguese administration of any arms which might, in its judgement, be used for military purposes in Portuguese territories overseas.[188]

The problem with the Canadian embargo of arms to Portugal was that Portugal was a N.A.T.O. ally. Thus Canada would still supply it with arms necessary to fulfil N.A.T.O. commitments, relying on Portugal not to use the arms in colonial repression.[189] This policy continued over the years.[190]

The U.N. adopted two resolutions in the General Assembly[191] and two in the Security Council[192] calling on states to prevent military supplies from being sent to Portugal.

Canada could have implemented this embargo by denying export permits as all arms were subject to export controls. This was in fact what was done.[193]

2. *Internationally Coordinated Sanctions*

(a) Soviet Union

(i) *Afghanistan.* In the aftermath of the Soviet invasion of Afghanistan, the U.S. announced measures against the Soviet Union on January 4, 1980.[194] Canada also condemned the Soviet actions in Afghanistan as early as January 7, 1980,[195] but took more cautious steps than did the U.S., perhaps in part since it did have a binding trade agreement with the Soviet Union.[196] It preferred to consult with other governments, proceed in the U.N., and consider measures affecting Afghanistan and bilateral Soviet-Canada relations.[197]

The consideration of the matter came before the Security Council of the U.N. on January 7, 1980. In a statement to the Security Council, the Canadian Ambassador to the U.N. strongly urged that it condemn the Soviet role in Afghanistan and called for the withdrawal of Soviet forces.[198] The Security Council did consider a resolution which would have called for the withdrawal of foreign troops from Afghanistan without naming the Soviet Union by name, but the Soviet Union vetoed it.[199]

Upon its defeat, the matter was brought before an emergency session of the U.N. General Assembly, pursuant to a reference from the Security Council.[200] The Canadian Ambassador called for the General Assembly to condemn the Soviet action as a clear violation of the *U.N. Charter* and to demand the withdrawal of Soviet troops.[201]

The General Assembly did in fact consider a resolution that was the same as that before the Security Council. It was adopted by a vote of 104–18 with 12 not voting.[202]

Canada supported the U.S. grain embargo as well:

> On the subject of grain exports, Mr. Clark reiterated that Canada will not take advantage of reductions in U.S. Grain Exports to the Soviet Union by making up the difference. He said Canada will refrain from grain sales to the Soviet Union in excess of "normal and traditional levels".[203]

The *Canada-USSR Trade Agreement* requires most favored nation treatment, but makes specific exception for "prohibitions or restrictions of any kind directed to the protection of its essential security interests."[204] While this exception appeared wide enough to admit the general export permit system in place with respect to the

Soviet Union, it could hardly support any additional measures taken in retaliation for the Soviet invasion of a third country. Canadian measures that limited shipments to normal and traditional levels, in support of the U.S. grain embargo, could be considered in breach of the Trade Agreement. The Canadian defence would have to be based on principles of reprisal (the breach of international law justified by the prior breach of international law by the other party). It is however very likely that Canada could not have invoked the Soviet breach of international law with respect to its invasion of Afghanistan as justification for the suspension of the Trade Agreement as there seemed to be no connection between the two, unless the invasion was breach of a duty *erga omnes*. Such a connection may be necessary to allow for an act of reprisal.

Canada also announced other measures and indications of its policy. Among them, it announced that it was prepared to tighten up the administration of the embargo on the export of strategic goods to the Soviet Union but that this would be in concert with "other major industrial exporters" (presumably CoCom partners). Canada also would not renew export credits for the Soviet Union which expired December 31, 1979, and would be prepared to consult with other countries about the future export credit policy and interest rates with respect to the Soviet Union.[205] This may have breached Article 4 of the Long Term Agreement between Canada and the Union of Soviet Socialists Republic to Facilitate Economic Industrial Scientific and Technical Cooperation.[206]

The N.A.T.O. Council issued a press statement through its Secretary General on the occasion of its January 15 meeting on the Afghanistan situation. The statement supported the U.N. General Assembly resolution of January 14, and stated "each member state will take appropriate individual measures and steps, and all agreed actions by one should be taken into account by other member states."[207] The communiqué implied that consultation was ongoing among N.A.T.O. countries but that there was no intergovernmental agreement on which measures were based. The consultation is however apparent in the comparison of the Canadian and U.S. measures.[208]

Canada clearly favoured collective action.[209] It was recognized that it would be impossible to have states agree on uniform measures.[210] However such measures would be taken only with the fullest consultation.[211] This position did not change despite the change of governments in February 1980.[212]

On April 22, 1980, the Canadian government announced it would not be supporting Canadian participation in the Olympics in Moscow,[213] although it would not coerce athletes to stay away.[214] It was not willing to try to preclude the National Hockey League (NHL) players from organizing the Canada Cup, although it left the NHL players to make the decision.

> ...il ne saurait être question que le gouvernement du Canada soit plus catholique que le pape, c'est-à-dire que le gouvernement du Canada aille plus loin à l'égard de l'Union Soviétique que celui des États-Unis, qui ont permis l'entrée sur leur territoire des athlètes soviétiques lors des jeux qui se sont déroulés à Lake Placid en février dernier.[215]

This passage reinforces what is clear on a comparison of the Canadian and U.S. state practice. There was clearly close consultation between the two countries, but it was the U.S. that was to take the initiative, and Canada would cautiously impose comparable measures, without going the full extent of the U.S.A.

There was one case in which the U.S. grain embargo did affect Canada although in a roundabout way. A U.S. parent of a Canadian company was denied a license to ship Canadian flour to Cuba, apparently because it was thought to be destined for the Soviet Union. This was similar to the way in which licenses had earlier been denied to ship wheat to the Soviet Union to prevent it reaching Cuba.[216] Nevertheless, the licenses were eventually granted.

Clearly the U.S. measures had extraterritorial effect either in their "voluntary application",[217] or in their normal application. One such issue that seemed to go unnoticed was the ambit of the *Transaction Control Regulations*.[218] These regulations prohibited persons "within the United States" from entering into any transaction anywhere including those which might result in an export to the Soviet Union.[219] Stretching the normal meaning of the words, the definition "within the United States" includes companies owned or controlled by U.S. persons, wherever organized.[220] Thus, Canadian companies owned or controlled by U.S. persons would generally have been prohibited from exporting to the Soviet Union without a U.S. license were it not for a limiting provision.[221] This provision permitted shipments licensed in Canada, including Canadian shipments to the Soviet Union.[222] Since the Soviet Union was on the Canadian Area Control List, and therefore licenses were required for such exports, the *Transaction Control Regulations* were ousted for those transactions. The problem remained however with respect to two issues. First, the fact that the *Transaction Control Regulations* applied to transactions with nationals of the Soviet Union as well, while the Canadian regulations applied only to the destination. Second, the Canadian export controls applied only to goods and technical data in material form, while the U.S. controls under the *Transaction Control Regulations* applied also to credit transfers, foreign exchange transactions and interest in property, none of which were covered by the Canadian export permit legislation. It is clear that this is an area for which the exempting provisions did not exempt Canadian companies owned or controlled by U.S. persons.

(ii) *Poland*. Canada had announced certain measures against the Soviet Union after its armed intervention in Afghanistan. It took no new measures with respect to the Soviet Union after the events in Poland, but did take measures against Poland.

Canada was one of the countries that protested the U.S. imposition of export controls on oil and gas technical data to be used in the construction of the Siberian pipeline. It was the fact that these controls purported to affect foreign companies that caused Canada to react. Canada sent a note to the U.S. Department of State on July 7, 1982 to protest the extraterritorial aspects of the U.S. regulations that had extended the oil and gas controls, June 18, 1982.[223]

The Secretary of State for External Affairs (S.S.E.A.), in a press conference, stated Canada had been concerned for many years about U.S. action applying its law to U.S. owned companies in Canada.[224] The June regulations had, however, gone further than before. Not only were they retroactive but they even extended to companies without U.S. ownership. The extension was rather on the basis of licenses granted by U.S. companies. The position was firmly stated in the Canadian note of July 7, 1982.[225] The note stated that the measures were an unacceptable infringement of Canadian sovereignty.[226] The note was significant in that it stood on principle and there seemed to be no Canadian companies immediately affected.[227] The S.S.E.A. stated in the press conference that there was a consideration of the use of the *Combines Investigation Act* provisions in this case.[228]

On August 9, 1982 it was announced that the influence of the U.S. *Export Administration Regulations* would be studied by the Director of Investigation and Research with a view to deciding whether a formal inquiry would be instituted under the *Combines Investigation Act*.[229] Despite allegations in the press that some Canadian companies were being affected directly or indirectly by the U.S. law[230] the investigation did not turn up anything that would lead to a formal inquiry.[231]

On the other hand, other countries were clearly affected. Several foreign firms had Temporary Denial Orders made against them by the U.S. export control authorities because they were going ahead with the completion of contracts for the supply of equipment and technology for the Siberian gas pipeline.[232] Some countries such as France,[233] the U.K.[234] and the Netherlands[235] ordered their companies to comply with their contracts. Others, such as the F.R.G., had no legal basis on which to do so.[236] Sweden was affected also.[237]

The European countries, members of the E.E.C., consulted each other and tried to present a solid front to the U.S.[238] The note sent to the U.S. by the E.E.C. stated the U.S. measures were "contrary to international law, and apparently at variance with rules and principles laid down in U.S. law."[239] Canada was not a party to this protest, organised by the E.E.C.

The E.E.C. comments that accompanied the note stated that the U.S. could not rely on either the territoriality principle or the nationality principle to support its regulations.[240] The comments relied on the *Barcelona Traction* case as standing for the proposition that the nationality of companies was to be determined by the place of incorporation or the place of the registered head office. It said no other test of corporate nationality had found general acceptance.[241] The E.E.C. comments also stated that international law also did not accept the notion that goods or technology can establish jurisdiction over persons controlling them.[242] It also stated that the protective principle could not be invoked by the U.S. because in this case it had expressly relied on the *Export Administration Act*'s foreign policy control power in section 5 rather than the national security controls in section 5.[243]

The E.E.C. comments also pointed out that it was doubtful that similar measures enacted in another country would pass the U.S. anti-boycott provisions test in the *EAA*.[244] Thus, arguing on the basis of reciprocity, it concluded the U.S. should not inflict such measures on the European Community.[245] It contued that, in any case, the U.S. had not even followed its own balancing of interests approach that had been enunciated in case law and the American Law Institute's Restatement.[246]

One incident in which Canada was directly affected was reported in the press on

October 6, 1982.[247] The U.S. Department of Commerce, as the report speculated, did in fact send a letter to a Canadian company informing it of the June 18 amendments to the U.S. export controls and seeking information.[248] The information sought was a description of products the company had supplied or planned to supply for the Siberian pipeline, and a description of technology that the company or its subsidiaries had transferred to any location outside the U.S. in the last seven years.[249] Rather than being subject to U.S. jurisdiction by U.S. ownership or control, the Canadian company in fact was the parent of a U.S. company.

The incident may be viewed as an application of enforcement jurisdiction of the U.S. in Canada. It appears, however, that no formal protest was made in this case, unlike the similar situation with respect to the *CACR*s in June 1982, in which case the Canadian Embassy in Washington did protest. But it is reported that the matter was raised in early November with the U.S. State Department.[250]

Canada did support the U.S. controls on U.S. origin goods by virtue of the denial of permits under item 9001 of its Export Control List. One of the companies involved in the Siberian Pipeline had a subsidiary in Canada which was refused permits in Canada for the export of equipment for a Soviet oil well project.[251] Perhaps for this reason the Soviet Union requested comfort letters from the Canadian government to the effect it would guarantee supply under contracts with Canadian firms.[252]

On November 13, 1982 the U.S. President announced that the U.S. controls were lifted.[253] The action was taken pursuant to an agreement among Western nations to study relations with the Soviet Union energy alternatives, and that no nation would enter into new Soviet gas contracts.[254] This deal was endorsed by Canada as well as Japan and the E.E.C.[255]

France however announced, within hours of the U.S. statement, that it was not party to the agreement. It did work out an agreement with the U.S. in the next month. The specific details of the agreement were reported after a midnight press conference following meetings with U.S. and French officials, on December 15th, 1982. CoCom was to broaden its activity and speed up its decision making. It was also to study whether it would include oil and gas controls under its aegis. The OECD was to study Western credit policy towards the Soviet Union, the East-West trade and how to keep the Soviet Union from getting preferential credit treatment. The OECD, the IEA and governments were to study energy alternatives to Soviet gas. NATO was to improve consultation and coordination and to study how economic relations with the Soviet Union affect Western security – a first for NATO.[256]

(b) Iran

On November 6, 1979, two days after the U.S. Embassy in Teheran was seized by militants, the Canadian Parliament approved a resolution protesting to the Iranian government the "act of criminal aggression."[257] By November 28, 1979 the Canadian Parliament condemned the government of Iran for breaching international law by encouraging and taking the U.S. diplomatic staff as hostages.[258] Canada initiated a meeting of Commonwealth High Commissioners in London to suggest that it would be valid for the Commonwealth to voice a common opinion on the situation in Iran.[259]

As a result of the Canadian initiative, a joint communiqué was issued protesting the actions of the Iranian militants and appealing for the release of the hostages.[260]

The U.N. Security Council called urgently for the government of Iran to release the U.N. Embassy personnel December 4, 1970.[261] On December 31, 1979 the Security Council Resolution 461 found the holding of the hostages to be in violation of international law and that it "could have grave consequences for international peace and security".[262] This language goes beyond the condition in Article 34 of the *U.N. Charter* giving the Security Council the right to investigate a dispute. Its investigation is to determine whether international peace and security are likely to be endangered. It would seem that Resolution 461 made the decision that it was likely that peace and security would be endangered by the continuance of the hostage taking. Thus it would seem that Resolution 461 met the requirement of Article 39 of the *U.N. Charter* for the imposition of mandatory measures, which may include economic sanctions under Article 41. The resolution decided that the Security Council would meet January 7 to review the situation and, if the hostages were not released, "to adopt effective measures under Articles 39 and 41 of the Charter of the United Nations."[263] Although this resolution seemed to have prejudged the issue with respect to mandatory economic sanctions against Iran if it did not comply, in fact it was not to have that result. The resolution contemplated that the Secretary General of the U.N., Kurt Waldheim, would travel to Iran before the January 7 meeting.[264]

On January 7 however the Security Council considered a resolution which would have called for the immediate and unconditional withdrawal of all foreign troops from Afghanistan. This resolution would have passed had the Soviet Union not vetoed it.[265] Then on the consideration of a U.S. sponsored resolution calling for economic sanctions against Iran, the Soviet Union again voted against.[266] It was modelled on the total embargo placed on Rhodesia by S.C. Resolution 253 of May 29, 1980.[267] It improved upon it in one crucial respect, however, by providing a termination date for the measures; "until such time as the hostages are released and have safely departed from Iran". It asserted that the Security Council opposed the holding of diplomats but that there was no threat to international peace and security.[268] The seeming contradiction with Resolution 461 in which such a threat seemed to be found, a resolution from which the Soviet Union abstained, can perhaps best be explained by the Security Council action with respect to Afghanistan.

Canada supported the U.S. freeze of Iranian government assets even before the U.N. resolution calling for a release of the hostages.[269] This position continued unaltered despite a change in government during the hostage taking.[270] The Canadian position was that, despite the Soviet veto in the Security Council on the economic sanctions resolution, the international community condemned Iran and this justified the imposition of economic sanctions.[271]

On this basis Canada imposed limited measures against Iran on April 23, 1980.

They responded to a call for support from the U.S. President earlier that month.[272] These could only have been denials of export permits with respect to items on the Export Control List, because Iran was not placed on the Area Control List until May 22, 1980.[273] Canada acted in concert with the E.E.C. and Japan, which also imposed measures, on April 22, 1980.[274] These countries had agreed to take further steps if there was no decisive progress by May 17, 1980.[275] There having been no such progress noted, on May 18 the E.E.C. and Japan implemented the measures proposed by the U.S. before the Security Council that the Soviet Union had vetoed.[276] Canada took the same step May 22.[277]

The Canadian action was two-fold. It put Iran on the Area Control List[278] under the *EIPA*. It also introduced legislation that was based on the draft resolution that had been defeated at the Security Council by the Soviet veto.[279] The bill was expedited by the consent of the opposition parties.[280]

The *Iranian Economic Sanctions Act* (*IESA*) was given Royal Assent and came into force, July 17, 1980.[281] The operative part empowered the Governor in Council to make regulations by reason of the breach of international law by Iran.[282] The *IESA* permitted regulations for purposes which were set out in the January resolution of the Security Council that had been vetoed. The *IESA*, section 3(a)-(f) allowed regulations:

(a) restricting or prohibiting the sale or supply by any person in Canada or by a Canadian outside Canada of goods or services to or destined for the Islamic Republic of Iran or any person situated therein;
(b) restricting or prohibiting the carriage or shipment by any means of goods through or from Canada destined for the Islamic Republic of Iran or any person situated therein;
(c) restricting or prohibiting the shipment of goods from Canada on vessels or aircraft registered in the Islamic Republic of Iran;
(d) restricting or prohibiting the making of loans, extensions of credit or the offering of deposit facilities to the Islamic Republic of Iran or any person situated therein by the person in Canada or by a Canadian outside Canada;
(e) restricting or prohibiting increases of non-Canadian or non-United States dollar deposits by the Islamic Republic of Iran or any person situated therein in deposit facilities in Canada or in deposit facilities operated by a Canadian outside Canada; and
(f) for the purpose of

    (i) ensuring that lenders or creditors who are in Canada or who are Canadians outside Canada do not allow the Islamic Republic of Iran or any person situated therein more favourable terms of loan or credit payment than those customarily used in international commercial transactions, and
    (ii) requiring lenders and creditors described in subparagraph (i) to act in such manner as is prescribed by the regulations to ensure that they exercise their rights in a business-like manner when payments due on

> their loans or credits made to the Islamic Republic of Iran or any person situated therein are not made on time.

The main purpose of the *IESA* seemed to be to empower the embargo that had been instituted under the *EIPA*. The *EIPA* would have required there to be an "intergovernmental arrangement or commitment" implemented before it would authorize regulation of goods.[283] Although it seems clear that Canada was coordinating its actions with that of the E.E.C. and Japan, it arguably did not have an arrangement or commitment that would meet the test of section 3 of the *EIPA*. It is probable that section 3 requires an obligation in international law before it will empower regulation with respect to specified items. Section 4 of the *EIPA* however allowed export controls to be placed on any country if "necessary". Thus, placing Iran on the Area Control List, on May 22, 1980, seemed amply justified in Canadian law under the *EIPA*.

The *IESA* was needed to implement the embargo on services, for which the *EIPA* has no provision. It also was needed to extend the embargo extraterritorially to Canadian citizens abroad.[284] It also served to consolidate the various measures in one statute. The *IESA* not only encompassed the export of goods and services, but also the control of the amounts in Iranian bank deposits[285] and treatment of Iranian debtors.[286] These measures could not have been implemented under the *EIPA* thus necessitating the *IESA*.

While the *IESA* empowered regulations with respect to the subject matters set out in it, no regulations pursuant to the authority were ever adopted. It is probable that Canada did in fact deny export permits on the matters coming under the *EIPA*. Iran was on the Area Control List since that was Canadian stated policy.[287] The *IESA* was to expire within a year,[288] although it could be renewed. The *IESA* however was terminated even before a year had run out.[289] On the same day Iran was removed from the Area Control List.[290] This action was taken a month and a half after the hostages had been released, January 20, 1981.[291]

Since that time Canada has been denying exports of arms and military supplies to Iran because of its war with Iraq. This is accomplished by the denial of permits for materials on the Export Control List where their ultimate destination is Iran or Iraq. Canada has also been controlling some chemicals that could be used in chemical warfare as the allegations of chemical use in the Iran-Iraq war have persisted.

(c) Argentina

On the invasion of the Falkland Islands by Argentina on April 2, 1982, the Canadian government took a "very serious view of the situation".[292] The next day the U.N. Security Council adopted Resolution 502 demanding the withdrawal of Argentine forces from the Falklands.[293] Canada announced an immediate export embargo on all military shipments to Argentina.[294]

The Canadian position was taken on the grounds that the U.K. had to have recourse to self-defence because of Argentinian aggression.[295] Canada also placed import measures on Argentinian goods similar to those of the E.E.C. countries.[296]

The E.E.C. took import measures on April 16, 1982[297] and also cut off arms sales.[298]

The U.K. had taken steps on April 3, 1982 to freeze Argentine assets held in Great Britain.[299] The measures were taken in the form of exchange control regulations which affected persons in Great Britain and British citizens normally resident there no matter where they were.[300] That was the only extraterritorial effect of the U.K. measures.

On April 23, 1982 the Canadian government exchanged letters with the E.E.C. and on April 26 issued regulations putting into effect import restrictions on goods from Argentina.[301] Apart from such measures it also suspended export credits for Argentina.[302] This and the embargo on military equipment were the only two export measures it would take.

Argentina took exception to the E.E.C., Australian and Canadian import suspension. It complained to the *GATT*[303] of violations of the most favored nation treatment obligations; non-tariff barriers prohibitions, discrimination prohibitions, and developing country provisions.[304] The Argentine complaint argued that the U.N. Security Council had not authorized third party measures under Article XXI(c) of the *GATT*.[305]

The complaint alleged the U.K. had no justification for its measures under Article XXI(b) of the *GATT*, since the Falklands were not British territory so that U.K. territory had not been threatened.[306]

It is difficult to appreciate the position of third countries with respect to Argentina under the *GATT*. Countries other than the U.K. would have trouble relying on the "essential security interests" under Article XXI(b) for any defence to the Argentinian complaint. Article XXI(c) of the *GATT* allows for measures taken:

> in pursuance of its obligations under the United Nations *Charter* for the maintenance of peace and security.

It is possible to argue that these included actions to maintain the principle of peaceful resolution of disputes,[307] by members of the U.N. other than those involved in the dispute, might fall under the *GATT* Article. The *GATT* Council merely voted to table the complaint however, and did not deal with the interpretation of the provisions of the *GATT*, although extensively discussing the matter.[308]

The Canadian government was pressed in Parliament to stop the export of nuclear technology or material from Canada to Argentina.[309] The government however, relied on undertakings the Argentine government had given and International Atomic Energy Agency inspection to guarantee the peaceful use of nuclear facilities.[310] The government stated it did not impose any export controls on nuclear materials as a result of the Argentine invasion of the Malvinas.[311] It stated no other country had done so[312] and it seemed clear the Canadian government would not act to surpass measures of the E.E.C.

The import controls of the Canadian government were formally removed July 8, 1982,[313] a couple of weeks after the E.E.C. had lifted its measures.[314] Canada continued its ban on military exports but recommenced export credits on June 22, 1982.[315]

The Falklands conflict thus did not involve Canadian export control measures save for those on military material. It did bring into focus the potential problem of trade measures contravening the *GATT*. Canadian measures were not extraterritorial in scope: the U.K. measures were extraterritorial only to the limited extent that they affected the British citizens abroad who were normally resident in the U.K. This is a marked contrast with the U.S. measures during the hostage crisis.[316]

B. Reaction to International Action in which Canada Did Not Participate

1. Arab Boycott of Israel

In 1954 the Arab League's Council adopted the *Unified Law on the Boycott of Israel*.[317] This resolution was enacted in the 20 member states.[318] It was the culmination of more than eight years of prohibitions of Jewish and Israeli goods.[319]

The 1954 *Unified Law* provided a prohibition to conclude any transaction or agreement with persons in Israel, of Israeli nationality, or working on behalf of Israel.[320] Any company with an office in Israel was assimilated to a person in Israel.[321] In addition there was a blacklist of firms, banks and ships.[322] In practice foreign firms seeking to do business in the Arab world needed to certify their compliance with the Arab boycott of Israel as a condition of doing business.[323]

In February 1964 the issue was brought before the Canadian Parliament. The Minister of Trade and Commerce stated:

> ... only a few Canadian firms have had their interests affected or threatened by the Arab boycott of Israel. If a Canadian firm is affected or likely to be affected, the firm's actions should be governed by its own policies and interests. Should a Canadian firm seek the assistance of the Canadian government we would certainly be prepared to consider what assistance might usefully and appropriately be provided in the circumstances pertaining thereto.[324]

It was not apparent from this statement what the Canadian government might do to assist a company requesting its assistance.

The Arab boycott was designed to affect activity carried on abroad by non-Arab persons or companies[325] and thus was extraterritorial in the sense that has always seemed most objectionable to Canada. Its extraterritorial features reached beyond its national jurisdiction. Canada, however, took no particular notice of the boycott for some twenty years.[326]

On October 21, 1976 the Canadian government issued a statement clarifying its position.[327] In it the Canadian government strongly opposed boycotts based on race, origin or religion.[328] Canada stated it would deny its support or facilities to sanction the discriminatory effects on Canadian persons.[329] Canada left it open to Canadian companies to forego Canadian support but nevertheless required reports of their compliance with boycott provisions in reports which were to be made public.

The Canadian position was based on its right to determine with which countries it will develop its trade.[330] The policy was sent to consulates with the direction that normal consular services were to be provided and that Ottawa should be consulted if services were requested with respect to acts complying with an international economic boycott offensive to Canada.[331] Where transactions were being entered into in countries where economic boycotts were in effect, an assurance had to be obtained that the transaction did not contravene Canadian government policy before consular services would be provided.[332]

The Canadian policy was applied in at least one instance. In order to have certain signatures authenticated, the Legal Bureau of the Department of External Affairs required an undertaking:

> ... that in meeting the terms of the Power of Attorney appointing an agent in Baghdad, Iraq to represent [the company, it] is not required to discriminate against any person on that basis of race, religion or national or ethnic origin, and is not required to refuse (a) to purchase from or sell goods and/or services to any other Canadian company, agency or individual, (b) to sell Canadian goods and/or services to any country, or (c) to purchase goods and/or services from any country.[333]

Canada was also closely watching legislative developments in the U.S. The Secretary of State for External Affairs told Parliament that he had met with the U.S. Secretary of State and had told him that Canada would take a dim view of extraterritorial foreign boycott legislation being passed in the U.S. Congress, and would have to take some action were it to happen.[334] Thus, while it had put itself clearly against boycotts based on race, origin or religion, Canada was unprepared to accept any extraterritorial means which other states with similar policies might choose to use to adopt to implement their policies.

The *EAA* amendments came into force on June 22, 1977.[335] Draft regulations were issued by the Department of Commerce September 20, 1977.[336] They were not finalized until January 18, 1978.[337] Before they came into force, Canada sent the U.S. State Department comments on the draft regulations pursuant to the notice accompanying them. The note stated that the particular comments were without prejudice to Canada's position on extraterritoriality.

Canada's note of November 21, 1977 referred to its previously expressed concern about the possible extraterritorial effects of the U.S. boycott legislation.[338] It noted the application of the law to foreign incorporated companies abroad, and stated:

> ... the Canadian government considers that a foreign state is not entitled to apply its laws to companies incorporated in Canada with respect to activities which occur outside that state.[339]

The Canadian note stressed that U.S. law could apply to foreign companies on the basis of as low as 25% voting securities, where there is no ownership at all if there is a U.S. management contract, or where the board of directors is also on a comparable U.S. corporation.[340] It also pointed out that even purely Canadian commerce could be affected by the imposition of penalties on U.S. parents or affiliates.[341] The note also pointed out:

> with respect to the transformation of U.S.A. components in a Canadian product, it has long been the Canadian view that imported goods and services incorporated into Canadian products take on the identity in completed form of a Canadian product.[342]

Finally, it commented that the rule which would have the whole of a transaction caught by the regulations if part was "in the U.S. Commerce" would catch a wholly Canadian consortium where one of its members is a subsidiary of or affiliated with a U.S. company.[343]

The British also sent comments on the draft regulations.[344] The British note was somewhat different in parts. It reaffirmed that Britain advocated that subsidiaries abroad "controlled in fact" were being affected where their activities fail to constitute any "direct substantial and foreseeable involvement ... in United States foreign commerce."[345] It also noted the extent of the application of the regulations would depend on the meaning given the word "affiliate": where "affiliate" was broadly interpreted the effect would be greater on British commerce.

On January 27, 1978 Canada sent another note to the Department of State, this time dealing with the proposed reporting requirements and the procedure for issuing interpretative letters.[346] The Canadian note pointed out that persons who appeared to be required to report included Canadian companies which were subsidiaries or affiliated U.S. concerns. While the U.S. parent could report on behalf of the Canadian company, it would still be liable for failure to report. It continued:

> The Canadian Government considers the United States authorities are not entitled to exercise extraterritorial jurisdiction over Canadian companies solely on the basis that those companies are deemed to be controlled by United States citizens. Such companies, as Canadian corporate citizens, cannot be regarded as United States persons. The proposed regulations pertaining to the reporting requirements are therefore unacceptable ...

It would also seem to conflict with the Ontario and Quebec legislation which prohibit the removal of business records from those jurisdictions.[347]

The Canadian government sent the U.S. State Department another note on July 31, 1978.[348] The note complained of the extraterritoriality of the U.S. anti-boycott regulations with respect to surveys to be conducted. It is reported that the U.S. response gave some satisfaction that Canadian concerns were being taken into account in preparing such surveys. The surveys were in fact to be voluntary, and, although public, would not name foreign subsidiaries, but rather report their information along with that of the parent.[349]

The U.S. laws also caught the attention of the press.[350] It was said that Canadian officials had alleged that U.S. companies were telling Canadian subsidiaries not to do business with the Arabs to avoid the consequences of U.S. law.[351]

The Canadian government announced several new measures. From October 1978 the Government would only allow certificates of origin that were positive in origin.[352] The Canadian government decided that negative certificates of origin, "those which certify that goods, services or components do not originate in a specified country, are unacceptable," effective Oct. 1, 1978. The government would allow statements of fact to be made about past or present commercial dealings but would continue to consider statements of future intent as unacceptable.[353]

Government support facilities were not denied during the first part of 1978. There were 38 cases in which undertakings were required of Canadian companies that contravened the Canadian policy on international boycotts. Of the 38, three companies declined to pursue their opportunities for various boycott-related reasons. The remaining 35 firms either removed the offensive clauses or managed to provide the qualified undertakings that Canadian policy would allow.

Consistent with its own practices, Canada recognizes the right of other states to a primary boycott. It is secondary and tertiary boycott clauses to which Canada objects. These clauses involve the restriction of the actions of companies in Canada to comply with the boycott as a precondition for doing business with the boycotting state.[354] This policy is implemented in part by the Export Development Corporation (EDC), which provides loans, investment guarantees and export credit insurance among its facilities.[355] The Corporation had a standard boycott endorsement form become part of the contract, and make the contract with the EDC inapplicable to the transaction.[356]

The necessity of government support in one form or another led the Canadian Prime Minister to conclude that the policy was effective.[357] Nevertheless, the Canadian government introduced Bill C-32 to make reporting of boycott requests mandatory.[358] Another private members bill would have mirrored legislation of the Province of Ontario.[359] The government of the day stated that it intended to bring in its own legislation.[360] This Bill died on the order paper at the end of Parliament in 1979, upon an election which saw a change of government. The Bill, its successors and others on the subject were never passed. Thus, the requirement that all firms report requests for compliance with boycotts has never been implemented. Only firms seeking government assistance need do so.

The Province of Ontario, however, adopted anti-boycott legislation.[361] The act does not apply to lawful action in a labour dispute nor to discriminatory practices in accordance with a policy of the federal or Ontario governments.[362] With these limitations the act prohibits refusals to enter into contracts, termination of contracts and failures to advance employees on the basis of any of their "attributes" which include those of persons to whom they were connected.[363] The prohibitions include the acts themselves, the provision of or requests for information to assist in a prohibited activity.[364] The Act also requires a report of any requests to engage in a prohibited activity, and the action taken.[365]

The Ontario law has no rules with respect to its application to transactions and persons not wholly within Ontario. The only rules that can be relied on are the general rules of statutory construction. Statutory construction does not suggest any application of the statute to persons outside Ontario, and the extraterritorial legislation incapacity of the provincial legislature, would seem to point to the same result.

C. Reaction to Unilateral U.S. Legislation or Practice Having Extraterritorial Effect

1. China, North Korea

U.S. controls with respect to China began with respect to exports to areas controlled by communists prior to the formation of the People's Republic of China in October 1949.[366] By December 29, 1949 Canada had added China to the Area Control List.[367] It was on the same day that Group 9 was added to the Export Control List controlling specific items.[368] This controlled all goods that were to be re-exported from Canada without further processing or manufacturing. Clearly the major use that would be made of this provision was to control U.S. goods that were imported into Canada from being exported to a destination to which they could not be exported directly from the U.S.[369]

The Korean War broke out June 25, 1950 and by June 30 the U.S. had a total embargo on exports to China.[370] By July 20, 1950, licenses requiring specific approval that had been granted for export to China were revoked by the U.S.[371] Canada cancelled all outstanding applications for strategic exports to China at the end of July 1950.[372] The immediate impact on export statistics could not be ascertained due to the fact that Canada compiled statistics that included both China and Taiwan (then called Formosa).[373]

Prior to Canadian membership in CoCom, it is hard to say what was considered a "strategic" export. Canada, however, met the U.S. once every 3 months[374] and it is reasonable to infer that there was some influence exercised by the U.S. in this regard. Some indication may be drawn from a comparison of the three *Battle Act* lists and the Canadian Export Control List. One *Battle Act* list is classified however and another generalized.[375] By May 15, 1952 the Canadian government stated that Canada had no trade at all with China.[376]

In 1952 the Consultative Group created a second working group to deal specifically with the China controls. It was known as ChinaCom.[377] The list of controlled items for export to China was more extensive than that to Soviet Bloc countries, although both were very restrictive.[378]

With the creation of ChinaCom the Consultative Group had four lists of items. There were CoCom lists, and one ChinaCom list. The ChinaCom list had items that were not to go to prohibited destinations. The second list was of items on which there was to be quantitative control. The third list was of items that were allowed to be shipped but they were to be watched "the watch list".[379] Canada applied these lists so that the quantitative control CoCom list was also completely embargoed with respect to China. Thus Canada applied the CoCom lists more stringently to China than to the Soviet Bloc.

Canada and the U.S. had meetings once every three months to discuss strategic trade with Area Control Countries.[380] The Minister of Trade and Commerce stated that to prevent U.S. controls being subverted:

> ... we have parallel arrangements which change from time to time as the joint committee decides in light of strategic considerations.[381]

This kind of cooperation explains the Canadian actions prior to membership in the Consultative Group to some extent.

It is difficult to say to what extent the Area Control listing of China resulted in a clamp-down on non-strategic exports, between December 1949 and May 1952. Tentatively it may be posited that Canadian participation in the China embargo had two stages: the first being the imposition of controls on exports of strategic items in consultation with the U.S., the second, and the more extensive, being the embargo based on membership in the Consultative Group. Most interesting is that the U.N. resolution recommending the embargo on some strategic items seems to have been redundant, although it would have provided easy justification to states whose measures conformed to it, even though they had been passed prior to it.

Canadian dissatisfaction was expressed with the extent of the U.S. measures in the Korean conflict in 1953 when President Eisenhower ordered a blockade of the Chinese mainland.[382] The Canadian government position was that the imposition of a blockade was a matter for U.N. decision.[383] On April 17, 1953 however, Canada set up a licensing system prohibiting Canadian ships from sailing from any port "whether within or outside Canada" except where licensed.[384] This action seems to have been taken pursuant to CoCom agreement.[385]

The armistice in Korea was signed shortly after on July 27, 1953.[386] A year later the CoCom list was shortened, but the ChinaCom list remained unchanged, greatly widening the gap between the two lists.[387] Pressure came to review the ChinaCom list however, and agreement to review it was announced by U.K. Prime Minister Eden and President Eisenhower on Feb. 1, 1956.[388] On May 14, 1956, the British Government formally announced it would make greater use of the procedure to have exports excepted from the ChinaCom list.[389] The U.S. however refused to discuss relaxation of trade restrictions with Chinese officials at Geneva.[390] During 1956 there was some trade with China, and thus the total embargo from Canada was no longer in effect.[391]

One year later the U.K. again announced weakening of its export controls to China. On May 30, 1957 the U.K. announced it would treat China on the same basis as the Soviet Union.[392] In that year there seem to have been two incidents in which U.K. companies had export sales vetoed by controlling U.S. ownership,[393] thus giving the U.K. good reason to pressure the U.S. for reduced controls on export to China.

One commentator found it difficult to understand why no complaint against the extraterritorial reach of U.S. export controls came to light in the period 1950–1957. He explained it by the subtlety of enforcement techniques used by the U.S.[394] A much better explanation suggests itself. If Canadian trade with China was broken off as completely as suggested in the House of Commons in 1952 (and by 1956 85% of the $2.4 million dollars trade was Canadian fertilizer)[395] there was not really much occasion for U.S. prohibitions to have effect when it seems Canadian prohibitions were practically total.

Prior to 1957 there had been some other problems experienced with exports by Canadian corporations owned by U.S. parents. The problem was that the U.S. corporation would monopolize the export business, perhaps allowing the Canadian subsidiary to export to Commonwealth countries.[396] Naturally when firms were questioned about restrictions on exports the U.S. parent firms would refer to U.S. law as restricting their exports to China.[397] But it was only once Canada had begun to allow trade which the U.S. had prohibited that U.S. parent restrictions on Canadian corporations' exports came to assume an extraterritorial dimension vis-à-vis Canadian exports.

With the U.K. announcement of 1957, the ChinaCom list was moribund. It was soon abolished, and China and North Korea placed under the lesser CoCom controls.[398] Before long the insistence by the U.S. on continuing its total embargo on China began to cause problems.

Perhaps the best known case is the refusal by the Ford Motor Company of the U.S. to permit its Canadian subsidiary to sell 1,000 vehicles to China.[399] The question of Canadian exports of cars to China was first raised in the House of Commons in mid-December, 1957, and reported in the press.[400] The government position stated in the House was that:

> ... the consent of the United States is not required before an export permit is granted for the shipment of automobiles to Communist China.[401]

Further clarification was given in the next year:

> ... the only law that is binding upon Canadians when in Canada or corporations that are doing business in Canada, to the extent to which they are doing business in Canada lawfully, is the law of Canada.[402]

The Ford case was to be studied by the government to see what could be done.[403] The government explained that it hoped to negotiate some relaxation of the U.S. rules.[404] This was in fact what occurred July 9, 1958 on the occasion of President Eisenhower's visit to Ottawa. The President and Prime Minister issued a joint statement. The Eisenhower-Diefenbaker joint communiqué of July 9, 1958 addressed the gaps between the Canadian and U.S. export controls with respect to China.[405] In it however, the method by which each case was to be considered was to look for "appropriate procedures".[406] Earlier that day the Secretaries of State had agreed to the wording as being "licensing procedures". There had also been agreement between the ministers that the U.S. would be prepared to grant a permit to parent companies in the U.S. when there was appreciable effect on the Canadian company and economy were the deal not to go through.[407] The U.S. minister stated U.S. laws ought not to operate to the disadvantage of a Canadian company but, on the other hand, he did not want to allow U.S. subsidiaries abroad to have the doors opened wide.[408]

The Leader of the Opposition, Lester B. Pearson, suggested that the problem was a lack of accord among CoCom countries as to a "uniform list of commodities which are on the strategic list and therefore not exportable to countries which we fear."[409] It would seem however that the problem was not lack of agreement on what CoCom countries considered strategic. Rather the problem was the desire of the U.S. to continue a total embargo on China, not merely a strategic one. The Opposition suggested that the government:

> introduce in Parliament a Canadian law requiring Canadian corporations to act in a business way to the advantage of this country and to make it a penalty for them to carry out the law of another foreign country if such a law is detrimental to our nation.[410]

But it seemed that the Eisenhower-Diefenbaker understanding worked to have U.S. licenses issued to the U.S. parents of Canadian corporations that wished to sell to China. The trouble was that it could hardly be assumed that every potential sale to China in which the U.S parent feared the sanctions of U.S. export control law would come to the attention of the Canadian government. Thus, it was only where companies came to the government and where the Canadian government subsequently made representations for a specific company that the understanding seemed to pay dividends.

Days after the agreement Rayonier Inc. sought a license for its subsidiary's (a Canadian corporation) export to China of bleached sulphite paper. It apparently requested the Canadian government to assist in obtaining the license.[411] On or about July 19, 1958 Canada sent an "aide mémoire" to the U.S. that outlined the steps necessary to exempt the U.S. parent Rayonier, and others considered by the U.S. to be "subject to U.S. law".[412] The license was issued by the U.S. July 30, 1958[413] but the deal was never completed.[414]

The fact that the understanding was not sufficient to give complete autonomy to Canadian corporations owned by U.S. parents, was demonstrated by the Aluminum Company of Canada (Alcan) case. Alcan refused an offer to purchase two thousand long tons of aluminum stating it feared a loss of business from its present customers. A look at its customers showed that U.S. customers were the potential problem.[415] There was no question that the sale would have been important to both the Canadian economy and company.[416] The Eisenhower-Diefenbaker understanding did not alter the situation, since it only came into play when the Canadian government made representations on behalf of a company that had already decided to go ahead with a sale and was awaiting export licenses before it did so. Alcan was likely to have received a license had it tried, and it was told so.

Late in January 1959, the issue was raised in Parliament that B.F. Goodrich did not pursue a potential sale of conveyor belting to China. The Canadian company forwarded a request for information to be supplied to the Chinese from its U.S. parent who wrote:

> Under the present regulations of our government, we are prohibited from dealing with China, even to the extent of communicating with nationals of Red China in any manner.[417]

Apparently this was a case in which the goods were only made in the U.S. In such a case Canadian policy had been expressed to respect the U.S. export controls.

Through the Group 9 mechanism of its regulations under the *Export and Import Permits Act* Canada would not allow re-export of U.S. origin goods unless they had been further manufactured in Canada.

During 1958, a small number of export permits were issued for exports from Canada to China with a value of (Cdn.) $11.3 million. Of that figure 62% ($7.02 million) were sales of wheat, and 19% ($2.17 million) sales of nickel.[418]

In March 1959, the Canadian Locomotive Company of Kingston, 77% owned by a U.S. parent, experienced difficulties obtaining a U.S. export license for the sale of 100 reconditioned Canadian built locomotives to China. On the basis of the Eisenhower-Diefenbaker understanding a U.S. export license was issued, however the sale was never completed.[419]

In May 1959 the Parliament and press discussed a U.S. ban on trucking in bond of Chinese shrimp and other food between British Columbia and eastern Canada.[420] Canada, which still did not have a good highway through the Rocky Mountains, invoked the *GATT* section, article V(2), which provides for "freedom of transit through the territory of each contracting party, via the routes most convenient".[421] The U.S. lifted these restrictions and notified the Canadian Embassy in Washington May 22, 1959.[422]

In February 1961, there was an allegation in the press and in Parliament that Massey-Ferguson Ltd. had lost a sale of 400 tractors to China due to U.S. law.[423] It seems to have been the case however that the tractors were only made in the U.S.[424]

The value of Canadian trade with China since 1956 had fluctuated:

1956	$2,426,620
1957	$1,398,613
1958	$7,808,965
1959	$1,720,033
1960	$8,737,363

China continued to be under export control in Canada until July 2, 1981[425] so all these exports were made under export permits.

In 1963 the Canadian government received applications to export automobile parts to China.[426] Where U.S. origin goods were involved they were refused but others were granted.[427]

There were complaints from one Canadian exporter however that it could not obtain automobile parts from two U.S. owned corporations, Chrysler Corporation of Canada Limited and Canadian Car Retailer, for shipment to China.[428] The Canadian government position seemed to be that were it asked for its assistance in securing the export permit from the U.S. for a U.S. parent, it would have been forthcoming,[429] but it would not become involved in the business decisions of corporations dealing with one another.[430]

Since 1960 Canadian trade with China had greatly expanded. In 1963, Canada exported (Cdn) $104.7 million worth of goods.[431] Nevertheless, from January 1, 1963 to June 30, 1967, the total number of export permits applied for was only 133. The implication is that transactions with China were large ones.[432]

In 1965 U.S. President Johnson introduced voluntary guidelines for U.S. corporations to help the U.S. with balance of payments difficulties.[433] The corporations were asked to restrain foreign investment and patriate earnings of their foreign subsidiaries.[434]

Perhaps using the U.S. idea, the Canadian Minister of Trade and Commerce issued guidelines for Canadian subsidiaries of foreign (i.e. U.S.) companies in March 1966.[435] The guidelines were sent by letter to selected corporations. It provided twelve desirable objectives, including the "maximum development of market opportunities in other countries as well as in Canada".[436] The response by companies to the guidelines was described by the government as highly encouraging.[437] Similarly, the response to the questionnaire, sent to the larger foreign-owned companies, was good.[438]

Canadian problems with U.S. export controls seemed to shift focus from China trade to Cuba at this point and both parliamentary and diplomatic attention were turned to Cuba. It is also possible that U.S. attention was diverted elsewhere as a result of a barrage of protests dealing with Cuban controls, and the 1965 French court action forcing through a sale by a French company despite its U.S. parent's direction not to complete the sale.[439] By 1969 the U.S. began phasing out some of its own export controls to China.[440] In June 1971 they were again watered down.[441] Until Feb. 14, 1972 China was controlled in the same manner as Soviet Bloc countries.[442] The U.S. controls remaining in force were still felt in Canada due to the working of Group 9 of its Export Control List. Under this provision, goods of U.S. origin could not be exported from Canada without export permits. The export permit for such goods to China would only be given where there was prior authorization under U.S. export control legislation.[443]

It seems doubtful that this situation was one in which Canadian action implementing export controls on China could not be criticised. In the first place, Canadian controls preceded U.N. action so it cannot be said to be taken for that reason. Second, the resolution of the General Assembly is doubtful legal justification for any measures. Third, even after the resolution, Canadian measures clearly went beyond the selected controls recommended by the U.N. The controls on arms and munitions can be supported as measures to contribute to the peace of nations. A total trade embargo can likely only be supported as a counter-measure based on a violation of international law (a reprisal or retortion). Continuation of the embargo after the armistice in 1953 raised the question of whether, the violation having ceased, there was any further legal justification for such measures. U.S. measures continued so long after the war that it is said that quite likely the U.S. measures violated the *U.N. Charter*.[444] The Canadian measures were not as drastic or as long-lasting after the end of the Korean war and thus were less open to criticism. If China had been a *GATT* member the measures would likely have violated the *GATT* but, that not being the case, the only violation of international legal obligations possible would depend upon the existence of a duty to trade or the measures being said to amount to aggression or intervention in Chinese affairs.

2. *Cuba*

Controls on exports to Cuba were imposed by the U.S. because of events following the overthrow of the government by Fidel Castro. The U.S. actions involved the control of both exports to and imports from Cuba. They also involved the attempt to control the exports to Cuba from third countries. The two main reasons for U.S. actions were the nationalization of U.S. interests in Cuba[445] and the subsequent threat posed by the Soviet military build-up there.[446]

Canadian action was taken to impose certain controls on exports to Cuba. Canada also reacted to the effect of the U.S. measures. The value of exports to Cuba in total terms however did not seem to be affected by either the Canadian action or the U.S. controls which affected Canadian trade, if a comparison is made of trade figures with those of previous years.

Year	*Value of exports (Cdn. $)*[447]
1956	15,283,863
1957	16,845,727
1958	17,548,726
1959	15,222,179
1960	13,037,868
1961	32,330,895
1962	11,498,060
1963	16,645,643

Canada did impose strategic controls on Cuba some time before Dec. 12, 1960.[448] In the House of Commons that day Prime Minister Diefenbaker stated:

> ... in trade relations with Cuba consideration is taken at all times of the strategic nature of any goods involved. In fact, in view of the troubled situation in the whole Caribbean area, we have not for some time permitted the export of arms, munitions and closely related goods to any part of that area including Cuba.[449]

The controls were obviously imposed by the exercise of discretion in granting permits for exports of strategic goods, because no special treatment of Cuba had been given in the regulations under the *EIPA*. Two weeks earlier, the Minister of Trade and Commerce was asked whether restrictions on strategic exports to communist countries applied equally to Cuba and answered they did not.[450]

Canada did have in place Group 9 of the Export Control List which would control re-export of U.S. origin goods. This was also the clear Canadian policy. Prime Minister Diefenbaker told the House that Canada did not intend to "exploit the situation arising from the United States embargo."[451] He also made it clear however, that there was no request from the U.S. for any particular action with respect to exports to Cuba.[452]

Days later Canada excluded Cuba as a destination for exports under the General Export Permit.[453] Thus proposed exports of strategic goods to Cuba had to undergo case by case consideration before they could be issued a permit. Canadian policy with respect to licensing strategic exports was expounded the same day in Parliament.

> The export control list incorporates materials which are classified as strategic by CoCom, the co-ordinating committee in Paris, in which agreement on strategic items is developed among NATO governments. The list includes arms and ammunition, military and related equipment, and raw materials which are of strategic significance. No permits have been, or will be, issued for export of these goods to Cuba.[454]

From this point it is clear that Canada was applying the CoCom list of strategic items with respect to Cuba, apparently on its own initiative.[455] Exports that were allowed in the previous two months were 17 in number and none of them strategic in nature.[456] The government understanding was that, where a Canadian exporter wished to ship non-strategic goods made in Canada to Cuba, no license was required.[457]

In 1961 76 export permits were issued for controlled items to Cuba having a value of (Cdn.) $3.27 million.[458] The exports included industrial grade dynamite, aircraft engines, synthetic rubber, sheet and strip steel and electric transformers.[459] Government insurance was granted for $270,000 worth of pharmaceuticals and supplies for making paper also exported to Cuba.[460]

The O.A.S. arms embargo to Cuba was adopted January 31, 1962.[461] It only resolved to study the imposition of other trade sanctions. The Prime Minister of Canada however, told the House that Canada had not been permitting the export of arms to Cuba "for more than two years", and had also not been allowing strategic materials to be exported to here.[462] Controls on U.S. origin goods were absolute. The Prime Minister stated it was his belief there was not even one instance of U.S. origin goods being re-exported to Cuba from Canada.[463] During 1961, 162 export permits were also issued under Group 9 at least one of which was in respect of U.S. goods.[464] It seems however that this involved permits issued with respect to shipments in bond through Canada and not re-exports. Canada required permits for U.S. origin goods and where goods were not on the Export Control List, the exporter would have to declare on customs form B-13 that the goods did not contain items imported from the U.S.[465] This double requirement prevented inadvertent re-exports of U.S. origin goods.

The O.A.S. Ministers of Foreign Affairs, meeting informally, agreed in October 1962 that it was "desirable to intensify individual and collective surveillance of the delivery of arms and implements of war and all other items of strategic importance to the communist regime of Cuba."[466] As the U.S. claimed:

> Our NATO allies have prohibited the export of any military items to Cuba, and they have indicated that they are not shipping any strategic items. They are also cooperating to assure that United States exports will not be diverted to Cuba through their ports.[467]

Whereas there was no CoCom arrangement to prohibit exports to Cuba,[468] certainly Canada was one of the "NATO allies" described in the U.S. claim.[469]

The Canadian export restrictions on Cuba up to this point would certainly have pleased the U.S. government, although it may have wished the Canadian controls to have been as restrictive as those of the U.S. The U.S. imposition of the *Cuban Assets Control Regulations* (*CACR*s)[470] on July 8, 1963 placed greater restrictions on Canadian companies. The *CACR*s froze Cuban assets and also extended the export controls to prohibit exports of persons "subject to the jurisdiction of the United States."[471]

The same definition of this phrase was used as under the *FACR*s with one major change. While the definition would encompass foreign companies owned or controlled by U.S. persons, an exemption was given to such companies.[472] It was however, known that, were the exemption to facilitate trade with Cuba, it would be withdrawn.[473] As well, the U.S. parent companies were "persuaded" to ensure their subsidiaries would not trade with Cuba.[474] There was no exemption made for directors or officers of the companies that were U.S. persons, although there was an exemption for the owner, if a U.S. person and not actually participating.[475]

Within a year there was evidence that the *CACR*s were affecting Canadian companies. In June 1964 the U.S. directors of a Canadian company were warned by the U.S. Treasury Department that they were liable to prosecution if the Canadian company went ahead with an export of drugs to Cuba without a Treasury license.[476] The Canadian Embassy made representations in support of the company to help it obtain a U.S. license. It also stated that if the U.S. Treasury insisted on maintaining extraterritorial control over the operations of Canadian companies, the situation it created in Canada would require examination at the highest level.[477] As a result a license was issued to cover the U.S. directors.[478]

July 8, 1964 the U.S. Treasury requested that Canadian banks provide information on U.S. dollar deposits held in head offices to the credit of Cuban interests.[479]

On July 26, 1964 the O.A.S. adopted a resolution that the governments of the American states suspend all trade "whether direct or indirect" with Cuba except in food and medical supplies.[480] The resolution was to be notified to the U.N. Security Council, as required by article 54 of the *U.N. Charter*. The Security Council had adjourned consideration of the U.S.-Cuba dispute pending a report from the O.A.S.[481] The Security Council, in the same resolution, also invited O.A.S. members to lend their assistance to achieve a peaceful solution to the dispute.[482] It also urged all other states however to refrain from any action which might increase the existing tensions between the U.S. and Cuba.[483] Thus the U.N. action was to encourage measures such as the Canadian embargo of arms and munitions[484] and to give the O.A.S. room to solve the dispute as a regional arrangement under Chapter VIII of the *U.N. Charter*.

The O.A.S. resolution could only bind its members in law and thus could be used by the U.S. as justification for its measures. It could have no direct legal effect on Canada however, as Canada had never been a member of the O.A.S. Even so, it is interesting to note that Canada-U.S. problems included exports of medical supplies, specifically excluded from the O.A.S. resolution, sent to Cuba for humanitarian reasons.

The Canadian Department of Trade and Commerce was briefed in August 1964 by the president of a Canadian pharmaceutical company, that the company had been told by its U.S. parent not to go ahead with two exports to Cuba. The board of directors of the Canadian company, a majority of whom were Canadian, managed to have issued a U.S. Treasury license for one transaction and a U.S. Commerce license for the other, which involved a re-export of U.S. origin goods.[485] The U.S. parent advised its subsidiary not to seek Canadian government assistance, and after the deal had gone through, to seek prior clearance with the parent in future.[486] This incident demonstrated the limitations of the Diefenbaker-Eisenhower agreement of 1958 on case by case consultation.[487] Where the incidents did not come to the Canadian government's attention, there was little its stand on the issue could accomplish.

Canada made informal representations through its Embassy in Washington again in September 1964. Its representations were to the effect that the State Department intercede to have a Treasury license issued to the parent of a Canadian company which had an order to fill with another Canadian company that was to ship to Cuba. The representations stated that Canada reserved its position on the question of principle. The company's parent told it that it could not do so without the license, and the parent filed for it. The State Department agreed to do so a month later, stressing that the case was exceptional because there was only a small amount involved and there was a pre-existing contract.[488]

In October 1964 the U.S. parent of a Canadian company was told its subsidiary was to cancel a service contract for Cubana Airlines flights in Canada or else U.S. airlines in Canada would be prohibited from using the subsidiary's service. The U.S. parent had been denied a Treasury license and had lost an appeal.[489] The Canadian government retaliated by threatening denial of Department of Transport contracts if the subsidiary did give up the contract.[490] The Canadian Embassy however also made informal representations on behalf of the companies involved and were told this was a case in which there was little room to manoeuver.

November 6, 1964 Canada sent the U.S. a note stating its position. The note relied on principle stating the *CACR*s were being administered in a way which interfered with Canadian companies in Canada and they "should not be given effect through the parent-subsidiary relationship or in any other way."[491] The note stated that Canada understood the *CACR*s would not be applied to U.S. subsidiaries in Canada, and control of directors or officers who were U.S. citizens would not accord with this understanding. Following this statement of principle an arrangement was made to have the U.S. directors replaced by Canadians, and a license was issued to a U.S. officer of the company.[492]

After the Canadian note there were no further known cases of Canadian companies being affected by U.S. export controls directly that could not be resolved. Indirect effects of the laws were more difficult to appreciate. The issue was raised by Canada at the March 1966 Joint Ministerial Committee on Trade and Economic Affairs.[493] The U.S. delegation agreed they would consult promptly where Canadian transactions were affected by U.S. foreign assets controls.[494] At about the same time Canada issued its guidelines for subsidiaries of foreign companies.[495]

Three months later another case was reported in the Canadian Parliament. Three Canadian flour mills owned by U.S. parents were alleged to have refused to bid on a contract to supply flour to Cuba.[496] The president of one company was quoted as stating his company would voluntarily act in a way to avoid conflicting with the U.S. Trading with the Enemy Act.[497] The Minister of Trade and Commerce replied that he had notified the company president of the Canadian guidelines, who said he subscribed to them.[498] The Minister said he told the company president that, were the Canadian industry to suffer, his attitude would be "quite different".[499] As a result this and other contracts were filled by Canadian controlled companies.[500]

Another incident occurred in April 1967 when a Canadian manufacturer of agricultural equipment was told by its U.S. parent that a Cuban order for parts would not be filled. The U.S. parent had apparently been told by the Treasury and State Departments it was preferable not to submit a license application. The Canadian company's president raised the matter with the Canadian Department of Trade and Commerce.[501] The matter was raised by Canada at the Joint Committee on Trade and Economic Affairs in June 1967.[502] The U.S. Secretary of the Treasury, wrote to the Canadian Minister of Trade and Commerce on July 7, 1967.[503] The letter stated that the *CACR*s exempted U.S. foreign subsidiaries because of Canadian "political sensitiveness" and that this was different "from the normal pattern of such regulations".[504] The controls could not be considered an invasion of Canadian sovereignty, he wrote. The problem was that the companies had U.S. officers or directors. This was perhaps the first indication of the U.S. view of the principles involved apart from its domestic practice.

A month later the Canadian Minister replied. Referring to the Eisenhower/Diefenbaker discussion in 1958, he wrote it was clear then that the Canadian government did not, nor could it, agree that nationality of directors could impede transactions by that company.[505] A formal note was sent to the U.S. State Department August 29, 1967 restating the same language.[506]

About a week later the Secretary of the Treasury replied that he agreed U.S. firms in Canada were to conduct themselves as good Canadian corporate citizens. He stated that there was a "seeming jurisdictional conflict" as well as a difference in trade policy.[507] A license was, however, granted to the U.S. parent some time later although U.S. officials emphasized it was a "one-time solution".[508] In April 1969 the same subsidiary apparently refused to fill an order for another Canadian company who intended to ship to Cuba. This intention had never been communicated to the company in question so it is uncertain what the problem was. Upon the Minister of Trade and Commerce sending the company a letter of enquiry however, the order was filled out of "increased production".[509]

The cases in which problems arose continued into the 1970s. In 1970 a Canadian company owned by a U.S. parent withdrew an offer to sell pulp to Cuba. It admitted to the Department of Industry, Trade and Commerce that a factor in its decision was that it was 90% held by its U.S. parent and its board of directors was composed largely of U.S. citizens. Later it admitted it had been told by its U.S.

parent to discontinue the negotiations. The Canadian company was referred to the Guidelines on Good Corporate Behaviour and that the Canadian government would support an application to the Treasury Department for a license. The company asked its parent to apply for a license[510] but in any case the sale never materialized.[511] Another case arose in June 1971 when an order was placed for drilling supplies with a Canadian company with a U.S. parent. The U.S. parent discouraged the order as it did a considerable volume of business with the U.S. government and only applied for a license when the president of the Canadian company contacted the Canadian Department of Industry, Trade and Commerce and threatened to resign. The U.S. parent applied to the U.S. Commerce Department rather than to the Treasury and, on discovering its error, did not wish to correct it. The Canadian government did not take action at this point because the order was successfully placed with a Canadian company.

In early 1974 a Canadian company, MLW-Worthington, received an order for 25 locomotives to be exported to Cuba.[512] The company was U.S. owned and its U.S. directors were subject to the *CACR*s. The U.S. parent's request for a license was denied. The Canadian government made representations to the U.S. government stating in part:

> The Canadian Government holds that the *Cuban Assets Control Regulations* of the U.S.A. should not be given effect in Canada through the parent-subsidiary relationship or in any other way ... the Canadian Government wishes to emphasize the significance of this issue and to urge the U.S.A. Government to remove on an urgent basis any restraint on the directors or officers of MLW-Worthington, who are also U.S.A. citizens, which might interfere with the proposed sale of the Canadian company.[513]

In the Canadian Parliament the Minister of Industry, Trade and Commerce stated that a solution to the problem would be the resignation of the U.S. directors which he expected would take place immediately.[514] The resignation of two U.S. directors was announced three days later, and the company announced its intent to pursue the deal. The deal was eventually closed.[515]

The MLW-Worthington incident was used by the government to gain support for its competition bill which provided a mechanism for the government to react to directions given from abroad to Canadian companies that would affect Canadian trade.[516] The deal was worth some $14 or 15 million and in 1972 all Canadian exports to Cuba were $58.9 million.[517]

During the years 1969 to 1973 a total of 575 applications for exports to Cuba were received, and only 34 (5.9%) were refused.[518] This suggests there was a high degree of understanding by Canadian exporters as to which exports would be allowed to go to Cuba by the Canadian government. In other words, Canadian trade policy seemed to be clear. Problems with U.S. controlled subsidiaries continued however and the Canadian government proposed measures to intervene where exports were prevented by a company's foreign owners.[519]

In late December 1974 Litton Industries of the U.S. instructed the president of its Canadian subsidiary to reject an offer for office equipment to be sold to Cuba.

On December 31, 1974 the Canadian government delivered a note to the U.S. State Department stating that a Canadian company had been effectively deterred from doing business with Cuba due to a corporate assessment of the relevance of U.S. legislation to the case in question. On Feb. 7, 1975 the State Department confirmed that a license was to be given in the case this case was discussed in Parliament.[520]

In mid-April 1975 another case arose in which the U.S. agreed to license a transaction by a Canadian company owned by the U.S. parent involving an export to Cuba. The license was given only after Canadian diplomatic intervention.[521]

On July 18, 1975 the Canadian government issued the "New Principles of International Business Conduct". The principles clarified the government's policy of having foreign-controlled business in Canada operate in such a way as to bring "significant benefit to Canada."[522] Principle 12 stated foreign-controlled firms should:

> give appropriate support to recognized national objectives and established government programs, while resisting any direct or indirect pressure from foreign governments or associated companies to act in a contrary manner.

Principle 5 specified that they should:

> aggressively pursue and develop market opportunities throughout international markets as well as in Canada.

The latter principle addresses the frequently voiced criticism that U.S. corporations tend to assign their Canadian subsidiaries restricted export territories or prohibit them from exporting altogether.[523]

The O.A.S. had made an attempt to remove its mandatory sanctions against Cuba but failed to obtain the necessary two-thirds majority.[524] On July 19, 1975 however the O.A.S. adopted a resolution that allowed each member to determine their own economic relations with Cuba.[525] This led the U.S. to change the *CACR*s in August 1975.[526]

The changes were made to the *CACR*s August 25, 1975.[527] Foreign subsidiaries were permitted to trade with Cuba if their government policy or law allowed it. U.S. origin goods were still subject to licensing, although a policy was expressed that they would be permitted where they made up no more than 20% of the value of an export to Cuba from a foreign country.[528] However the provision which had exempted U.S. owned or controlled companies abroad from the *CACR*s was revoked in October 1975.[529] The result was that the foreign subsidiaries were subject to U.S. licenses on a case-by-case basis.[530]

In the Spring of 1976 the Chief of the U.S. Office of Foreign Assets Controls, in the Department of Treasury, told a House subcommittee that some deals with foreign subsidiaries had been denied licenses. The Canadian government ordered the Director of Investigation and Research to begin an investigation under the provisions of the *Combines Investigation Act*. The investigation did not reveal that any Canadian firms had been thwarted in their attempts to export to Cuba.[531]

The final amendments to the *CACR*s allowed licensing of certain transactions where local law of policy favored trade with Cuba.[532] These 1977 amendments required the exports to meet six criteria before they could be exported from foreign owned subsidiaries.[533] The criteria required the commodities be non-strategic,[534] not to include technical data, where having U.S. origin parts, to have been licensed by the Commerce Department under the *Export Administration Act*, and not to involve U.S. dollar accounts.[535]

The most interesting part of the amendments required the foreign subsidiary to be "independent" to qualify for a license.[536] This provision was to prevent abuse of the restrictions on U.S. firms by use of their foreign subsidiaries.[537] Independence was to be determined on consideration of the conduct of the subsidiary in transactions of the same type, but was to be considered not independent when "there [were] a substantial number of officers or directors of the foreign affiliate who [were] also officers or directors of a person within the United States."[538]

Shortly after these *CACR* changes two other incidents arose. In November 1977 a Canadian company, wholly owned by a U.S. parent, wanted to sell chemicals to Cuba for use on its fishing vessels. The Office of Foreign Assets Control considered the subsidiary was not "independent" and stated that resignations of directors would not change the opinion as the material time was the time of contracting.

Another case in which the "independent" test caused a Canadian company problems was with respect to the sale to Cuba of X-ray equipment in 1978. Four of the seven directors of the Canadian company were also on the board of its U.S. parent. While the Canadian company was told it was not "independent" it was given a license on "an exceptional basis".[539]

Following these two cases the Canadian government delivered a note to the U.S. State Department on September 29, 1978. The note stated that Canada had frequently expressed serious concerns "at the highest level" regarding the extraterritorial application of U.S. law to control Canadian exports to Cuba. It continued that the 1977 *CACR* amendments raised questions of extraterritoriality, and that Canadian opposition to extraterritoriality was based on international law which is "particularly relevant to an economic boycott not accepted by Canada."[540]

The objections based on international law are illuminated by a memorandum of the Legal Bureau of the Secretary of State for External Affairs.[541] The memorandum stated that, while public international law allows states a wide discretion to exercise enforcement jurisdiction, it is only to be exercised within their territory unless based on a permissive rule of customary international law or treaty. This jurisdiction is even extended with respect to events outside its territory on certain grounds but is limited. One such limit is that:

> it appears a state is prevented from requiring such acts from its citizens abroad as are forbidden to them by the municipal law of the state in which they reside and from ordering them not to commit such acts as they are bound to commit according to the municipal law of the state in which they reside.[542]

It appears that with respect to imports the U.S. was interested in Canadian trade with Cuba as well. For instance, in 1979 the U.S. requested that U.S. Customs officials be allowed to visit Canadian sugar refineries to determine whether sugar of Cuban origin was adequately segregated from non-Cuban sugar so that none was in fact being exported to the U.S. The Canadian reply of April 24, 1979 was that one visit satisfied the U.S. Customs official and that now the Canadian government would investigate further.[543]

Despite the protest about the new amendments to the *CACR*s, the problems with their application continued. In February the U.S. parents of two Canadian corporations were told they would not get licenses to sell wheat to Cuba because of the presidential directive to limit wheat sales to the Soviet Union. By March 6, the licenses were reported to be issued.[544]

In October of 1980 a Canadian company owned by a British company which in turn was owned by a U.S. company, was frustrated in its attempt to export to Cuba. Its U.S. parent refused to apply for a license. In this case the Canadian government did not intervene.[545]

Despite the more prominent examples of U.S. export controls which affected foreign subsidiaries at about this time, for example the Soviet pipeline sanctions, it appears that Canada had continued to feel the effects of the U.S. controls on Cuba throughout the 1980s. One type of problem arose from occasional telephone calls to Canadian companies from U.S. consular officials to inform the companies of the reach of U.S. export control legislation. The Canadian Government had protested such calls as an attempt to inhibit Canadian firms from complying with Canadian policy promoting trade with Cuba.[546]

In 1982 a Cuban firm's Montreal branch is reported to have been refused an order in Canada by a wholly owned U.S. subsidiary. When the matter came to its attention, the Canadian government assured the Canadian company that it favored trade with Cuba. Despite the fact that the sale would have been of 100% Canada origin goods, it was not completed.[547]

There appear to have been some recent signs that the U.S. position with respect to Cuba is not merely to treat each case separately. For example, a Canadian company that had only been allowed to sell Canadian marine products to Cuba after the Canadian government had made strong representations to the U.S. State Department in earlier years, had a license given to its U.S. parent without government intervention in May 1980. In another example, spare parts for X-ray equipment were allowed to be shipped to Cuba.[548] While the examples are not numerous enough to indicate a trend, it may be suggested that in future one may look for examples of the U.S. licensing of categories of items that have been the subject of successful diplomatic intervention before.

These cases do not suggest a softening U.S. attitude with respect to exports to Cuba in general. The export of journalistic services was the subject of one recent press report.[549] A Canadian reporter, working in the U.S. for the partly Cuban-owned Prensa Latina of Canada Ltd., was told to apply for a license under the Treasury regulations. He left the U.S. in the belief that the license would be denied. Prensa Latina had had its U.S. license revoked in 1969 in retaliation for the Cuban closing of the Havana offices of UPI and Associated Press.[550]

The Canadian government in recent years has focused its diplomatic energies on the debate within the U.S. dealing with the renewal of the *Export Administration*

Act. The *CACR*'s continued existence however, leave no reason to assume that their application will not cause effects in Canada which the Canadian government may find objectionable.

3. Uganda

The U.S. embargo of Uganda was said to be the "first embargo imposed unilaterally by the U.S. for non-defence purposes."[551] It lasted only eight months from October 10, 1978 to May 17, 1979.[552] The regulations proposed by the Department of Commerce to implement the legislation imposing the embargo were never adopted in final form.[553] Nevertheless they did cause Canada to react.

Canada controlled the re-export of U.S. origin goods, through its regulations, by requiring permits for them.[554] The general rule applicable was that for U.S. origin goods Canada would determine what U.S. policy was with respect to any specific item and deny permits where the U.S. policy would be to prevent the re-export. This is what occurred for items of U.S. origin which were to be shipped to Uganda. Canada determined it would consult the U.S. with respect to U.S. origin items where there was doubt about what U.S. policy was.[555]

Despite any sympathy Canada might have shared for the aims of the U.S. embargo on Uganda, it was clear Canada would not accept the means by which the U.S. regulations proposed to implement it. Canada is reported to have commented critically upon the proposed regulations[556] in January 1979; since they purported to apply U.S. laws to Canadian corporations controlled in fact by U.S. persons.[557]

This example is a good one with which to illustrate the Canadian approach to unilateral U.S. controls. First, under its own regulations, Canada would control U.S. origin goods in the same way that the U.S. would have done. Second, regardless of the merit of the goals, or the justification of the measures, Canada would object to control of Canadian corporations being used as a lever to apply U.S. law.

4. Libya

The U.S. instituted export controls on Libya after the amendment of its *Export Administration Act* in 1979. Section 3(8) of the *EAA* specified that the policy of the U.S. was to use export controls to fight international terrorism. Section 6(a)(1) made it clear that the controls are part of the *EAA* foreign policy controls when instituted to fight terrorism.

The U.S. State Department named Libya as one of the states to which anti-terrorism controls would apply.[558] It was only in May 1980 that regulations specifically implementing special anti-terrorism controls were implemented.[559] Until then it had been supposed that the existing framework would suffice to control the flow of exports to designated countries supporting terrorism. The existing controls had been used to prevent the exports and re-exports of militarily significant items to Libya.[560] The re-export from Canada took place under the authority of a valid Canadian export permit. The transaction occurred in August 1977 and shows that even then there was a lack of harmony between the U.S. and Canadian measures with respect to Libya, despite the U.S. anti-terrorism export controls not yet having been put in place.[561] The main effect of the anti-terrorism controls on Canada was their control of the re-export of U.S. origin goods. Thus any U.S. component in a Canadian good might suffice for the U.S. to claim jurisdiction over the re-export.

Canada was more affected when U.S. policy changed to prohibit export of a greater number of items to Libya in March 1982.[562] The new regulations generally prohibited the export of all national items, oil and gas equipment and data not available outside the U.S. to Libya. There was considerable leniency with respect to contracts or exports made before the regulations came into force, and re-exports where the U.S. origin item was 20% or less were generally allowed.[563]

Canada imposed controls on all U.S. origin goods which had not been substantially changed in Canada.[564] In assessing items with U.S. components however, the Canadian position was that, if they amounted to 50% of the value or were readily removable, they would be considered of U.S. origin. As a practical matter the Canadian government recognized that the Canadian company might have its supplies interrupted by the U.S. supplier if it did not follow the U.S. rule so it did not object to the Canadian company seeking U.S. re-export authorization. Canada, being of the view that its controls were sufficient for the needs of Canadian and Western defence and foreign policy, declined to adopt the parallel of the U.S. regulations.[565]

It appears that at this time the only major Canadian sales to Libya would have involved civil aircraft. Although the Canadian government licensed at least one such export, the sale did not go through, although the aircraft had approximately 20% U.S. content and would likely have met even the U.S. test. This may have resulted from concern on the part of the Canadian company involved of losing sales in the more lucrative U.S. market – essentially a business decision. In another case a Canadian company was prosecuted for selling U.S. origin parts for airplanes to Libya.[566] On January 10 1986, Canada placed Libya on the Export Control List.[567]

5. Nicaragua

The U.S. regulations with respect to Nicaragua were made effective May 7, 1985. In this case the U.S. Treasury regulations implementing the embargo on exports to and imports from Nicaragua are largely territorial.[568] There is however, the likelihood of an effect on Canada that will be greater than that for other nations.

A provision in the Treasury rules specifies that the prohibitions do not apply to exports from outside the U.S.[569] The licensing requirements of the Commerce Department remain applicable however,[570] and, due to the Presidential order, any export licenses required under the Commerce Department's regulations will likely be denied. Thus, the re-export of U.S. origin goods is unlikely to be allowed. The same is true for U.S. technical data.

A specific problem with the Treasury regulations, the *NTCR*'s, for Canada is that transshipment through the U.S. of goods destined for Nicaragua, or coming from there, is prohibited.[571] Canada finds itself with the U.S. between it and Nicaragua. Thus, the most convenient routes for international transit are denied by the U.S. transshipment ban. Canada could invoke Article V(2) of the *GATT* for the right to such routes. The U.S. would have to invoke its "essential security interests" pursuant to Article XII(b) to justify denial of the right of transshipment.

While the *NTCR*'s do not have extraterritorial application, they do have extraterritorial effects. They will influence both the cost of Canadian trade with Nicaragua and the items that foreign countries may trade. U.S. origin goods may be exported to Nicaragua, however, if they are first "substantially transformed" abroad.[572] Canada will not be in a position to complain about this criterion as it matches the extent to which the Export Control List item 9001 requires permits for U.S. origin goods. Canada is likely to deny permits for shipment of U.S. origin goods not substantially changed in the same cases in which the U.S. would not allow them to be exported to Nicaragua.

The Canadian position has been to deny arms exports to countries where armed conflict exists. This is the policy which it has applied to deny arms exports to Nicaragua.[573] Canada sought and received assurances that the U.S. actions with respect to Nicaragua would not be extraterritorial prior to their introduction.[574]

Notes

1. A.F. Lowenfeld, *International Economic Law*, 2nd ed., vol. III (U.S.A.: Matthew Bender, 1983) [*Trade Controls for Political Ends*] at 432–33 [hereinafter *Lowenfeld*].
2. *Ibid.* at 436.
3. 20 UN SCOR 1257 3–8 (1965) as cited in *Lowenfeld*, *ibid.*
4. UNGA Res. 2024, 20 UN GAOR, Supp. 14 at 55, UN Doc. A/6014 (1965).
5. UNSC Res. 216, 20 SCOR Res. & Decs. at 8, UN Doc. S/Res. 216 (1965).
6. H.C. Debates, 1965, vol. I, pp. 775–76, Hon. Paul Martin, Secretary of State for External Affairs.
7. Press Release, Nov. 11, 1965 "Statement by the Prime Minister of Nov. 11, 1965" as cited in "Canadian Practice in International Law, 1965 and 1966" in (1967) 5 C.Y.I.L. at 334. See also the state of the measures on Feb. 2, 1966 in H.C. Debates, 1966, vol. I, Feb. 2, 1966, The Hon. Mr. R.H. Winters, the Minister of Trade and Commerce.
8. UN SC Res. 217, 20 SCOR Res. & Decs. at 8–9, UN Doc. S/Res. 217 (1965).
9. *Ibid.*
10. U.N. *Charter*, art. 34.
11. U.N. *Charter*, art. 39–51.
12. Note of the Secretary of State for External Affairs, the Hon. Paul Martin, to the British High Commissioner in Ottawa, Sir Henry Lintott, November 26, 1965, tabled in Parliament, H.C. Debates, 1966, vol. 1, p. 668, Feb. 3, 1966, Mr. Martin.
13. Note of the British High Commission, Ottawa, signed by A. Currall, to the Secretary of State for External Affairs, the Hon. Paul Martin, November 26, 1965.
14. P.C. 1965–2252, Dec. 20, 1965, SOR/66–4, 100 Can. Gaz. Pt II 6, Jan. 12, 1966.

15. H.C. Debates, 1966, vol. I, p. 499, Feb. 1, 1966, Mr. Paul Martin.
16. *Supra*, note 8.
17. C.C. Joyner, "International Sanctions – United Nations Security Council Resolution – Economic Sanctions against Southern Rhodesia" (1974) 14 Va. J. Int'l L. 319 at 323 [hereinafter *Joyner*].
18. *Lowenfeld, supra*, note 1 at 437.
19. *Ibid.*
20. *Ibid.*
21. *Ibid.* Britain acted under authority of the *Southern Rhodesia Act*, (Nov. 16, 1965) reprinted in *Lowenfeld, supra*, note 1 at DS–509.
22. The Southern Rhodesia (Prohibited Exports and Imports) Order 1966, (Jan. 20, 1966) reprinted in *Lowenfeld, ibid.* at DS–515.
23. H.C. Debates, 1966, vol. I, p. 645 at 646, Feb. 3, 1966, Mr. Martin.
24. *Ibid.* at 645.
25. SOR/66–89, Feb. 4, 1966, 100 Can. Gaz. Pt II 237, Feb. 23, 1966.
26. S.C. 1953–54, ss. 5–6 [hereinafter *EIPA*].
27. *Ibid.* at s. 3.
28. *Ibid.* at s. 3(a).
29. *Ibid.* at s. 3(b).
30. H.C. Debates, 1966, vol. I, p. 653, Feb. 3, 1966, Mr. Martin.
31. It was in effect by virtue of P.C. 1965–2252, *supra*, note 14, which placed Rhodesia on the Area Control List. See H.C. Debates, 1966, vol. I, p. 653, Feb. 3, 1966, Mr. Nesbitt.
32. H.C. Debates, 1966, vol. I, p. 699, Feb. 3, 1966, the exchange between Mr. Martin and Mr. Churchill.
33. R.S.C. 1952, c. 275 [hereinafter *U.N. Act*], later R.S.C. 1970, c. U–3, now R.S.C. 1985 c. U–3, which, in s. 2, requires a U.N. Security Council decision pursuant to article 41 of the *U.N. Charter*.
34. The government referred to the Commonwealth, in speaking of the sanctions, quite frequently, and the Commonwealth Sanctions Committee was referred to in H.C. Debates, 1967, vol. III, p. 3058, Oct. 12, 1967, Mr. John R. Matheson at 3059.
35. H.C. Debates, 1966, vol. X, p. 10,921, Dec. 9, 1966, Mr. Martin in response to the questions of Mr. Olson.
36. H.C. Debates, 1966, vol. X, p. 10,165, Nov. 22, 1966, Right Hon. Lester B. Pearson, the Prime Minister.
37. *Ibid.*
38. SC Res. 221, 5 UN Doc. S/INF/21/Rev. 1 (1966), April 19, 1966.
39. SC Res. 232, 21 SCOR, Res. & Decs. at 7, UN Doc. S/Res.232 (1966).
40. *Ibid.* at para. 2(d), (e).
41. *Ibid.* at para. 2(f)).
42. See *ibid.* at para. 3.
43. *Ibid.*
44. P.C. 1967–323, Feb. 21, 1967, SOR/67–93, 101 Can. Gaz. Pt II 324, Mar. 8, 1967.
45. *Supra*, note 39 at s. 31.
46. *Ibid.* at s. 9.
47. The resolution also required ships and aircraft registered in the member state be prohibited from shipping oil to Rhodesia. In this regard see ss. 7 and 8 of the Canadian regulations, *supra*, note 44.
48. *Supra*, note 44, s. 2(i)
49. *Ibid.* at s. 2(d))
50. *Ibid.* section 2(i) read:

    "person" in respect of the doing of any act or thing in any place other than Canada means, *except in section 10*, a Canadian citizen or a Canadian corporation ... (emphasis added).

51. *Supra*, note 44 at s. 10(3).
52. P.C. 1968–2339, Dec. 20, 1968, SOR/69–14, 103 Can. Gaz. Pt II 58, Jan. 8, 1969. See s. 2(i) thereof.
53. H.C. Debates, 1967, vol. II, p. 2380, July 7, 1967, Mr. Martin.
54. H.C. Debates, 1967, vol. III, p. 3058, Oct. 12, 1967, Mr. John R. Matheson, Parliamentary Secretary to the Prime Minister paraphrasing the address to the U.N. General Assembly given by the Secretary of State for External Affairs, September 27, 1967.
55. *Ibid.*
56. *Ibid.* at 3059.
57. Except for some goods of a humanitarian nature, SC Res. 253, 23 UN SCOR Res. & Decs. at 5, UN Doc. S/Res.253 (1968); reprinted in (1968) 7 Int'l Leg. Mat. 897.
58. H.C. Debates, 1967–68, vol. III, p. 7859, Mar. 20, 1968, The Hon. Paul Martin, Secretary of State for External Affairs.
59. P.C. 1968–2339, Dec. 20, 1968, SOR/69–14, 103 Can. Gaz. Pt II 58, Jan. 8, 1969.
60. *Ibid.* at s. 3(1).
61. *Ibid.* at s. 4.
62. *Ibid.* at s. 8.
63. *Ibid.* at s. 14.
64. *Supra* note 57, para. 3(d).
65. H.C. Debates, 1969, vol. II, p. 1253, the Hon. Mitchell Sharp, Secretary of State for External Affairs (Nov. 26, 1969).
66. H. C. Debates, 1968, vol. II, p. 2246, Oct. 31, 1968, Mr. Robert L. Stanfield and the Hon. Mitchell Sharp, Secretary of State for External Affairs.
67. SC Res. 277, 25 UN SCOR, Res. & Decs. at 5, UN Doc. S/Res./277 (1970); also see *Joyner*, *supra*, note 17 at 325.
68. *Joyner*, *ibid.* at 326.
69. SC Res. 314, 27 UN SCOR, Res. & Decs. at 7, UN Doc. S/Res./314 (1972), and SC Res. 318, 27 UN SCOR, Res. & Decs. at 8, UN Doc. S/Res./318 (1972).
70. E.A. Paschall, "The Price of United States Noncompliance with the United Nations Rhodesian Sanctions" (1975) 5 Ga. J. Int'l & Comp. L. 558 at 559 gives the legislative history of the bill which became section 503 of the *Military Procurement Act* of 1971, Nov. 17, 1971, H.R. 8687, Pub. L. 92–156, 85 Stat. 423 at 427.
71. *Ibid.* at 564.
72. H.C. Debates, 1972–1973, vol. IV, p. 3872, May 17, 1973, the Hon. Mitchell Sharp.
73. SC Res. 333, UN Doc. S/Res./333, May 22, 1973, para. 4.
74. *Ibid.* at para. 4(e).
75. *Ibid.* at para. 5.
76. Dec. 17, 1979, 80 Dep't State Bull. 12, Feb. 1980.
77. P.C. 1979–3509, Dec. 19, 1979, SOR/80–30, 114 Can. Gaz. Pt II 103, Jan. 9, 1980, effective Dec. 28, 1979.
78. UN Doc. S/13699 (1979).
79. 18 UN SCOR, UN Doc. S/P.V. 5386 (1963). See also M.J. Mehlman, T.H. Milch, and M.V. Toumanoff, "United States Restrictions on Exports to South Africa" (1979) 73 Am. J. Int'l L. 581 [hereinafter *Mehlman*] for a good history of the U.N. measures and U.S. action.
80. GA Res. 1761, 17 UN GAOR Supp. No. 17, at 102; UN Doc. A/5217 (1962). In this regard see also J. Davis, J. Cason and G. Hovey, "Economic Disengagement and South Africa: The Effectiveness and Feasibility of Implementing Sanctions and Divestment" (1983) 15 L. & Pol. Int'l Bus. 529 at 530–31, n. 8.
81. The U.N. Security Council Resolution 181 was recommendatory and not binding under Chapter VII of the *U.N. Charter*.
82. H.C. Debates, 1963, vol. IV, p. 3800, Oct. 21, 1963, Hon. Paul Martin, Secretary of State for External Affairs.
83. *Ibid.*

84. *Ibid.*
85. *Ibid.*
86. Since April, 1969, the Department of Industry, Trade and Commerce; in 1985 this Export Permits Branch was placed in the Department of External Affairs.
87. Except with respect to spare parts for items supplied prior to Resolution 181.
88. SC Res. 182, 18 UN SCOR, UN Doc. S/P.V. 5471 (1963).
89. See H.C. Debates, 1966, vol. I, p. 696, Feb. 3, 1966, Mr. Martin.
90. See H.C. Debates, 1966, vol. VI p. 6133, June 8, 1966, the Hon. Mr. Winters, Minister of Trade and Commerce.
91. H.C. Debates, 1972–83, vol. V, p. 4924, June 19, 1973, Mr. Gus Mitges.
92. H.C. Debates 1966, vol. VI, p. 6133, the Hon. Mr. Winters.
93. H.C. Debates, 1968, vol. II, p. 2246, Oct. 31, 1968, the exchange between Mr. Robert Stanfield and The Hon. Mitchell Sharp, Secretary of State for External Affairs.
94. *Ibid.*
95. UN Doc. A/Res. 2621 (XXV), adopted by a vote of 86 to 5 with 15 abstentions, Oct. 12, 1970.
96. A case which will be examined below.
97. UNGA Res. 2621, para. 3(3)(b)(iii).
98. H.C. Debates, 1971, vol. III, p. 2930, Feb. 1, 1971, Mr. Bruce Howard.
99. H.C. Debates 1976, vol. I, p. 938, Nov. 10, 1976, Mr. C. Wagner. This was not called for until the UNSC Res. 282, UN Doc. S/Res./282, July 23, 1970, in paragraph 4(c) called for termination of supply of spare parts. This, however, was not mandatory.
100. H.C. Debates, 1972–73, vol. IV, p. 3337 at 3338, June 21, 1972, Mr. Bruce Howard, Parliamentary Secretary to the Minister of Industry, Trade and Commerce.
101. H.C. Debates, 1972–73, vol. V, p. 4924, June 19, 1973, Mr. Gus Mitges.
102. *Ibid.*
103. H.C. Debates, 1972–73, vol. V, p. 5503, July 11, 1973, Hon. Mitchell Sharp, Secretary of State for External Affairs. It also announced that it neither encouraged nor discouraged investment in South Africa.
104. UN Doc. S/11712 (1975); reprinted at 73 U.S. Dep't State Bull. 45 July 7, 1975.
105. *Ibid.* at para. 10,
106. Letter of Leslie O. Harriman, Chairman, Special Committee Against Apartheid, of Sept. 9, 1976 to Mr. Kurt Waldheim, Secretary General, United Nations, New York.
107. Adopted by 101 to 15 (including Canada) with 16 abstentions. Canada apparently voted against because it condemned all states with economic ties with South Africa.
108. The states implicated in the letter were France, the Federal Republic of Germany, the U.K. and the U.S.
109. H.C. Debates 1976, vol. I, p. 938, Nov. 10, 1976, Mr. Claude Wagner and Hon. Donald C. Jamieson referring to GA Res. 31/6D (XXXI), Nov. 9, 1976, which was adopted by a vote of 110 to 8 with 20 abstentions (including Canada).
110. E.g. see GA Res. 32/105K of Dec. 14, 1977, adopted by a vote of 113 to 0, with 27 abstentions (including Canada); UNGA Res. 3411G (XXX), of Dec. 10, 1975 adopted by vote of 101 to 15 (including Canada) with 16 abstentions.
111. UNGA Res. 31/6H (XXXI), quite similar to 32/105K, condemning all economic activity with South Africa as collaboration which was said to be a "hostile act". It was adopted by a vote of 110 to 6 with 24 abstaining (including Canada). Canada abstained for the same reasons as it did for resolution 32/105K.
112. SC Res. 418, Nov. 4, 1977, UN Doc. S/Res.418 (1977), para. 1.
113. *Ibid.* at para. 2.
114. *Ibid.* at para. 4.
115. P.C. 1973–1105, May 8, 1973, effective May 23, 1973, SOR/73–253, 107 Can. Gaz. Pt II 1100, May 23, 1973, item 10,003.
116. E.g. U.K.: The South Africa (United Nations Arms Embargo Prohibited Transactions) Order 1978, S.I. 1978, No. 277, Mar. 1, 1978, effective Mar. 24, 1978.

117. UNSC Res. 421, Dec. 9, 1977, UN Doc. S/Res./421 (1977).
118. *Ibid.* at para. 1(a) and (b).
119. *Ibid.* at para. 1(c).
120. A church group wanted the Canadian federal government to prevent Canadian banks from doing business with South Africa. See "Churches Oppose S. African deals" *Ottawa Journal* (Nov. 7, 1977) National News Section 5.
121. "Canadian Policy Towards South Africa", No. 77/23 Statements and Speeches, External Affairs Canada, Dec. 19, 1977; also at H.C. Debates, 1977–78, vol. II, p. 2000, Dec. 19, 1972, Mr. Donald Jamieson.
122. *Ibid.* at 2.
123. The main task of these officers is to promote Canadian exports.
124. *Supra*, note 121.
125. European Community Information Service, Ottawa, N.R. (77) 32, Oct. 4, 1977.
126. *Ibid.* at para. 7.
127. "A South African Code of Employment Practice", South African Employers' Consultative Committee on Labour Affairs, Press Release, Dec. 7, 1977, the "Sullivan Code", or the "State of Principles of U.S. Firms with Affiliates in the Republic of South Africa" March 1977; "ASSOCOM's 40 Principles" (ASSOCOM is the Associated Chamber of Commerce) Information Digest Issue 37/1978, Sept. 16, 1978, Durban Chamber of Commerce; and the Newsome Code of 1973, the British and Dutch Codes which are cited in M.D. Copithorne, "Codes of Conduct for Foreign Business in South Africa: the Canadian Experience" Notes for a speech to the J.B. Moore Society, University of Virginia, Charlottesville, April 24, 1979 [hereinafter *Copithorne*].
128. UNGA Res. 32/1050, Dec. 16, 1977.
129. Also see: UNSC Res. 191, UN Doc. S/INF/19 (1964); and UNSC Res. 282, UN Doc. S/INF/25 (1970).
130. H.C. Debates, 1977–78, vol. IV, p. 3994, Mar. 21, 1978, Mr. Rodriguez at 3995.
131. *Ibid.*
132. Communiqué No. 44, Department of External Affairs.
133. But see *Copithorne*, *supra*, note 127 at 7, who says Codes are to address change within limits of South African law.
134. *Copithorne*, *supra*, note 127 at 5.
135. Canadian Press, Ottawa, Wire Report AG141, Dec. 7, 1978.
136. H.C. Debates, 1980–83, vol. II, p. 2176, June 17, 1980, Hon. Flora MacDonald.
137. UN Doc. S/14179, Sept. 19, 1980 at 7–8.
138. The U.K. has had a *Code of Practice* since 1974 (Cmnd. 5845), and a new *Code of Conduct* since 1978 (Cmnd. 7233). See also John Smite, Secretary of State for Trade, *Code of Conduct for Companies with Interests in South Africa*, Feb. 15, 1979, which included lists of reporting companies.
139. H.C. Debates, 1980–83, vol. XI, p. 11763, Oct. 4, 1981, The Hon. Mark MacGuigan.
140. SC Res. 473, June 13, 1973, UN Doc. S/Res.473 (1980), para. 11.
141. UN Doc. S/14179, Sept. 19, 1980.
142. *Ibid.* at 27.
143. *Ibid.* at 28–29 with the U.K., France and the U.S. objecting to some or all.
144. Items such as aircraft, electronic, and telecommunications equipment and computers. (see *ibid.* recommendation (vi)).
145. Task force on the Churches and Corporate Responsibility, "Canadian Policy Towards Southern Africa", May 5, 1981.
146. *Ibid.* at 3.
147. *Ibid.* at 4, para. 14–15. Texas Gulf, 30.7% owned by the Canada Development Corporation (CDC) and Connaught Laboratories, Ltd., 100% owned by the CDC were the examples. It was also alleged that Ford of Canada should be held accountable for a Ford, U.S. subsidiary building vehicles for the South African Defence Force under

contract, although no government ownership was involved. The U.N. Security Council committee recommended that four-wheel drive vehicles destined for the army or police should not be exported (UN Doc. S/14179, p. 18, recommendation (vi)) There is no indication if the Ford contract was for four-wheel drive vehicles.

148. *Supra*, note 145 at 8.
149. *Ibid.* at 12.
150. *Ibid.*
151. "South Africa: Nuclear Safeguards and Exports and Announcement" 84 Dep't State Bull. 57, Mar. 1984.
152. *Ibid.*
153. SC Res. 558, UN Doc. S/Res.558, Dec. 13, 1984.
154. UN Doc. S/14179, Sept. 19, 1980.
155. *Legal Consequences for States of the Continued Presence of South Africa in Namibia (South West Africa)* [1971] I.C.J. Rep. 1 at 51–53.
156. SC Res. 276 preamble and para. 2, UN Doc. S/Res.276, Jan. 30, 1970,
157. SC Res. 264, UN Doc. S/Res./264, Mar. 20, 1969.
158. SC Res. 269, UN Doc. S/Res./269, Aug. 12, 1969.
159. SC Res. 283, UN Doc. S/Res./283, July 29, 1970, para. 4.
160. *Ibid.* at para. 5–7.
161. *Ibid.* at para. 11.
162. UN Doc. A/AC.131/L.155; Official Records of the General Assembly, 29th session, Supplement No. 24A (A/9626/Add.1, para. 84) approved by UNGA Res. 3295 (XXIX), Dec. 13, 1974.
163. *Ibid.* at para. 1 and 2.
164. *Ibid.* at para. 4 and 5.
165. UNGA Res. 1803 (XVII), Dec. 14, 1962.
166. *Supra*, note 159, para. 4.
167. UN Doc. S/11713 (1975); reprinted in 73 Dep't State Bull. 45, July 7, 1975.
168. *Ibid.* at para. 10.
169. H.C. Debates, 1974–76, vol. XII, p. 12,136, Mar. 25, 1976, Mr. Bill Clarke and Hon. Allan J. MacEachen, Secretary of State for External Affairs, and H.C. Debates, 1974–76, vol. VI, p. 5543, May 6, 1975, Mr. Maurice Foster.
170. H.C. Debates, 1974–76, vol. VI, p. 5543, May 6, 1975, Mr. Maurice Foster.
171. See, for example, *ibid.* Mr. John Rodriguez.
172. "Council for Namibia asks 'Urgent' Meeting of Security Council to Impose 'Comprehensive and Mandatory Sanctions' against South Africa", U.N. Press Release NAM/517, June 3, 1980.
173. L. Meret, "Canada and Namibia" (1979) 17 C.Y.I.L. 314 at 318–21.
174. *Supra*, note 145.
175. *Ibid.* at p. 17.
176. The C.B.C. news programme, The National, Sept. 15, 1981 at 11:00 p.m.
177. Information from officers of the Department of External Affairs.
178. Dec. 16, 1975 from which Canada abstained.
179. *Ibid.* at art. 16.
180. *Ibid.* at art. 17.
181. "Seminar on Legal Issues Concerning the Question of Namibia", UN Doc. A/AC.131/SLI/PV.3, Sept. 8, 1981 at 7.
182. *Ibid.*
183. "Implementation of Decree No. 1 for the Protection of the Natural Resources of Namibia", UN Doc. A/Conf. 120/11, April 8, 1983 at 9.
184. *Supra*, note 104 at 12.
185. *Supra*, note 106 at 10.
186. *Ibid.* at 11.
187. UN Doc. A/Res./1699, Dec. 19, 1961.

188. H.C. Debates, 1963, vol. IV, p. 3800, Oct. 21, 1963, Hon. Paul Martin, Secretary of State for External Affairs.
189. H.C. Debates, 1963, vol. VI, p. 6309, Dec. 21, 1963, Mr. Douglas and Mr. Martin.
190. "Canadian Practice in International Law, 1973" (1974) 12 C.Y.B.I.L. 304 at 311–12; also see H.C. Debates, 1974, vol. II, p. 1616, Apr. 22, 1974, Hon. Mitchell Sharp.
191. UNGA Res. 1807 (XVII), and UNGA Res. 1913 (XVIII).
192. SC Res. 5380, UN Doc. S/Res./5380, July 31, 1963 and SC Res. 218, UN Doc. S/Res./218, 23 Nov. 1965.
193. H.C. Debates, vol. IV, p. 3800, Oct. 21, 1963, Hon. Paul Martin.
194. "Soviet Invasion of Afghanistan", President's Address, Jan. 4, 1980, 80 U.S. Dep't State Bull., Special, Jan., 1980.
195. SC Plenary Session of January 7, 1980; UN Doc. S/PV.2190 and Corr. 1 and Add.1, p. 8, para. 72.
196. *Trade Agreement Between Canada and the Union of Soviet Socialist Republics*, instruments of ratification exchanged, May 26, 1956, Can. T.S. 1956 No. 1.
197. *Supra*, note 195.
198. *Ibid.*
199. U.N. Doc. S/P V./2190, Jan. 7, 1980; reprinted in 80 Dep't State Bull. A, Special, Jan., 1980.
200. The reference was SC Res. 462, UN Doc. S/Res./462, Jan. 9, 1980.
201. UNGA 6th Emergency Special Session of 11 January 1980, UN Doc. A/ES–6/L.1, p. 16, para. 19.
202. GA Res. ES–6/2; UN Doc. A/Res./ES–6/2 Jan. 15, 1982; reprinted in (1980) 19 Int'l Leg. Mat. 246.
203. M. Trueman, "Clark Would Consider Moving Olympics to Montreal" *Toronto Globe and Mail* (Jan. 12, 1980) 2.
204. *Supra*, note 196, article III, para. 2.
205. *Supra*, note 203.
206. Concluded in Ottawa, July 14, 1976, Can T.S. 1976 No. 9.
207. Statement of Secretary General Luns. Document in the files of the Department of External Affairs.
208. Especially the grain embargo and high technology measures.
209. H.C. Debates, 1980–83, vol. I, p. 62, April 16, 1980, Right Hon. P.E. Trudeau.
210. *Ibid.* See also H.C. Debates, 1980–83, vol. I, p. 298, April 22, 1980, Hon. Mark MacGuigan, Secretary of State for External Affairs.
211. *Ibid.*
212. MacGuigan, *ibid.*
213. *Ibid.* at 298.
214. *Ibid.* at 299.
215. H.C. Debates, 1980–83, vol. I, p. 558, April 29, 1980, Mr. Louis Duclos, reprinted in "Canadian Practice in International Law, 1980" (1981) 19 C.Y.I.L. 347 at 357–58.
216. Information made available by the Department of External Affairs.
217. As was requested for the U.S. grain embargo.
218. 31 C.F.R. 505 (1983).
219. *Ibid.* at 505.10.
220. *Ibid.* at 500.330, made applicable to part 505 by virtue of *ibid.* 505.20.
221. *Ibid.* at 505.31.
222. *Ibid.* at 505.31(a)(2).
223. Note of July 7, 1982, Canadian Embassy in Washington to the U.S. Dept. of State.
224. Press Conference July 7, 1982, transcripts in files of S.S.E.A.
225. *Ibid.*
226. *Ibid.*
227. E.P. Mendes, "U.S. Uses Export Rule as a Foreign Enforcer", *Globe and Mail* (Aug. 9, 1982) 7.

228. *Ibid.*: *Combines Investigation Act*, R.S.C. 1970 c. C–23 as am. S.C. 1974–75–76 & 77, ss. 31.5 and 31.6 now ss. 54 and 55 of the *Competition Act*, S.C. 1986, c. 26.
229. Department of External Affairs, Communiqué No. 121, Aug. 9, 1982. Also see "Siberian Pipeline Dispute" Nov./Dec. 1982 International Perspectives, Supp. 12.
230. Editorial, "Push v. Shove" *Globe and Mail* (Sept. 1, 1982) 7.
231. In a letter dated Feb. 9, 1983, Hon. André Ouellet, Minister of Consumer and Corporate Affairs, wrote to the Secretary of State for External Affairs advising that the inquiry pursuant to section 14(2) of the *Combines Investigation Act* (CIA) with respect to the U.S. trade sanctions had been discontinued. He reported that one large Canadian company which was the subsidiary of a U.S. firm refrained from making shipments to the U.S.S.R. due to the U.S. *EAA* but within days of this event the U.S. sanctions were lifted and the company had then proceeded with shipments to the Soviet Union. The Director of Research and Investigation under the *CIA* did not discover any other situation.
232. See Chapter VI, Section A.2(a)(ii).
233. Requisition Order for Services issued pursuant to Ordinance No. 59.63 of Jan. 6, 1959 and Decree No. 62.367 of March 26, 1962, as cited in Bransvold at 325, note 210.
234. *The Protection of Trading Interests (U.S. Re-export Control) Order* 1982, S.I. 1982, No. 885, in force July 1, 1982.
235. "Geosource Unit Told to Honor Pipeline Contract" Dow Jones, Sept. 17, 1982, LZ 09/17 reported a Court ordering a Dutch company, Sensor Nederland B.V., owned by a U.S. parent to comply with its contract to supply equipment for the Soviet pipeline, *Compagnie Européenne des Pétroles, S.A.* v. *Sensor Nederland, B.U.* (Dist. Ct., The Hague, Sept. 17, 1982) 36 Rechtspraak Vaude, Week-Kort Gerding 167, reprinted (1983), 22 Int'l Leg. Mat. 66; *Lowenfeld, supra*, note 1 at 297.
236. "Bonn Splits with Paris over U.S. Licenses Pipeline Orders" Dow Jones, July 23, 1982, I. LNG 01/27 LG.
237. "Volvo Unit says U.S. Stops Oil Rig Rental to Soviets" Dow Jones, Sept. 29 1982, G/EXE 01/34 OG.
238. "Europe Trade Officials to Meet on Pipeline Sanctions" Dow Jones, Sept. 2, 1982, I/LNG 01/28 LO. But their most united action came in the form of a formal protest from the Commission of European Communities to the U.S. Department of State of August 12, 1982 accompanied by Comments [hereinafter *Comments*]; reprinted in A.V. Lowe, *Extraterritorial Jurisdiction* (Cambridge, England: Grotius, 1984) at 197–211 [hereinafter *Lowe*].
239. *Lowe, ibid.* at 198, para. 2.
240. *Ibid.* Comments at para. 4.
241. *Ibid.* Comments at para. 7.
242. *Ibid.* Comments at para. 8, pointing out there was jurisprudence to the contrary: *American President Lines* v. *China Mutual Trading Co.* [1953] A.M.C. 1510 at 1526 (Hong Kong Sup. Ct.) and *Moens* v. *Ahlers North German Lloyd*, (1966) 30 R.W. 360 (Tribunal of Commerce, Antwerp).
243. *Ibid.* Comments at para. 13.
244. *Ibid.* Comments at para. 15.
245. *Ibid.* Comments at para. 161.
246. *Ibid.* Comments at para. 17–23.
247. C. Waddell, "U.S. Writes – but Why to Nova?" *Financial Post* (Oct. 16, 1982) 18.
248. Letter of Sept. 27, 1982, from Lawrence J. Brady, Assistant Secretary for Trade Administration, U.S. Department of Commerce, International Trade Administration, to Nova, an Alberta Corporation, Calgary, Alberta.
249. *Ibid.* See also "U.S. Seeks Export Data from Pipeline Suppliers" *New York Times* (Oct. 1, 1982) Business Day 1 cont'd. on D–15.
250. Information from officers of the Department of External Affairs.
251. It was Dresser (France) S.A. which was the object of a temporary Denial Order issued

against it by the Department of Commerce, 47 Fed. Reg. 38,170 (Aug. 30, 1982).
252. Files of Department of External Affairs.
253. Implemented by 47 Fed. Reg. 51,858 (Nov. 18, 1982).
254. "East-West Trade Relations and Soviet Pipeline Sanctions", Nov. 13, 1982, 83 Dep't State Bull. 28, Jan. 1983; 18 Weekly Comp. Press. Docs. 1475 (Nov. 13, 1982).
255. "U.S. Pact with Allies Seen as Step to Harder Line on East" Dow Jones, Nov. 15, 1982 I/LMG 01/31 MV.
256. After a meeting of Secretary of State George Schultz and French Foreign Minister Claude Cheysson, B. Gwertzman, "U.S. and France Agree on Studies to Unify Strategy on Soviet Trade" *New York Times* (Dec. 15, 1982) A–1.
257. H.C. Debates, 1979, vol. I, p. 984–85, Nov. 6, 1979.
258. H.C. Debates, 1979, vol. II, p. 1782, Nov. 28, 1979.
259. H.C. Debates, 1979, vol. II, p. 1684, Nov. 26, 1979, Right Hon. Joe Clark, Prime Minister.
260. H.C. Debates, 1980–83, vol. III, p. 2982 at 2983, July 16, 1980, Hon. Flora MacDonald.
261. UNSC Res. 457, UN Doc. S/Res./457 (1970).
262. UNSC Res. 461; UN Doc. S/Res./461 (1970).
263. *Ibid.* at para. 6.
264. *Ibid.* at para. 5. See also A.F. Lowenfeld, *International Economic Law*, 2d ed., vol.I (U.S.A.: Bender Pub., 1981) [*International Private Trade*] at 565–66 [hereinafter *Lowenfeld Vol. I*].
265. UN Doc. S/P.V./2190, Jan. 7, 1980.
266. UN Doc. S/13,735 (1980).
267. UN Doc. S/Res./263 (1968).
268. *Lowenfeld Vol. I, supra*, note 264 at 566.
269. H.C. Debates, 1980–83, vol. I, p. 62, April 16, 1980, Hon. Ray Hnatyshyn and Right Hon. P.E. Trudeau, Prime Minister.
270. *Ibid.* The Canadian election was held Feb. 18, 1980.
271. H.C. Debates, 1980–83, vol. III, p. 2981, July 16, 1980, Hon. Mark MacGuigan, Secretary of State for External Affairs reprinted in "Canadian Practice in International Law, 1980" (1981) C.Y.I.L. 347 at 372.
272. *Ibid.*
273. P.C. 1980–1397, May 22, 1980, SOR/80–374, 114 Can. Gaz. 1928, Extra, May 22, 1980.
274. H.C. Debates, 1980–83, vol. III, p. 2981, Hon. Mark MacGuigan, July 16, 1980.
275. *Ibid.*
276. *Ibid.*
277. *Ibid.*
278. *Supra*, note 273.
279. *Supra*, note 274 at 2982.
280. H.C. Debates, 1980–83, vol. III, p. 2982, July 16, 1980, Hon. Flora MacDonald, and at 2984, July 16, 1980, Hon. Stanley Knowles.
281. H.C. Debates, 1980–83, vol. III, p. 3051, July 17, 1980.
282. S.C. 1980–81–82–83, c. 39, s. 3.
283. R.S.C. 1970, c. E–17, s. 3(b).
284. *IESA*, *supra*, note 282 at s. 2 defines a Canadian corporation as one incorporated in Canada.
285. *Ibid.* at section 3(e).
286. *Ibid.* at section 3(f).
287. H.C. Debates, 1980–83, vol. III, p. 2981, Hon. Mark MacGuigan, July 16, 1980.
288. *Supra*, note 282 at section 9(1).
289. "Iranian Economic Sanctions Act Proclamation Declaring that the Act Ceases to be in Force March 3, 1981" S.I./81–62, March 3, 1981, 115 Can. Gaz. Pt II 1231, April 22,

1981.

290. P.C. 1981–560, March 3, 1981, SOR/81–210, 115 Can. Gaz. Pt II 820, March 25, 1981.
291. Lowenfeld Vol. I, *supra*, note 264 at 591.
292. H.C. Debates, 1980–83, Vol. XIV, p. 16,097, April 2, 1982, Hon. Mark MacGuigan, Secretary of State for External Affairs.
293. UN Doc. S/Res./502, April 3, 1982, April 5, 1982.
294. H.C. Debates, 1980–83, vol. XIV, p. 16,134, April 5, 1982, Hon. Mark MacGuigan.
295. H.C. Debates, 1980–83, vol. XV, p. 16,694, April 28, 1982, Hon. Mark MacGuigan.
296. *Ibid.*
297. 25 O.J. Eur. Comm. (No. L 102), 1 (1982).
298. J.L. Amine, "Economic Sanctions: Falkland Islands (Malvinas)" (1983) 23 Harv. J. Int'l L. 404 at 406 [hereinafter *Amine*]. Also see J.-L. Dewost, "La Communauté, les Dix, et les "sanctions" économiques: de la crise iranienne à la crise des Malvines" (1982) Ann. Fr. Dr. Int'l 215 at 222–24.
299. The Control of Gold, Securities, Payments and Credits (Argentine Republic) Directions 1982, S.I. No. 512 (1982). See *Amine*, *ibid.* at 405 for a description.
300. Bank of England Notice 3–7, April 13, 1982, as cited in *Amine*, *ibid.* at 405 n. 3.
301. P.C. 1982–1276, April 26, 1982, SOR 82–442, 116 Can. Gaz. Pt II 1611.
302. Files of S.S.E.A.
303. *GATT* Doc. L/5317, April 30, 1982.
304. *Ibid.* See also *Amine*, *supra*, note 298 at 407-08.
305. *Ibid.* at para. III.
306. *Ibid.* at para. V.
307. Article 33 of the U.N. *Charter*.
308. *Amine*, *supra*, note 298 at 408.
309. H.C. Debates, 1980–83, vol. XVI, p. 17,864, May 28, 1982, Mr. Douglas Roche, Hon. Flora MacDonald.
310. *Ibid.* Hon. Mark MacGuigan.
311. *Ibid.*
312. *Ibid.* also at 17,980, June 1, 1982, Hon. Mark MacGuigan.
313. P.C. 1982–2008, July 8, 1982, SOR 82–667, 116 Can. Gaz. Pt II 2549, July 28, 1982, revoking P.C. 1982–1276, April 26, 1982, SOR 82–442, 116 Can. Gaz. Pt II 1611, May 12, 1982.
314. E.E.C. Council Reg. No. 1577/82/23 O.J. L/177 (June 22, 1982), The European Coal and Steel Community had also imposed measures: 82/211/ECSC, O.J. No. L/102 (April 4, 1982) 3; 82/320/ECSC O.J. No. L/136 (May 18, 1982) 2; 82/324/ECSC O.J. No. L/146 (May 25, 1982), 2. These were repealed by 82/413/ECSC (June 21, 1982).
315. "Argentina, Sanctions Lifted" (Sept./Oct. 1982) International Perspectives, Supp. at 8.
316. *Amine*, *supra*, note 298 at 409.
317. League of Arab States Resolution No. 849, Dec. 11, 1954, as cited in A.F. Lowenfeld, "... 'Sauce for the Gander': The Arab Boycott and United States Political Trade Controls" (1977) 12 Texas Int'l L.J. 25 at 26 [hereinafter *Lowenfeld 'Sauce'*].
318. *Ibid.* at 26.
319. See *Lowenfeld*, *supra*, note 1, at 313–14.
320. *Lowenfeld 'Sauce'*, *supra*, note 317. This is very much like typical trading with the enemy legislation used by common law countries in time of war: compare with M. Domke, *Trading with the Enemy in World War II* (New York: Central Book, 1943) at 154, and the legislation appended to that book.
321. *Lowenfeld 'Sauce'*, *supra*, note 317 at 27.
322. *Ibid.* at 27.
323. *Ibid.* at 27–28.
324. H.C. Debates, 1964, vol. I, p. 9, Feb. 19, 1964.
325. *Lowenfeld*, *supra*, note 1 at 322.

326. One statement that was made by the then Prime Minister of Canada was that "the boycott is alien to everything the government stands for and indeed to what Canadian ethics stand for", cited in *Lowenfeld*, *supra*, note 1 at 409.
327. *Ibid.*
328. Statement on Motions by the Secretary of State for External Affairs, the Honourable Don Jamieson, on Boycott Policy, at H.C. Debates, 1976, vol. 1, p. 302-03, Oct. 21, 1976.
329. *Ibid.*
330. *Ibid.*
331. *Ibid.* also found at H.C. Debates, 1976, vol. I, p. 302, Oct. 21, 1976.
332. Circular Document Consular No. 23/77 (CSR) May 11, 1977, File No. 81–4, signed by the Acting Under-Secretary of State for External Affairs.
333. Circular letter to All Posts, Operations 77–3/Action, International Economic Boycotts, signed by K.D. Taylor, General Director, Trade Commissioner Service, Feb. 15, 1977. Bracketing in the passage as reprinted in "Canadian Practice in International Law" (1978) 16 C.Y.I.L. at 369.
334. H.C. Debates, 1976, vol. I, p. 296, Oct. 21, 1976, Hon. J.G. Diefenbaker and Hon. Donald C. Jamieson.
335. *Export Administration Reports, 116th Report on U.S. Export Controls April-Sept. 1977* at 18–19 describes their implementation.
336. 42 Fed. Reg. 48,556 (Sept. 23, 1977).
337. 43 Fed. Reg. 3508 (Jan. 25, 1978).
338. The Sept. 1976 meeting of Secretary of State for External Affairs, Mr. Donald Jamieson, and the U.S. Secretary of State Henry Kissinger; the meeting of Canadian Ministers with Attorney General Bell in Ottawa, June 1977 and Canada-U.S. discussions in Washington, July 1977.
339. Note No. 591, November 21, 1977 of Canadian Embassy in Washington, to the U.S. Department of State, files of the S.S.E.A.
340. *Ibid.*
341. *Ibid.*
342. *Ibid.*
343. *Ibid.*
344. Note No. 266 of Nov. 18, 1977, the Washington Embassy of the U.K. to the Department of State, reprinted in part in *Lowe*, *supra*, note 238 at 148.
345. *Ibid.*
346. Note No. 49, of Jan. 27, 1978, the Canadian Embassy in Washington to the State Department. Britain sent a similar note the same day.
347. The January 27 note also stated that the Canadian government should also be given the right to obtain "interpretative letters" about the application of the *EAA* as amended.
348. Note No. 374, July 31, 1978 of the Canadian Embassy in Washington to the U.S. State Department, in files of the S.S.E.A.
349. Information from officers of the Department of the External Affairs.
350. J. Rusk, "Extraterritorial Aspect of U.S. Boycott Law is Affecting Canada" *Globe and Mail* (April 8, 1978) B–1.
351. *Ibid.*
352. Export Development Corporation, *International Economic Boycotts Third Semi-Annual Report* (Feb. 1, 1978 to July 31, 1978.)
353. *Ibid.*
354. *Ibid.* at 3. Tertiary boycott clauses are those which require certification that goods or services are not procured from companies with which the boycotting state refuses to do business.
355. *Supra*, note 352.
356. *Ibid.* Appendix 1. The EDC and other government offices required a written

declaration of all persons seeking their assistance which read:

We can assure you that in meeting the terms of this contract the seller, is not required to discriminate against any person on the basis of race, religion or national or ethnic origin, and is not required to refuse to purchase from or sell goods and/or services from any country, except that it would be the right of the purchaser to refuse to accept goods, components and/or services of specified non-Canadian origin that would be prohibited entry if imported directly.

357. H.C. Debates, 1978, vol. VI, pp. 6093–94, June 6, 1978, also at p. 6479, June 16, 1978, The Rt. Hon. P.E. Trudeau.
358. Bill C–32 died on the order paper at the end of the last session of Parliament before the 1979 election which saw the Conservative Party form a new government. Bill C–203 was moved to be read a second time Oct. 25, 1979 by a member of the opposition Liberal Party as a private members bill. See H.C. Debates, 1979, vol. I, p. 611, Oct. 25, 1979, Mr. Bob Kaplan, at 612 and Oct. 29, 1979, 695, The Rt. Hon. P.E. Trudeau.
359. See H.C. Debates, 1979, vol. I, p. 615, Oct. 25, 1979, Mr. David Orlikow at 616.
360. See H.C. Debates, 1979, vol. I, p. 649, Oct. 26, 1979, Rt Hon. Joe Clark, Prime Minister.
361. *An Act to Prohibit Discrimination in Business Relationships*, R.S.O. 1980, c. 119.
362. *Ibid.* at section 3(2).
363. *Ibid.* at section 5 is the prohibition and section 4 the prohibited situations. In as much as the act applies to primary boycotts, it is a piece of human rights legislation as it serves the interests of the person who is the subject of the primary boycott.
364. *Ibid.* at s. 5.
365. *Ibid.* at s. 5(8). Arguably this sort of provision may be inconsistent with the *Canadian Charter of Rights and Freedoms* to the extent that it requires self-incrimination, s. 13, unreasonable search or seizure, section 8, or infringes upon the right to life, liberty and security of the person, s. 7. If it is inconsistent it may be struck down.
366. L.T. Lee & J.B. McCobb Jr., "United States Trade Embargo on China, 1949–1970: Legal Status and Future Prospects" (1971) 4 N.Y.U.J. Int'l. L. & Pol. 1 at 3 [hereinafter *Lee & McCobb*].
367. P.C. 6562, SOR 49–549, 84 Can. Gaz. Pt II 211 (1950).
368. P.C. 6561, SOR/49–552, 84 Can. Gaz. Pt II 224 (1950).
369. This can be deduced from the fact that a large volume of Canadian trade was with the U.S. while the provision only dealt with goods exported to a destination other than the U.S.
370. *Lee & McCobb*, *supra*, note 366 at 4.
371. *Ibid.*
372. H.C. Debates, 1951, vol. III, p. 2746, Mr. McIllraith.
373. *Ibid.* at 2746–47.
374. H.C. Debates, 1952, vol. II, p. 2230, the Hon. Mr. Howe, Minister of Trade and Commerce.
375. H.J. Berman and J.R. Garson, "United States Export Controls – Past, Present and Future" (1967) 67 Column. L. Rev. 791 at 838–39 [hereinafter *Berman & Garson*].
376. *Supra*, note 374.
377. *Berman & Garson*, *supra*, note 375 at 835.
378. 17th *Battle Act* Report, 1964, reprinted in part in 51 U.S. Dep't State Bull. 148, Feb. 1, 1965 at 149.
379. *Berman & Garson*, *supra*, note 375 at 835.
380. H.C. Debates, 1952, vol. II, p. 2230, Hon. C.D. Howe.
381. *Ibid.*
382. For example, H.C. Debates, 1952–53, vol. II, p. 1981, Feb. 16, 1953 Mr. H. Argue.
383. H.C. Debates, 1952–53, vol. II, p. 2005, Feb. 17, 1953 Mr. Pearson.
384. P.C. 1953–604, SOR/53–138, 87 Can. Gaz. Pt II 346 at 347, s. 3 (1).

385. H.C. Debates, 1952–53, vol. IV, p. 4197, Mr. Howe said "this action to prevent the movement of contraband was not taken by Canada primarily: it was taken by agreement among the NATO countries". At that time COCOM was referred to as "NATO countries" action.
386. "Third *Battle Act* Report", 29 (748) U.S. Dep't. State Bull. 569 at 574, Oct. 26, 1953.
387. *Lee & McCobb*, *supra*, note 366 at 9.
388. H.C. Debates, 1956, vol. I, p. 791–92, Mr. Claude Ellis, and Mr. Hower.
389. *Lee & McCobb*, *supra*, note 366 at 9.
390. "Ambassadorial Talks at Geneva with Chinese Communists" Sept. 24, 1956, 35 U.S. Dep't. State Bull. 553, Oct. 8, 1956.
391. $2,426,780 worth of Canadian products were licensed. H.C. Debates, 1957–58, vol. II, p. 1402, The Hon. Gordon Churchill, Minister of Trade and Commerce.
392. *Lee & McCobb*, *supra*, note 366 at 9.
393. Canadian Secretary of State for External Affairs files reveal that Ford (G.B.) had an export order for tractors vetoed, and a Bahamian firm's contract for non-strategic goods cancelled by the U.S. majority shareholder, who would otherwise have been subject to proceedings in the U.S. under U.S. export control laws.
394. J.I.W. Corcoran, "The Trading with The Enemy Act and the Canadian Controlled Corporation" (1968) 14 McGill L.J. 174 at 193 [hereinafter *Corcoran*].
395. H.C. Debates, 1957–58, vol. II, p.1402, Nov. 21, 1957 the Hon. Gordon Churchill.
396. H.C. Debates, 1956, vol. III, p. 2858–59, Mr. Mitchell; 1957, vol. I, p. 1156, Mr. Diefenbaker; 1957, vol. III, pp. 2462–63, Mr. Macdonnell.
397. H.C. Debates, 1959, vol. I, pp. 5188–89, June 25, 1959 Mr. Harold Winch, (also quoted in *Corcoran*, *supra*, note 394 at 190–91, n. 38).
398. *Berman & Garson*, *supra*, note 375 at 835, H.C. Debates, 1958, vol. IV, p. 3649, Aug. 16, 1958 Mr. H. Argue and Mr. Churchill.
399. *Lee & McCobb*, *supra*, note 366 at 9; *Corcoran*, *supra*, note 394 at 193, 194–95.
400. "Tories Dodged Question on U.S. Ban on Canadian Car Exports to Red China" *Toronto Star* (March 24, 1958) 6.
401. *Ibid.*
402. H.C. Debates, 1958, vol. II, July 10, 1958, p. 2090, Hon. Donald M. Fleming, Minister of Finance.
403. *Corcoran*, *supra*, note 394 at 194–95.
404. H.C. Debates, 1958, vol. II, 24 June, 1958, p. 1559 The Hon. Gordon Churchill, Minister of Trade and Commerce.
405. 39 U.S. Dep't State Bull. 209, Aug. 4, 1958.
406. *Ibid.*
407. Minutes of the meeting, in the files of the Canadian Secretary of State for External Affairs.
408. *Ibid.*
409. H.C. Debates, July 11, 1958, vol. II, p. 2143, Mr. Pearson.
410. H.C. Debates, July 18, 1958, vol. III, p. 2392–93, Mr. Argue.
411. H.C. Debates, 1958, vol. III, pp. 2859–60, Hon. Gordon Churchill, Minister of Trade and Commerce.
412. Files of the S.S.E.A.
413. *Ibid.*
414. H.C. Debates, 1958, vol. III, p. 2859, July 30, 1958.
415. H.C. Debates, 1959, vol. I, pp. 274–5, Mr. Howard.
416. *Ibid.* see also H. C. Debates, 1959, vol. I, p. 394–95, Mr. Winch.
417. Mr. Winch, *ibid.*
418. H.C. Debates, 1959, vol. I, p. 937, Hon. Gordon Churchill, Minister of Trade and Commerce. However only $7.8 million worth of sales was actually made.
419. *Corcoran*, *supra*, note 394 at 200.
420. H. Morrison, "Canada Trucks Barred by U.S.: Food from China Held 'Peril to

Security'" *Montreal Gazette* (May 2, 1959) A–1.
421. "Frozen Shrimp Rift Under Way" *New Orleans Times-Picayune* (May 14, 1959): extract from the files of the Department of External Affairs.
422. H.C. Debates, 1959, vol. IV, p. 4023, May 26, 1959, The Rt. Hon. John Diefenbaker, Prime Minister.
423. H.C. Debates, 1960–61, vol. II, p. 1852, Feb. 8, 1961, Mr. Argue.
424. *Ibid.* The Hon. George Hees, Minister of Trade and Commerce.
425. P.C. 1981–1793, SOR/81–543, 115 Can. Gaz. Pt II 2059, July 22, 1981.
426. H.C. Debates, 1963, vol. II , p. 1228, June 17, 1963, Mr. Pépin.
427. *Ibid.* see also H.C. Debates, 1964, vol. II, p. 1398, March 24, 1964 Hon. Mitchell Sharp, Minister of Trade and Commerce as reprinted in "Canadian Practice in International Law as Reflected in Public Statements, 1964" (1966) 4 C.Y.I.L. 220 at 225–26.
428. Mr. Sharp, *ibid.* see also H.C. Debates, 1964–66, vol. XII, p. 12,630–31, March 22, 1965, Hon. Mitchell Sharp, Minister of Trade and Commerce, as reprinted in "Canadian Practice in International Law as Reflected in Public Statements, 1965 and 1966" (1967) 5 C.Y.I.L. at 308-09.
429. *Ibid.*
430. *Ibid.* at 201.
431. H.C. Debates, 1964–66, vol. III, p. 7458–59, Aug. 31, 1964.
432. H.C. Debates, 1967, vol. IV, p. 4175–76, Nov. 13, 1967 Mr. Jean-Charles Cantin.
433. H.C. Debates, 1966, vol. I, p. 324–26, Jan. 27, 1966, Hon. M. Sharp excerpted in "Canadian Practice in International Law as Reflected in Public Statements, 1965 and 1966" (1967) 5 C.Y.I.L. at 313–14 [hereinafter *Canadian Practice (1965–66)*].
434. *Ibid.*
435. H.C. Debates, 1966, vol. IV, p. 3643–44, Mar. 31, 1966, Hon. Robert Winters.
436. The letter and the guidelines were appended to H.C. Debates, 1966, vol. IV, at 3713–14, March 31, 1966.
437. H.C. Debates, 1966, vol. X, p. 10,052, Nov. 18, 1966, Mr. Winters.
438. *Ibid.* at 10,053 states 300 of 389 companies responded to the questionnaire. The guidelines have been reprinted in *Canadian Practice (1965–66)*, *supra*, note 433 at 316.
439. *Freuhauf* v. *Massardy*, Judgement of May 22, 1965, Cour d'appel, Paris, 1965, Recueil Dalloz-Sirey Jurisprudence, 147, English translation in (1966) 5 Int'l Leg. Mat. 476.
440. *Lee & McCobb*, *supra*, note 366 at 10–13 for Treasury Department Controls, and at 13–15 for Commerce Department controls.
441. "President Nixon Reduces Controls on Trade with Mainland China" Press Release, June 10, 1971, 64 U.S. Dep't State Bull. 815 (June 28, 1971).
442. "Restrictions Eased on Exports to People's Republic of China" Press Release Feb. 14, 1972, 66, U.S. Dep't State Bull. 291 (March 6, 1972).
443. H.C. Debates, 1971, vol. VII, p. 7598, Hon. Jean-Luc Pépin, Minister of Industry, Trade and Commerce.
444. *Lee & McCobb*, *supra*, note 366 at 20.
445. 43 U.S. Dep't State Bull. 715 at 716 (1960); also see P.A. Shneyer & V. Barta, "The Legality of the U.S. Economic Blockade of Cuba Under International Law" (1981) 13 Case W. Res. J. Int'l L. 451 at 457.
446. Oct. 3, 1962, S.J. Res. 230, Pub. L. 87–733, 76 Stat. 697.
447. H.C. Debates, 1962, vol. I, p. 757, Feb. 12, 1962, Mr. Morris for 1956 to 1960 and H.C. Debates, 1964, p. 522 at 523, March 4, 1964 Mr. Latulippe for 1961 to 1963.
448. H.C. Debates, 1960–61, vol. I, p. 700-01, Dec. 12. 1960 The Rt. Hon. J. Diefenbaker, Prime Minister.
449. *Ibid.*
450. *Ibid.* at 339, Nov. 30, 1960 Hon. George H. Hees.

451. *Ibid.* at 701, Dec. 12, 1960.
452. *Ibid.*
453. General Export Permit No. Ex. 2 amended, Dec. 16, 1960, SOR/60–652, 94 Can. Gaz. Pt II 1532, Dec. 28, 1960.
454. *Supra*, note 448 at 867, Dec. 16, 1960, Hon. G. Hees.
455. H.C. Debates, 1962, vol. I, p. 953, Feb. 16, 1962 Hon. G. Hees.
456. *Ibid.*
457. *Supra*, note 448 at 1032, Dec. 21, 1960, Hon. G. Hees, Minister of Trade and Commerce in response to question of Mr. Pearson, the Leader of the Opposition.
458. *Supra*, note 455 at 912, Feb. 15, 1962, Mr. Martin.
459. *Ibid.* at 910.
460. *Ibid.* at 958, Feb. 16, 1962, Hon. G. Hees, Minister of Trade and Commerce.
461. 46 U.S. Dep't State Bull. 282.
462. *Supra*, note 455 at 480, Feb. 2, 1962, Rt. Hon. J. Diefenbaker.
463. *Ibid.*
464. *Ibid.* at 1461, Mr. Morris.
465. *Supra*, note 455 at 575, Feb. 6, 1962, Hon. G. Hees, Minister of Trade and Commerce.
466. "Text of Final Communiqué", Press Release 598, Oct. 3, 1962, 47 U.S. Dep't State Bull. 598, Oct. 22, 1962 at 600.
467. "Trading Relations Between the Free World and Cuba" Statement by Under Secretary Ball before the House Select Committee on Export Control, Oct. 3, Press Release 595, 47 U.S. Dep't State Bull. 591 at 592, Oct. 22, 1962.
468. *Lowenfeld*, *supra*, note 1 at n. 13.
469. This was equally true upon the defeat of the Conservative government and the election of the Liberals. See, for example, H.C. Debates, 1973, vol. III, p. 2127, July 12, 1963, Hon. Mitchell Sharp, Minister of Trade and Commerce.
470. 31 C.F.R. 515.
471. *Ibid.*
472. 31 C.F.R. 515.541; revoked by 40 Fed. Reg. 47,108 (1975).
473. S.L. Sommerfield, "Treasury Regulations of Foreign Assets and Trade" (1964) 19 Bus. Law. 861 at 868.
474. *Ibid.*
475. 31 C.F.R. 515.541(e).
476. Information from officers of the Department of External Affairs.
477. Information from officers of the Department of External Affairs.
478. *Ibid.*
479. *Ibid.*
480. 51 U.S. Dep't State Bull. 181 (Aug. 10, 1964).
481. UN Doc. S/4395, July 19, 1960.
482. *Ibid.*
483. *Ibid.*
484. H.C. Debates 1964, p. 5997, July 27, 1964, Mr. Martin.
485. Information from files of the Department of External Affairs.
486. *Ibid.*
487. 39 U.S. Dep't State Bull. 209, Aug. 4, 1958.
488. Information from files of the Department of External Affairs.
489. *Ibid.*
490. *Ibid.*
491. *Ibid.*
492. *Ibid.*
493. Communiqué, March 5, 1966, 54 U.S. Dep't State Bull. 464, Mar. 21, 1966; H.C. Debates, 1964–66, vol. III (Appendix A, March 7, 1966)
494. *Ibid.*
495. H.C. Debates, 1966, vol. IV, pp. 3643–44, Mar. 31, 1966, Hon. Robert Winters.

496. Robin Hood, Quaker, and Pillsbury, H.C. Debates, 1966, vol. VII, pp. 7607-08, July 12, 1966, Mr. L. Sherman and Hon. Robert Winters.
497. H.C. Debates, 1966, vol. VII, p. 7650, July 14, 1966, Mr. T.C. Douglas.
498. *Ibid.* at 6758, July 14, 1966, Hon. Robert Winters.
499. *Ibid.*
500. H.C. Debates 1969, vol. III, p. 8491, May 8, 1969 Mr. J.L. Skoberg.
501. Information from files of the Department of External Affairs.
502. *Ibid.*
503. *Ibid.*
504. *Ibid.*
505. Letter of Robert Winters to Secretary Fowler, Aug. 11, 1967, Files of the Department of External Affairs.
506. Files of the Department of External Affairs.
507. Letter of U.S. Secretary of the Treasury Fowler to Robert Winters, September 7, 1967, files of Department of External Affairs.
508. Files of the Department of External Affairs.
509. Information obtained from the files of the Department of External Affairs.
510. It is uncertain whether it was granted.
511. Information made available by the Department of External Affairs.
512. H. C. Debates, 1974, vol. I, p. 20, Feb. 28, 1974.
513. Note of Feb. 13, 1974, Canada to the U.S. State Department, released to the public, Mar. 6, 1974.
514. H.C. Debates, 1974, vol. I, p. 165, Mar. 5, 1974, Hon. Alastair Gillespie, Minister of Industry, Trade and Commerce.
515. H.C. Debates, 1974, vol. I, p. 707, Mar. 20, 1974, Mr. Wicher.
516. *Ibid.* see also *Combines Investigation Act*, R.S.C. 1970 c. C–23 as am S.C. 1974–75–76 & 77, ss. 31.5 and 31.6 now ss. 54 and 55 of the *Competition Act* S.C. 1986, c. 26 which are identical save for removing wording about affording the person to be subject to such an order the reasonable opportunity to be heard first.
517. H.C. Debates, 1972–73, vol. VII, p. 8002, Nov. 21, 1973 Mr. Herb Breau.
518. H.C. Debates, 1974, vol. II, p. 1221, Apr. 8, 1974, Mr. Raynald Guay.
519. H.C. Debates, 1974–76, vol. I, p. 7, Sept. 30, 1974 speech from the Throne.
520. H.C. Debates, 1974–76, vol. IV, p. 3310, Feb. 18, 1975, Mr. Alan Martin, and Hon. Allan J. MacEachen.
521. Files of the Department of External Affairs.
522. Reprinted in J.G. Castel, A.L.C. de Mestral, W.C. Graham, *International Business Transactions and Economic Relations* (Toronto: Emond Montgomery, 1986) at 390.
523. H.C. Debates, 1979, vol. I, p. 253, Oct. 16, 1979, Mr. Roy MacLaren. Some lawyers interviewed acting for U.S. companies in export licensing matters feel that in the majority of cases the subsidiary in Canada is given extensive export authority.
524. 72 U.S. Dep't State Bull. 9, Jan. 6, 1975, the vote was 12 for, 3 against and 6 abstentions including the U.S.
525. See (1975) 14 Int'l Leg. Mat. 1354.
526. Aug. 21, 1975, 73 U.S. Dep't State Bull. 404, Sept. 15, 1975.
527. *Ibid.*
528. 31 C.F.R. 515.559. It incorporated the 20% rule by reference to Dep't of Commerce licensing of U.S. origin parts which include the rule in 25 C.F.R. 385.1(b).
529. 40 Fed. Reg. 47,108 (1975) revokes 31 C.F.R. 515.541.
530. M.P. Malloy, "Embargo Programs of the United States Treasury Department" (1981) 20 Colum. J. Trans. L. 485 at 509 [hereinafter *Malloy*].
531. Information obtained from the files of the Department of External Affairs.
532. 42 Fed. Reg. 1472, 16,621 (1977).
533. 31 C.F.R. 515–559(a)(1).
534. I.e. not to be on the Commodity Control List of Dep't of Commerce, 31 C.F.R.

559(b).
535. *Ibid.*
536. 31 C.F.R. 515.559(c) (1981).
537. *Malloy*, *supra*, note 530 at 509.
538. 31 C.F.R. 515.559(c) (1981).
539. Information from officials at the Department of External Affairs.
540. Note on file at the Department of External Affairs.
541. Dated Oct. 20, 1977, "The Exercise of Extraterritorial Jurisdiction" reprinted in "Canadian Practice in International Law as Reflected in Public Statements, 1977" (1978) 16 C.Y.I.L. 362.
542. *Ibid.* at 362–63.
543. Information from the files of the Department of External Affairs.
544. *Ibid.*
545. *Ibid.*
546. Information from officials of the Department of External Affairs. In a note sent in early 1983 the Embassy stated:

> We cannot accept ... that U.S. officials take steps in Canada in support of the application of U.S. law to inhibit Canadian firms from pursuing express Canadian government policy of promoting trade with Cuba in non-strategic goods ... if they are indeed long-standing U.S. practice they should be discontinued.

547. *Ibid.*
548. *Ibid.*
549. M. McDowell, "U.S. Curbs Canadian over Cuba Connection" *Globe and Mail* (Feb. 1, 1984) 20.
550. Oct. 1, 1966, 61 U.S. Dep't State Bull. 335, October 20, 1969.
551. H. Alan Talkington, "International Trade: Uganda Trade Embargo" (1979) 20 Harv. Int'l L.J. 206 at 209.
552. *Export Administration Report, 120th Report on U.S. Export Controls*, Semi-annual: April 1979-Sept. 1979, U.S. Dep't of Commerce, Industry and Trade Administration at 18.
553. *Ibid.*
554. C.R.C. 1978, c. 601, item 9001.
555. Information from files of the Department of External Affairs.
556. 43 Fed. Reg. 58,573 (Dec. 15, 1978).
557. *Supra*, note 555.
558. 45 Fed. Reg. 33,956 (May 21, 1980).
559. *Ibid.*
560. In one case a U.S. company agreed to a Consent Order for selling to another U.S. company in the U.S., items it knew the latter intended to sell to Libya. See *In the Matter of Applied Systems Corporations* Sept. 30, 1982, Munitions Control Newsletter No. 97 10/82. In the same case a Canadian working for the Canadian parent of the U.S. company which exported the item to Canada and then to Libya, was charged under the *Arms Export Control Act* 22 U.S.C. 2778. See *U.S.A.* v. *Robert Antonio Manina* U.S. Dist. Ct. E. Dist. of Virginia, Alexandria Division Criminal No. 82–99176-A.
561. A. Kamen and D.L. Vaughan, "Wilson Associate Indicted Over Exports to Libya" *Washington Post* (Mar. 8, 1982) A–11.
562. 47 Fed. Reg. 11249 (Mar. 16, 1982).
563. *Ibid.* implemented 15 C.F.R. 385.7 subsection (a)(2)(i) of which give the exceptions.
564. Item 9001 of the Export Control List.
565. Information from officials of the Department of External Affairs.
566. *Ibid.*
567. P.C. 1986–108, Jan. 10, 1986, SOR 86/110, 1986 Can. Gaz. Pt II p. 467.
568. *Nicaragua Transaction Control Regulations*, 31 C.F.R. 540.401 (1985) [hereinafter

NTCR's].

569. *Ibid.*
570. *Ibid.*
571. 31 C.F.R. 540.404.
572. 31 C.F.R. 540.406 (1985).
573. "Nicaragua, Military Supplies from Abroad" July/Aug. 1983 International Perspectives, Supp. at 8–9.
574. H.C. Debates, 1985, vol. III, p. 4474–75, May 7, 1985, Rt. Hon. Joe Clark, Secretary of State for External Affairs, also at 4435, May 6, 1985.

CHAPTER VI

STATE PRACTICE – U.S.

A. Participation in International Action

1. U.N. Sanctions

(a) Mandatory Sanctions

(i) *Rhodesia*. U.S. measures with respect to Rhodesia began December 28, 1965 when all exports of petroleum were placed under special controls. Where goods were being shipped under a general license under the *Export Control Act* (*ECA*) it was required that the bill of lading and commercial invoices, as well as a sworn statement, contain an anti-diversion notice listing Rhodesia as a country to which diversion was prohibited by U.S. law.[1] These measures were in response to the Security Council recommendation that U.N. members not provide arms, military equipment or oil to Rhodesia.[2]

The U.S. authority for implementing Security Council recommendations could not, however, be based on its *United Nations Participation Act of 1945* (*UNPA*).[3] It required mandatory measures under Article 41 of the *U.N. Charter* before the *UNPA* gave the President authority to regulate and prohibit international economic relations.[4] Thus prior to mandatory sanctions the U.S. measures, like those of Canada, could not be based on U.N. decisions. The U.S. actions had to be based on its *ECA*.

On February 26, 1966, prior to any mandatory sanctions of the U.N. Security Council,[5] the U.S. announced that almost all exports to Rhodesia would require validated licenses.[6] This U.S. measure was in addition to those previously taken to embargo the exports of arms, military equipment and all petroleum products to Rhodesia,[7] and to discourage travel to Rhodesia.[8] The mandatory embargo was placed on those items by the Security Council Resolution 232 on December 16, 1966.[9] It was only then that the U.S. could rely on its *UNPA* to issue regulations. Regulations under the *UNPA* were issued January 5, 1967.[10]

The *ECA* and the regulations under it were only extraterritorial with respect to controls on U.S. origin goods.[11] Thus the measures preceding the invocation of the *UNPA* were extraterritorial only in that regard. Nevertheless, the U.S. *Rhodesia Regulations* applied to persons "subject to the jurisdiction of the United States" according to Executive Order 11,322.[12] The Regulations that were issued pursuant to the Executive Order[13] were very similar to the *CACR*s and the *FACR*s under the *TWEA*.[14] The one salient difference was that subsidiaries abroad, controlled or owned by U.S. persons, were not included in the definition of "persons subject to U.S. jurisdiction".[15] The only exceptions were those persons incorporated in or having their principal place of business in Rhodesia[16] which included only:

[a]ny partnership, association, corporation, or other organization organized

> under the laws of, or having its principal place of business in, Southern Rhodesia which is owned or controlled by (U.S.) persons ...

Officers, directors and chief management of foreign subsidiaries were still subject to the regulations, however.[17] They were considered to be involved if they authorized or permitted the subsidiary's transaction, even if they themselves were not involved.[18] This seemed more far-reaching than either the *CACR*s or *FACR*s because mere passivity was subject to liability.[19] The U.S. parent corporation was, however, unlikely to fall within the definition.[20] A separate provision prevented the parent from entering into a transaction that either involved goods destined for Rhodesia, or had the effect of avoiding the prohibitions.[21] Nevertheless, appointment of non-U.S. persons as directors with the direction they export to Rhodesia appeared permitted by the wording.[22]

Thus the U.S. *Rhodesia Regulations* were based on the U.N. Security Council, but went further. Where Resolution 232 required prohibitions based on nationality and territory they did not extend to owned or controlled business organizations.[23] The U.S. provision with respect to officers and directors can be read as consonant with Resolution 232.

The U.S. position was that Britain was sovereign over Rhodesia and that the regime that had declared independence was illegal.[24] Part of the U.S. justification for its policy was that the action was taken pursuant to Security Council Resolutions pursuant to a request by Great Britain.[25] It seems somewhat incongruous that the U.S. would specifically control U.S. owned or controlled Rhodesian companies when its position implied they were under British jurisdiction. If U.S. action was in support of Britain surely it would be Britain which best appreciated its own interests. The explanation that suggests itself is that the U.S. could effectively control these companies whereas Britain could not. This suggests the degree to which U.S. measures are based on effective control in fact, rather than abstract principles of sovereignty.

On May 29, 1968, Security Council Resolution 253[26] imposed a total trade embargo on Rhodesia. Two months later the President implemented the resolution in U.S. law.[27] Among the provisions was a ban on travel to Rhodesia, to be implemented under the *Immigration and Nationality Act*.[28] Only exceptions of a humanitarian nature were made by the Security Council, and by U.S. law. On August 13, 1968 the regulations implemented the Executive Order.[29]

The U.S., like Canada, did not support recourse to force in Rhodesia.[30] It did not support the extension of economic sanctions to South Africa and Portugal either.[31] Thus it abstained from voting for a Security Council Resolution which would have imposed mandatory sanctions against South Africa and Portugal, and called for the British to use force.[32] The draft resolution did not pass, although no vote was cast against it, because it could not muster the necessary 9 votes in favor.[33]

In 1971, the U.S. adopted the *Byrd Amendment* which prevented the President from prohibiting imports of certain strategic materials.[34] This was seen as a violation of the U.N. mandatory embargo by commentators[35] and the U.N. General Assembly.[36] The Security Council Resolution 320 urged the U.S. to comply.[37] The

U.S. executive opposed the legislation[38] but it became law January 1, 1972.

The U.S. delegation to the U.N. stated that U.S. imports from Rhodesia amounted only to 2 or 3 percent of all Rhodesian exports, thus suggesting that the U.S. was being singled out unfairly.[39] The U.S. told the Security Council that only two of the Security Council members had actually taken adequate enforcement measures and some had not even enacted the appropriate laws and regulations.[40] The problem was not the *Byrd Amendment,* it argued, it was rather the evasion of the sanctions,[41] notably the transactions that accounted for the 97 or 98 percent of Rhodesian exports the U.S. was not importing.[42] The U.S. delegation pointed out that the U.S. was making its imports a matter of public record while others were not, and that is why it was being singled out.[43]

The U.S. joined the U.K. in vetoing a resolution which would have made mandatory a limit on imports from South Africa and Mozambique (then still a Portuguese colony) to pre-1966 levels to deal with the refusal by these states to implement import restrictions by these states.[44] Nevertheless, it only abstained on Security Council Resolution 333 which called on states to provide severe penalties for natural or juridical persons evading sanctions. This U.S. action can be best explained by the provisions of Resolution 333 relating to imports, and the condemnation of South Africa and Portugal therein. U.S. international action is better understood in the light of the problems caused by the *Byrd Amendment.* The U.S. could not be quick to point the finger at South Africa or Portugal when its own hands were not clean and could not support resolutions which contradicted its internal law.

The *Byrd Amendment* was repealed in March 1977 under President Carter.[45] Following upon the removal of that obstacle to its participation in the Rhodesia sanctions, the U.S. could lead an expansion of sanctions against Rhodesia.[46] Its initiative resulted in Security Council Resolution 409[47] which made mandatory a prohibition on the transfer of funds within member territories by Rhodesian agents. This went along with the prohibition on the export of funds to Rhodesia found in Resolution 253.[48]

U.S. compliance with the sanctions was questioned nevertheless. A church group accused Mobil Oil of providing oil to its South African subsidiary which was then providing it to Rhodesia.[49] South African law and policy prohibited any resale conditions on sales made within it, thus making it illegal to restrict sales that were destined to Rhodesia.[50] The U.S. Treasury Office of Foreign Asset Controls interpreted the regulations to allow a foreign company to do whatever it wished as long as no U.S. citizens were involved. The knowledge of the U.S. parent of an arrangement to ship oil to Rhodesia was irrelevant.[51]

There was evidence that British and French firms were involved in swapping oil to avoid the sanctions.[52] The British government acquiesced in the arrangement, however, and did not take the step of banning oil exports to South Africa which, given South African law, would have been the only effective way to prevent re-exports to Rhodesia.[53]

As a trend toward free elections was apparent in Rhodesia, the pressure mounted in the U.S. for the repeal of U.S. controls against Rhodesia. The President was required to cease the enforcement of the sanctions after December 31, 1978 if certain conditions had been met.[54] The conditions to be met were a demonstration of willingness to negotiate in good faith by the government of Rhodesia and a government that had been chosen in free elections. As of June 7, 1979 President Carter stated he was convinced lifting the sanctions would not be in the best interests of the U.S.[55] He also stated the Rhodesian situation was not sufficient to meet the two conditions in the *ISAA* of 1978.

Another statute required sanctions be terminated unless the President determined it would not be in the national interest to do so and so reported to Congress.[56] It was adopted as a result of the June 7 Presidential determination.[57] President Carter made another such determination on November 14, 1979[58] with the following justification:

> Encouraging progress has been made in recent months toward a peaceful resolution of the conflict in Zimbabwe-Rhodesia ... A termination of sanctions at this stage could lead all the parties to harden their positions and would jeopardize the changes for a successful settlement for Zimbabwe-Rhodesia.[59]

On December 12 the U.K. assumed legal and constitutional authority in Rhodesia and the process of free elections was begun.[60] The U.K. lifted its sanctions the same day[61] and, effective midnight of December 16, 1979, the U.S. sanctions were lifted.[62] The U.S. declared that the U.N. aims had been achieved.[63]

The problem was that the U.N. sanctions were not terminated until Security Council Resolution 460 was passed on December 21, 1979.[64] The U.K. was in a position similar to the U.S. having lifted its sanctions prior to the resolution.[65] The U.K. argued the obligation to impose sanctions fell away on the return of Rhodesia to British rule.[66] The U.S. seems to have taken a similar position by stating that the aims of the U.N. had been achieved.[67] Be that as it may, there was some opinion that the *U.N. Charter* had been violated.[68]

It may be said that the lifting of the sanctions unilaterally was a mere technical violation if at all. What would have been the situation in the Security Council had a veto been cast against Resolution 460?[69] Since the sanctions had been justified on the basis of U.N. action, in other words multilateral action, on the premise that the Rhodesian situation constituted a threat to international peace and security, it was legally inconsistent to then contend that each state might unilaterally interpret the end to such threat. The better route to have followed would have been to have voted on Resolution 460 first and, in the case of a veto, deal with the consequences afterwards. The Canadian action seems much more respectful of international law than were the British or U.S. actions.[70]

(b) Recommended Sanctions

(i) *South Africa – Apartheid.* The United States told the Security Council it expected to bring to an end the sale of all military equipment to South Africa by the end of 1963. This statement was made as the Security Council was deliberating the question of sanctions against South Africa.[71] The U.N. Security Council did call for all nations to embargo the sale of arms to South Africa[72] and then equipment and materials for their manufacture.[73] The U.S. applied these measures subject only to honouring pre-existing contracts and reserving the right to provide arms if international peace and security required it.[74]

From 1964 the U.S. had guidelines, which were not made public, prohibiting the sale of all items prohibited by the U.N. Security Council resolutions.[75] Pre-existing contracts however, accounted for sales worth $30 million in the next 10 years.[76] They included sales of spare parts.[77] Still the U.S. controls were extensive, calling for the close scrutiny of dual use equipment.[78]

The guidelines were implemented without regulatory changes, merely by exercise of discretion in issuing licenses.[79] Until February 1978, there was no legislative or regulatory indication of the U.S. policy. The guidelines by which licenses were issued however, were the manifestations of the U.S. policy.

In 1968 the guidelines were extended to include the use of U.S. origin components in the foreign manufacture of arms destined for South Africa.[80] The embargo was strictly maintained.[81] New investment in South Africa was neither encouraged nor discouraged.[82]

With the coming into office of the Nixon Administration the policy toward South Africa was reviewed and changes made. Relaxation of controls was implemented in 1970 to encourage some[83] modification of South African "racial and colonial policies". In practice this meant the relaxation of controls on dual-use equipment but maintenance of the rest of the embargo.[84] Publicly no change was admitted.

In practice transport aircraft, computers, helicopters all were allowed to South Africa. With the relaxation of the controls aircraft sales quickly doubled in 1971 and were almost triple the 1971 levels by 1974.[85]

The embargo was tightened by the Carter administration which came into office in 1977. Dual use items were once again brought under the embargo.[86] Aircraft sales that had been allowed under the Nixon dual-use policy were now restricted.[87] Still, in fiscal year 1977 (U.S.), $5 million worth of exports to South Africa of goods on the Munitions Control List were approved by the State Department.[88]

The U.S. action preceded the U.N. mandatory sanctions on South Africa that were adopted by Security Council Resolutions 418.[89] Several months later the U.S. took cognizance of this resolution in its regulations.[90] The regulations stated that an embargo was in effect on South Africa for items listed[91] and for any exports or re-exports to the South African military or police.[92] They also included in the embargo technical data relating to embargoed commodities[93] and U.S. origin parts.[94] Crime detection and crime control exports to South Africa also required a license.[95] The regulations also required a "destination control statement" prohibiting resale or delivery to military or police on shipping documents for exports to South Africa.[96] South African law however would seem to have prohibited such clauses and made the U.S. requirement meaningless.[97] The significance of the U.S. regulation went beyond the fact that it was a codification of government policy into the *Export Regulations*. The embargo on arms was extended to all items to be exported to the South African military or police if they were under Department of

Commerce jurisdiction. In other words the U.S. embargo went beyond any recommended by the U.N. There is doubt that the embargo[98] was effective although the measures did extend to foreign subsidiaries with respect to the extent of U.S. origin goods and technology.[99]

Coincident with the embargo program, the U.S. gave publicity to the labour practices of U.S. controlled firms in South Africa.[100] Some goals these firms ought to achieve were made public, including the goal of equal pay for equal work.[101]

It is difficult to describe the U.S. measures as following international action. Its embargo had gone beyond what was necessary for all of the years since 1963. But the U.S. objected to some recommendations of the Security Council on how to make the mandatory arms embargo against South Africa more effective.[102] Among them were recommendations for states to prohibit their corporations' investment in arms manufacture in South Africa, exports of dual purpose items, and nuclear collaboration with South Africa.[103] Of its objections it seems surprising that one was made for the dual use items. In view of its policy to restrict dual use exports to South Africa, it is likely that the question of the extent of the U.N. recommendations kept the U.S. from agreeing to that item.

The political flexibility left by the U.S. objection to the dual-use item was welcome when the U.S. relaxed the embargo on South Africa.[104] Certain items were removed from the controls, and non-strategic items would be licensed if they were determined not to contribute significantly to military or police functions. Foreign exports with 20 percent or less U.S. origin components would also be considered for export to the military or police on a case by case basis.[105] Computers needed licenses only for exports to certain South African Government departments.[106] As result there were no licenses denied for aircraft or computers to South Africa in fiscal year 1982.[107] The destination control statement was changed to a stamp on the license.[108] As well, a policy statement was included indicating that licenses would be denied for exports to the South African police and military, but there were some exceptions that may be made on a case by case basis.[109] Crime control equipment, air craft and computer exports specifically required validated licenses.[110]

On January 25, 1983 the export controls on South Africa were brought into line with those for most communist countries.[111] This meant broad categories of items that previously were non-strategic could be sold to the South African police or military without a license.[112]

Congress saw a number of bills that would have further restricted trade with South Africa.[113] They would have imposed the controls lifted by the President in 1982 and 1983, giving the President power to prohibit investments in South Africa, prohibited transfers of nuclear materials or technology and required U.S. firms with more than 20 employees to comply with the "Sullivan Code" on fair employment practices in South Africa.[114]

The comprehensive *Anti-Apartheid Act* of 1986 came into force on October 2, 1986[115] over a Presidential veto. This Act sets out a comprehensive and coordinated set of policies and measures designed to combat apartheid in South Africa. The very purpose of the Act is extraterritorial in that it seeks to influence the policies and actions of the South African government and of private corporations and individuals in South Africa with a view to ending apartheid. A series of measures were adopted to assist the victims of apartheid both in and outside South Africa, including the withdrawal of U.S. economic assistance to those not complying with a code of conduct for activities in South Africa which involves fair and equal employment practices with respect to black employees in the workplace and in their daily lives beyond the workplace. The Act also sets out a range of trade measures designed to undermine apartheid including a ban on new investment in South Africa and the tightening of the panoply of existing export controls. As well, the Act includes the imposition of new specific export prohibitions on computers, crude oil, nuclear technology, loans to the South African Government and air transportation to South Africa.

The comprehensive *Anti-Apartheid Act* of 1986 contains a range of specific prohibitions. A further range of measures, directed mainly to exports were adopted by amendments to the *Export Administration Regulations,*[116] the new *South Africa and Fair Labour Standards Regulation,*[117] revised *International Traffic in Arms Regulations*[118] and amendments to the *South Africa Transactions Regulations.*[119]

As stated above the whole thrust of the regulations is to change governmental policy in South Africa and in this sense constitutes the extreme of extraterritoriality, only justified by the nature of the injustice and human tragedy to which it is addressed. The Act applies to "nationals of the U.S.," defined as citizens or permanent residents, and "corporations, partnerships or other business associations organised in the U.S.". Certain parts of the Act also apply to "controlled South African corporations."

(ii) *Namibia.* Unlike Canada, the U.S. had always made it quite clear what its position was with respect to exports to Namibia. For the most part its position was identical to that with respect to South Africa. The U.S. supported U.N. General Assembly Resolution 2145 (XXI)[120] which purported to terminate the mandate of South Africa in Namibia. It did not support mandatory sanctions for Namibia, however.[121] It did seek to refrain from dealings which were inconsistent with the position that the presence of South Africa in Namibia was illegal.[122]

The U.S. did take some special measures with respect to Namibia.[123] These measures included officially discouraging U.S. nationals from investing in Namibia,[124] refusing export credit guarantees for trade with Namibia, and U.S. diplomatic protection was not to be extended to investments made in Namibia after General Assembly Resolution 2145 (XXI).

The U.S. also supported Security Council Resolution 283 which called upon states to ensure companies owned by or under the direct control of the state cease all dealings with Namibia,[125] as well as to discourage investment in or tourism to Namibia. It felt it supported decolonization although it could not always agree with the text of resolutions brought to a vote at the U.N.[126] The U.S. also was one of the countries to veto the proposed mandatory arms embargo on South Africa in 1975.[127] The proposed resolution would have affected pre-existing contracts, which the U.S. had not favored in respect of South Africa since 1963.

The Regulations issued effective February 16, 1978, dealing with the embargo on South Africa applied equally to Namibia.

(iii) *Portugal.* As with Canada, the U.S. embargoed the supply of arms to Portugal.[128] The U.S. asked the Portuguese government for formal assurances that any embargoed arms would only be used in the N.A.T.O. area.[129]

The U.S. however had even more difficult relations with Portugal than did Canada due to its use of Portuguese islands as bases.[130] It too invoked General Assembly Resolution 1699 (XVI), as well as the subsequent U.N. resolutions, as justification for its measures.

2. *Internationally Coordinated Sanctions*

(a) Soviet Union

(i) *Afghanistan.* The U.S. has had extensive controls on the export of a wide range of commodities to the Soviet Union since World War II. Their ambit has ebbed and flowed since 1945. The number of items was reduced during the years of "peaceful coexistence" until the controls existed mostly on items that were of a strategic nature according to the U.S. To a considerable degree these items were also subject to export controls of allied nations through CoCom. The U.S. controls however required licenses for many items that were not agreed by CoCom to be strategic.

In October 1972 the U.S. and the U.S.S.R. concluded a Trade Agreement which gave each most favoured nation treatment with respect to customs and duties for the products of the other.[131] But in January 1975, in reaction to legislation passed by Congress, the Soviet Union would no longer accept the terms of the Trade Agreement.[132] It collapsed without ever having been formally put into effect.[133]

Political relations with the Soviet Union were troubled in the late 1970s with regard to Soviet observance of the Helsinki accords and treatment of dissidents.[134] To increase the pressure upon the Soviet Union[135] licenses for petroleum equipment were required by August 1978.[136]

It was becoming clear that foreign policy considerations were entering into U.S.-Soviet trade relations to a greater degree than in the early 1970s. More precisely, it was becoming clear that U.S. export controls for exports to the Soviet Union were foreign policy oriented as well as national security based.

On December 27, 1979 the President of Afghanistan was arrested and executed by revolutionaries. The Soviet Union had already sent troops to Afghanistan prior to the arrest[137] and continued to send more afterwards.[138] On January 4, 1980 the President responded with a television announcement of measures including the suspension of exports of high technology items, including computers and oil drilling equipment, curtailment of Soviet fishing privileges and a limit on the amount of grain that would be exported.[139] The Department of Commerce revoked the general licence to export agricultural commodities to the Soviet Union and announced that it would deny licenses for grain exports beyond the limit set by the

President.[140]

The U.S. also supported a Security Council resolution which called for the immediate and unconditional withdrawal of all foreign troops from Afghanistan.[141] It was vetoed by the Soviet Union. It was clear there was no use trying to pursue the U.N. Security Council route to have mandatory sanctions imposed; they were sure to meet with a Soviet veto.

The President also sent a memorandum to the Secretary of Commerce requiring him not to issue any licenses for goods or technical data to the Soviet Union and to suspend those that had been issued pending the implementation of the new policy.[142] This was implemented by regulations under the *EAA* on January 11, 1980.[143] As well exports to the Soviet Kama River truck plant were prohibited.[144]

The new policy was not an outright denial of high technology exports to the Soviet Union. Rather, they would be licensed more strictly.[145] The U.S. would no longer consent to any exceptions being made by CoCom either. This would have the effect of denying the export as CoCom requires unanimous consent of its members for an exception to the items on its list of prohibited exports to the Soviet Bloc.[146]

After a series of requests to the olympic committees of the U.S. and other countries to boycott the Moscow Olympics of 1980, the President decided on February 20, 1980 that the U.S. would not participate.[147] The U.S. Olympic Committee went along with this decision.[148] So did some other countries,[19] including Canada, the F.R.G. and Japan.[149]

March 13, 1980 the President requested a voluntary embargo on exports of products related to the Olympics.[150] Two weeks later the embargo was made mandatory.[151] The embargo was implemented on the basis of the foreign policy power allowed the President in section 6 of the *EAA*.[152] The earlier export measures relating directly to the Soviet invasion of Afghanistan had straddled the national security power in section 5 and the foreign policy power of section 6 to avoid Congress blocking the export prohibition with respect to agricultural commodities.[153]

The regulations were implemented under the *EAA* which prohibit the export from the U.S. of all commodities and technical data without a license.[154] In addition, all re-exports were prohibited without a license.[155] The prohibition on supplying the Moscow Olympics[156] applied to persons "subject to the jurisdiction of the United States".[157] In these regulations the term was defined differently from earlier regulations.[158] The same term did not in this case include foreign corporations owned or controlled by U.S. persons.[159] Some control was however exercised over the U.S. persons who might own or control such a foreign company. They were subject to the regulations where they "actually" authorized, or participated in a transaction by a foreign company.[160] The provision specified that the mere ownership, financial interest in or a position with another person would not suffice to consider the U.S. person to have performed the transaction.[161]

> A person subject to the jurisdiction of the United States who actually authorizes, arranges, directs or actually participates in the authorization, arrangement or

> direction of a particular export transaction may be considered to have performed that transaction, but no person will be deemed to have so participated solely by reason of having an ownership or financial interest in or position with another person.

The regulations which dealt with the control of grain exports applied only to "U.S. origin" agricultural commodities.[162] In practice this meant only U.S. grown grain.[163] In January, 1980, the U.S. requested that grain companies operating in the U.S. voluntarily refrain from selling grain grown elsewhere to the Soviet Union as well.[164] Apparently the companies complied.[165] This involved foreign operations of companies with respect to foreign grown grain, and thus was extraterritorial with little jurisdictional link to the U.S. The request was withdrawn in June 1980.[166]

The U.S. grain contract offered by the Commodity Credit Corporation required a certification stating that the company had complied with the restrictive policies of any foreign country with respect to the Soviet Union for grain produced or transshipped through them.

> The Exporter certifies that both it and its affiliates have complied and will comply with any lawful restrictions or announced restrictive policies with respect to the exportation of agricultural commodities and products to the U.S.S.R. which have been or may be imposed by any foreign countries with respect to commodities which have been produced in, or are being transshipped through, such country.[167]

It is most interesting to note the extent to which the U.S. was willing to enforce foreign export restrictions where the policy coincided with its own. The breach of a certification was stated in the contract to be a material breach allowing the Commodity Credit Corporation to rescind the contract.[168]

While the imposition of the voluntary extraterritorial grain embargo caused protest from other countries,[169] not applying it to foreign produced grain drew protest in the U.S. Congress.[170] The motivation may have been as much to protect the U.S. grain companies as to reflect concern for intrusion in the affairs of other countries.[171]

Ronald Reagan became President in January 1981. The grain embargo in particular had been a significant election issue.[172] At first there was speculation that the new President found the embargo could be effective and was inclined to keep it despite campaign promises to lift the grain embargo if he were elected.[173] Shortly after the inauguration, it was stated that the grain embargo had been kept only as a temporary measure by the new administration and it was lifted April 24, 1981.[174] Agreement was reached August of 1981 to extend the grain agreement with the Soviet Union for another year.[175] On the imposition of martial law in Poland, one of the U.S. sanctions against the Soviet Union included postponement of negotiations of a new agreement.[176] The agreement was in fact extended for another year on its expiry.[177]

(ii) *Poland.* December 13, 1981, martial law was declared in Poland.[178] Ten days later President Reagan announced sanctions had been taken against the Polish government.[179] The measures included the suspension of government sponsored agricultural exports to Poland, a decision not to renew export credits for the Polish government, suspension of Polish fishing rights in U.S. waters, and a proposal to U.S. allies to further restrict high technology exports to Poland.[180]

Shortly thereafter, new sanctions against the Soviet Union were also announced.[181] They included the suspension of issuance or renewal of export licenses for electronics, computers and other high technology materials and greater controls on oil and gas equipment exports and denial of all such licenses.[182] The oil and gas equipment controlled heretofore had been that used in exploration and production. Now the controls extended to equipment for transmission or refining of oil and gas,[183] meaning that the U.S. intended to hinder the Soviet natural gas pipeline.[184] Prior to this time the case of a French company proposing a sale of computerized gas flow control equipment, had come before CoCom.[185] The sale was allowed with the proposal changed to not exclude the latest technology.[186] On December 9, 1981 the Commerce Department licensed an export of 200 pipelayers for the pipeline by Caterpillar Tractor.[187] The President's sanction on the Soviet Union resulted in the revocation of the Caterpillar Tractor license, and rotors and nozzles, intended for export by General Electric, needed licenses.[188] The policy was to deny such licenses.[189]

January 23, 1982 NATO countries agreed to deny further credits to Poland but not the Soviet Union.[190] The same day France signed an agreement to buy gas from the Soviet Union for the next 25 years.[191] There was an "agreement" between the United States and European governments about the measures to be taken. It was interpreted by the F.R.G. however to mean the U.S. would not interfere with any deal they chose to make, while it was interpreted by the U.S. to mean the Europeans would not defeat any measures it took against the Soviet Union.[192]

The original export controls did not apply to foreign companies.[193] But after the June summit that year they were extended by the President to include "equipment produced by subsidiaries of U.S. companies abroad, as well as equipment produced abroad under licenses issued by U.S. companies."[194]

The regulations that implemented the President's order affected foreign companies owned by U.S. parents. The regulations also affected them retroactively with respect to technology licensing agreements already existing when the regulations were issued. The regulations applied as well to foreign companies which were not controlled or owned by U.S. persons. One way in which this was done was to prohibit exports of foreign products of U.S. technical data retroactively,[195] although they were only affected where there was some ongoing contact with persons subject to U.S. jurisdiction by virtue of a licensing agreement or continuing payments.[196] The material definition of "person subject to the jurisdiction of the U.S." included foreign companies owned or controlled by U.S. persons.[197] Thus foreign companies, which had an agreement with a second foreign company allowed or controlled by a U.S. person with respect to U.S. technical data, were subject to the regulations. Foreign companies were also made subject to the U.S. law by virtue of a clause required by regulation in the technology transfer agreement, submitting them to U.S. law.[198] Submission to U.S. law was achieved by the recipient agreeing to abide generally by U.S. export control regulations[199] or having the export of the technological data conditional on written assurances that it would not be re-exported to the Soviet Union.[200] The foreign company would need a license from the Department of Commerce before it could re-export technological information.[201] Foreign governments and the E.C. protested the re-export prohibitions and the control asserted over foreign companies.[202]

They also ordered their companies to complete contracts entered into prior to the U.S. regulations of June 18, 1982.[203] The result was that several firms were denied U.S. export privileges.[204]

On October 9, 1982 the President announced that Poland would be denied the most favored nation treatment it was receiving pursuant to a treaty with the United States.[205] The export prohibitions were lifted November 13, 1982.[206] Days later the Temporary Denial Orders revoking export privileges to certain firms in Europe were also removed.[207] These measures represent the apogee of U.S. extraterritorial export controls. The measures were highly controversial. Their domestic legality was challenged[208] and they were unanimously condemned by the closest allies of the U.S.[209] as violations of international law. One may speculate that these criticisms had much to do with their early withdrawal. As a result of these measures the issue of extraterritoriality, long an irritant, became for a brief moment a major issue of foreign policy disagreement between the U.S. and its allies. Ironically, for once, Canada suffered little direct harm from the U.S. regulations.

(b) Iran

On November 4, 1979 the U.S. Embassy in Teheran was overrun and about 60 U.S. citizens held by the occupiers.[210] Ten days later the President acted pursuant to the *International Emergency Economic Powers Act*[211] to order all Iranian government entity interests in property blocked if they

> are or become subject to the jurisdiction of the United States or which are in or come within the possession or control of persons subject to the jurisdiction of the United States.[212]

It became clear that half of the assets blocked were in deposits in banks outside the U.S.[213]

The regulations that were enacted, pursuant to the Presidential invocation of the *IEEPA*, formed part of the *Iranian Assets Control Regulations*.[214] They only froze government interests, not those of Iranian persons.[215] This was based on the belief that it might be possible to continue normal commercial transactions and only affect financial operations[216] but that was not entirely possible.[217] In effect the freeze affected commercial dealings with Iranian government entities and any private transactions dependent on financial services in which the Iranian government had an interest.[218]

The freeze order extended to foreign subsidiaries which were subject to the jurisdiction of the U.S.[219] thus deposits in any U.S. owned banks were affected.[220]

But on November 19, 1979, assets held in currencies other than U.S. dollars were "unblocked".[221] Even so, the U.K. was upset about the U.S. application of its law to U.S. banks in Britain.[222]

There is one reported case which came out of the controversy. In *Chase Manhattan Bank, N.A.* v. *State of Iran*[223] Chase sued in a U.S. court for an injunction restraining Iran from pursuing its suit in England to have returned the dollar deposits which totalled about $315 million (U.S.), from Chase's London Branch. The judge deciding the case held the standard of a vexatious or unreasonable choice of forum by Iran had not been met. In *obiter dicta* the judge said Chase went too far in urging that the controversy should be decided solely under U.S. law in order to prevent evasion of the President's blocking order. He continued:

> Perhaps the ultimate legal question involved is whether the President's blocking order, and the regulations thereunder, are valid under English law with respect to an English branch of an American bank.[224]

Thus the U.S. court could not use any enforcement mechanism at its disposal to enforce the freeze order.

The Security Council of the U.N. adopted a resolution urgently calling upon Iran to release the U.S. Embassy personnel.[225] But the Security Council could not decide to adopt measures under Chapter VII of the *U.N. Charter* due to the veto of the Soviet Union.[226] It thus only decided to meet and take Chapter VII action in the event of non-compliance with S.C. Res. 461 which called for the release of U.S. Embassy personnel once again. On meeting to consider a draft resolution which would have provided mandatory export prohibitions of all goods save for food and medical supplies, of all credit facilities and service contracts, the Soviet Union, and the German Democratic Republic voted against the U.S. sponsored resolution.[227]

The freeze of assets was at first said to be a response to a threat of Iranian attack on the U.S. economy but, even prior to the imposition of an export embargo, was officially stato have as its purpose to pressure the Iranian government into releasing the hostages.[228] In April 1980 the regulations were amended to impose an export embargo and extend the assets freeze to Iranian persons other than the government.[229] These regulations were administered by the Treasury Department.

Unlike other Treasury administered embargoes, the export embargo did not apply to foreign corporations owned by U.S. parents.[230] Although the foreign corporations were excepted, the U.S. parents were required to:

> report to the Office of Foreign Assets Control any prospective transaction with Iran ... ten days before any subsidiary enters into such a transaction.[231]

This was likely a cause of some U.S. based multinationals establishing corporate policies that went beyond the regulations and banned their foreign subsidiaries' trade altogether.[232] The ten days notice implied a threat that if the exception for foreign non-banking subsidiaries was used it would be closed.[233]

The export embargo was removed in February 1980.[234] It was not lifted until a month after the U.S. and Iran had come to an agreement with Iran and the hostages had been released.[235] The month was spent reviewing the agreement that had been reached and whether to implement it.[236] This rather extraordinary review took place due to the change in U.S. Presidents the day the hostages were released.

The Iran regulations were lifted with respect to the embargo[237] but remained in effect with respect to financial transactions. Military items had been denied throughout. In order to circumvent the export controls unscrupulous exporters often used false ultimate destinations.[238] By 1984 the export controls were back.[239] This time they were imposed as anti-terrorism measures[240] and implemented under the Department of Commerce regulations issued under the *EAA*. The export controls included denials of licenses for all sorts of aircraft items, vehicles and crime fighting equipment.[241] In addition to the anti-terrorism controls on items not controlled for national security purposes, the items subject to the national security controls were to be denied any Iranian military end use or user.[242]

(c) Argentina

The U.S. took some time to respond to the crisis in the Falkland Islands and only announced sanctions equivalent to the E.E.C., Canada and Australia on April 30, 1982, almost a month after the Argentine invasion had occurred.[243] One reason for this delay was that the U.S. was a member of the Organization of American States (OAS) and as such was bound by the *Rio Treaty*.[244] Article 3 of the Treaty provided for response to the armed attack against of a member. Argentina considered the Falklands as its territory so that according to this view the British action fell within Article 3, and therefore was "an attack against all the American States." Article 6 provided for situations other than an armed attack which might endanger the peace of the region. The U.S. was torn between the demands of two allies the U.K. and Argentina. It did however assist the U.K. military effort early on.[245] The U.S. stated its position as being that the first use of force did not come from outside the hemisphere.[246]

The announced U.S. measures included the suspension of all military equipment exports and all military assistance to Argentina. As well, export credits and guarantees were suspended. Both Export-Import Bank and Commodity Credit Corporation facilities were revoked. On the other hand, the U.S. publicity stated it would allow exports for the British forces.[247]

The U.S. measures came in for much criticism from the OAS. In Resolution I of April 28, 1982 the majority of OAS members deplored the "measures taken by states prejudicial to the Argentine nation."[248] Resolution II adopted on May 29, 1982 urged the U.S. to immediately lift the coercive measures it applied.[249] The U.S. abstained from both resolutions. It explained that it would lift its measures once the U.N. Security Council Resolution 502 was complied with.[250]

The Inter-American Economic and Social Council of the OAS adopted a resolution declaring measures adopted against the Argentine Republic to be in violation of the OAS *Charter*, and the *U.N. Charter*.[251] The U.S. was bound to pay a serious political price for its support of the British. In the circumstances, the adoption of strictly territorial measures was calculated to avoid irritating the other belligerent and traditional O.A.S. allies.

The special controls that remain on Argentina are for crime control and detection equipment. Military vehicles and some machinery which could manufacture military equipment are all controlled.[252] This is the same as has existed for all of the Americas, except Canada, since the end of the Malvinas crisis.[253]

B. Reaction to International Action in which the U.S. Did Not Participate

1. Arab Boycott of Israel

Although the Arab boycott of Israel had already caused much concern in the U.S., only after the OPEC countries embargo of the U.S. in 1973 had it assumed major political dimensions.[254] The boycott first began in 1954 when the Council of the Arab League adopted a resolution to boycott Israel.[255]

Like Canada, the U.S. did not pay any special attention to the Arab boycott of Israel for its first 20 years. It did have legislation that set out its policy in general terms.[256]

> It is the policy of the United States to oppose restrictive trade practices or boycotts fostered or imposed by foreign countries against any country that is friendly.[257]

The statute merely required that a report of a boycott request was to be made to the Secretary of Commerce.[258] The *Export Control Act* had added to it a provision encouraging and requesting domestic concerns to refuse to take any action furthering restrictive trade practices or boycotts.[259] Beginning October 7, 1965 reports were to be made within 15 days.[260] Later the reporting was changed to within two weeks of the close of a quarter of a calendar year[261] due to the number of reports received.

In the 9 months following imposition of reporting requirements 5,235 such reports were filed, and over three quarters were as a result of the Arab boycott of Israel.[262] This volume continued.[263] By 1975 it had increased to 7,396 transactions concerned in 6 months, with 4,143 of those stating they would comply.[264]

On October 1, 1975 the *Export Administration Regulations* were amended to require a statement from the exporter as to whether he would comply or not.[265] Little more than a month later President Ford issued a Presidential statement that it had been decided that comprehensive measures would be taken against discrimination that might arise from foreign boycotts.[266] The President stated that these measures "are being taken with due regard for ... the sovereign rights of other nations."[267] The same day the regulations were amended.[268]

In the amended regulations the reporting requirements were to continue.[269] Where the reports dealt with discrimination against U.S. citizens on the basis of race, color, religion, sex or national origin, compliance was prohibited.[270] Compliance with other measures was only discouraged.[271] Section 4(b)(1) of the *Export Administration Act of 1969* provided that all "domestic concerns" must report. The regulations included all exporters and others involved in the "export or negotiations leading towards the export from the United States".[272] Thus the question was open as to the extent to which foreign persons were addressed by these provisions.

In 1976 there was more concrete legislative action by the U.S. The *Tax Reform Act of 1976* amended the *Internal Revenue Code* (I.R.C.) to include a penalty on U.S. taxpayers and related companies who agreed to refrain from doing business with persons linked to Israel.[273] There were some exceptions, the most relevant being that the penalty would not be imposed where the person agreed not to import from or export to Israel itself. Thus the secondary boycott was the aim of the section.[274]

The *Tax Reform Act* of 1976 also included participation in corporations controlled by a person so that the act of either of them was presumed to be the act of the other. Using this provision it seems that foreign subsidiaries were being reached by the legislation. It is surely the case that, using its jurisdiction over U.S. taxpayers, the provisions reached into transactions in foreign commerce on the basis of ownership in foreign corporations.[275]

Late in 1976 and in 1977 the U.S. Congress saw several bills proposing to strengthen the anti-boycott provisions. They resulted in amendments to the *Export Administration Act* in 1977.[276] The prohibitions on discrimination were basically taken from the 1975 regulations made under President Ford's order.[277] The new part was that all refusals by a "U.S. person" to do business with a boycotted country could be prohibited.[278]

The amendments applied extraterritorially without any doubt. The definition of a "U.S. person" included foreign subsidiaries which were "controlled in fact" by a domestic concern.[279] It seems that "domestic concern" restricted the definition of "U.S. person" to corporations controlled by other corporations only.[280] The regulations elaborated that "controlled in fact" meant where the domestic concern established the general policies or controls the day to day operations of the foreign subsidiary.[281] There were also rebuttable presumptions of such control in fact where the domestic concern a) owned 50% voting securities;[282] b) owned 25%, but the largest single block;[283] c) ran the subsidiary by a management contract;[284] d) a majority of the subsidiary's board of directors were directors of the parent,[285] it could appoint the majority of directors of the subsidiary[286] or; f) could appoint the subsidiaries' chief executive officer.[287]

Simply stated the new anti-boycott provisions in the *EAA* applied extraterritorially to foreign companies.[288] The prohibition however applied only with respect to "interstate or foreign commerce of the United States."[289] For a foreign subsidiary that was "controlled in fact", the definition of "foreign commerce of the United States"[290] was quite complex. If the foreign subsidiary transacted with a U.S. person it was clearly caught.[291] The direction by the U.S. parent of the foreign subsidiary was also caught.[292]

The more complex cases were those where the foreign subsidiary dealt with others abroad. If acquired from a person in the U.S. and goods or services were involved, the transaction was caught when they were acquired for the purpose of a transaction with another person abroad.[293] The purpose of the transaction may have been determined by the filling of an actual order, a customary order, or an anticipated demand.[294]

There were also separate rules for goods and for services. Goods were also caught if they were merely "ultimately used without substantial alteration or modification" in a transaction outside the U.S.[295] Otherwise they were not caught.[296] Commingled goods were presumed caught unless there was sufficient foreign-origin inventory to fill the order.[297]

Services acquired from the U.S. without the purpose of filling a transaction were not caught if they were primarily for the foreign subsidiary's use, and not that of the client.[298] A chain of transactions with U.S. goods or services would still have been caught.[299] Even if the subsequent transaction was not caught the export from the U.S. would be.[300] If any part of the transaction was in U.S. commerce then it "tainted" the rest of the transaction and the whole was caught.[301] But if there was no transfer of goods or services from the U.S. then the transaction would not be caught.[302]

The anti-boycott regulations thus covered transactions with goods or services coming from the U.S. and to this extent narrowed the degree to which they applied to corporation-controlled foreign subsidiaries. While the provision that effected this limit of the U.S. law was the requirement that activities take place "in U.S. commerce", that requirement was not present in a subsection that permitted the Department of Commerce to "request" foreign subsidiaries to provide information for transactions not caught because they were "outside U.S. commerce."[303]

The regulations applied to the foreign subsidiaries directly[304] and not only to their U.S. parent.[305] They determined where the foreign subsidiary may have been in breach of them without the parent breaching.[306] The foreign subsidiary was also required to file reports.[307]

The U.S. regulations have been enforced with respect to transactions in U.S. commerce by foreign subsidiaries.[308] In the typical case, consent judgements were arranged. In such consent judgements, there is customarily a recital that the Department of Commerce has jurisdiction.[309] The consent agreement was somewhat different however in one of the cases with the largest fines. The foreign subsidiary of 3M company in the F.R.G. was alleged to have provided more than 90 negative certificates of origin. Although it entered into a consent agreement, it did so only in the following terms:

> 3M Deutschland waives its objection to the assertion of jurisdiction of the Department on the specific transactions identified … 3M Deutschland does not waive its objections to jurisdiction asserted by the Department … on matters other than the specific transactions …[310]

Jurisdiction in international law is not something that an individual may confer - it may only be conferred by a state's consent to another exercising its jurisdiction. By having individuals enter into consent agreements admitting jurisdiction however, the U.S. puts those individuals in positions in which it is more unlikely that their host state will take up their case, or that they will bring their case to the attention of their host state.

The regulations may also be enforced by private action according to some U.S. case law. In one case two Jewish physicians excluded from surgical teams sent to a Saudi Arabian hospital sued their employer. The District Court Judge ruled they could bring an action under the anti-boycott provisions of the *EAA*.[311] Another case has held that there is no such right of private action under the statute.[312]

C. Unilateral Action, Legislation or Practices Having Extraterritorial Effect

1. China, North Korea

U.S. export controls applicable to China began even before the establishment of the People's Republic of China (China) in October 1949.[313] By March 1950 they were equivalent to those on exports to the Soviet Bloc.[314]

Within five days of the outbreak of the Korean War, on June 25, 1950, a total embargo on exports to North Korea and China was in place.[315] Licenses requiring specific approval were revoked July 20, 1950.[316] Controls of the CoCom were extended to China in July 1950.[317]

Petroleum from any source was voluntarily embargoed by major U.S. oil companies in August, 1950, and in November under the authority of the *Defence Production Act* of 1950[318] the transportation of goods in U.S. ships or aircraft was prohibited to the Soviet Bloc and more strictly to China and N. Korea.[319] On December 3, 1950 all exports to China required specific approval and no general license could be used,[320] and on December 16, 1950 the *Foreign Assets Control Regulations*[321] were enacted as the result of an emergency declared by the President[322] the previous day. The U.S. government stated: "It is not our desire that this be a permanent restriction."[323] The *Foreign Assets Control Regulations* (*FACR*s) were issued under the *Trading With the Enemy Act* of 1917.[324]

Under the *FACR*s the Treasury Department, which was responsible for their administration, compiled a list of specially designated nationals who supposedly acted for the benefit of China. In this way nationals of foreign countries were and are affected by the *FACR*s outside the U.S.[325] Another way in which foreign persons outside the U.S. could be affected by the *FACR*s is the provision applying the regulations to business entities owned or controlled by U.S. persons.[326]

These U.S. measures pre-dated the U.N. sanctions that were called for by the General Assembly on May 18, 1951 in Resolution 500 (V).[327] The U.N. General Assembly has only the power to recommend measures to its members and not to bind them in international law.[328] Only the Security Council may bind U.N. members.[329] The Security Council may specifically use measures that include requiring members of the U.N. to sever or interrupt economic relations.[330] Thus Resolution 500 V of the General Assembly could not be considered as binding in international law. Nevertheless, it did recommend an embargo on arms and strategic materials to China and North Korea.

Among the General Assembly recommendations was that each state:

> [p]revent by all means within its jurisdiction the circumvention of controls on shipments applied by other States pursuant to the present resolution.[331]

As well the recommendations called for cooperation in carrying out the purposes of the General Assembly recommended embargo.[332] These obligations to cooperate could not be considered to be obligations of international law. In any case they refer specifically to controls "pursuant" to the resolution. In as much as U.S. controls preceded the resolution they would not qualify for the purposes of the resolution. It may only be said that the general cooperation provision, "[c]ooperate with other States in carrying out the purposes of this embargo",[333] might be of avail to the U.S. in support of its controls. It must be noted that the resolution did recite that states had already taken measures prior to its passing, thus perhaps giving them legitimacy for all purposes in the context of the resolution.[334]

On the heels of the U.N. resolution the U.S. passed the "*Battle Act*".[335] This act provided three lists of items on which the decisions to refuse U.S. foreign aid are based. The first list is of strategic items and results in mandatory termination of aid. The second list is of items that may be used to manufacture military items and results in termination unless the President determines otherwise. The third list contains items the control of which is to be by negotiation rather than sanction.[336] In September 1952, the Consultative Group formed the China Committee (ChinaCom) with more extensive lists than those of the CoCom.[337] Japan joined the Consultative Group at this time and enforced a list even more comprehensive than the ChinaCom one.[338] The actions of the Consultative Group can be seen as similar to other international sentiment. As of May 1952, 45 countries had notified the U.N. that they had accepted and were applying the General Assembly Resolution 500(V) embargo on strategic items.[339] If the resolution by its nature was not a binding instrument in international law, at least it subsequently received the approbation of state practice, although it is not a necessary conclusion that a rule of customary international law was formed.

The U.S. commitment to the embargo resulted in its exports to China dropping in value from U.S. $354 million to U.S. $273 million in 1948, U.S. $83 million in 1949, and U.S. $47 million in 1950.[340] Trade with China would not have dropped correspondingly for some other countries that had placed an embargo on China, due to the fact that they were often unwilling to cooperate on non-strategic items.[341] The third report on the *Battle Act* to Congress stated:

> ... we had to recognize that other sovereign countries were entitled to make judgements of their own with respect to their own trade, and that we could not stop their nonstrategic shipments without taking measures that in the long run would do the free world and the United States far more harm than the existing trade could possibly do.[342]

The U.S. added still another measure on June 29, 1953 when the Treasury Department issued the *Transaction Control Regulations*.[343] These regulations prohibited trade in strategic merchandise to China and Soviet Bloc countries, they extended to U.S. owned or controlled corporations abroad. Clearly these regulations had the potential of irritating foreign governments.

July 27, 1953 the armistice in Korea was signed[344] but the U.S. position was that controls should be maintained and the U.N. Resolution continued in force.[345] U.S. control of arms was subsumed under the *Mutual Security Act* of 1954[346] section 414 of which is known as the *Munitions Control Act,*[347] and under which the *International Traffic in Arms Regulations* (*ITAR*s)[348] were issued.[349] These regulations separated arms controls from other controls, at least making clear just which controls aroused the protests that were to follow.

From this period until late in the 1960s the U.S. controls did not change. This remained the case despite the gradual lessening of CoCom controls and British leadership doing away with the ChinaCom controls in 1956 and 1957. While CoCom controls were the standard for its allies, the U.S. maintained its total embargo.[350]

The U.S. imposition of its law on owners of foreign companies for the foreign companies' acts created much resentment in Canada,[351] Britain[352] and France.[353] U.S. *Battle Act* lists were said by the French paper *Combat* to contain 1700 items.[354] As well, travel restrictions to China were in effect, based on the fact it "would seriously impair the conduct of U.S. foreign affairs."[355] Minor changes to the U.S. *FACR* controls on exports to China occurred June 23, 1969, and significant changes December 22, 1969.[356] These were mostly with respect to imports from China.[357] One other change was that ships and aircraft could "export" their services with respect to Chinese goods between foreign countries, but not to or from China.[358]

The one major change of concern to other countries was the lifting of the most far reaching extraterritorial control of foreign companies.[359] Foreign companies were allowed to trade with China in CoCom non-strategic[360] and in Chinese goods, removing the major feature of the *Foreign Asset Control Regulations* that caused protest from U.S. allies, such as Canada.[361] This helps explain the lack of Canadian protest about export controls to China after the latter half of the 1960s.

The *Export Administration Act* (*EAA*) was amended in 1969 to be used primarily to control militarily significant items.[362] Further the Commerce Department indicated that it would give permits for some U.S. origin items that were to be used as components in some foreign-made products destined for China.[363] Clearly this is another way in which potential friction with its allies, such as Canada, was avoided and thus likely contributed to the apparent lack of protests from Canada since 1968.

U.S. dollar transactions and some securities were still controlled.[364] The same was true of U.S. origin goods and technical data.[365] Currency controls were relaxed however in April 1971.[366] Travel restrictions were also dropped to China in April.[367] There then remained the travel restrictions to Cuba, N. Korea, and N. Vietnam.[368] Since July 1969 "almost anyone with a legitimate purpose to travel to mainland China" was allowed to do so.[369]

A further reduction occurred June 10, 1971 when a general license on exports of certain goods to China was created.[370] Then on Feb. 14, 1972, the U.S. ceased to treat exports to China more stringently than to the Soviet Union.[371] First, all goods available to the Soviet Union by general license were made available to China in the same way. Second, goods made abroad with U.S. technical data were limited only to the same extent as they were to the Soviet Union.[372]

As well as changes to lists under the *Export Control Act,* the *FACR*s were also amended. U.S. controlled companies in CoCom countries were no longer required to obtain a U.S. Treasury license for exports of strategic goods to China. The host country's export license would suffice. Similarly only the host CoCom country's license would suffice for the export of "foreign technology" by U.S. controlled firms.[373]

U.S. ships and aircraft were allowed to go to China by amendment of transportation orders in November 1972[374] but it was not until Jan. 1979 that relations were "normalized".[375] The "normalization" involved a policy where some technology transfers might be allowed that would not be allowed to the Soviet Union. As well, military support equipment such as trucks, some types of radar and communications equipment would be considered on a "case by case basis".[376] The control of re-exports was required of these sales, and it was enforceable by the control of the supply of spare parts.[377]

By the 1980s the China differential had thus turned into the "China preferential".[378] The 1100 items available to the Chinese from other CoCom countries in 1969 that only the U.S unilaterally controlled, were largely eliminated by 1972.[379] China was in the same group as the USSR until April 1980 but since then has been in a separate one.[380]

Other steps that President Reagan's administration has instituted include a greater likelihood of permit approval where required and the availability of U.S. government insurance for exports and investment in China.[381]

While the imposition of controls on China and N. Korea were simultaneous, relaxation of them has not been equivalent. Controls on N. Korea remain.[382]

2. Cuba

Fidel Castro seized power in Cuba in early 1959. U.S. export controls on arms were in place before that. They were announced in March 1958[383] but it was not until October 19, 1960 that the U.S. put into effect more general export prohibitions.[384] They were put into effect through the *Export Control Act* of 1949, which does not apply to subsidiaries of U.S. companies that are incorporated abroad.[385] Only food and medical supplies were exempt. The U.S. pressed Canada for assurances that U.S. origin goods would not be re-exported from Canada to Cuba without control.[386] Canada already controlled re-exports of U.S. origin goods[387] so the only change needed to abide by U.S. wishes was to revoke General Export Permits that would allow some items to be exported regardless of origin of the goods, and without case-by-case consideration. The action was taken by Canada on December 16, 1960.[388]

On September 4, 1961 the U.S. Congress enacted section 620(a) of the *Foreign Assistance Act of 1961*.[389] It empowered the President to "establish and maintain a total embargo upon all trade between the United States and Cuba."

The Organization of American States considered the problems of having a communist Cuba. The final Acts of the January 1962 meeting included a resolution to immediately cease trade in arms with Cuba.[390] The resolution also mandated the O.A.S. Council to study other trade sanctions.

Days later the U.S. imposition of a total trade embargo on Cuba was announced by Presidential Proclamation.[391] Only some food and medical supplies were exempt.[392] The Proclamation recited the *Foreign Assistance Act* of 1961 as authority, but directed that export controls be continued under the *Export Control Act* of 1949.[393] There was no change for export controls, only the addition of import controls and the addition of the *Foreign Assistance Act* as authority for the export controls.

At first the justification for export controls was retaliation for what the U.S. called a "deliberate political policy to divert trade away from the United States."[394] In the measures listed, the U.S. included the Cuban nationalizations.[395] Their effect on U.S. trade with Cuba was enormous. In 1958 trade was worth more than one billion dollars, but during the first 6 months of 1962 was only worth U.S. $373,000, all of which was exports from the U.S.[396]

The U.S. alleged that exports of military items to Cuba were prohibited by NATO allies as well as the O.A.S.[397] Apparently CoCom controls were never applied to Cuba despite U.S. pressure to do so.[398] U.S. controls were a complement to its stated policy to prevent an "externally supported military capability endangering the security" of the U.S.[399] In other words, it would prevent Soviet use of Cuba as a military base or as a missile launching ground.

February 6, 1963 the White House announced it would not permit government financed cargoes to be shipped on vessels that engaged in trade with Cuba.[400] This sanction further attempted to control the actions of foreign persons without any link to the U.S. used as justification.

Exports to Cuba from non-communist countries dropped from some U.S. $773 million in 1958 to U.S. $100 million in 1962.[401] Nevertheless, in the ame period, exports from Communist countries increased from U.S. $2 million to U.S. $550 million. Thus Cuba largely switched to importing from Communist countries.[402] Overall Cuban exports declined in value over the same period by nearly twice the amount that its imports declined.[403] Its exports also were directed towards Communist countries.[404]

The U.S. instituted the *Cuban Assets Control Regulations* on July 8, 1963.[405] The Regulations were administered by the Treasury Department and required licenses for all transactions not covered by the *Export Control Act* licensing of the Department of Commerce.[406] The *Export Control Act* only applied to U.S. origin goods, so for these transactions a general license was available under the *CACR*s, with the result that the exporter would only be subject to the Department of Commerce controls.[407]

The *CACR*s were very much like the *FACR*s that were instituted some ten years earlier. The one major difference was the apparent lack of extraterritorial features. The means by which this was accomplished was that, while the regulations applied to "persons subject to the jurisdiction of the United States", there was an exemption for foreign companies controlled by U.S. parents.[408] The officers or directors of those corporations were still controlled[409] although no one was liable merely by the ownership of the foreign company.[410]

The difference was more illusory than real. The threat was made that if this measure in fact permitted trade by U.S. controlled foreign companies, it would be amended.[411] The Treasury Department also found early in the *CACR*s application that foreign firms could be controlled by "persuading" their parents to ensure the subsidiary would not trade with Cuba.[412]

Apart from the export implications of the *CACR*s they also froze all Cuban government and nationals' assets in the U.S. Parallel restrictions prevented export of tourist dollars to Cuba by making U.S. passports invalid for Cuba unless specifically so endorsed by the Secretary of State.[413]

The U.S. restrictions were not eased until the O.A.S. resolution which allowed each state to determine its economic policies with respect to Cuba and to lift the mandatory embargo.[414]

Not only Canada had been making representations to the U.S. A most celebrated case was that of Argentina. Argentina declared that corporations within its borders, whether U.S. subsidiaries or not, were to follow only Argentinian law.[415] The result of the declaration was that Argentinian companies with U.S. parents secured orders for automobiles. Licenses for those goods were issued as an "exception to the United States regulations concerning foreign assets controls, which will continue to be maintained."[416] Secretary of State Henry Kissinger stated that some Argentinian and Canadian deals were licensed, despite the extraterritorial features of the U.S. law, so as to allow the behaviour of U.S. companies in those countries to comply with the policies of the host countries vis-à-vis Cuba.[417]

The U.S. measures only changed once the O.A.S. rescinded the mandatory sanctions against Cuba. Until that time any changes were only ascertainable on the administrative level – namely which licenses were granted and which were not. On that level it seemed that the embargo with respect to Cuba was complete and the only exceptions were due to diplomatic intervention by other countries, such as was the case with Canada.

The O.A.S. voted on a resolution to rescind the sanctions on Cuba about six months prior to the date on which the sanctions were ended. The first vote[418] failed to obtain the required a two-thirds majority. The result was that the *Rio Treaty* which constitutes the O.A.S. had to be amended to allow for the resolution to pass by a simple majority.[419] With that amendment made, the resolution to rescind the sanctions passed July 29, 1975.[420]

Following the O.A.S. action the U.S. announced that its policy was to license transactions between "U.S. subsidiaries and Cuba for trade in foreign-made goods when those subsidiaries are operating in countries where local law or policy favors trade with Cuba."[421] While such licenses were to be granted, restrictions would continue on U.S. origin parts, components, strategic goods and technology.[422]

The way in which most of these changes were implemented was by amendment of the Treasury *CACR*s.[423] The *CACR*s' section 515. 541 allowed foreign subsidiaries to conduct business with Cuba where the transactions were "incidental to the conduct of business activities abroad."[424] Section 515.541(e) specifically exempted persons who would otherwise be caught by the *CACR*s by the mere fact of their financial interest in a foreign subsidiary. Even so, the Office of Foreign Assets Control in the Treasury Department, which administered the *CACR*s, interpreted the *CACR*s to apply to U.S. officers and directors of the foreign subsidiaries and any U.S. person could act to prevent the foreign subsidiary's export to Cuba.[425] This view was incorporated into the *CACR*s in 1974 when it was stated in section 515.412 that section 515.541

> does not authorize United States citizens who are officers, directors or principal management personnel of such firms to engage, participate or be involved in transactions with Cuba; nor does it authorize such persons to allow firms which they control to engage in prohibited transactions with Cuba or its nationals. ... Such persons are regarded as being involved in prohibited transactions when they set policy or permit the foreign firm to engage in such transactions even if they do not themselves actually engage in such transactions.[426]

The changes after the O.A.S. resolution made licensing of foreign subsidiaries possible even with respect to foreign-made goods where U.S. origin items accounted for up to 20% of their value.[427] Section 515.541 was revoked however,[428] so that rather than being under a general license, each transaction required a specific license.[429]

Fifteen months later there were further amendments made to the provisions of the *CACR*s,[430] designed to prevent abuse by U.S. firms with foreign subsidiaries. Section 515.559(c) specified that the regulations applied to "persons within the United States"[431] however, it is basically the same definition as a "person subject to the jurisdiction of the United States" save that U.S. citizenship is not included within the definition. "Persons within the United States" include:

> Any partnership, association, corporation, or other organization, wheresoever organized, or doing business, which is owned or controlled by any person or persons specified in paragraphs (a)(1), (2) or (3) of the section.[432]

The *CACR*s did authorize the granting of specific licenses for transactions involving U.S. controlled firms in third countries. According to the regulations:

> Specific licenses issued pursuant to the policies set forth in this section do not authorize any person within the United States to engage in, participate in, or be involved in a licensed transaction with Cuba or Cuban nationals. Such involvement includes, but not by way of limitation, assistance or participation by a U.S. parent firm, or any officer or any officer or employee thereof, in the negotiation or performance of a transaction which is the subject of license application. Such participation is a ground for denial of a license application, or for revocation of a license. To be eligible for a license under this section, the affiliate must be generally independent, in the conduct of transactions of the type for which the license is being sought, in such matters as decision-making, risk-taking, negotiation, financing or arranging of financing, and performance. For purposes

> of this section, an affiliate is not independent if there are a substantial number of officers or directors of the foreign affiliate who are also officers or directors of a person within the United States.[433]

This "independence" test seems to preclude only active participation, although broadly covering any such participation. It seems that, unlike the previous wording of s. 515.412, the meaning of 515.541 was extended to failure to prevent action of a foreign firm, or in other words passive "participation". The definition of "person within the United States" does, however, narrow the number of foreign firms which may avail themselves of the provisions to have licenses issued for specific trades under 515.559(a)(1).[434] Persons "within the United States" include foreign firms owned by residents, or U.S. corporations.[435] In other words the only firms exempted are those that are owned by U.S. citizens not in the U.S. and perhaps firms owned by foreign subsidiaries of U.S. corporations.

The application of the "independence" test to Canada in two occasions show that the Treasury Department considered two of five and four of seven directors were a "substantial number" and sufficient to disqualify the Canadian corporations from the *CACR* exemption.[436]

In late 1977 there was a major reorganization of export control laws. The *Trading with the Enemy Act* (*TWEA*) was changed, the *International Emergency Economic Powers Act* (*IEEPA*) was adopted, and provision was made for the control of non-U.S. origin exports from foreign companies in the *Export Administration Act*.[437] The *CACR*s could no longer have been passed under the revised *TWEA*. Nevertheless, the *CACR*s remained in force under the authority of the *TWEA* due to provisions that grandfathered them and the *FACR*s as long as each was renewed by the President.[438]

Travel restrictions to Cuba were lifted on March 18, 1977.[439] They were however put back into place under President Reagan.[440]

Although the U.S. modified its foreign policy trade controls in 1982 to allow for the export of civil aircraft when assured they would not be used for military end-use, this was not to apply to Cuba and Libya.[441]

3. Uganda

The U.S. imposed an embargo on Uganda October 10, 1978.[442] Rather than a Presidential action on the basis of existing legislation, Congress adopted special legislation. The *Uganda Embargo Act*,[443] added as a rider to the *Bretton Woods Agreements Act*,[444] recited the commission of genocide by the Idi Amin regime as the reason it was enacted.[445] This gave the U.S. the possibility of justifying any unilateral act it took on the basis of a breach of international law by Uganda.[446]

The legislation dealt with both exports and imports. It banned all exports save for food.[447] It applied to "persons subject to the jurisdiction of the United States"; the proposed regulations referred to the definitions in the anti-boycott provisions to define the term.[448] Thus, "person subject to the jurisdiction of the United States" was said to mean "United States persons," which included "controlled in fact" subsidiaries. The basic definition in the proposed regulations was the same as that for the anti-boycott regulations, but was expanded to include foreign corporations owned by individuals as well as corporations.[449] This was achieved by expanding the definition of "controlled in fact" foreign subsidiaries to include those controlled by U.S. residents or nationals wherever they may be.

The Department of Commerce proposed use of this expanded definition for all of the *EAA* regulations.[450] This would have extended the extraterritorial jurisdiction of the Act however beyond its application to the re-export of U.S. origin goods, so it was criticized.[451] The result was that the proposal was withdrawn.[452] Nevertheless, the amendments to the *EAA* in 1977 appear to give the President the power to regulate exports extraterritorially.[453] The amendment extends the Presidential power to persons, as well as to goods subject to the jurisdiction of the U.S.[454] The amendments also restricted the *TWEA* to wartime use only and created the *International Emergency Economic Powers Act*[455] for non-wartime use.

There was thus no real objection to the extraterritorial application of U.S. Uganda regulations, nor extraterritorial regulations under the *EAA* generally after the 1977 amendments from the standpoint of U.S. law. The situation did not last long enough for the proposed Uganda regulations to be adopted in final form however.[456] The *Uganda Embargo Act* stated that export controls were to continue until the President determined and certified to Congress that Uganda was no longer committing gross human rights violations.[457] This he did effective May 17, 1979.[458] The eight month embargo did not give rise to much controversy because its application in practice did not seem to pit countries against one another. There was protest however from other governments with respect to the extent of jurisdiction claimed in the proposed regulations.[459]

4. Libya

The U.S. export controls on Libya came about as the result of a series of legislative acts to combat terrorism.[460] In 1977, the *Export Administration Act* amendments included a policy to use export controls to fight terrorism if international cooperative means were ineffective.[461] Several bills were introduced in the late 1970s which would have required presidential action and consideration of trade sanctions against countries supporting terrorism.[462] These Bills were reintroduced prior to the 1979 amendments to the *EAA*.[463] They would have provided for automatic sanctions when certain tests were met.

The amendments to the *EAA* in 1979 provided for the notification of Congress in cases of exports with a value of more than $7 million (U.S.) to a country that supports international terrorism.[464] The notification was to be before any license for the export was approved. Thus mandatory controls were not imposed by the amendment,[465] rather it dealt with the controls that already existed.

The terrorism amendment to the *EAA* assigned to the Secretary of State the determination of which states support terrorism. Among the states named by the State Department was Libya.[466] Validated licences were required by the regulations for all goods valued at $7 million (U.S.) or more for military use or users, as well as crime control equipment, vehicles, aircraft and similar items.[467] The regulations were only enacted after it became apparent that the existing regulatory scheme was inadequate to cover some situations where foreign countries included U.S. components in finished products for sale to listed countries.[468] The regulations also extended the controls to all exports to military end users or for a military end use.[469]

It was an export of engine cores for frigates destined for Iraq, which was also on the U.S. terrorism list, that caused the implementation of the more restrictive regulations in May of 1980.[470] Because only the U.S. imposed controls on exports to terrorist supporting countries,[471] the U.S. controls were said to be "relatively easy and lucrative to evade".[472]

In March 1982, all U.S. origin goods and technical data exports to Libya were placed under case-by-case export licensing scrutiny with the policy made clear that licenses for national security equipment would generally be denied.[473] There were exceptions made to the national security controls. Licences would be issued "where failure to obtain a license would not excuse performance" under pre-existing contract.[474] Licenses would also be issued where the goods exported prior to the regulations were not national security controlled.[475]

There was also a rule allowing for licensing of re-exports from foreign countries where the U.S. origin items made up 20% or less of the value of the goods.[476] As well there was a general rule that license applications would be favourably considered for re-exports of goods or data subject to national security controls that had been exported from the U.S. prior to the regulations if "not contrary to specific foreign policy objectives of the United States."[477] All other exports and re-exports would likely be approved.[478]

It appears that in July 1983 the U.S. urged Western countries and others that might have excess aircraft that could be offered to Libya in July 1983 to restrict the sale of such aircraft or aircraft parts to Libya.[479]

Further important measures were taken against Libya during the course of 1986. These included the *Libyan Sanctions Regulations*.[480] Perhaps in response to mounting criticism of such measures, the extraterritorial aspect of these amendments is surprisingly muted given the level of hostility between the two states. Apart from the application of the Regulations to U.S. nationals and a prohibition upon transshipment and transactions for the purpose of evasion, they are largely territorial in scope.

5. Nicaragua

On May 7, 1985 the *Nicaragua Trade Control Regulations* came into effect.[481] They implemented the President's Executive Order of May 1,[482] which invoked the *IEEPA* as authority for both import and export prohibitions on goods and services to and from Nicaragua, by declaring a national emergency. The national emergency was stated to be due to a finding

> that the policies and actions of the Government of Nicaragua constitute an unusual and extraordinary threat to the national security and foreign policy of the United States...[483]

There appears to be very broad Presidential discretion to determine the existence of a threat to the U.S. Once the regulations were enacted the Secretary of the Treasury was delegated to implement them.

The U.S. administration seems to have gone to some pains to avoid conflict with allies as a result of extraterritorial extension of its laws. The Treasury Department regulations specifically state they do not apply to the export of goods to, or destined for, Nicaragua "from locations outside the United States."[484] Possible extraterritorial effects were eliminated from the Treasury Department regulations. Nevertheless, there is still a license requirement which serves to control U.S. origin goods under the Commerce Department regulations. That Department may deny its license for re-exports of U.S. origin goods and thus the Regulations may be extraterritorial.[485]

In light of the Presidential Order the Commerce Department policy is to deny goods to Nicaragua as well.[486]

Notes

1. H.J. Berman & J.R. Garson, "U.S. Export Controls – Past, Present and Future" (1967) 67 Colum L. Rev. 791 at 814–15 [hereinafter *Berman & Garson*].
2. UNSC Res. 217, UN Doc. S/Res./217 (1965).
3. Dec. 30, 1945, S. 1580, c. 583, Pub. L. 79–264, 59 Stat. 619 codified at 22 U.S.C. 287.
4. *Ibid.* Pub. L. 79–264 at s. 5(a).
5. The first was April 9, 1966, SC Res. 221, 5 UN Doc. S/INF/21/Rev. 1 (1966).
6. "All U.S. Exports to Rhodesia to Require Validated Licenses", 54 U.S. Dep't State Bull. 466, March 21, 1966.
7. *Ibid.* See also 54 U.S. Dep't State Bull. 27, 85 and 157, Jan. 3, 17, and 31, 1966 (respectively).
8. "Southern Rhodesia and the United Nations: The U.S. Position" 56 U.S. Dep't State Bull. 366, Mar. 6, 1967 at 370.
9. 21 UN SCOR, Res. & Decs. at 7, UN Doc. S/Res./232 (1966).
10. Executive Order 11,322, 32 Fed. Reg. 119 (1967); reprinted in 56 U.S. Dep't State Bull. 146, Jan. 23, 1967.
11. Under its successor, the *Export Administration Act* (*EAA*), the situation changed in 1977 at which time the *EAA* first gave the president the power to reach exports of foreign origin goods extraterritorially under the *EAA*. See R.B. Thompson, "United States Jurisdiction over Foreign Subsidiaries: Corporate and International Law Aspects" (1983) 15 L. & Pol. Int'l Bus. 319 at 344–47 [hereinafter *Thompson*], for the legislative history of this change.
12. 56 U.S. Dep't State Bull. 146, *supra,* note 10.
13. 31 C.F.R. 525 (1967) added by 32 Fed. Reg. 3448 (1967), later replaced by 31 C.F.R. 530 as per 33 Fed. Reg. 11524.
14. *Thompson, supra,* note 11 at 334.
15. 31 C.F.R. 530.307, see also at 334.
16. 31 C.F.R. 530.307(4) (1970).

17. 31 C.F.R. 530.404 (1970).
18. 31 C.F.R. 530.405 (1970).
19. See *Thompson, supra,* note 11 at 335.
20. *Ibid.* at 336.
21. 31 C.F.R. 530.201(a)(3) and (b).
22. *Thompson, supra,* note 11 at 336.
23. This may raise the question whether the President had exceeded his powers under section 5(a) of the *UNPA*.
24. *Supra,* note 3.
25. *Ibid.* at 375.
26. UN Doc. S/Res./253, (1968).
27. "U.S. Extends Program Banning Trade with Southern Rhodesia", Press Release 176, July 29, 1968, 59 U.S. Dep't State Bull. 199, Aug. 19, 1968; Executive Order 11,419 implemented by 33 Fed. Reg. 11,524, Aug. 13, 1968.
28. *Ibid.* 59 U.S. Dep't State Bull. 199.
29. 33 Fed. Reg. 11,524, revoked 31 C.F.R. 525 and created 31 C.F.R. 530.
30. U.S./U.N. Press Release 67, June 24, 1969, 61 U.S. Dep't State Bull. 57, July 21, 1969 at 58.
31. *Ibid.*
32. The resolution is reprinted *ibid.* It is UN Doc. S/9270/Rev.1.
33. *Ibid.*
34. Section 503 of the *Military Procurement Act* of 1971, Nov. 17, 1971, H.R. 8687, Pub. L. 92–156, 85 Stat. 423 at 427. See E.A. Paschall, "Price of United States non-compliance with United Nations Rhodesian Sanctions" (1975) 5 Ga. J. Int'l & Comp. L. 558 at 559 [hereinafter *Paschall*] for the legislative history of the provision.
35. *Paschall, ibid.* at 564.
36. UNGA Res. 2765 (XXVI), UN Doc. A/Res./2765 (XXVI) A/C.4/L.988/Rev. 1, which adopted the resolution by a vote of 106 to 2 with 13 abstentions. Reprinted in 65 U.S. Dep't State Bull. 690, Dec. 13, 1971.
37. UN Doc. S/Res./320 (1972) S/10804/Rev.1, September 29, 1972, adopted by a vote of 13 to 0 with 2 abstentions (U.K. and U.S.).
38. "U.S. Abstains on Security Council Resolutions on Southern Rhodesia", U.S./U.N. Press Release 109, September 29, 1972, 67 U.S. Dep't State Bull. 543.
39. *Ibid.* at 544.
40. *Ibid.* The U.S. delegation mentioned that one of them was the U.S. and it is a likely inference that the other was the U.K.
41. *Ibid.* at 544–45.
42. *Ibid.*
43. *Ibid.*
44. UN Doc. S/10928; reprinted in 69 U.S. Dep't State Bull. 43, July 2, 1973.
45. March 18, 1977, H.R. 1746, Pub. L. 95–12, 91 Stat. 22.
46. 77 U.S. Dep't State Bull. 66, July 11, 1977.
47. UN Doc. S/Res./409, adopted by consensus, May 27, 1977.
48. *Supra,* note 27.
49. *Thompson, supra,* note 11 at 336–38 and A.F. Lowenfeld, *International Economic Law,* 2nd ed., vol. III (U.S.A.: Matthew Bender, 1983) [*Trade Controls for Political Ends*] at 485–89 [hereinafter *Lowenfeld*].
50. *Thompson, ibid.*
51. *Ibid.* at 338.
52. *Ibid.* at 338–39.
53. *Ibid.* at 339.
54. *Internal Security Assistance Act of 1978,* s. 27, Sept. 26, 1978, S. 3075, Pub. L. 95–384, 92 Stat. 730 at 746, Sept. 26, 1978.
55. 15 Weekly Comp. Press. Docs. 1012 (1979), as cited in *Lowenfeld, supra,* note 49 at

519, note 1.

56. Section 408(b) of the *Department of State Authorization Act,* Fiscal Years 1980 and 1981, (*DSAA*), Aug. 15, 1979, H.R. 3363, Pub. L. 96–60, 93 Stat. 395 at 405.
57. See P.F. Hurst Jr., "Economic Sanctions: The Lifting of Sanctions against Zimbabwe-Rhodesia by the United States" (1980) 21 Harv. Int'l L.J. 253 at 256 [hereinafter *Hurst*].
58. 15 Weekly Comp. Pres. Docs. (Nov. 19, 1979); reprinted in 80 U.S. Dep't State Bull. 10, Feb., 1980.
59. *Ibid.* Congress could, by resolution, within 30 days have rejected the President's report and ended sanctions. Section 408(b) of the *DSAA*.
60. 80 U.S. Dep't State Bull. 11, Feb. 1980.
61. *Lowenfeld, supra,* note 49 at 525.
62. 80 U.S. Dep't State Bull. 11, Feb. 1980. Exec. Order 12, 183 of Dec. 16, 1979, 15 Weekly Comp. Pres. Docs. 2251, 44 Fed. Reg. 74,787 (Dec. 18, 1979).
63. 80 U.S. Dep't State Bull. 11, Feb. 1980.
64. U.N. Doc. S/13699 (1979).
65. Which it had itself introduced. See *Lowenfeld, supra,* note 49 at 350.
66. *Ibid.* at 530.
67. Also see *Hurst, supra,* note 57 at 259.
68. The Soviet Union circulated a letter to that effect, U.N. Doc. S/13702 of Dec. 21, 1979. Also see *Lowenfeld, supra,* note 49 at 530. See also *Hurst, ibid.* at 253.
69. See *Lowenfeld, ibid.*
70. In fact the U.N. General Assembly passed Resolution 192 on Dec. 18, 1979 which deplored unilateral lifting of sanctions by a vote of 95 to 17.
71. M.J. Mehlman, T.H. Mitch & M.V. Tourmanoff, "United States Restrictions and Exports to South Africa" (1979) 73 Am J. Int'l L. 581 at 582 [hereinafter *Mehlman*] .
72. SC Res. 181, UN SCOR, UN Doc. S/P V. 5386 (1963).
73. *Ibid.*
74. *Mehlman, supra,* note 71 at 582–83.
75. *Ibid.* at 583.
76. *Ibid.*
77. Press Release 104, April 6, 1973, 68 U.S. Dep't State Bull. 581, May 7, 1973.
78. I.e., equipment that may have either military or civilian use such as computers, communication equipment etc. See *Mehlman, supra,* note 71 at 583.
79. Government to government arms sales require Presidential determination, 22 U.S.C., s. 2753(a)(1)(1976). Commercial sales of items on the Munitions List require a State Department license pursuant to its regulations, 22 C.F.R., s. 121.1 is the list. Some dual-use items, U.S. components exported abroad, military-related materials, as well as technical data are under the aegis of the Department of Commerce regulations when a communist state is contemplated, 15 C.F.R. 370.3(a).
80. *Mehlman, supra,* note 71 at 583.
81. "Southern Africa: Constant Themes in U.S. Policy", address by David D. Newsom, Asst. Sec. for African Affairs, before the Mid-America Committee at Chicago, June 28, 1972, 67 U.S. Dep't State Bull. 119, July 24, 1972 at 120. See also 68 U.S. Dep't Bull. 581, May 7, 1973 at 584.
82. 67 U.S. Dept. State Bull., *ibid.* at 124.
83. *Mehlman, supra,* note 71 at 584.
84. *Ibid.*
85. $30 million to $60 million to $170 million in *Mehlman, ibid.* note 20.
86. *Ibid.* at 585.
87. *Ibid.* at 584–585, compare notes 20 and 24.
88. *Ibid.* at 586.
89. S.C. Res. 418, November 4, 1977, U.N. Doc S/Res 418 (1977).
90. Feb. 16, 1978 by 43 Fed. Reg. 7,311 (Feb. 22, 1978) created the policies found in 15

C.F.R. 385.4 (1978).
91. 15 C.F.R. 385.4(a)(1) and list at 15 C.F.R. 379, Supp. 2 (1978).
92. 15 C.F.R. 385.4(a)(1) (1978).
93. 15 C.F.R. 385.4(a)(3) (1978).
94. 15 C.F.R. 385.4(a)(4) (1978).
95. 15 C.F.R. 385.4(a)(5).
96. 15 C.F.R. 386.6(a)(2) (1978) by virtue of 43 Fed. Reg. 7,314 (1978).
97. *Mehlman, supra,* note 71 at 593.
98. *Ibid.* at 594–96.
99. *Ibid.* at 596.
100. Employment Practices of U.S. Firms in South Africa, Department of State, Bureau of African Affairs, Feb. 1973.
101. Statement on Employment Practices to U.S. Firms Operating in South Africa, Sept. 1974.
102. U.N. Doc. S/14179, Sept. 19, 1980.
103. *Ibid.* at 28–29, recommendations (v), (vi), (viii), (x), and (xv) were those to which it objected. The last two recommendations were to prohibit the enlistment of mercenaries or armed services and police personnel for South Africa, and the creation of a Sanctions Branch in the U.N. Secretariat.
104. 47 Fed. Reg. 9201 (March 4, 1982); 47 Fed. Reg. 40,538 (Sept. 15, 1982).
105. *Export Administration Annual Report, For Year 1982,* U.S. Department of Commerce at 30.
106. *Ibid.*
107. *Ibid.* at 31.
108. *Ibid.*
109. 15 C.F.R. 385.4(a)(5) (1983).
110. 15 C.F.R. 385.4(a)(6),(8),(9) (1983) respectively.
111. *Export Administration Annual Report, For Year 1983,* U.S. Department of Commerce at 34.
112. *Ibid.*
113. Business International, Aug. 19, 1983 at 258.
114. *Ibid.* See "'Sullivan Code': A South African Code of Employment Practice", South African Employers' Consultative Committee on Labour Affairs, Press Release, Dec. 7, 1977.
115. Oct. 2, 1986, Pub. L. 99–440, 100 Stat. 1086, 22 U.S.C. 5001. This Act and supporting Regulations (15 C.F.R. 371 *et al.*; 22 C.R.F. 60–65, 121, 123–128; 34 C.F.R. 545.) are reprinted in (1987) 27 Int'l Leg. Mat. 77–136.
116. 15 C.F.R. Parts 371, 373, 379, 385, 386, 399. 50 Fed. Reg. 47,363 (November 18, 1985).
117. 22 C.F.R. Parts 60–65, 50 Fed. Reg. 39,655–6 (Dec. 21, 1966).
118. 22 C.F.R. Parts 121, 123–128, 51 Fed. Reg. 47,013–16 (December 30, 1986).
119. 31 C.F.R. Part 545, 50 Fed. Reg. 41,682–84 (October 15, 1985); 50 Fed. Reg. 46,726–28 (Nov. 12, 1985); 51 Fed. Reg. 41, 906–11 (Nov. 12, 1987); 51 Fed. Reg. 46,853–56 (Dec. 29, 1986).
120. Reprinted at 55 U.S. Dep't State Bull. 871, Dec. 5, 1966.
121. "U.S. Abstains on Security Council Resolution on Namibia", 61 U.S. Dep't State Bull. 252, Sept. 15, 1969.
122. The U.S. voted for SC Res. 276, UN Doc. S/Res./276, 1970.
123. "The U.S. Stake in Effective United Nations", U.S./U.N. Press Release 68, May 19, 1970, 62 U.S. Dep't State Bull. 705 at 709, June 8, 1970.
124. The U.S. was alone among major countries in doing so it should be noted, 67 U.S. Dep't State Bull. 119 at 121, July 24, 1972.
125. UN Doc. S/Res. 283, July 29, 1970.
126. E.g. UNGA Res. 2621 (XXV); UN Doc. A/Res./2621 (XXV), Oct. 12, 1970.

127. UN Doc. S/11,1713; reprinted in 73 U.S. Dep't State Bull. 45, July 7, 1975.
128. Statement April 6, 1973, 68 U.S. Dep't State Bull. 581, May 7, 1973.
129. *Ibid.*
130. 7 U.S. Dep't State Bull. 119 at 121, July 24, 1972.
131. *Agreement between the Government of the United States of America and the Union of Soviet Socialist Republics Regarding Trade,* (1972) 11 Int'l. Leg. Mat. 1321, Oct. 18, 1972, Article 1.
132. *Lowenfeld, supra,* note 49 at 177 states in note c) that the Soviet Union seems not to have made any official statement of this action, relying on Secretary of State Kissinger to announce it.
133. *Ibid.* at 191.
134. *Ibid.* at 226.
135. *Ibid.* at 227–28.
136. 43 Fed. Reg. 33,699 (Aug. 1, 1978).
137. *Lowenfeld, supra,* note 49 at 234.
138. *Ibid.* at 235.
139. "Soviet Invasion of Afghanistan", President's Address, Jan. 4, 1980, 80 U.S. Dep't State Bull. A, Special January 1980; 16 Weekly Comp. Docs. 25, at 26 (Jan. 4, 1980), as cited in *Lowenfeld, ibid.* at 236, note c). It was implemented Jan. 7, 1980 by 45 Fed. Reg. 1,883 (Jan. 9, 1980) with respect to "agricultural commodities", and then 45 Fed. Reg. 8,289 (Feb. 7, 1980) identified grain and 45 Fed. Reg. 8,293 (Feb. 7, 1980) requiring validated licenses for phosphates. See generally H.E. Moyer & L.A. Mabry, *Export Controls as Instruments of Foreign Policy* (Washington, D.C.: International Law Institute, 1984) at 25–58 [hereinafter *Moyer & Mabry*].
140. 45 Fed. Reg. 1,883 (Jan. 9, 1980). See *Lowenfeld, supra,* note 47 at 238 for the mechanism by which the grain policy was to be implemented. See also "Final Draft of Commodity Credit Corporation Contract to Be Offered to U.S. Grain Exporters (Test)" Economic Developments, Feb. 1, 1980, No 23 M–1, Bureau of National Affairs, Inc. [hereinafter *Final Draft*].
141. See 80 U.S. Dep't State Bull. A, Special, January 1980, at B-D. For the text of the resolution see p.D. or U.N. Doc. S/P.V./2190, Jan. 7, 1980.
142. Jan. 8, 1980, 16 Weekly Comp. Pres. Docs. 43 (Jan. 9, 1980) as cited in *Lowenfeld, supra,* note 49 at 239, note (a).
143. 15 C.F.R. 390.6 and 390.8, by virtue of 45 Fed. Reg. 3,027 (Jan. 16, 1980).
144. 15 C.F.R. 385.2(e) (1983).
145. 45 Fed. Reg. 29,568 (1980). See also Export Administration Bulletin No. 205, pp.36–40, June 9, 1980, as cited in *Lowenfeld, supra,* note 49 at 240, note (f).
146. *Lowenfeld, supra,* note 49 at 240.
147. *Ibid.* at 248. See also J.A. Nafgizer, "Nonaggressive Sanctions in the International Sports Arena" (1983) 15 Case W. Res. J. Int'l L. 329.
148. By vote of April 12, 1980, *Lowenfeld, supra,* note 49 at 248.
149. *Ibid.* at 249. See also "Canada, F.R.G. to Boycott Olympic Games", April 23, 1980, 80 Dep't State Bull. 34, June 1980.
150. *Lowenfeld, supra,* note 49 at 250.
151. 16 Weekly Comp. Pres. Docs. 559, 560, March 28, 1980, as cited in *Lowenfeld, supra,* note 49 at 250, note (o), subsequently in 15 C.F.R. 385.2(d).
152. Implemented by 45 Fed. Reg. 21,612 (April 2, 1980); 15 C.F.R. 371, 379, 385 and 499.
153. A power given Congress under section 7(g)(3) of the *EAA* of 1979 with respect to short supply and foreign policy controls.
154. 15 C.F.R. 370.3(a), incorporating the definition of technical data found in 379.1. Only exports to Canada are excepted and only where the items are for consumption in Canada, see s. 370.3(a).
155. 15 C.F.R. 374.1 for goods and 15 C.F.R. 379.8 for technical data.

156. 15 C.F.R. 385.2.
157. 15 C.F.R. 385.2(d)(d).
158. Compare for example the definition in the *Foreign Assets Control Regulations,* 31 C.F.R. 500.329 (1983).
159. See 15 C.F.R. 385.2(d)(3), and *Thompson, supra,* note 11 at 353.
160. *Ibid.* 385.2(d)(3)(iii), and *Thompson, ibid.* at 353.
161. *Ibid.*
162. 45 Fed. Reg. 1,883 (Jan. 9, 1980) and later 45 Fed. Reg. 8,289 (Feb. 7, 1980).
163. *Thompson, supra,* note 11 at 351.
164. *Ibid.*
165. *Ibid.*
166. *Ibid.* at 352.
167. *Final Draft, supra,* note 140, sec. II Certification by the Exporter, para. E., which reads in part:
The Commodity Credit Corporation was to issue a list of such policies, and "In no case shall any announced restrictive policy be applied retroactively."
168. *Ibid.* sec. II para. G.
169. *Thompson, supra,* note 11 at 352, and note 152 thereon mentions the case of Argentina.
170. *Ibid.* at 352.
171. *Ibid.*
172. L. Cannon & L. Lescaze, "U.S. to Keep Embargo on Grain Sales" *Washington Post* (Feb. 5, 1981) A–1.
173. *Ibid.*
174. "U.S. Lifts Agricultural Sales Limitations to the U.S.S.R.", President's Statement, April 24, 1981, 81 U.S. Dept't State Bull. 41, June 1981.
175. "U.S.-Soviet Grain Sales Agreement", July 30, 1982, 82 U.S. Dep't State Bull. 40 at 42, October 1982.
176. *Ibid.*
177. *Ibid.* at 40.
178. *Lowenfeld, supra,* note 49 at 270.
179. 17 Weekly Comp. Press. Docs. 1401, Dec. 23, 1981 at 1406 cited in *Lowenfeld, supra,* note 49 at 271, note (g) as Dec. 23, 1980.
180. *Ibid.*
181. 17 Weekly Comp. Press. Docs. 1429, Dec. 29, 1981 as cited in *Lowenfeld, supra,* note 49 at 272, note (i).
182. *Ibid.*
183. 47 Fed. Reg. 141 (Jan. 5, 1982).
184. *Lowenfeld, supra,* note 49 at 273. See generally R. Ergec, *La compétence extraterritoriale à la lumière du contentieux sur le gazoduc euro-sibérien,* (Bruxelles: Bruylant, 1984) [hereinafter *Ergec*], and *Moyer & Mabry, supra,* note 139 at 59–90.
185. *Lowenfeld, supra,* note 49 at 277.
186. *Ibid.*
187. *Ibid.*
188. *Ibid.*
189. *Ibid.*
190. *Ibid.* at 279.
191. *Ibid.*
192. W. Safire, "Helmut's Pipeline" *New York Times* (Feb. 19, 1982) A–31. As he wrote: "Some agreement."
193. *Thompson, supra,* note 11 at 354.
194. June 18, 1982, 18 Weekly Comp. Press. Docs. 820 (June 21, 1982) as cited in *Lowenfeld, supra,* note 49 at 281, reprinted as "Export Sanctions on Gas and Oil Equipment" June 18, 1982, 82 U.S. Dep't State Bull. 31, Sept. 1982. Implemented by

47 Fed. Reg. 27,251 (1982) and also extending the ban on any foreign subsidiary to include these exports 47 Fed. Reg. 27,250 (1982).

195. 47 Fed. Reg. 27,251 (1982) was to amend 15 C.F.R. 379.8(a)(3) to:

...any foreign produced direct products of U.S. technical data, or any commodity produced by any plant or major component thereof which is a direct product of U.S. technical data...

It would also add 15 C.F.R. 379.8(a)(4) which covered the data excepted from (3):

...any foreign produced direct products of U.S. technical data excepted from (3) if:

(i) a written assurance was required under these regulations when the data was exported from the U.S.;

(ii) the U.S. technical data is the subject of a licensing agreement with, or the use of the data is contingent upon royalty payments or other compensation to, any person subject to the jurisdiction of the United States... regardless of when the data were exported from the U.S.; or

(iii) the U.S. technical data are the subject of a licensing agreement or other contract, whereby the recipient of the technical data has agreed to abide by U.S. export control regulations.

196. See *ibid.*

197. 47 Fed. Reg. 27,252 (1982) amending 15 C.F.R. 385.2(c)(2).

198. 47 Fed. Reg. 27,251 (1982) amending 15 C.F.R. 379.8(a)(4)).

199. *Ibid.* to be 15 C.F.R. 379.8(a)(4)(iii).

200. *Ibid.* to be 15 C.F.R. 379.8(a)(4)(i).

201. *Ibid.* For an analysis of the legality under U.S. municipal law of these provisions see B.G. Brunsvold & J.M. Bagarazzi, "Licensing Impact of Foreign Policy Motivated Retroactive Re-export Regulations" (1983) 15 Case W. Res. J. Int'l L. 289 [hereinafter *Brunsvold*]. For a brief descriptive account see *Thompson, supra,* note 11 at 354–56. J.J. Zaucha, "The Soviet Pipeline Sanctions: The Extraterritorial Application of U.S. Export Controls" (1983) 15 L. & Pol. Int'l Bus. 1169; or the first of them in K. Abbott, "Linking Trade to Political Goals: Foreign Policy Export Controls in the 1970's and 1980's" (1981) 65 Minn. L. Rev. 739 at 790–94. For a review of the European response and an evaluation of the conformity of these regulations with international law, see *Ergec, supra,* note 184.

202. *Thompson, supra,* note 11 at 356; *Lowenfeld, supra,* note 49 at 281–82, *Brunsvold, ibid.* at 324–25.

203. *Thompson, supra,* note 11 at 356; Lowenfeld, *supra,* note 49 at 294–95.

204. Temporary Denial Orders were issued against Creusot-Loire S.4., Aug. 26, 1982, 47 Fed. Reg. 38,169 (1982); Nuovo Pignone Ltd., Sept. 4, 1982, 47 Fed. Reg. 39,709 (1982); John Brown Engineering Ltd., Sept. 9, 1982, 47 Fed. Reg. 40,205 (1982); AEG-Kanis GmbH and Mannesmann Anlagenbau AG, Oct. 5, 1982, 47 Fed. Reg. 44,604 (1982).

205. *The Agreement Relating to Settlement of Claims of Nationals to the United States Nationals against Poland,* concluded July 16, 1960, 384 U.N.T.S. 169; 11 U.S.T. 1953; T.I.A.S. No. 4545 and the Trade Agreement Letter of Nov. 16, 1960, 3 C.F.R. 885 (1959–63 Comp.) was suspended by 18 Weekly Comp. Press. Docs. 1289, Oct. 9, 1982, as cited in *Lowenfeld, supra,* note 49 at 301-02, notes (c) and (d).

206. See "East-West Trade Relations and Soviet Pipeline Sanctions", Nov. 13, 1982, 83 U.S. Dep't State Bull. 28, January 1983, implemented by 47 Fed. Reg. 51, 858 (Nov. 18, 1982).

207. 47 Fed. Reg. 52,489–91 (Nov. 22, 1982).

208. *Brunsvold, supra,* note 201, see also *Moyer & Mabry, supra,* note 139 at 91–134.

209. See *Ergec, supra,* note 184.

210. *Lowenfeld, supra,* note 49 at 539.

211. Dec. 28, 1977, H.R. 7738, Pub. L. 95–223, 91 Stat. 1625 Title II [hereinafter *IEEPA*].

212. Executive Order 12,170, Nov. 14, 1979, 44 Fed. Reg. 65,729 (Nov. 15, 1979); also

see 79 U.S. Dep't State Bull. 50, 1979.
213. *Lowenfeld, supra,* note 49, at 548.
214. 31 C.F.R. 535.201-03 (1982) by virtue of 44 Fed. Reg. 65,956 (1979) [hereinafter *IACR*s].
215. M.P. Malloy, "Embargo Programs of the United States Treasury Department" (1981) 20 Colum. J. Trans. L. 485 at 512 [hereinafter *Malloy*], see also *Moyer & Mabry, supra,* note 139 at 7–25.
216. *Malloy, ibid.*
217. *Ibid.* at 512–13, give two reasons as being: 1) goods awaiting shipment to which Iran already had title would be affected; and (2) payment mechanisms for private transactions in which Iranian controlled banks might have an interest would also be affected thus indirectly affecting commercial transactions.
218. *Ibid.*
219. 31 C.F.R. 535.329(d).
220. *Thompson, supra,* note 11 at 348.
221. 31 C.F.R. 535.566 by virtue of 44 Fed. Reg. 66,833 (Nov. 21, 1979).
222. C. Farnsworth, "Iran Freeze and British Wrath" *New York Times* (Dec. 10, 1979) D–2.
223. U.S.D.Ct., S.D.N.Y., 1980) 484 F. Supp. 832.
224. *Ibid.* at 835
225. UN SC Res. 457, Dec. 4, 1979, UN Doc. S/Res./457 (1979).
226. UN SC Res. 461, Dec. 4, 1979, received 11 votes for, 4 abstentions (Soviet Union), UN Doc. S/Res./461 (1979).
227. See 80 U.S. Dep't State Bull. 70–71, Feb. 1980. See *Lowenfeld, supra,* note 49 at 567–68 for details of the Soviet motivation.
228. R.W. Edwards Jr., "Extraterritorial Application of the U.S. *Iranian Assets Control Regulations*" (1981) 75 Am. J. Int'l L. 870 at 872.
229. Exec. Order 12, 205, April 7, 1980, 45 Fed. Reg. 24,099 (1980); Exec. Order 12,211, April 17, 1980 and the amendments to the *IACR*s in 45 Fed. Reg. 26,685 (1980) resulting in 31 C.F.R. 535.207 prohibiting exports to Iran.
230. 31 C.F.R. 535.207(b) excepted both foreign organized entities which were not banking entities and those that were doing business abroad.
231. *Ibid.*
232. *Thompson, supra,* note 11 at 349, n. 141.
233. *Ibid.* at 349.
234. 46 Fed. Reg. 14,337 (Feb. 26, 1981).
235. The agreement was signed Jan. 19, 1981 and the hostages released Jan. 20, *Lowenfeld, supra,* note 49 at 591.
236. "Implementation of Hostage Agreements", Feb. 18, 1981, 81 Dep't State Bull. 17, Mar. 1981.
237. Exec. Order 12,282, 46 Fed. Reg. 7925 (1981).
238. See, for example, an attempt to list Pakistan as the recipient of M60 tank parts. "Attempt to Sell Parts to Iran Hit a Custom's Snag" *Washington Post* (Dec. 14, 1981) A–1.
239. "U.S. Imposes Additional Export Controls on Iran", 84 Dep't State Bull. 68.
240. The 1977 *EAA* amendments created section 3(8) which endorsed export controls to discourage other countries to support international terrorism.
241. *Ibid.*
242. *Ibid.* from Sept. 28, 1984. For a legislative history of the origin of anti-terrorism export controls see D. Flores, "Export Controls and the U.S. Effort to Combat International Terrorism" (1981) 13 L. & Pol. Int'l Bus. 521.
243. D.E. Acevedo, "The U.S. Measures Against Argentina Resulting from the Malvinas Conflict" (1984) 78 A.J.I.L. 323 at 325–26 [hereinafter *Acevedo*].
244. Sept. 2, 1947, TIAS 1838, 62 Stat. 1681, 21 U.N.T.S. 77.
245. *Acevedo, supra,* note 243 at 325, and note 7 thereon.

246. "The Falkland Islands", Secretary Haig OAS, May 27, 1982, 82 Dept. State Bull. 87, July 1982.
247. *Acevedo, supra,* note 243 at 326.
248. *Ibid.* at 338, cites OEA/Ser. F./ II.20, doc. 28/82m rev. 3, April 28, 1982.
249. *Ibid.* cites OEA/Ser.F./II.20, doc. 80/82, rev. 2, (May 29, 1982); reprinted at 82 U.S. Dep't State Bull. 90, July, 1982.
250. "The Falkland Islands", Ambassador Middendorf, OAS May 28, 1982, 82 U.S. Dep't State Bull. 90, July, 1982.
251. Final report, XVII Annual Meeting of the Inter-American Economic and Social Council at the Ministerial Level, OEA/Ser. H./XII.40, CIES/3772, rev. 1 at 12 (1982), as cited in *Acevedo, supra,* note 243 at 338, n. 56.
252. 15 C.F.R. 385.5 (1983).
253. By virtue of 46 Fed. Reg. 31,408 (June 16, 1981).
254. S.J. Marcuss, "Extraterritoriality: U.S. Antiboycott Law and the *Foreign Corrupt Practices Act*" (1983) 15 L. & Pol. Int'l Bus. 1135 at 1136 [hereinafter *Marcuss*].
255. League of Arab States, Resolution No. 849, Dec. 11, 1954 adopting the "Unified Law on the Boycott of Israel", as cited in A. F. Lowenfeld," '... Sauce for the Gander': The Arab Boycott and United States Political Trade Controls" (1977) 12 Texas Int'l L.J. 25 at 26 [hereinafter *Lowenfeld, "Sauce"*]. Lowenfeld states the unified law was enacted by all 20 states member of the Arab League with only minor variations at 26.
256. June 30, 1965, H.R. 7105, Pub. L. 89–63, 79 Stat. 209 amending the *Export Control Act of 1949.*
257. 15 C.F.R. 369.1 added by virtue of 30 Fed. Reg. 12,121 (1965).
258. 15 C.F.R. 369.2 dealt with the questions of what was to be reported. While the request had to be reported the compliance or intention to comply was an optional question. See *Lowenfeld, "Sauce", supra,* note 255 at 36.
259. *Export Control Act* of 1949, Feb. 26, 1949, S. 548, c. 11, Pub. L. 11, 63 Stat. 7 at s. 2(4) and (b). Also see *73rd Quarterly Report under the Export Control Act of 1949,* U.S. Dep't of Commerce, Nov. 15, 1965 at 20–21.
260. *75th Quarterly Report under the Export Control Act of 1949,* U.S. Dep't of Commerce, May 15, 1966 at 7.
261. *76th Quarterly Report under the Export Control Act of 1949,* U.S. Dep't of Commerce, Aug. 15, 1966 at 23.
262. *Ibid.* at 23. This number is based on the reports received in the 2nd quarter of 1966. The other reports were almost all Israeli restrictions against Arab countries, Indian restrictions against Pakistan, or Pakistani restrictions against India.
263. See, for example, *84th Quarterly Report under the Export Control Act of 1949,* U.S. Dep't of Commerce, Aug. 14, 1968 at 30.
264. *Report on Export Administration covering the second and third quarters, 1975,* required by the *Export Administration Act of 1969,* U.S. Dep't of Commerce at 14.
265. 15 C.F.R. 369.2 (1976) by virtue of 40 Fed. Reg. 45,421 (1975).
266. Nov. 20, 1975, 11 Weekly Comp. of Pres. Docs. 1305 (1975), as cited in *Lowenfeld, "Sauce", supra,* note 255 at 37, n. 59.
267. *Ibid.* and reprinted in *Lowenfeld, supra,* note 49 at D5–416.
268. 40 Fed. Reg. 54,770 (1975).
269. 15 C.F.R. 369.2, 369.3 (1976).
270. 15 C.F.R. 369.2.
271. 15 C.F.R. 393.3.
272. 15 C.F.R. 369.2.
273. Oct. 4, 1976, H.R. 10612, Pub. L. 94–455, 90 Stat. 1520 at 1649–54.
274. *Marcuss, supra,* note 254 at 1142.
275. *Ibid.* at 1143.
276. Dec. 30, 1969, H.R. 4293, Pub. L. 91–184, 83 Stat. 841 was amended by June 22, 1977, H.R. 5840, Pub. L. 95–52, 91 Stat. 235, codified at 50 U.S.C. app., ss.2402-07,

2409–10 (Supp. V, 1981).

277. Section 4A(1)(1)(B) and (C).
278. Section 4A(a)(1)(A).
279. *EAA*, s. 11(2). See also the description of the regulations in *Marcuss, supra,* note 254 at 1137–42.
280. *Thompson, supra,* note 11, at 343, note 106.
281. 15 C.F.R. 369.1(c)(1).
282. *Ibid.* 369.1(c)(2)(i)
283. *Ibid.* 369.1(c)(2)(ii).
284. *Ibid.* 369.1(c)(2)(iii)).
285. *Ibid.* 369.1(c)(2)(iv).
286. *Ibid.* 369.1(c)(2)(v).
287. *Ibid.* 369.1(c)(2)(vi).
288. *Marcuss, supra,* note 254 at 1139.
289. 15 C.F.R., 369.2(a)(10) (1983).
290. 15 C.F.R., 369.1(d) (1983).
291. 15 C.F.R., 369.1(d)(2), and (d)(6).
292. 15 C.F.R., 369.1(d)(2).
293. 15 C.F.R., 369.1(d)(8)(b)(i)-(iii).
294. 15 C.F.R., 369.1(d)(9)(i)-(iii).
295. 15 C.F.R., 369.1(d)(8)(iv).
296. 15 C.F.R., 369.1(d)(12).
297. *Ibid.*
298. 15 C.F.R., 369.1(d)(13)-(15).
299. 15 C.F.R., 369.1(d)(17).
300. 15 C.F.R., 369.1(d)(16).
301. 15 C.F.R., 369.1(d)(10).
302. 15 C.F.R., 369.1(d)(11))
303. 15 C.F.R., 369.6(a)(7).
304. 15 C.F.R., 369.1)(d)(16).
305. *Marcuss, supra,* note 254 at 1141.
306. *Ibid.*
307. 15 C.F.R., 369.6 required a "United States person" to report. This definition includes "controlled in fact" foreign subsidiaries.
308. *Lowenfeld, supra,* note 49 at 374. For more general information on enforcement of the regulations see *Lowenfeld, ibid.* at 373–87.
309. *Ibid.* at 374.
310. *Ibid.* at 376.
311. *Lawrence M. Abrams, M.D.* v. *Baylor College of Medicine* 581 F. Supp. 1570 (U.S.D.Ct, S.D. Texas, 1984).
312. *Bulk Oil (Zug) A.G.* v. *Sun Co., Inc.* 583 F. Supp. 1134 (U.S.D.Ct, S.D.N.Y., 1983).
313. L.T. Lee & J.B. McCobb, "United States Trade Embargo on China 1949–1970: Legal Status and Future Prospects" (1971) 4 N.Y.U.J. Int'l & Pol'y 1 at 4 [hereinafter *Lee & McCobb*].
314. *Ibid.* at 4.
315. *Ibid.*
316. *Ibid.*
317. *Ibid.*
318. 64 Stat. 798 (1950).
319. Transportation Orders T–1 and T–2 32 A.C.F.R. c. VII (1970) as cited in *Lee & McCobb, supra,* note 313 at 5.
320. Press Release Dec. 16, 1950, 23 U.S. Dept. State Bull. 1004.
321. 31 C.F.R. 500.101–500.808 (1967).
322. Pres. Proc. No. 2914, 3 C.F.R. 99 (comp. 1949–53).

323. 23 U.S. Dept. State Bull. 1004, *supra,* note 320.
324. As am. (1946) III U.S.C. 1760 at 1762.
325. *Lee & McCobb, supra,* note 313 at 6 citing 31 C.F.R. 500.302 (1970).
326. *Ibid.* citing 31 C.F.R. 500.329 (1970).
327. 5 UN GAOR Supp. 20A, UN Doc. A/1775/App. 1 at 2 (1951).
328. Except when the Security Council is considering a matter the General Assembly may make recommendations to the U.N. members. Article 10, U.N. *Charter,* concluded at San Francisco June 26, 1945.
329. *Ibid.* art. 25.
330. *Ibid.* art. 42.
331. *Supra,* note 327, para. 1(c).
332. *Ibid.* para. 1(d).
333. *Ibid.*
334. *Ibid.* para. (b).
335. *Mutual Defense Assistance Control Act of 1951,* Oct. 26, 1951, H.R. 4550, c. 575, Pub.L. 213, 65 Stat. 644.
336. *Lee & McCobb, supra,* note 313 at 7–8, and *Berman & Garson, supra,* note 1 at 836–37.
337. *Lee & McCobb, ibid.* at 8.
338. *Ibid.*
339. J.M. Allison, "Problems and Accomplishments in the Far East" 27 U.S. Dep't State Bull. 97, July 21, 1952 at 100; see also 28 U.S. Dep't State Bull. 532 April 13, 1953 at 533.
340. "Enforcing Strategic Trade Controls, Third Report to Congress on the *Battle Act*" 29 U.S. Dep't State Bull. 569 October 26, 1953 at 571.
341. *Ibid.*
342. *Ibid.* at 572.
343. 31 C.F.R. 505.01–505.60 (1970).
344. "Third *Battle Act* Report", *supra,* note 340 at 574.
345. *Ibid.*
346. Aug. 26, 1954, H.R. 9678, c. 937, Pub.L. 665, 68 Stat. 833.
347. *Ibid.* at 848.
348. 22 C.F.R. 121.01–128.01 (1970).
349. See generally *Lee & McCobb, supra,* note 313 at 8.
350. *Ibid.* at 9.
351. J.I.W. Corcoran, "The Trading With the Enemy Act and the Controlled Canadian Corporation" (1968) 14 McGill L.J. 174 at 188–201 [hereinafter *Corcoran*].
352. Hansard, H. C., (U.K.) 1960–61, vol. 631, pp. 196–97. Nov. 29, 1960, Mrs. Castle, and Mr. Langford-Holt.
353. Paris, May 22, 1965, *Fruehauf* v. *Massardy,* D. 1965, Jur. 147, reprinted in translation in (1966) 5 Int'l Leg. Mat. 476.
354. Translation of "World Commerce and U.S. Barriers", by A. Baturin, (original in Russian) *Trud,* in files of the Department of External Affairs.
355. Public Notice 256, 56 Dep't State Bull. 564 April 3, 1967 32 Fed. Reg. 4140.
356. *Lee & McCobb, supra,* note 313 at 10, see also "Restrictions Eased on Trade with the Communist China", 62 U.S. Dep't State Bull. 31, Jan. 12, 1970.
357. *Ibid.*
358. *Ibid.* at 11.
359. *Ibid.*
360. 62 U.S. Dep't State Bull. 31, at 32.
361. *Ibid.* For the regulation itself see 31 C.F.R. 500.541 (1970).
362. 83 Stat. 841 *supra,* note 276. Cited in *Lee & McCobb, supra,* note 313 at 13–14.
363. *Lee & McCobb, ibid.* note 313 at 14 citing U.S. Dep't Commerce, Export Control Bull., No. 16, Apr. 7, 1970, pt. 2.

364. *Lee & McCobb, ibid.* note 313 at 11–12.
365. *Ibid.* at 12 citing 31 C.F.R. 500.541(d), (c) (1) (1970) and 31 C.F.R. 500.541 (c) (3), .543 (b) and .543 (c) (1970) respectively.
366. "U.S. Foreign Policy for the 1970's" a report to Congress by R. Nixon, Feb. 9, 1972, 66 U.S. Dep't State Bull. 350 Mar. 13, 1972.
367. "Department Lists Steps Taken on Contracts with Mainland China" Mar. 15, 1971, 64 U.S. Dep't State Bull. 510 Apr. 12, 1971.
368. 36 Fed. Reg. 5439, as cited in "U.S. Passports Remain Invalid for Travel to Certain Areas", March 23, 1971, 64 U.S. Dep't State Bull. 510 Apr. 12, 1971.
369. "Department Lists Steps ...", *supra,* note 367.
370. 36 Fed. Reg. 11,808 (1971), as cited in "President Nixon Reduces Controls on Trade with Mainland China" Press Release June 10, 1971, 64 U.S. Dep't State Bull. 815, June 28, 1971.
371. "Restrictions Eased on Exports to People's Republic of China", Feb. 14, 1972, 66 U.S. Dep't State Bull. 291, Mar. 6, 1972.
372. *Ibid.*
373. *Ibid.* The precise ambit of this term is not clear.
374. Nov. 22, 1972, 37 Fed. Reg. 25,041, as cited in Dept. Commerce Press Release G72–214, "Restrictions on Visits to China by U.S. Aircraft and Ships Relaxed" 68 U.S. Dep't State Bull. 4, Jan., 1973.
375. R.C. Holbrooke, "Procedures for Sale of Military Support Items to the P.R.C." Statement before the Subcommittee on Asian and Pacific Affairs of the House Foreign Affairs Committee on April 1, 1980, Press release 99 of April 24, 1980, 80 U.S. Dep't State Bull. 24, June, 1980 at 25.
376. *Ibid.* at 25.
377. *Ibid.* at 25–26.
378. S.A. Meese, "Export Controls to China: An Emerging Trend for Dual Use Exports" (1981–82) 7 Int'l Trade L.J. 20.
379. *Ibid.* at 23.
380. *Ibid.* at 30–31.
381. *Ibid.* at 36–37.
382. See *Thompson, supra,* note 11 at 328.
383. "Facts Concerning Relations Between Cuba and the United States", 43 U.S. Dep't State Bull 690, Oct. 31, 1960 at 693.
384. "United States Institutes Controls on Exports to Cuba", Press Release 600, 43 U.S. Dep't State Bull. 715 Nov. 7, 1960.
385. *Corcoran, supra,* note 351 at 202.
386. Information from files of Department of External Affairs.
387. P.C. 1953–1213, Aug. 5, 1953, SOR/53–329, 87 Can. Gaz. Pt II 750 Schedule 2, group 9.
388. General Export Permit No. Ex. 2, amended, Dec. 28, 1960, SOR/60–562, 94 Can. Gaz. Pt II 1532.
389. Sept. 4, 1961, S. 1983, Pub. L. 87–195, 75 Stat. 424 at 444–45.
390. Adopted by a vote of 16 to 1 (Cuba), with 4 abstentions, Jan. 31, 1962, 46 U.S. Dep't State Bull. 282.
391. Pres. Proc. 3447, Feb. 3, 1962, 27 Fed. Reg. 1085; "President Proclaims Embargo on Trade with China", Press Release, 46 Dep't State Bull. 283, Feb. 19, 1962.
392. *Ibid.*
393. 43 U.S. Dep't State Bull. 690, *supra,* note 383 at 715.
394. *Ibid.* at 716.
395. "Trading Relations Between the Free World and Cuba", Statement by Under Secretary Ball before the House Select Committee on Export Control on Oct. 3, Press Release 595, 47 U.S. Dep't State Bull. 591, Oct. 22, 1962 at 592.
396. *Ibid.*

397. *Ibid.*
398. Lowenfeld, *supra,* note 49 at 13, note (c).
399. Oct. 3, 1962, S.J. Res. 230, Pub. L. 87–733, 76 Stat. 697.
400. "U.S. Will Not Ship Aid Cargoes on Vessels Engaged in Cuban Trade" 48 U.S. Dep't State Bull. 283, Feb. 25, 1963.
401. "East-West Trade", Statement by Secretary Dean Rusk to Senate Committee on Foreign Relations, Mar. 13, 1964, 50 U.S. Dep't State Bull. 474, Mar. 30, 1964 at 483, Chart 5.
402. *Ibid.*
403. *Ibid.*
404. *Ibid.*
405. 31 C.F.R., s. 515 [hereinafter *CACR*s].
406. M.P. Malloy, "Embargo Programs to the United Treasury Department" (1981) 20 Colum. J. Trans. L. 485 at 502-03, and notes therein.
407. *Ibid.*
408. 31 C.F.R. 515.541, revoked by 40 Fed. Reg. 47,108 (1975).
409. Made clear by 31 C.F.R. 515.412, added by 39 Fed. Reg. 25,317 (1975) and later revoked by 40 Fed. Reg. 47,108 (1975).
410. 31 C.F.R. 515.541(e), see also *Thompson, supra,* note 11 at 331.
411. S.L. Sommerfield, "Treasury Regulations of Foreign Assets and Trade" (1964) 19 Bus. Law. 861 at 868.
412. *Ibid.*
413. See, for example, Public Notice 257, 32 Fed. Reg. 4140, also reprinted in 56 U.S. Dep't State Bull. 564 Apr. 3, 1967 at 564–65.
414. "Freedom of Action of the States Parties to the Inter American Treaty of Reciprocal Assistance to Normalize or Conduct Their Relations with the Republic of Cuba at the Level and in the Form as Each State Deems Advisable", July 29, 1975, reprinted at 14 Int'l Leg. Mat. 1354 (1975).
415. H. C. Debates, 1974, vol. I, p. 105, Mar. 4, 1974, Mr. Broadbent.
416. "Remarks by Assistant Secretary Kubisch", April 18, 1974, 70 U.S. Dep't State Bull. 516, May 13, 1974 at 517.
417. Press Release 159, April 26, 1974, 70 Dep't State Bull. 537, May 20, 1974 at 544.
418. "Text of Draft OAS Resolution to Rescind the Sanctions Against Cuba", 72 U.S. Dep't State Bull. 9, Jan. 6, 1975.
419. July 25, 1975 the protocol of amendment was adopted, Aug. 21, 1975, 73 U.S. Dep't State Bull. 404, Sept. 15, 1975.
420. *Ibid.* for the text of the resolution see *supra,* note 414.
421. *Ibid.* 73 U.S. Dep't State Bull. 404.
422. *Ibid.*
423. 31 C.F.R. 515.
424. 31 C.F.R. 515.541(a).
425. *Thompson, supra,* note 11 at 331, and note 44 therein.
426. 31 C.F.R. s. 515.412.
427. 31 C.F.R. 515.559, added by 40 Fed. Reg. 47,108 (Oct. 8, 1975) deferred to *Commerce Regulations* including the 20% rule in 15 C.F.R. 385.1(b)(2) (1983) which reads in part:

    (2) On August 21, 1975, the U.S. Government announced modifications in those aspects of U.S. restrictions on trade with Cuba which affect third countries, in order to bring them into accord with the policy of the Organization of American States to allow each member state to determine for itself the nature of its economic and diplomatic relations with the Government of Cuba. In this context, the Department of Commerce generally will consider favorably on a case-by-case basis requests for authorization for the use of an insubstantial proportion of U.S.-origin materials, parts, or components in nonstrategic foreign-made products to be exported to Cuba, where

local law requires, or policy in the third country favors, trade with Cuba. U.S.-origin content will generally be considered insubstantial when it amounts to 20 percent or less of the value of the product to be exported from the third country. Approval of requests for authorization for the use of U.S.-origin materials, parts, or components amounting to more than 20 percent by value of the foreign-made product to be exported from the third country to Cuba will be less likely.

428. 40 Fed. Reg. 47,108, *ibid.*
429. 31 C.F.R. 515.559(a) (1983).
430. 42 Fed. Reg. 1472 (Jan 7, 1977), and 16,621 (Mar. 29, 1977); see also *Thompson, supra,* note 11 at 332.
431. 31 C.F.R. 515.559(c).
432. 31 C.F.R. 515.330.
433. 31 C.F.R. 515.559(c).
434. Which specified that licenses would be issued if 6 criteria are met as to the type of item.
435. 31 C.F.R. 515.330 (1), (2), (4).
436. See, *supra,* cases described in the Canadian state practice with respect to Cuba, Chapter V.C.2.
437. Dec. 28, 1977, H.R. 7738, Pub. L. 95–223, 91 Stat. 1625 codified at 50 U.S.C. App., s. 1705(b)(2), (3) (Supp. V, 1981).
438. 91 Stat 1625, *ibid.* at s. 101(b).
439. "Exploration of Area Restrictions on Use of Passports", Press Release 114, March 18, 1977, 76 U.S. Dep't State Bull. 346, April 11, 1977.
440. 47 Fed. Reg. 17,030 (Apr. 20, 1982) and 47 Fed. Reg. 32,060 (July 23, 1982); 31 C.F.R. 515.560.
441. "Foreign Policy Export Controls", statement before a Subcommittee of the Senate Foreign Relations Committee on Mar. 18, 1982, 82 U.S. Dep't State Bull. 66, June, 1982 at 66.
442. Oct. 10, 1978, H.R. 9214, Pub. L. 95–453, 92 Stat. 1051 codified at 22 U.S.C. 286–7 (Supp. V, 1981).
443. *Ibid.*
444. H.A. Talkington, "International Trade: Uganda Trade Embargo" (1979) 20 Harv. Int'l L.J. 206 at 206.
445. *Uganda Embargo Act, supra,* note 442 at s. 5(a) and (b).
446. It is difficult to conceive how the breach of international law by one state will give another greater latitude to affect third states by the assertion of its jurisdiction. This is not the case of asserting jurisdiction over the person committing the international delict. Rather it is a case in which the international breach by one country is being used to justify assertion of jurisdiction in a third, over the third country's nationals.
447. 15 C.F.R. 385.7 (1978).
448. 43 Fed. Reg. 58,573 (Dec. 15, 1978).
449. *Ibid.*
450. 43 Fed. Reg. 58,571 (Dec. 15, 1978).
451. *Thompson, supra,* note 11 at 344, and note 108 therein.
452. 44 Fed. Reg. 31,010 (May 30, 1979).
453. Dec. 28, 1977, H.R. 7738, Pub. L. 95–223, 91 Stat. 1625 at s. 301(a) codified at 50 U.S.C. 1701-06 (1976).
454. *Ibid.*
455. 50 U.S.C. 1701–1706 (Supp. V., 1981) [hereinafter *IEEPA*].
456. *Export Administration Report,* 120th Report on U.S. Export Controls, Semiannual, April 1979-September 1979, U.S. Dep't of Commerce, Industry and Trade Administration at 18.
457. *Supra,* note 442 at s. 5(c) and (d).
458. *Supra,* note 452.

459. Canada made representations to the U.S. State Department in January 1979 protesting the extent of the jurisdiction of the proposed regulations, reaching to Canadian corporations. Information from Officers of the Department of External Affairs.
460. D.A. Flores, "Export Controls and the U.S. Effort to Combat International Terrorism" (1981) 13 L. & Pol. Int'l Bus. 521 at 538–42 [hereinafter *Flores*]. He lists the *Anti-hijacking Act of 1974,* Aug. 5, 1974, Pub. L. 93–366, 88 Stat. 409, Title I; the *Foreign Assistance Act of 1961* as amended June 30, 1976, H.R. 13680, Pub. L. 94–329, 90 Stat. 753 at s. 303; the *International Security Assistance Act of 1977,* Aug. 4, 1977, H.R. 6884, Pub. L. 95–92, 91 Stat. 614 at s. 15; the *Omnibus Multilateral Development Institutions Act of 1977,* Oct. 3, 1977, H.R. 4262, Pub. L. 95–118, 91 Stat. 1067, title VII, s. 701; and a 1978 amendment to the *Export-Import Bank Act,* Oct. 18, 1978, H.R. 12931, Pub. L. 95–481, 92 Stat. 1591 at s. 607.
461. June 22, 1977, H.R. 5840, Pub. L. 95–52, 91 Stat. 235 at s. 115 adding s. 3(8) to the *EAA*.
462. *Omnibus Anti-terrorism Act of 1977,* S. 2236 95th Cong., 1st Sess. and H.R. 13387 95th Cong. 2d. Sess., pt 1 at 5 (1978) as cited in *Flores, supra,* note 460 at 545 and 554 respectively.
463. *Flores, ibid.* at 556 and 557 cites S. 333 96th Cong., 1st Sess. (1979), and H.R. 2441, 96th Cong. 1st Sess. (1979).
464. *EAA* of 1979, s. 6(i).
465. *Flores, supra,* note 460 at 567.
466. 45 Fed. Reg. 33,956 (May 21, 1980), as cited in *Flores, ibid.* at 570. See at 581–82 for some of the reasons Libya was listed. The regulations were codified at 15 C.F.R. 385.4(d) and remain in force despite Libya not being specifically mentioned in subsequent codifications. 15 C.F.R. 385.7(b) (1983).
467. *Ibid.*
468. See *Flores, supra,* note 460 at 571–76.
469. 15 C.F.R. 385.4(d) (1983).
470. *Flores, supra,* note 460 at 571–76.
471. Bingham & Johnson, "A Rational Approach to Export Controls" (1979) 57 Foreign Affairs 894 at 912.
472. *Flores, supra,* note 460 at 588.
473. 15 C.F.R. 385.7, by virtue of 47 Fed. Reg. 11,249 (Mar. 16, 1982). See also "Foreign Policy Export Controls" 82 U.S. Dep't State Bull. 55, June 1982 at 57.
474. 15 C.F.R. 385.7(a)(2)(i)(A).
475. 15 C.F.R. 385.7(a)(2)(i)(B).
476. 15 C.F.R. 385.7(a)(2)(i)(C).
477. 15 C.F.R. 385.7(a)(2)(ii)(A).
478. 15 C.F.R. 385.7(a)(3).
479. Information from officers of the Department of External Affairs.
480. U.S. 51 Fed. Reg. 1354–59 (January 10, 1986), 31 CFR 550.101–807. Reproduced in (1986) 25 Int'l Leg. Mat. 173 at 192.
481. 31 C.F.R. 540, by virtue of 50 Fed. Reg. 19,980, (May 10, 1985) [hereinafter *NTCRs*].
482. Executive Order 12,513, 50 Fed. Reg. 18,629 (May 2, 1985).
483. *Ibid.*
484. 31 C.F.R. 540.401(b) (1985).
485. 31 C.F.R. 540.101(b) expressly provides for the continued application of the Commerce regulations.
486. The Executive Order 12,513, 50 Fed. Reg. 18,629, does not deal with technical data except inasmuch as it is covered by the word "goods". Technical data in tangible form was included in the term "goods" for the purpose of the Treasury *NTCR*s. 31 C.F.R. 540.402 (1985).

CHAPTER VII

EUROPEAN STATE PRACTICE

This Chapter is devoted to a summary review of European state practice.[1] It is designed to set the Canadian and American practice in a broader perspective so that the reader should be better able to judge positions taken by the governments of Canada and the United States.

A. France

Few states have been more conscious of the need to protect the integrity of national sovereignty than France since 1945. Perhaps for this reason the classic cases of adverse response to the extraterritorial extension of U.S. export controls have come from France. In the *Fruehauf* v. *Massardy* case, and equally in its response to the attempt by the U.S. government to inhibit Dresser S.A. (France) from participating in the construction of the Euro-Siberian gas pipeline, the French government intervened vigorously to require the companies to perform their contractual commitments in the face of the U.S. prohibitions.[2] There is little doubt that in the face of any similar well-publicized efforts by a foreign power to regulate business transactions within France in the future the French government will react in the same manner. The government of France views the prescription of extraterritorial export controls as potentially violative of its sovereignty and the attempt to enforce such controls is viewed as a breach of international law. In particular, France objects to any attempt to control business decisions in France through the various channels of corporate control or licensing, and denies that the law of a foreign state can follow technology once it has entered France. Any attempt at investigation in France or attempts to influence business conduct in France by officials of a foreign power is also rejected as violating French sovereignty and hence international law.

The starting-point of any policy is therefore the exclusivity of French control over national territory. Certain legal traditions however, in particular the assertion of a strong link based upon nationality, as well as a strong, if unexpected, degree of pragmatism, make the French legal and policy positions somewhat less clear than might otherwise be the case.

French export controls are based on four groups of laws: *Le Code des douanes* and related customs legislation;[3] the lois, décrets and arrêtés dealing with the export of arms;[4] the regulations of 1985 and 1986 dealing specifically with import and export controls[5] and finally the rules of the *Code pénal* defining criminal offences, in particular conspiracy and the various arrêtés setting penalties for their violation, since export control violations are deemed to be penal offences.

Despite its position on principle of exclusive control over all business transactions within national territory France has been a party to the CoCom arrangements since their inception. French officials insist strongly on the non-binding nature of CoCom but it is French policy to cooperate fully in CoCom and to ensure that all export restrictions taken by France subsequent to CoCom deliberations be respected. This is ensured primarily by the *Avis aux exportateurs* of 1985[6] which contains extensive provisions for the licensing of exports of strategic goods and the effective implementation of the IC/DV system of controls. Roughly similar controls exist for exports and imports of strategic goods from NATO countries plus Japan, and a second group of neutral European states while different requirements pertain to exports and re-exports to all others. The *Avis aux exportateurs* of 1985 is completed by an extensive, CoCom-inspired list of strategic goods, the export of which requires a permit.

The *Avis aux exportateurs* of 1985 is essentially a territorially-based system designed to implement a multilaterally agreed system of controls. One can point out two potential elements of extraterritoriality, the first specific, the second systemic in character. Article 7 of the *Avis* of 1985 requires that any purchase abroad of technology in the French list by "un opérateur résident en France" is subject to the requirements of the *Avis* governing final destination of the goods. By virtue of Article 7.3 the resale of these goods by the "opérateur résident en France" is subject to the prior authorisation of the French export control authorities. Such authorisation is obtained only after the submission of documentation concerning the final destination of the goods. The second extraterritorial aspect results from the general principles of French penal law. Penal law is in principle applicable to French nationals abroad; this flows from a long legislative tradition in France maintaining a close link with French nationals abroad. The general principles of French penal law governing conspiracies will often have the effect of submitting the violation of a French export permit abroad, even by non-French nationals, to the jurisdiction of the French courts. The sufficient condition for jurisdiction is the existence in France of some of the acts constituting the offence.[7]

The second recent legislative act dealing with export controls is resoundingly territorial in scope and purpose. The *Arrêté* of 1986[8] is a response to U.S. efforts to submit foreign corporations to the requirement of proving an effective internal auditing system in order to qualify for a general distribution licence. Since any such attempt to control internal corporate activity by a foreign power is viewed as a violation of French sovereignty, France protested U.S. efforts to implement and verify such controls in France, but undertook to establish and police a similar system, thus allowing French-based companies to qualify for the advantages of the scheme. Like the *Avis aux exportateurs* of 1985 the Arrêté of 1986 is enforced by the Service des Autorisations Financières et Commerciales (SAFICO). The information to be supplied to the SAFICO and the auditing procedures which must be established in order to qualify are very close to those required under the U.S. *Export Administration Act of 1985*.[9] This is an example of a case where the French government has insisted on respect for the principle of territoriality when a number of other governments have preferred not to become directly involved.

With respect to the practice of submission clauses by the U.S., the French government has taken no public position and has not yet protested U.S. actions. This is an example of one of several cases where the French government leaves the decision to the companies involved. In principle companies are required to conduct themselves in a manner which respects French sovereignty. To date complete discretion has been left to companies, and there is no reason to think that submission clauses are not included in contracts involving the export of strategic goods from the U.S. to France. It is the policy of French authorities to promote the free flow of high technology from the U.S. to France when needed by French companies. Thus, on a day to day basis, one may presume that compromises of principle have been made when French companies have needed to obtain technology subject to U.S. extraterritorial export controls.[10]

Another example of pragmatism winning out over principle is the French reaction to the U.S. black list. In principle France objects to the maintenance of such a list in the U.S. when it affects French companies. When the situation arises however, French authorities seek to assist their companies in reaching a suitable accommodation with U.S. export control officials rather than seeking to combat this enforcement technique in the public political arena.

B. Federal Republic of Germany

The Federal Republic of Germany, as perhaps the greatest single importer of high technology and a country with unique defence ties with the U.S., is highly vulnerable to the extraterritorial impact of U.S. export controls. The situation is thus less clear than is the case with France or the U.K. The degree of ambiguity is increased by the nature of the German private legal system, based on a long tradition of the plurality of laws and federalism, to which have been added new elements of international law since the adoption of the Constitution in 1947 and adhesion to the Treaty of Rome in 1957.

Export controls are established by virtue of the general legislation on foreign trade and related subordinate legislation.[11] By virtue of this legislation the federal authorities are empowered to regulate exports and in particular to manage the F.R.G.'s participation in CoCom, including the establishment of an IC/DV system. The legislation is not extraterritorial in character.

As a proposition of international law the federal authorities do not deny the existence of extraterritorial prescriptive jurisdiction. They admit the legitimacy of extraterritorial prescriptive jurisdiction where there is a genuine link between the legislating state and the subject-matter of the rules. The link, to be genuine, must reflect a factual situation of considerable intensity. Examples of genuine links, justifying some forms of prescriptive jurisdiction, are laws governing nationals and to a lesser extent residents. Other examples include laws governing piracy, currency violations, laws prohibiting the use of chemical weapons, areas where custom and international public policy provide a sound basis and tax and cartel legislation where the economic effects with the F.R.G. are considerable. To a lesser degree federal authorities are prepared to countenance a measure of prescriptive jurisdiction on the basis of the protective principle.[12] Foreign policy controls, in their view, have no such link and hence have no justification.

Where federal officials draw a very clear line is between prescription and enforcement. Officials of the F.R.G. are not prepared to admit the legitimacy of most forms of extraterritorial enforcement. Their legal position is based on the sovereign equality of states, which places limits on the enforcement jurisdiction of all. Their reading of the *Lotus* case is that with respect to enforcement, the proper starting point is not to ask whether international law places any specific limit, but rather does international law allow this form of enforcement. In their view the issue of extraterritorial enforcement of laws cannot be placed on the basis of private law but raises issues of public international law. Extraterritoriality is not a matter of comity but rather a matter of strict law.

In the view of federal authorities the only legitimate enforcement techniques of extraterritorial legislation are those which do not affect the sovereignty of other states. Short of the rare cases of universal jurisdiction admitted by international law, or enforcement measures adopted by the Security Council of the U.N., it is difficult to conceive of any legitimate extraterritorial enforcement unless it has the prior agreement of the state affected. Thus, in the view of the Federal German authorities, the attempts of the U.S. to enforce export control laws on the basis of nationality, the U.S. parent subsidiary relationship or U.S. control, violate international law. A licence, even with a submission clause, does not justify extraterritorial enforcement. Federal officials deny that U.S. law can follow goods once they enter the territory of the Federal Republic.

The position of principle with respect to enforcement is thus a strong one. Nevertheless, as a state with a unique trading and security relationship with the U.S., some compromise has been necessary. Thus the Federal Republic of Germany has not adopted blocking legislation. While the U.S. "Black List" is objectionable in principle as an enforcement technique, there is little that the F.R.G. can do about it except to help German firms when in difficulty. The establishment of internal auditing procedures by German companies to qualify for a U.S. general distribution license raises delicate questions. Federal officials consider that such audits serve a valuable purpose in reinforcing CoCom measures. Thus a private audit organised within the company raises no problems. There would be objection to any attempts at oversight in the F.R.G. by U.S. officials but there has been no confrontation on this matter.

Submission clauses also appear to pose interesting questions in the Federal Republic of Germany. There have been no judicial decisions on the subject to give guidance as to the characterisation of such clauses under German law. Officials interviewed indicated that thinking may be torn between several views. In the first place, firms are left to their own discretion as to whether to sign a submission clause as part of their private agreements. There is however recognition that submission clauses can raise issues of public law and that it might be necessary to intervene before a court to take this position some day. As yet they do not appear to be viewed as a problem.

Interestingly the issue of submission clauses has been the object of doctrinal consideration in the F.R.G.[13] Basedow notes the difference between clauses justifying non-performance through force majeure, and clauses such as these which presume performance, but limit the buyer's right of disposition of the goods after delivery. While recognising that such clauses raise problems of public as well as private law, as well as potential conflict between the public policy of the exporting and importing (forum) state, Basedow suggests that the clause may be enforceable if the policy of the forum is indifferent to the outcome. Basedow also rejects the view that such clauses are accepted only under duress, suggesting they be viewed as potentially facilitating international transactions. On the balance Basedow considers that the potential value of a submission clause in a court outside the prohibiting-exporting country is not likely to be great.[14]

One result of Basedow's analysis which suggests itself is that a submission clause may well be effective where the public policy concerning re-exports of the exporting state and of the importing (forum state) are the same, as is the case where both are parties to the CoCom arrangements.

On March 27, 1986, in the context of an agreement on the U.S. Strategic Defense Initiative, the Federal Republic undertook to tighten its enforcement of export controls generally, and in particular to take further steps to guarantee against the re-export of U.S. technology exported to the F.R.G.[15]

In conclusion the extraterritorial extension of U.S. export controls has been viewed by the F.R.G. as a major foreign policy issue during the years 1982-86. As a result of regulatory changes in late 1986 in the U.S. however and a perceived change of heart within the U.S. Administration on the subject, it is expected that this problem will rapidly diminish if not disappear. There would thus be left, in the German view, the non-extraterritorial issue of enforcing CoCom, and from time to time the potentially irritating but short-term problems posed by the extraterritorial enforcement of measures designed to stop dangerous armed conflicts, or a trade or foreign policy boycott by the U.S. The latter policy is opposed in principle by the F.R.G. except when imposed by the Security Council of the United Nations.[16]

C. Belgium

Of all the economies of the E.C., Belgium is the most open to intra-community and international trade and, given the size of its economy, must import a wide range of technologies from the U.S. Belgium is thus highly vulnerable to the extraterritorial reach of U.S. export controls.

In principle Belgium adopts a territorialist position with respect to both prescription and enforcement of laws abroad and has from time to time protested the extension of U.S. export controls to its territory. There would appear to be a tendency to look to the E.C. as the safest bulwark against the extension of U.S. measures. In principle Belgium objects to the extension of U.S. laws to business transactions in Belgium on the basis of nationality, the U.S. parent-subsidiary relationship and U.S. control.

Despite its basic position of principle Belgium is prepared to countenance the extraterritorial extension of laws where based on universal custom, multilateral agreement to which it is a party or bilateral agreement.

Exports and imports are controlled by the *Loi du 11 septembre 1962*[17] and a series of regulations.[18] This legislation allows the Belgian government to regulate exports to protect vital economic interests, national security and to implement international economic treaties and arrangements – in particular the CoCom and IC/DV system. In principle the legislation is territorial in scope except that any permit for Belgium is also valid for Luxemburg and the Netherlands. Article 10 of the *Loi du 11 septembre 1962* makes offences against the Act and Regulations subject to general provisions, which govern penal offences and customs legislation. In this respect there may be an element of extraterritoriality in that offences by Belgians abroad or by others abroad, where some elements of the offence (fraud or conspiracy) are present in Belgium, will subject the offenders to liability for prosecution under the general principles of Belgian penal law.

Submission clauses are known to be current in Belgium but up to the present time they have not given rise to any governmental action. On the other hand the Belgian government became concerned by the auditing requirements of the 1985 amendments to the *Export Administration Act.*[19] A protest was lodged with the U.S. by Belgium in 1986 and a system of audits overseen by Belgian authorities was offered in lieu of visits by American officials or their agents.[20]

Belgium has been the scene of one of the few court cases in Europe involving U.S. export controls. In its decision in the case of *Moens* v. *Ahlers et al.*[21] the Commercial Tribunal of Antwerp rejected the attempt of the U.S. government (intervenor) and the defendant to claim that a shipping company could refuse to deliver goods listed on a bill of lading, pursuant to orders from the U.S. export control authorities.

Perhaps, as befits the country which hosts the seat of the E.C., Belgium looks more and more to the E.C. to carry the burden of the dialogue on extraterritoriality with the U.S. and fully subscribes to the principles set out in the protection note of 1982 concerning the U.S. extraterritorial measures against the Euro-Siberian pipeline.[22]

D. Switzerland

As a long-standing neutral country Switzerland has always been concerned with ensuring the integrity of its territory. Switzerland adopts a strongly territorialist position with respect to the extraterritorial extension of laws.[23] Nevertheless, Switzerland does accept the right of extraterritorial prescription based on nationality, or protection of the fundamental interests of the state.[24] The Tribunal fédéral has also recognised the possibility of extraterritorial prescription on the basis of the effects doctrine.[25] Thus Article 24 of the *Loi du 8 décembre 1934 sur les banques et les caisses d'épargne*[26] requiring secrecy concerning the operations of Swiss banks applies regardless of the place of commission of the offence.[27] Certain penal offences also apply to Swiss nationals regardless of where the offences are committed. It is recognised by Swiss authorities that any attempt to regulate corporations extraterritorially on this basis raises delicate and difficult questions. In their view such jurisdiction can only be exercised where there is a sufficient degree of contact between the institution of the event and the legislating state.

Where the Swiss authorities draw an absolute line is with respect to the attempt to enforce extraterritorially.[28] This position was reiterated a number of times in diplomatic notes and an amicus brief in the *Marc Rich S.A.* litigation in the U.S., where Switzerland vigorously fought the attempt to obtain information concerning Swiss banking operations.[29] The only extraterritorial enforcement acceptable in the eyes of the Swiss federal authorities is that pursuant to prior agreement.

Export controls have not provided any major test of these principles within Switzerland. As a neutral state Switzerland is not a member of NATO, but has, for economic and political reasons, maintained export controls and an IC/DV system paralleling those of the CoCom.[30] Switzerland is a member of the IAEA and a party to the *Nuclear Non-Proliferation Treaty*. Since it is not a CoCom participant, the CoCom type controls on radio-active substances and nuclear technologies come under its general legislation on nuclear technology.[31] This legislation is not extraterritorial either as to prescription or as to enforcement in itself. The only possible extraterritorial aspect might be with respect to conspiracies to violate an export permit which are partially committed in Switzerland and partly abroad.

Submission clauses have never been considered by the federal authorities, so that it is not possible to determine the legal issues which they might raise. It is clear however that any attempt by U.S. officials or their private agents to verify an auditing system within a Swiss company would involve a serious penal offence. Switzerland has no general blocking statute, although it does have legislation in the field of bank secrecy to the same effect.

The *Restatement of the Law, Third, Foreign Relations Law of the United States*[32] and the balancing of interests approach which it espouses in the chapter on jurisdiction, are welcomed, insofar as they help U.S. courts look to the interests of other states, but they are not regarded as an adequate or fair approach to extraterritoriality generally or with respect to export controls. Krafft states:

> ... cette méthode risque de conduire à des résultats contraires au droit international, dans la mesure en particulier, où elle fait dépendre la solution d'un conflit juridique de considérations relevant de la "courtoisie internationale" ("principles of international comity") et se prête à des appréciations éminemment subjectives.[33]

In the field of export controls, as elsewhere, the Swiss federal authorities would support an approach to extraterritorial extension of laws upon the basis of moderation and restraints. These they view as legal obligations flowing from the principles of territory and non-intervention in the affairs of other states.[34]

E. The Netherlands

The basic stance of the Government of the Netherlands concerning the extraterritorial extension of laws is territorialist. Making perhaps less moment than many governments of the distinction between prescription and enforcement, the Dutch government denies the right of a foreign state to regulate business transactions within Dutch territory. The Dutch government accepts that in certain contexts, where justified by a sufficiently close link, a state may legislate extraterritorially on the basis of nationality and the protection of national security. This view has been confirmed by a Dutch court in the case of *Compagnie européenne des pétroles* c. *Sensor Nederland*.[35] The Dutch government also accepts the legitimacy of extraterritorial controls in the case of U.N. Security Council binding sanctions. The Dutch government has traditionally rejected the legitimacy of the effects doctrine as a basis of jurisdiction. There is legislation in the Netherlands which applies extraterritorially in the case of currency violations, attacks on the person of the Head of State and in the event of multilaterally agreed economic sanctions.[36]

The legislation governing export controls[37] provides for the imposition of export controls based in substance upon the CoCom list, which for all intent and purposes is binding in the Netherlands. The IC/DV system is used to guarantee against deviation of exports. There is also legislation which covers related financial transactions. The Netherlands has adopted a comprehensive blocking statute as well as a narrower provision to the same end in the competition legislation. This legislation is not extraterritorial in reach.

The Netherlands was the scene of one of the very few cases before the courts arising out of the U.S.-European pipeline dispute in 1982. In this case, Sensor Nederland, the Dutch subsidiary of an American firm, Geo Source Corp. of Houston, Texas, followed the orders of its U.S. parent not to proceed with delivery of 2000 seismic devices (made in the Netherlands) to a French corporation, engaged in the construction of the Euro-Siberian pipeline. In mitigation of its contractual obligation to deliver the goods, Sensor pleaded its own and the U.S. parent's obligation to respect the U.S. embargo. The court of the Hague, while not rejecting outright that certain types of extraterritorial jurisdiction might be justified to protect national security, rejected the defence of Sensor Nederland in this case on the grounds that the attempt by the U.S. to regulate the sale of products made in the Netherlands for reasons of foreign policy constituted a breach of international law.[38]

Like other governments, the Government of the Netherlands has had to make certain compromises in the interests of trade with the U.S. Thus it appears that no protest has been made of the U.S. practice of requiring submission clauses, perhaps because no Dutch company has complained of the issue to the government. The practice of reviewing auditing systems in Dutch companies by U.S. officials is objected to in principle, but in practice, after negotiations, it was agreed that such verifications could be made, subject to the authority of a Dutch official. The traditional methods of extending U.S. export controls via U.S. nationals, corporations and subsidiaries is objected to but, where it can, the Dutch government seeks to exercise its discretion in a manner designed to promote commerce and assist the Dutch company out of its difficulties.

No official position has been expressed on the American Law Institute's *Restatement of the Law, Third, Foreign Relations Law of the United States*.[39] It appears that the Dutch delegation to the OECD has been an active supporter of the recent work of the OECD Subcommittee on Conflicting Requirements to define the content of the obligations of moderation and restraint.[40]

F. The European Economic Communities

At first blush it may seem curious to consider the position of the European Economic Communities ("E.C.") on this issue. Nevertheless, a review of developments since 1980 in the E.C. reveals a complex and fascinating picture which highlights many of the problems dealt with elsewhere in this study. At the present time there is a debate on export controls within the EC which raises all the traditional questions of the legitimacy of their extraterritorial extension at international law, together with complex problems relating to the extent of the E.C.'s own jurisdiction to establish such controls, and hence to conduct the dialogue on extraterritoriality with the U.S. This debate may ultimately give rise to the most fundamental debate of all on export controls, namely the debate between those who see security in restricting trade in certain technologies and those who see long-term security best served by freer trade.

Much of this debate is still speculative, and will depend upon positions to be taken by the Commission and upon the subsequent reaction of the Council. But the issues are now emerging and in all probability will give rise to such a debate.

Under the *Treaty of Rome* the E.C. is charged with promoting the adoption of a common commercial policy, the elements of which either inherently or specifically are binding upon member states and their citizens. The E.C. has no export controls at the present time, nor does it have a blocking statute, however, there is little doubt that the E.C. is empowered to adopt both should the Council be prepared to do so.[41]

The E.C. is one of the rare jurisdictions in Europe to have made notable use of extraterritorial legislation. This fact is often cited by U.S. authorities[42] in justification of U.S. extra-territorial legislation. Some reservations and clarifications are in order. The examples of E.C. extraterritorial legislation are limited essentially to antitrust legislation cases. There have been proposals relating to the issuance of securities as well as the Vredeling proposal[43] which would have required foreign companies to provide information to their employees in Europe about their corporate activities around the world.

There have been a number of cases[44] where the Commission and the Court of the European Communities have had occasion to give extraterritorial reach to Articles 85 and 86 of the *Treaty of Rome* and have had to elaborate a legal rationale for such extension. Certain caveats are necessary however. In the first case, Articles 85 and 86 speak of cartels and restrictive practices "between" member states and not generally international practices. Secondly, until recently, the Court has not had occasion to pronounce upon a practice taking place entirely outside the E.C. territory and producing effects within.[45] The Commission has lately offered the Court the opportunity to espouse the pure effects doctrine.[46] In substance, the Court of Justice of the European Communities has done so[47] but in a manner which appears to create a new basis of extraterritorial jurisdiction rather than relying on the effects doctrine as developed in the U.S. and in the E.C. Commission. Up to the *Wood Pulp Cartel* litigation, E.C. antitrust law had been applied against subsidiaries of foreign companies, doing business in the E.C., on the ground that these foreign companies were violating Articles 85 and 86 through the agency of their subsidiaries. In matters of service of process, production of evidence and penalties, where U.S. laws reached out to control subsidiaries abroad or to require the production of documents from abroad, the E.C. has been much more circumspect. The E.C. sought to respect the distinction between prescription and enforcement and thus generally avoided clashes with the public policy of foreign states.[48]

The *Wood Pulp Cartel* litigation applied to acts committed entirely outside the territory of the E.C. The Commission and Advocate General Darmon were prepared to espouse the effects doctrine fully in this case. The Court, however, based its decision on the principle that sales by the offending cartel to purchasers established in the community offended E.C. competition law and thus could be caught.[49] This may be read as an attempt to maintain the primacy of the principle of territoriality, but it is in reality more akin to some kind of "stream of commerce" doctrine and hence perhaps as broad as the effects doctrine. In sum, the E.C. Commission has adopted a position on extraterritoriality in the field of anti-trust which parallels that of the United States. The Court of Justice has given extraterritorial scope to Articles 85 and 86 but in doing so has acted on a new basis whose full implications are difficult to assess. In the field of Competition Law some kind of Rubicon has been crossed.

The E.C. took a position on the extraterritorial extension of U.S. export controls in 1982 and 1983. This was done both in response to the measures adopted by the U.S. to embargo the Euro-Siberian pipeline and subsequently in response to the renewal of the *Export Administration Act*. These documents are interesting both for their content and for their implications for the role of the E.C.[50]

In response to the changes to the *Export Administration Regulations*, the E.C. submitted a Note and Comment to the U.S. on 12 August 1982.[51] The Note described the U.S. measures, which applied retroactively to products manufactured entirely out of the U.S. under licence from U.S. companies, as "contrary to international law,"[52] as well as highly damaging both to European and U.S. industry. The accompanying comments are much more expansive and cover a wide range of legal issues. The U.S. measures are described as:

> ... unacceptable under international law because of their extraterritorial aspects. They seek to regulate companies not of U.S. nationality in respect of their conduct outside the U.S. and particularly the handling of property and technical data of these companies and within the U.S.[53]

The measures are described as violating the territoriality principle "since they purport to regulate other activities of companies ... not under the territorial competence of the U.S.". They violate the nationality principle by "seeking to impose its [U.S.] corporate nationality on companies the great majority of which are incorporated and have their registered office elsewhere...".[54] The effect of this, according to the Comments, is to replace the "ordre public" of the E.C. with the public policy of the U.S. by pressing the E.C. companies into the service of U.S. policy. The Comments also suggest that the criteria required by the effects doctrine and the protective principle had not been met, although the caveat is placed that these bases of jurisdiction "have found less than general acceptance under international law."[55] In this the Comments mirror the divergence of views between E.C. states like the U.K. and the Netherlands, which still reject the effects doctrine, and those like the F.R.G. which support it.

Interestingly, the Community chose to predicate its Comments on the assumption of a number of principles which positively authorise extraterritorial legislation, rather than the assertion of general prohibitive rules which have been violated by the U.S. There are however, from time to time in the Comments, references to more general prohibitory standards such as non-intervention and abuse of rights.[56]

The Comments also condemn the implication of the U.S. measures that goods produced in the E.C. using U.S. know-how under a U.S. licence "should somehow be considered as unalterably American".[57]

The Comments reject the use of submission clauses by the U.S. In the view of the E.C. "[p]rivate agreements should not be used in this way as an instrument of foreign policy," since by doing so "... freedom of contract is misused in order to circumvent the limits imposed on national jurisdiction by international law."[58] In the concluding paragraphs the Comments also argue that the balancing of interests approach of the Third Restatement, which is not accepted by the E.C. as a principle of international law, should have led the U.S. not to adopt these measures against the pipeline.[59]

The Aide-Mémoire of 14 March 1983, sent by the E.C. and its Member States on the amendments to the U.S. *Export Administration Act*, is a much more compact document. It is based essentially on the argument that assertions of jurisdiction over U.S. companies and their subsidiaries or controlled companies, as well as goods manufactured by them abroad, violate the territorial sovereignty of the E.C. The Aide-Mémoire states:

> According to a basic principle of international law any natural or legal person doing business in the Community should abide both by Community and national legislation in force therein.[60]

The Aide-Mémoire returns to submission clauses which are described as "a clear abuse for foreign policy purposes, of the freedom of contract."[61] Interestingly the Aide-Mémoire also argues that foreign policy controls, unlike national security or short supply controls, run counter to the exemptions to the *G.A.T.T.* provided in Articles XX and XXI.[62]

Partly as a result of the E.C. actions in 1982 and 1983 and partly as a result of the commitment to complete the unification of the internal market of the E.C. by 1992,[63] there is now a debate within the E.C. as to the extent to which export controls constitute a barrier to the free movement of goods within the market and the role that the Community should play in removing or enforcing them in the future. This is primarily a debate as to E.C. jurisdiction and policy but the outcome is of great interest to other states since, if the E.C. Commission achieves a central or coordinating role, it may become the primary interlocutor of Europe in questions of extraterritoriality.

The emerging debate is twofold: a) the role of the E.C. in eliminating the regulating export controls and b) the substance of export controls and their ambit. In the first issue, on the hypothesis that export controls constitute a barrier to internal trade,[64] it will be necessary to remove them and to reconstitute a new system of controls on the periphery of the E.C. Given that most export controls are imposed upon products of military or strategic significance, this raises the issue of the extent to which export controls are justified under the exception Article 223 of the *Treaty of Rome*. Views as to future action range from the creation of an E.C. system, the creation of a new harmonised system on the periphery by Member States, to the maintenance of the existing system.[65]

Inevitably there is also an emerging debate on the substance of export controls within the E.C. Insofar as it is public, this debate is taking place within the European Parliament. In a major report of the Committee on Energy, Research and Technology on Transfer of Technology,[66] serious questions were raised as to the consequences of export controls, the propriety of the extraterritorial operation of U.S. controls and the role of CoCom. The Metten Report suggested that the U.S. was seeking to cast the net of export controls much too broadly both domestically and in CoCom. A subsequent Report of the Committee on External Economic Relations[67] and Draft Resolution[68] is also critical of U.S. export controls and their extraterritorial reach. The draft resolution, while falling short of a call to transfer jurisdiction to the E.C., did call for the harmonisation of the positions of Member States. It also called for the eventual conclusion of a treaty between members of the E.C. to replace CoCom and better define the goods covered, the method of application and the scope of the system. The Draft Resolution also noted the potential conflict between CoCom and the rules of E.C. law.

This debate is note yet over. Clearly, a unified E.C. speaking with a single voice on the extraterritorial application of export controls would constitute a major change in the existing situation.

Notes

1. Time and information available to the authors did not allow us to do justice to the complexity of European state practice studied. This Chapter is based essentially upon a review of legislation and interviews conducted in Departments of Foreign Affairs and International Trade as well as the E.C. Commission. The Committee on Extraterritorial Jurisdiction of the International Law Association is preparing a study of this subject which will be published in 1990 under the editorship of Professor Karl Meessen.
2. *Fruehauf* v. *Massardy*, Judgement of May 22, 1965, Cour d'appel, Paris, Recueil Dalloz-Sirey "Jurisprudence", 147, English translation in (1966) 5 Int'l Leg. Mat. 476. Fully detailed in R. Ergec, *La compétence extraterritoriale à la lumière des contentieux sur le gazoduc euro-sibérien* (Bruxelles: Bruylant, 1984) at 4 ff.

3. It is important because the customs officers are charged with the enforcement of import and export controls.
4. Some of these predate World War II. Collected in *Matériel de guerre, armes et munitions, Régime*, Publication No. 1074, tiré du J.O. (Edition, 1985) at 6, 21, 95–126.
5. Avis aux importateurs et aux exportateurs relatif aux produits et technologies soumis au contrôle de la destination finale, J.O. le 5 décembre 1985. Arrêté du 13 janvier 1986 modifiant et complétant l'arrêté du 30 janvier 1967 sur les procédures d'importation et d'exportation, J.O. le 30 janvier 1986.
6. *Ibid.*
7. The general principles have recently been set out by the Cour de cassation (C. criminelle) in the affaire *Ampelio Bolis*, Gazette du Palais, 3, 4, décembre 1986, p. 5.
8. *Supra*, note 5.
9. July 12, 1985, S. 883, Pub. L. 99–64, 99 Stat. 120, 50 USC App. 2401–20 at s. 104 (West Supp. 1951–1986) concerning validated licenses for multiple exports.
10. Much of the information in this section was obtained by the author from officials of the Ministère des Affaires étrangères and the Ministère du commerce extérieur. See generally, *L'application extraterritoriale du droit économique*, Cahiers du Centre de Droit International de Nanterre, No 3 (1987).
11. Aussenwirtzschaftsgesetz, vom 28 April 1961, Bundesgezetsblatt 1, Seite 481 and regulations; conveniently set out in the Commerzbank A.G. Publication, *Leitfaden durch das Aussenwirtzschaftsrecht* (Ausgabe, 1986).
12. An example might be the "Vredeling Proposal" in the E.C. to require multinational enterprises to submit to certain obligations designed to protect their workers before closing a plant. See Section F, *infra*.
13. J. Basedow, "Private Law Effects of Foreign Export Controls - An International Case Report" (1984) 17 German Y.B.I.L. 109. This volume of the Yearbook contains a number of valuable articles on the European response to the Euro-Siberian pipeline controversy.
14. *Ibid.* at 138–99.
15. "F.R.G.-U.S.A.: Arrangements on the Transfer of Technology and the Strategic Defense Initiative" (1986) 25 Int'l Leg. Mat. 956 at 974–77.
16. Much of the information in this section was obtained by the author from officials of the Ministry of Foreign Affairs and the Ministry of International Trade of the Federal Republic of Germany.
17. *Loi relative à l'importation, à l'exportation et au transit des marchandises*, Moniteur belge, October 27, 1962, p. 9491.
18. Arrêté royal du 24 octobre 1962, Moniteur belge, October 27, 1962. Arrêté ministériel du 23 novembre 1978, Moniteur belge, December 5, 1978. Arrêté ministériel du 31 décembre 1982, Moniteur belge, January 23, 1963.
19. *Supra*, note 9.
20. It would appear that in order to avoid sending U.S. officials to Belgium to verify company auditing procedures, the U.S. export control authorities sent chartered accountants working out of international firms in England. Belgium is also reported to have protested the extraterritorial provisions of the 1986 U.S. drug abuse legislation.
21. Rechtskundig Weekblad, Vol. 30 (1966–67), Col. 630–33 cited by P.J. Kuyper, "The E.C. and the U.S. Pipeline Embargo" (1984) 27 German Y.B.I.L. 72 at 82.
22. Much of the information in this section was obtained from officials of the Ministère des affaires étrangères et du commerce extérieur et de la coopération au développement, Bruxelles.
23. See statements of the Conseil fédéral, June 7, 1982, Bulletin officiel de l'Assemblée fédérale, Conseil national 1982, pp. 1455–57 and December 5, 1983, pp. 1884–85. See also the section on state practice in the annual volumes of the *Annuaire suisse de droit international*.
24. M.-Ch. Krafft, "Secret bancaire et conflit de juridiction – Le point de vue d'un

internationaliste" in von Graffenried, ed., *Butträge zum Schweitzerischen Bankenrecht* (Bern: Verlag Stämpfli, 1987) 207 at 216 [hereinafter *Krafft*].
25. Affaire *Banque commerciale S.A.* c. *Commission fédérale des banques*, 1ère Cour civile, ATF 1081b, 513.
26. R.S. 952.0.
27. M. Aubert, "The Limits of Swiss Banking Secrecy Under Domestic and International Law" (1984) 2 Int'l Tax & Business Lawyer 284 at 284–85.
28. *Krafft*, *supra*, note 24 at 214.
29. Bulletin officiel de l'Assemblée fédérale, Conseil national, 1985, pp. 1366–68.
30. *Loi fédérale du 25 juin 1982 sur les mesures économiques extérieures*, R.O. 1982, 1923; Ordonnance du 7 mars 1983 sur les exportations de marchandises, R.S. 946.221 amended December 16, 1985. The latter ordonnance contains a provision to back up efforts made by other countries, particularly the U.S., to avoid unauthorised re-exports of exported technology. This mirrored steps taken by Austria, Law of December 12, 1984, reprinted (1986) 25 Int'l Leg. Mat. 848; Sweden, Ordinance of Feb. 27, 1986, and F.R.G. in March 1986, see *supra*, Section B.
31. Ordonnance du 18 janvier 1985, sur les définitions et autorisations dans le domaine de l'énergie atomique, R.S. 732.11.
32. (St. Paul: American Law Institute, 1987) [hereinafter *Third Restatement*].
33. Krafft, *supra*, note 24 at 244. Ambassador Krafft writes with particular authority as Chef de la Direction du droit international public du Département fédéral des affaires étrangères.
34. Much of the information in this section was obtained from officials of the Departement fédéral des affaires étrangères, Berne.
35. President District Court, The Hague, September 17, 1982, translated and reprinted in (1983) 22 Int'l Leg. Mat. 66.
36. *Foreign Boycotts Notification Act*, Stb. 1984, 215 which is based on a moderate effects doctrine, see P.J. Kuyper, "The EC and the US Pipeline Embargo" (1984) 27 German Y.B.I.L. 72 at 87 [hereinafter *Kuyper*].
37. Wet van 5 juli 1962 as amended and subsequent regulations of April 26, 1963 and March 11, 1981.
38. *Supra*, note 36.
39. *Supra*, note 32. Privately officials express reservations. One official suggested to the author that one problem with the balancing test was that, while it might suit multinational companies, small Dutch businesses were hardly likely to be able to make such an assessment.
40. It would appear that Dutch officials would welcome work in this Subcommittee specifically directed to the issue of export controls. Much of the information in this section was obtained from officials of the Ministries of Foreign Affairs and Economic Affairs of the Kingdom of the Netherlands.
41. Kuyper, *supra*, note 36.
42. Sometimes in a rather uncritical fashion - even by the *Third Restatement*, *supra*, note 32. See Introductory Note at 283 and Reporters' Note 9 at 294.
43. E.C.O.J., 1980, No. C297/3, November 15, 1980.
44. *Inter alia I.C.I.* v. *E.E.C.* Case (No. 48/69), [1972] E.C.R. 619; *Commercial Solvents Corporation*, Decision of the Commission, December 14 1972, [1973] CMLR D50; *Franco- Japanese Ball Bearings Agreement*, Decision of the Commission, November 29 1975, [1975] CMLR D8; *Béguelin Import Co.* v. *SASL Import-Export* [1971] E.C.R. 949; *Walrare & Koch* v. *Union Cycliste Internationale* [1974] E.C.R. 1407; *Continental Can & Europemballage* v. *E.C.C* [1973] E.C.R. 223.
45. P.J. Kuyper, "European Community Law and Extraterritoriality: Some Trends and New Developments" (1984) 33 I.C.L.Q. 1013 at 1017.
46. In the *Wood Pulp* litigation, Cases IV/29.725, 85/102/EEC, 89/85, 104/85, 114/84, 116–117/85, 125–129/85, [1988] 4 C.M.L.R. 901.

47. See *Re Wood Pulp Cartel: A. Anlström OY and Others* v. *E.C. Commission*, Decision of the Court, September 27, 1988, [1988] 4 C.M.L.R. 901.
48. The two protests received by the E.C. came 1) from the U.K. after the I.C.J. decision, (before the U.K. joined the E.C.) reprinted in A.V. Lowe, *Extraterritorial Jurisdiction* (Cambridge, England: Grotius, 1983) at 144 [hereinafter *Lowe*] and 2) from the U.S. after the Commission's 1981 investigation of activities of I.B.M. In Europe; *Kuyper*, *supra*, note 45 at 1013, note 3.
49. See *Wood Pulp Cartel*, *supra*, note 47 para. 12 at 940.
50. Some states protested separately and it is unclear whether the E.C. protest binds them or was designed to give the weight of numbers to their contents. Officials of all states interviewed expressed support for the Note, Comments and Aide-Mémoire.
51. Reproduced in *Lowe*, *supra*, note 48 at 197.
52. *Ibid.* at 198.
53. *Ibid.* at 201.
54. *Ibid.* at 202.
55. *Ibid.* at 204.
56. The somewhat hybrid nature of the Comments has been remarked upon by *Kuyper*, *supra*, note 36 at 77. In this respect the Comments are clearly the product of a committee reflecting a variety of national positions.
57. Comments in *Lowe*, *supra*, note 48 at 203.
58. *Ibid.* at 204.
59. *Ibid.* at 211.
60. *Ibid.* at 216.
61. *Ibid.* at 217.
62. *Ibid.* at 218.
63. *Completing the Internal Market*, White Paper from the Commission to the Council, June 1985.
64. Estimates suggest that export controls potentially affect as much as 40% of trade in manufacturers between Member States, and 45% of extra-E.C. trade in manufactures.
65. Views as to the possible future role appear to differ widely between member states.
66. European Parliament Working Documents 1985–86, Doc. PE 96.409/fin, September 30, 1985, known as the "Metten Report".
67. Parlement Européen, Commission des Relations Économiques Extérieures, Projet de Rapport sur la firme Pegard, Doc. PE 92.714/B, July 14 1986.
68. *Ibid.* Proposition de Résolution, Doc. Pe 92.716/A.16, October, 1986.

CHAPTER VIII

CONCLUSIONS

A. General Considerations

This Chapter seeks to draw conclusions from the state practice reviewed above. The record is complex and often contradictory; it has given rise to major foreign policy disputes between some of the most closely allied states of the late Twentieth Century and holds promise of doing so again. Passions have cooled in 1989, partly as a result of a somewhat relaxed U.S. position on export controls, but none of the major issues of principle in contention have been resolved to the general satisfaction. The search for an acceptable international rule is still under way, but the international community may be at something of a watershed with respect to the extraterritorial application of export control laws. Much has been said and done by governments in recent years and there has been considerable effort by commentators to reassess and redefine the applicable rules of international law. The moment may be ripe to bring these disparate strands together with a view to reaching some long-lasting conclusion.

This book concentrates on state practice, in the expectation that this practice would reveal much concerning the views of governments as to their powers and the limits of these powers when they came into conflict with those of other states. The legislative and executive record of the U.S. and the manner in which it has been defended does indeed reveal much concerning the exercise of power by the strongest military and economic power in the world. The review of state practice reveals the U.S. record to be the benchmark for claims as to the maximum extraterritorial application of laws. Few, if any, states in any sphere have claimed the right to apply their laws more broadly, and none have attempted to do so by more diverse means. It would be quite wrong to suggest that there is no sense of the limits or restraints upon the exercise of prescriptive or enforcement jurisdiction in the U.S. However, the fact remains that the most extensive claims to the right to apply laws extraterritorially are to be found in the legislative and administrative practice of the U.S.

Canada is a middle power. Canada is also a state which espouses a functionalist view of the philosophical basis of the rules of international law and of their development. The Canadian practice reveals much both as to the state of international law in this area and equally as to the dilemmas facing a middle power in the late twentieth century.

Canada can rely upon the law or develop the law and on occasion is able to bend the law in its own direction, but unlike the U.S. it cannot purport to make international law by virtue of its practice alone. The practice of Canada has often been responsive rather than innovative with respect to extraterritoriality. Canadian positions are likely to be closer to the generally accepted norms of international law since Canada usually invokes the law in protection of its territorial sovereignty and in defense of a more static interest than does the U.S.

Canada's defense of territorial sovereignty in the face of U.S. arguments based upon the necessity of enforcing national policies across international boundaries, in order to guarantee the efficacy of these policies in a highly interdependent world, is in a sense paradoxical in the light of Canadian sympathy for the functionalist view of the basis of international law. In many circumstances the Government of Canada is likely to be of one mind with the U.S. in seeking to ground the rules of modern international law in a just calculus of national interest, properly adjusted to the regulatory functions which they are to serve. The rules which emerge from this process, if properly adjusted to the interests of a sufficient number of states, should be conducive to the maintenance of a stable world order. At first blush Canada appears to have laid greater emphasis on the abstract idea of sovereignty than upon the functional exigencies of interdependence. The answer to this seeming paradox lies in the fact that interdependence is a two-sided coin. On one side are the advantages of interdependence, on the other are the risks. Each state, according to its situation, must make an assessment of the benefits and dangers of interdependence and seek to strike a balance between the two. A widely accepted rule of international law governing the extraterritorial application of export controls will emerge when enough states have been able to agree upon this balance of interests.

The dilemma of interdependence is central to the definition of rules of public international law governing the extraterritorial application of laws. The ever-increasing degree of economic and political interdependence of the western trading nations and to a lesser degree the rest of the world is a fact which none can ignore. Commerce and communications are bringing these states and their peoples ever closer together; products and immaterial property traverse international boundaries with great speed and the production patterns of enterprises great and small virtually always involve multinational sourcing of components for products. In such circumstances the pressure to apply laws in respect of products which leave national territory is often very great, especially for a major military power such as the U.S. The advantages of the international trading system and the degree of interdependence which it has brought are so widely accepted that one is tempted to conclude that a broad measure of extraterritoriality is inevitable and should be accepted and practised by all states. Why have states like Canada resisted this impulse in the past and why are they certain to continue to do so in the future? Objections are framed in function of differing understandings as to the appropriate rule of international law, but they surely go beyond differences as to interpretation of abstract legal principles. What is revealed here is the continuing vitality of the nation state as the primary decision-making organ in the international community and a desire to preserve the integrity of national governments.

The net result of the dilemma of interdependence, as revealed by the state practice reviewed in this book, is that no state has been able to have its way entirely. State practice reveals clearly that international law and the reaction of other states has set limits to the capacity of the U.S. to extend its laws abroad. On the other hand, state practice also reveals that other states have had to accommodate the U.S. in practice and sometimes even on matters of principle; furthermore, the domestic practice of certain states with respect to extraterritoriality also indicates that the picture is not without ambiguity. The policies of the U.S. have involved that government in serious disputes with closely allied governments. These governments in turn have had to enter into collaborative multilateral arrangements to control certain exports and beyond this in varying degrees these governments have had difficulty in maintaining the strict integrity of the traditional rules of international law in the extraterritorial application of laws. At the very least they have been forced into a process of reaffirmation of the territoriality rule and in that process they have had difficulty in not accepting that changing circumstances may be provoking a change in the rules themselves.

The contemporary debate over extraterritoriality is also a debate about rules. Despite the fact that it deals with a broad range of security and economic issues, where well-defined rules are not always welcome, a preoccupation with rules is clearly evident. Indeed, rules play so important a part that many maintain that debate over rules simply masks a debate over differing interests and policies. As is shown by the state practice reviewed, governments are preoccupied by the state of the rules and most of them appear to desire the formulation or at least the reaffirmation of more precise rules. Again, one can wonder at the paradox of Canada and the U.S. disagreeing on the content of rules, when often these two governments place more emphasis on the processes of negotiation, decision-making and dispute resolution. A similar preoccupation with rules is also and less surprisingly evident in Europe. Rules still matter. Well-defined rules continue to play a significant role in the definition of the international political and economic order. Those who hold that precise rules are an impediment to the protection of important political and economic values in the international community and that international law can be best studied from the standpoint of power and process would do well to consider the debate over extraterritoriality. It would seem that the values at stake are simply too important to be left to the vagaries of a dispute settlement process when difficulties arise. Governments need to know where they stand on such fundamental issues as the limits of their jurisdiction. Governments at the end of the Twentieth Century may still hesitate to submit their conduct to the test of third-party settlement, but they want rules upon which to base their conduct.

The approach to the definition of the appropriate rules depends fundamentally upon the legal culture of the states involved. The U.S., being committed to a functionalist and policy-oriented view of the basis of law, quite naturally adopts a broad extraterritorial position which is not simply explained by the fact that this position suits its political and economic interests. The U.S. espouses a functional approach as a result of its prevailing legal culture, which is based on federalism, the interaction of state laws, the great complexity of jural relations in the U.S., all tempered by a policy-oriented concept of law itself. It is not by chance that the European state which displays the greatest tendency to resort to extraterritorial measures is the Federal Republic of Germany, itself a federal state with a long history of the interplay of different legal systems of each principality and the overplay of Roman Law on customary law. Nor is it surprising that the European entity which makes greatest use of extraterritoriality in the field of competition law is the E.C., itself the amalgam of the legal orders of its member states. At the opposite end of the spectrum is the U.K. which, despite its potential as a multi-jurisdictional state, has chosen to ignore this important aspect of its personality, and in its essentially common law inspired public law, stresses the undesirability of mixing legal orders by the extraterritorial extension of laws. Despite the presence of Scotland in the U.K., English public law stresses the unity of the judiciary and through the judiciary, the unity of the legal order itself. For this reason of legal culture the U.K. government has consistently taken the view that no foreign laws should be applied to persons or acts in the U.K.without the consent of the U.K. government. The fundamental stance of the other governments of Europe is also territorialist. The occasional variation from this stance can also be ascribed to the differing legal cultures of each country.

The most difficult stance to explain is probably that of Canada, given that there are a number of similarities between the legal cultures of Canada and the U.S. However, there are a number of subtle and important differences which do explain the position of Canada. The first is the heritage of British public law. Many of the fundamental principles of public law governing territory and the exercise of jurisdiction over territory have been received from the U.K. by way of common law or constitutional statutes. The Canadian approach to many issues of international law and in particular fundamental principles of public and private law governing jurisdiction have also been received from the U.K. Beyond this, the prevailing legal culture of Canada, both of civil and common law, has been positivist for a large part of the Twentieth Century. Until recently the Canadian legal system has restricted its borrowing in this Century to the British common law and the French civil law. It is only in the last decades that Canada has been ready to accept the policy-oriented approaches to the law of the U.S. Despite ever-increasing integration with the U.S. on the economic front, Canada has sought to maintain its integrity and stress its differences with the U.S. One very important aspect of this effort to protect its autonomy and integrity has been the stress laid by successive generations of public lawyers and successive Canadian governments on the preservation of the territorial and political integrity of the country. They have been spurred on in this effort by the fundamental economic and political vulnerability of Canada beside its great neighbour. Canada has been uniquely vulnerable and for this reason has been uniquely vigilant with respect to extraterritoriality.

But if Canada has been vigilant it has also had to make compromises. Throughout the years Canada has been faced with the dilemma of maintaining a close and valued economic association with the U.S., while at the same time seeking to maintain its political independence and the integrity of its international personality in the world. This effort has not been easy. The Government of Canada has had to learn to choose its moment carefully so that its declarations of principle should have maximum effect. It has not always been easy to maintain continuity and the pressure to tolerate quietly rather than put valuable business relationships at risk has often been great. The Canadian experience illustrates a dilemma facing the European governments whose practice is reviewed in Chapter VII. In the same way, albeit to a lesser extent, these governments have also had to make their calculus of principle and tolerance. Doubtless the easiest situations to judge have been those where extraterritorial orders from abroad had the effect of restraining production or sales which were already planned. But in some cases a judgment has had to be made essentially on matters of principle with a view to protecting the very concept of sovereignty. These are the most difficult cases to call. The Canadian government appears to react with particular vigour when such situations assume a high public profile. If there is a uniform criterion of selection it would appear that the Government of Canada, while not seeking confrontation, does not wish to appear to be seen backing off from the defense of Canada's sovereignty.

B. Relevance of Legal Categories

Many authors cited in this book and a number of diplomatic notes appear to presume that jurisdiction at international law is based upon a number of established legal categories. The first categories mentioned are territory and nationality; they are followed by the categories discussed in Chapter II such as the protective principle, the active and passive personality principles and the effects doctrine to name those most generally cited. The *Third Restatement* while using these categories as part of its analysis also uses the distinction between jurisdiction to prescribe, to adjudicate and to enforce in a variety of circumstances throughout the text. These categories are clearly of great utility as aids to analysis, but do they reflect international practice and in the final analysis are they part of the corpus of international law?

On the basis of the practice reviewed it is clear that these categories are widely used in diplomatic correspondence. Such categories serve to refine the analysis of complex factual situations and assist in determining how the basic principles of law operate in different contexts. In this sense they are invaluable. But having said this, it is difficult to maintain that they are all clearly defined and widely accepted rules of international law. There is too much disagreement on the content and scope of these principles to allow the conclusion that they are all rules of jurisdiction in themselves. One need only cite the instinctive reaction of Canada and of many other states against the extension of U.S. laws to foreign subsidiaries of U.S. corporations to illustrate the point. The concepts of territorial sovereignty, and to a lesser degree, sovereignty over nationals meet the test of acceptance of rules of international law, but even here there is disagreement as to the content and scope of the rules.

Having said this, with respect to export controls it is necessary to accept that international law and state practice make an important distinction between prescription and enforcement. Control over territory, as well as the principles of nationality, protection (national security) and the related effects doctrine, are used to justify a wide range of prescriptive measures, some of which may well come into conflict with the laws and policies of other states. Thus, international law does not prohibit the U.S. from threatening sanctions within its territory against its nationals who violate export licenses abroad or from requiring its nationals not to trade with certain foreign firms or states. Given the importance of the U.S. economy, the threat of sanctions within the U.S. for actions abroad by U.S. nationals can be a heavy one. But provided the measures adopted by the U.S. apply within its territory, they are perfectly legitimate, whatever their direct or indirect effects may be abroad. Similarly where there is a close link, as manifested by a significant governmental interest, between the state and the person, organization or action regulated, a measure of extraterritorial prescriptive jurisdiction is permissible. To have enforcement jurisdiction a state must also have such prescriptive jurisdiction.

The line must be drawn between the threat of action within the U.S. for acts accomplished abroad over which the U.S. has prescriptive jurisdiction and legislation bearing directly upon the disposition of goods abroad where generally the U.S. does not have prescriptive jurisdiction. Laws in respect of business transactions and the disposition of goods wholly accomplished outside the U.S. violate international law in that they seek to prescribe rules of conduct which fall wholly within the jurisdiction of foreign states. By so legislating, the U.S. supplants the legitimate and exclusive control each state exercises over activities within its territory.

The significance of the distinction between prescription and enforcement is thus very great. A state may go a long way in prescribing conduct abroad, particularly if it is involved in a host of international business transactions via its citizens and multinational companies as is the U.S. But a state cannot purport to enforce these measures by punitive actions when the individuals, goods or transactions are out of its territory and beyond its reach. Enforcement is essentially a territorially- based phenomenon. Thus, while state practice reveals a variety of approaches to prescription, there is a far greater degree of unanimity against the enforcement of extraterritorial export controls.

With respect to prescription, the most troublesome area is nationality. On its face, a law which prohibits in advance U.S. nationals abroad, on penalty of sanction within the U.S., from trading with a particular foreign company or state would seem to be acceptable under international law. In such a case, however, there is potential conflict with foreign laws or policies which may require commission of the acts prohibited by U.S. laws. Where the line must be drawn is with respect to laws, administrative action and judgments requiring U.S. nationals to violate foreign law and policy in given cases. The U.S. national who knowingly braves the threat of sanction in the U.S., by breaking U.S. law abroad, is free to take his own risks upon return to the U.S. If he does not wish to do so he can refrain from such types of conduct. But where U.S. law reaches out and requires that certain transactions not be made in foreign states in specific cases, using as vehicles U.S. nationals, corporations, corporate subsidiaries or controlled corporations, it exceeds the limits of both prescriptive and enforcement jurisdiction.

The only exceptions to this rule revealed by state practice which prohibits enforcement of extraterritorial export controls are those situations where good neighbourhood, and the impracticality of policing private conduct, make it unwise or impossible to stop certain forms of extraterritorial extension of laws. Even here, the position, in principle, against such actions has generally been communicated to the U.S. Government by Canada and other foreign states.

C. What is the U.S. Position?

The best indicator of the U.S. position appears to be the legislative record. Review of legislation and regulations provides a degree of continuity and certainty to what is otherwise often a confusing and multifaceted phenomenon.

The legislative record reveals a willingness to apply U.S. laws abroad to a very wide range of situations and for this purpose to define the concept of "U.S. person" very broadly. The scope of the reach of the legislation changes from one law or regulation to another. The fundamental criterion appears to be the degree of the intensity of the U.S. governmental interest in ensuring the full and effective enforcement of the law or regulation in question. The highest degree of intensity is that of military security and arms control. Here the extraterritorial reach is most sweeping in terms of prescription and in terms of the means adopted to enforce sanctions. With respect to controls adopted for economic security or for foreign policy reasons there is a wider array of internal legislative controls and the extraterritorial scope of specific regulations often varies considerably.

Underlying the U.S. legislative record appear to be certain fundamental assumptions of international law. The basic assumption appears to be that international law does not specifically prohibit the extraterritorial application of export controls. This circumstance implies a general freedom to act on the part of states. Where there is no prohibition there is a presumption of freedom. The next basic assumption is that of governmental interest as a basis of action. The existence of a governmental interest constitutes a justification for acting extraterritorially: the interest is the foundation of jurisdiction. Military or economic security constitute interests as do the domestic effects of foreign actions upon the U.S. economy or upon U.S. citizens. In the final analysis the existence of a strong legislative policy appears to constitute an interest justifying extraterritorial action.

There is no doubt that multilateral or bilateral agreement greatly facilitates the process of justification of extraterritorial application of laws. Such prior agreement assists in justifying measures of extraterritorial enforcement or adjudication and the U.S. administration is often at pains to demonstrate the existence of such agreement. Similarly, wherever appropriate, such measures are based on the enforcement of universally accepted standards of human rights.

The U.S. willingness to countenance extraterritorial application of its export control laws, when there exists a strong policy interest, is remarkably consistent. The one important exception is the case of the extraterritorial extension to the U.S. of the Arab boycott of Israel. In this case many of the arguments used by the U.S. Administration and in debates in Congress resemble strangely those of other governments contesting the legality of U.S. extraterritorial measures. Two explanations are possible. In the first place, it may be too much to expect the totality of U.S. interests to go the same way. Consistency is the bugbear of small minds. More serious is the fact the U.S. refusal to countenance the extension of the Arab boycott of Israel and of persons of Jewish extraction reflects fundamental values of domestic and international human rights to which the U.S. is committed.

If the U.S. is right in maintaining that there is no prohibitory rule then, as is argued by the U.S., the many examples of extraterritorial extension of U.S. export controls by legislative, executive and judicial action are justifiable under international law. Similarly, should the various heads of jurisdiction argued by the U.S. – nationality principle, effects doctrine, protective principle – cover the various types of export controls, then again their extraterritorial extension is justifiable under international law.

Based on the review of the law and the state practice set out above, the answer to these questions must be in the negative. However powerful the state asserting a position and however strongly the position is argued, one state cannot make international law. In the case of export controls one is constantly struck by the loneliness of the U.S. position. Proponents of the U.S. position have skilfully broken the debate into many fragments. They have sought to show the contradictions in the positions of others by pointing to practice in other areas of law and they have sought to wrap the U.S. in the cloak of multilateral or bilateral agreement on the substantive rules. But on the basic issue of principle, as to whether the various forms of extraterritorial jurisdiction asserted by the U.S. are justified by international law, the U.S. stands alone. The rules of international law governing territory and governing the duty of non-intervention in the affairs of a foreign state act as a break upon the extraterritorial extension of U.S. export controls. The positions of Canada and the European states reviewed amply bear this out.

In the field of export controls, one justification advanced by the protagonists of the U.S. position is that of the U.S. role as guarantor of the military security of its allies and major trading partners. This goes to the most potent justification, national security, a manifestation of the protective principle. The allies of the U.S. have met this concern by participating in CoCom and enforcing the CoCom prohibitions. It is also with respect to the control of the export and re-export of armaments that there is the least protest of U.S. extraterritorial controls. While there may be a degree of tolerance here, there is no evidence of an acceptance in principle of the legality of all forms of U.S. extraterritorial controls and their enforcement in general, and still less so when such controls are imposed in specific cases for foreign policy reasons. CoCom involves prior multilateral agreement of lists of specific strategic goods, but is based upon national enforcement of multilaterally coordinated measures. CoCom is not a justification of U.S. unilateralism, quite the contrary.

The other great argument advanced by the protagonists of the U.S. position is essentially one based upon modern conceptions of functionalism. In other words, because the international economy is highly interdependent and is characterized by effective systems of transportation and commerce and is dominated by multinational and global corporations whose allegiance to any one state is very much in doubt, states must be free to exercise jurisdiction in function of world trading patterns regardless of national frontiers. U.S. lawyers trained in a functionalist, if not instrumentalist, legal culture often have trouble understanding how foreign lawyers can reject this functionally-based view of the legitimacy of extraterritoriality, especially when the same foreign lawyers have recourse to functionalism when it suits their interests, such as with the law of the sea for example. No state appears to have a monopoly on self-interest or logical consistency. What is evident, is that the review of the law and state practice does not support the U.S. functionalist view of extraterritoriality.

D. What is the Canadian Position?

The position of the Government of Canada can be discerned from analysis of a variety of the sources reviewed in this book. The picture which emerges is at once clear and shaded. Clear because Canada has been consistent in its approach, shaded because at various moments in its history Canada has made certain compromises for a variety of policy reasons and not least out of a desire to keep harmonious commercial relations with the U.S.

In the first place, a review of the legislative record reveals that Canada has not opted for a system of extraterritorial export controls. Canada's basic approach has been to legislate with respect to acts in Canada; no attempt has been made to apply Canadian laws to the acts of Canadians or of Canadian companies abroad simply by virtue of their nationality. Instead, Canada has sought to deal with the problem of diversion to undesirable destinations by multilateral agreement and by restraining the original export. As a matter of general policy, the Government of Canada has taken the position that persons and products are subject to the laws of the place where they are. This was stated with particular clarity in the House of Commons on July 10, 1958, when the Minister of Finance stated that "the only law that is binding upon Canadians when in Canada or corporations that are doing business in Canada ... is Canadian law."[1]

The response to the unilateral extension of U.S. export controls has been particularly clear. The Government of Canada has publicly and privately made known its opposition to the extraterritorial extension of U.S. export controls as they have been developed since the Second World War. On a number of important occasions the Government of Canada has intervened to secure the withdrawal of U.S. orders affecting products or proposed transactions involving Canadian products. Thus the Government of Canada has long been on record as objecting to the extension of U.S. export controls to Canada through the vehicle of subsidiaries or controlled corporations.[2] Successive Canadian guidelines have stressed the illegitimacy of pressure being brought to bear by parent companies on their Canadian subsidiaries to follow U.S. export controls with respect to their production in Canada.[3] Similarly the Government of Canada has long objected to the application of U.S. export controls to U.S. nationals in their capacity as directors of Canadian corporations.[4] For the same reason Canada has taken the position that U.S. laws do not follow U.S. origin goods; once they have entered Canada they are in principle subject to Canadian laws governing their disposition and eventual re-export. The Government of Canada takes the position that a product made in Canada from goods sourced abroad is a Canadian product for the purposes of the eventual disposition of that final product.[5] The Government of Canada is also firmly of the view that goods made outside the U.S. under a U.S. origin license are subject to the laws of the country where they are made.[6] The Government has also objected to attempts by officials of the U.S. Government to contact or visit Canadian companies without prior Canadian authorization, with a view to securing compliance with extraterritorial export controls.[7] Finally, Canada has even objected to the extraterritorial aspects of the U.S. anti-boycott legislation, itself designed to counteract the extraterritorial Arab boycott of Israel.[8]

Chapter V reviews a number of specific incidents, some well-known others less so, in which the Government of Canada intervened with the U.S. Administration and with the Canadian corporations involved to ensure that a proposed contract go forward and that the threat of sanctions under U.S. export controls be withdrawn. From time to time, there have been working arrangements with U.S. Administrations to deal with problems as they arose,[9] although these arrangements have tended to fall into desuetude as the intensity of the original crisis faded. In essence, the Government of Canada has sought to protect Canadian sovereignty by objecting to unilateral extensions of U.S. export controls to Canada regardless of the form of the extension. To back up this position the Parliament of Canada has recently adopted the *Foreign Extraterritorial Measures Act*,[10] a law similar to many others now in existence which empowers the Government of Canada to intervene in situations where the U.S. seeks to extend its export controls to Canada. The signature of the *Canada-U.S.A. Free Trade Agreement* in 1988 has not changed this position of principle.

Canada has on occasion adopted extraterritorial export controls. It would appear that such controls existed during the Second World War with a view to promoting the war effort. Apart from this case based on military necessity, Canada has only legislated extraterritorial export controls when they had a multilateral basis. This was most evident with respect to the *Rhodesia Regulations*[11] which were based on mandatory United Nations sanctions. The situation is somewhat similar with respect to the sanctions which have been taken against South Africa. Here the legal basis is provided by United Nations resolutions condemning apartheid and the very strong international and domestic policies against officially imposed racial segregation. The basis of the Canadian legislation against Iran in the wake of the hostage-taking crisis was that of a serious and universally condemned breach of international law.[12] What emerges from this practice is a commitment to the principle of a multilateral basis to legitimize extraterritorial export controls in all circumstances, with the possible exception of military necessity.

If Canada's reaction in principle to U.S. extraterritorial export controls has been unequivocal, it has in practice been prepared to make certain accommodations. The first accommodations involve parallel action to that of the U.S. The second form of accommodations involve a measure of replacement of U.S. extraterritorial rules by Canadian measures.

In the case of the U.S. sanctions against China, Cuba, Libya, Poland, Afghanistan, the USSR, Uganda and Nicaragua, reviewed in Chapter V, Canada has always objected to their extraterritorial extension. However, while insisting on its right to make an independent judgment of the necessity for any such international sanctions, on a number of occasions Canada has been prepared to impose its own territorially-based sanctions as a gesture of solidarity with the U.S. Administration.

Doing so implied no acceptance by the Government of Canada of the extraterritorial features of the U.S. laws and regulations in question, but by acting in concert with the U.S. the threat of extraterritoriality was somewhat alleviated.

The second and more complex situation involves the insertion in the Canadian Export Control List in 1973 of Item 9001 (now Item 5400)[13] which specifically required an export permit for the re-export from Canada of all goods of U.S. origin. In doing this the Government of Canada sent a strong signal to the U.S. Administration that Canada would not be used as a back door to allow illegal exports from the U.S. Canada thus ensured that the U.S. border would remain largely open to the movement of goods from the U.S. and that Canadian businesses would be able to be operated on a closely integrated basis with their American counterparts and that they would be viewed with a greater measure of trust by U.S. export control officials. This step inevitably involved Canadian officials in a closer degree of cooperation with U.S. export control authorities than might otherwise have been the case. For this approach to work it has been necessary to build up a system of cooperation and trust between the two administrations. To a very large degree Canadian officials have to defer to U.S. views. This was exemplified by the refusal of an export permit by Canada in 1982 to a U.S. subsidiary for the export of U.S. origin goods destined for the Siberian gas pipeline, despite the Canadian position of neutrality on the issue.[14]

Where difficulties inevitably have arisen is with respect to the determination of precisely when U.S. origin components included in a Canadian product cease to be subject to U.S. extraterritorial controls and can be exported from Canada as Canadian products. As reviewed in Chapter V, the Canadian position has always been that this was solely a Canadian decision.[15] In practice a measure of negotiation and mutual accommodation has always been necessary in such cases.

Canada has thus consistently maintained that many aspects of U.S. extraterritorial export controls violate Canadian sovereignty and hence violate international law. But can it be said that Canada rejects the legitimacy of any recourse to extraterritorial measures? It would seem not. The Government of Canada spelled out its position fairly explicitly in a series of speeches and diplomatic notes during the 1980s. In a major address in 1982, the Canadian Ambassador to the U.S. stated that in the Canadian view territory and nationality no longer provided the exclusive basis of international jurisdiction, while in the same speech noting that extraterritoriality "almost always engages the sovereign interest of another state."[16] The position of the Government of Canada stresses respect for sovereignty and rejects most of the techniques of extraterritorial application of export controls adopted by the U.S. and stresses the need to take into account the interests and policies of other states. Extraterritorial measures must be based on "self-restraint and non-interference".[17] In a diplomatic note in 1983 Canada suggested that most of the problems of extraterritoriality would disappear if states restricted the adoption of extraterritorial measures to areas where they would be prepared to accept such measures applied to themselves.[18] It would seem that the Golden Rule is of universal application. In recent years, as revealed in Chapter IV, Canada has stressed the commitment to diplomacy to resolve the problems arising from conflicting policies on extraterritoriality. To this end Canada has sought to build up a network of arrangements to ensure prior consultation on such questions. It would seem to be the view of the Government of Canada that there now exists a duty of consultation and Canada is working towards the consecration of a duty of prior notification. Until such time as all difference as to the substantive rules can be removed Canada is working towards a process-oriented solution.

E. Has Canada Compromised its Sovereignty?

Canada is more highly integrated into the economy of its neighbour than any other important economy in the world, with the possible exception of the Benelux countries. Over 26% of Canada's GNP is exported to the U.S. There is considerable Canadian investment in the U.S. and more U.S. investment in Canada. U.S. multinationals and their subsidiaries control large sectors and have played and continue to play a major and vital part in the development of the Canadian economy. Exchange controls have not existed between the two since the end of the Second World War. Movement across the border is a mere formality for citizens of both countries and immigration, although restricted, is still common. Since January 1, 1989 Canada and the U.S. have been linked by the *Canada-U.S.A Free Trade Agreement*.

Critics in Canada have suggested that the costs of this situation outweigh the undoubted advantages. Particularly in the realm of foreign investment, they suggest that the price is too high and that Canada has suffered a serious diminution of its national sovereignty. The same question can be raised with respect to the extraterritorial application of U.S. export controls. Setting aside the more general argument that no state can claim complete sovereignty in the highly interdependent world of the late Twentieth Century and that a middle power like Canada cannot claim the same degree of sovereign independence as a superpower or a state possessed of nuclear weapons, can it be said that by its actions, the Canadian government has diminished Canadian sovereignty by not taking what steps it could to counter the application of U.S. export controls in Canada ?

The basic issue appears to be one of tolerance. To what degree has Canada tolerated the application of U.S. export controls in its territory? To what extent can Canada be said, by its practice, to have given credit to the U.S. assertions that its extraterritorial export controls were applied in conformity with international law, thereby contributing to the development of state practice favourable to such extensions?

The close economic ties joining Canada and the U.S. have already been noted. The political ties are, if anything, even closer. Air defense is fully integrated in NORAD; defense production is fully integrated; Canada is a NATO member; a host of other bilateral ties of a political nature unite the two states. Beyond this there exists a deep bond of sympathy between the two peoples on questions of political and cultural life, which in many ways transcend the differences of policy commanded by national interest and outlook. The U.S. is, in every sense, Canada's closest ally and this situation does not appear likely to change. This does not mean that important differences in outlook on foreign policy may not exist but it does imply that Canada is unlikely to take steps which openly challenge the vital interests and policies of the U.S. "Bon Voisinage" and a calculus of Canada's own national interest suggest that differences of outlook and policy be treated in a manner which reflects these basic facts.

All this has not led Canada to tolerate the strong U.S. policy in favour of extraterritorial export controls to the detriment of Canadian sovereignty. A review of the law and Canadian state practice reveals that Canada has not adopted extraterritorial export controls itself, except in wartime, and with broad international support, and that, within the constraints of the Canada-U.S. relationship, Canada has been careful to avoid compromising its position of principle.

The record reveals that Canada is opposed in principle to many forms of extraterritorial prescription and to most forms of extraterritorial enforcement. The exceptions made by Canada can be shown to involve bilateral agreement, assistance on an administrative basis, or action based on multilateral agreements or universal jurisdiction created by international law. Canada has also shown a willingness to adopt adequate measures to deal with the problem of illegal re-exports through CoCom or through direct bilateral arrangements with the U.S. The contrast of the Canadian and U.S. practice in the field of export controls revealed by this study is striking. Where Canada has steadily refused to adopt any such extraterritorial export controls and has resolved problems of re-export by multilateral and bilateral agreements, the U.S. has shown an extraordinary degree of inventiveness in the range and complexity of the extraterritorial export controls that it has adopted. For two close allies the differences could hardly be more striking.

Where Canada is most open to the charge of tolerance and even acceptance is with respect to Section 5400 (previously 9001) of the Export Control List which requires a Canadian permit for the reexport of all U.S. origin goods, except those further processed in Canada. This measure involves not only the imposition of controls in Canada but active consultation with the U.S. on a daily basis and deferral to the U.S. export control authorities on their decision as to whether a Canadian permit should be issued or not when the request involves U.S. origin goods. In some measure Canada is enforcing U.S. controls. In response, it can be said that this is done by agreement, and that Canada itself imposes and enforces these controls. Canada could do otherwise on both counts. Furthermore, the alternative would be great hardship to importers and long delays in the importation of many commodities into Canada. Both Canadian and U.S. industry would suffer. To act in this way implies no acceptance of U.S. extraterritorial controls, since this could be done regardless of the extraterritorial reach of U.S. measures.

It can also be seen that on a number of occasions Canada has been forced to debate extraterritorial export controls on ground chosen by the U.S. Canada has thus often been on the defensive and has reacted to incidents provoked by the U.S. But again, how could this have been otherwise, given that Canada has no extraterritorial export controls, while the U.S. has many? The record shows that wherever the extraterritorial application of U.S. export controls have reached public notice, wherever the Canadian position has been openly challenged, successive Canadian governments have been quick to reiterate Canada's opposition to such measures and have taken steps to stop their imposition upon persons or companies doing business in Canada. Furthermore, since the advent of a more vigorous policy of extraterritoriality in Washington since 1980, the Canadian government and Canadian officials have not been content to express views on given incidents but have also on a number of occasions stated Canada's view on questions of general principle and the general rules of international law in a variety of official and unofficial contexts.

It may also be alleged, in support of the argument of Canadian tolerance, that the instances which come to public notice are only the tip of the iceberg and that, in fact, compliance with U.S. extraterritorial export controls by companies doing business in Canada is widespread. On the basis of observations made by the authors during the conduct of their research, this possibility cannot be ruled out. The precise degree of compliance in Canada cannot be calculated but there are certainly incidents which have not come to the attention of the public and others which have not come to the attention of the Canadian government. But in this, Canada is in exactly the same position as the countries of Europe reviewed here. From the standpoint of a company, U.S. extraterritorial export controls represent a bureaucratic hurdle to be overcome. It may often be preferable to comply with the demands of U.S. export control authorities than risk losing a contract. The vast majority of companies are sensitive to the national interest and comply with export controls conscientiously. It is the companies which are caught in the web of what the OECD terms "conflicting requirements". When a company is caught in the dilemma of respecting U.S. extraterritorial export controls, or not doing business, or risking future U.S. business because of a position of principle of their home government, many companies may well choose to comply quietly. It is difficult to blame them, given the alternative, which in many cases can be devastating.

In the Canadian case, in the face of the degree of integration of the Canadian and U.S. economies it is unthinkable that the Canadian government should destroy a mutually beneficial economic relationship by engaging in a witch-hunt against Canadian companies complying with U.S. controls and by engaging in a daily battle with the U.S. Administration. The cost would be too great for our government and the companies. The calculus of "Bon Voisinage" and self-interest commands that the Government of Canada choose the moments to make known its position of principle carefully. Too much is at stake for both countries to allow the issue of extraterritoriality to poison a basically sound relationship.

This being the case it is hard to escape the conclusion that the Government of Canada and officials charged with handling this issue over the years have done an excellent job of issue management by responding to major incidents which raised questions of principle and in general maintaining a credible international position in opposition to most forms of extraterritorial export controls.

F. Is it Possible to Define an International Rule?

On the basis of the practice reviewed, is it possible to define the international rules governing the extraterritorial application of export controls? It would appear that a cautiously positive answer is justified. The difficulty lies not so much in the absence or obscurity of the applicable general principles but rather from the highly situation-specific nature of the problem. The answer will often be ascertainable only when the facts of the particular case are fully known and when all the relevant variables can be weighed. However, despite this difficulty, the practice reviewed does provide guidance as to the applicable rules of international law. This Section outlines those forms of extraterritorial extension which appear to be unjustified on the basis of the practice reviewed and those areas where it may be justified.

1. Forms of Extraterritorial Application which Appear Difficult to Justify

Nationality clearly is a basis upon which a state may legitimately found jurisdiction. Under international law a state is authorized to create duties for its nationals which it would not be empowered to require of other physical persons. The duties flowing from citizenship can follow citizens when they leave national territory, as is also the case with respect to the concomitant power of protection of nationals abroad. However, this power is not unlimited. The power to regulate the acts of citizens abroad must be exercised in a manner which respects the authority of other states over persons who enter their territory. The duty which may be imposed upon a state's nationals to respect its export control laws must be framed in a way which reflects its legitimate prescriptive powers and must thus reflect the limits of its authority. In essence this implies limiting extraterritorial export controls over nationals to acts or effects on national territory. It is perfectly proper for a state to require that its nationals respect national export controls with respect to goods in the territory or with respect to the conditions of their export and to require that nationals do nothing in the territory which frustrates the conditions of export abroad. Any act abroad by a national which is designed to frustrate the conditions of export can also quite legitimately subject the national to enforcement and adjudication in the domestic courts.

Nationality ceases to be a legitimate basis for the extraterritorial application of export controls when it is used as a means of justifying a duty to perform acts in respect of exported goods when these goods have come under the authority of other states by virtue of their entering the territory of these states and thus being submitted solely to the laws of these states. A state may if it wishes continue to threaten its citizens with punishment for events occurring abroad, but they can do so with no legitimate expectation that their citizens will behave as required by such laws, since they and the goods will be subject to the laws of another state which will have the sole legitimate jurisdiction over the disposition of the goods in question. It is possible to argue that this is a case where prescriptive jurisdiction is unlimited but that enforcement and adjudicative jurisdiction is limited to situations where the citizen returns to the national territory. However, even this would overstate the case. The practice reviewed suggests that jurisdiction over nationals is in the final analysis limited by territorial jurisdiction. If, by exercising jurisdiction over its nationals abroad, a state genuinely seeks to have them perform acts abroad which would conflict with the laws of the state where the goods have been exported, the first state not simply involves its nationals in a conflict of loyalties, but also is attempting to prescribe conduct in respect of things now exported, in the territory of the second state, with respect to something it has no legitimate interest recognized by the international community. This is something which it has no authority to do.

The application of laws to corporations abroad on the basis of incorporation or domicile in the territory raises a number of serious difficulties. These difficulties go far beyond those inherent in determining which corporations are subject to the jurisdiction of a state or the basis of nationality in the age of the multinational and the global corporation. They are of the same order as those pertaining to physical citizens. As suggested above, nationality does not suffice to found jurisdiction over nationals in all circumstances. This is even more true of corporations, joint-ventures, partnerships or other forms of business associations. The mere fact of the original creation or the physical location of the direction of the enterprise is not recognized as an adequate basis for the control of all aspects of the business decisions of an enterprise. These decisions must be in conformity with the legislation applicable in the territory where they are taken. The practice reviewed does not allow the use of business enterprises as vehicles for imposing rules in conflict with those in force where the enterprise does its business. Again, business enterprises lay themselves open to a form of double jeopardy if they do not follow abroad the rules set for them by the laws of their home base. However, this fact gives no legitimacy to the attempt by the home state to influence business conduct abroad, except in the cases where this standard of behaviour reflects some universally-agreed international norm.

If it is inappropriate to use domestic business institutions as instruments of national policy by seeking to make them subject to domestic laws with respect to their business abroad, it is even more so with respect to the business done by subsidiary institutions. Apart from the fact set out above that such business activities are inherently subject to the laws of the foreign state where they are undertaken, subsidiary corporations and other business enterprises are normally the creation of the laws of that state and not of the state of the parent corporation. The state of the parent corporation has therefore even less colour of right to seek to apply its laws to the activities of subsidiaries. *A fortiori* the justification for the extraterritorial application of domestic export control laws to controlled foreign business institutions is even more tenuous.

The position outlined above is galling to those trained in the functionalist tradition. There is little doubt that subsidiaries and controlled corporations are often separate only in form from the parent and that their business activities are an extension of the activities of the parent. The answer to this lies in the painful necessity of controlling the parent corporation at source. If there is a real danger that the parent will use its subsidiaries and affiliates as vehicles for the illicit re-export of controlled products then such parents should not be permitted to possess, and still less to export, such products. To claim the right to lift the international corporate veil in this way is to claim the power to regulate the business activities of such institutions throughout the world. The U.S. would not tolerate other states to regulate business activities in the U.S. Why should it expect to do so abroad unchallenged?

Is it appropriate for export control laws to be applied abroad by attaching them to the goods exported? Can a supercomputer and all those who possess and operate it remain subject to the laws of the exporting state by virtue of their association with the machine? There can be no legal objection to the imposition of sanctions in the state of export or the future denial of business to persons who violate the original conditions of export of controlled products. Conditions of export freely assumed should be honoured and the exporting state is free to cut off foreigners from business dealings with its nationals at any time, subject to any GATT, other multilateral, or bilateral obligations. But this is a far cry from purporting to have export control laws follow the goods into the hands of any third party, wherever they may be and regardless of whether the goods remain in their original state or are incorporated into a new and different product. *A fortiori* the claim made by the U.S. during the Siberian Pipeline dispute[19] that U.S. export control laws could apply to goods made abroad under a licence originating in the U.S. is quite untenable, as was maintained by Canada and all of the European allies of the U.S.

The private international law issues raised by submission clauses are of the type best clarified and resolved by the courts. In practice the problems posed by submission clauses are unlikely to arise before the courts in Canada in light of the Canadian Government's commitment to control the re-export of goods of U.S. origin. In theory two factors are in conflict: one is the attempt to prescribe public policy in a foreign state by imposing conditions upon the export of products which may well violate the host state's public policy; the other is the right of any exporting state to set conditions upon the export of products from its territory. It is probable that if left to the courts the conflict of principles could be resolved on the basis of recognized principles of conflicts of laws. In this case it would seem appropriate to regard submission clauses which cover goods subject to multilateral export control commitments as enforceable, on the ground that public policy in the state imposing the clause as a condition of export and the public policy of the host state are in conformity. If however there is no identity of public policies, then the submission clause clearly is unenforceable in the host state and constitutes an unwarranted attempt to set public policy in a foreign jurisdiction.

The requirement that the importing company prove to the satisfaction of the U.S. export control authorities that its internal auditing procedures are of a sufficiently high standard appears to be a perfectly legitimate condition of exportation. What is unacceptable is the attempt to inspect these procedures *in situ*, whether by governmental officials or by private persons acting on behalf of the exporting government: any such attempt to perform inspections abroad without the express authorization of the host state is a violation of its sovereignty.

2. *Is the Extraterritorial Application of Export Control Laws Entirely Unjustified?*

While there is a strong prohibition against the extraterritorial enforcement of export controls, and while their extraterritorial prescription can only be partially justified, one cannot maintain that all forms of extraterritoriality are illegitimate under international law. This Section attempts to suggest certain examples of justifiable extraterritorial application and to explain why these exceptions to the general rule may exist.

Setting aside the examples of extraterritorial export controls justified by the link of nationality, which are enforced by sanctions within the prescribing state, what other examples of extraterritorial export controls can be distinguished? The only example which is likely to go unchallenged on the basis of the law and state practice studied is that of controls imposed during the course of a war. A state must, at international law, be given wide latitude in determining the measures it must take to protect its security. Beyond this the preservation of military secrets and the broadly accepted core of interests relating to military security (weapons, army organization and plans) in time of peace are unlikely to be challenged.

Once one goes beyond measures designed to protect national security, in the identifiable military sense, the possibility of justification becomes much less clear. It is admitted that the difference in risk between military and civilian technology is very unclear and the time lag between the incorporation of new technology into military systems is now much longer than civilian applications. But the record shows wide disagreement on the extent to which extraterritorial controls can be placed on new technologies simply because of an alleged military significance – immediate or potential. The record studied shows a willingness of the CoCom partners of the U.S. to submit some new technologies to multilateral controls, but no general willingness to accept unilaterally imposed extraterritorial controls on such items. Beyond this the record shows no acceptance of extraterritorial export controls to protect economic interests and still less to protect foreign policy concerns.

In short, some limited forms of extraterritorial prescription of export controls and much more limited forms of extraterritorial enforcement can be justified at international law. But this limited justification cannot be generalised to cover the whole range of measures and techniques employed by the U.S. Rather, this is an exception which proves the rule.

A number of disparate factors are invoked in justification of the extraterritorial extension of export controls. They are briefly reviewed here to show that they go to other issues and do not in fact prove the point they are alleged to support.

The first point often made is that even those states most opposed to extraterritoriality in principle can be shown to have resorted to it in certain cases. Apart from wartime measures, examples include laws governing piracy and slavery, nationality, counterfeiting, drug trafficking, aerial piracy, some forms of terrorism and in some cases crimes against humanity. In some jurisdictions the general rules of criminal law relating to conspiracies may have strong extraterritorial overtones.

To list these examples is to show that none of them, except possibly criminal law, relate directly to extraterritorial export controls and that most of them enjoy a broad acceptance in international law and state practice on a case by case basis.

A second major argument is based upon the fact that some justifications of extraterritorial actions, particularly the protective principle, which is related to the effects doctrine, national security and nationality, are widely accepted in other contexts as the basis for certain forms of extraterritorial action. Although still controversial with some states, the best example here appears to be the growing acceptance of very limited extraterritorial extension of competition legislation, and perhaps securities legislation, justified by an invocation of the effects doctrine. Again, to state specific examples is one thing but to generalize these examples into a principle applicable in all contexts is quite another. It does not appear on the basis of the law and the practice reviewed that this argument can be sustained. There may be a measure of interrelationship between the principles governing extraterritoriality in different spheres of activity, but it is dangerous to transpose these principles without taking into account the degree of agreement which may exist on underlying policies. Competition policy and export controls are very different phenomena. For example, there has been consensus at the U.N. on the *Set of Multilaterally Agreed Equitable Principles and Rules for the Control of Restrictive Business Practices*[20] although no similar international consensus in the export control area has been reached.

A third general example cited is the very fact of the existence of private international law rules of conflict which imply the recognition and enforcement of broad categories of foreign private law, particularly those relating to personal and corporate status and contract. But private international law is not an example of deliberate extension, quite the reverse. It involves the recognition and acceptance of foreign law, subject always to the supervision by domestic courts, the procedural law of the forum and doctrines of public policy.

A further complicating factor is that the positions of states, at least as to detail, differ widely on various aspects of extraterritoriality. Their views on certain rules and justifications may differ and generally their perception of the legal issues raised in different contexts are by no means as uniform as might be expected. Protagonists of the U.S. position have sought to use this discrepancy to prove the absence of a rule prohibiting the types of measures adopted by the U.S. and they have often been successful in luring their opponents into the quicksands of arguments dealing with exceptions and details rather than principle. The answer to this seems to be that, whatever differences exist on points of detail for reasons of legal culture and national interest, there is unanimity on the principle with respect to export controls. The principle runs against the U.S. interest and is revealed by the laws and the state practice reviewed above.

It must be admitted that there exists a measure of tolerance of certain forms of U.S. extraterritorial export controls, as shown by the review of state practice in Canada and Europe. This relates especially to certain areas of private corporate decision-making where policing would be both very difficult and in all probability unacceptable to the companies concerned. Does this imply acceptance of the general principle legitimising all forms of extraterritorial export controls? No, rather it involves a situation where practicality and, occasionally, political pressure make it impossible to plug every hole. At least as far as Canada is concerned the stated objectives of principle appear to cover these cases.

The functional justification, already discussed above, is a potent one and cannot be dismissed lightly. This is all the more so as extraterritorial measures have been included in export controls imposed as a result of Security Council mandatory sanctions and other widely agreed measures, such as those against Iran in 1982 during the hostage-taking crisis. The functional argument has to be admitted as a matter of practicality for a major state such as the U.S.; whether it is as strong for states with less economic power may well be doubted. But as a matter of law, as already stated above, in the absence of general agreement the functionalist position is not borne out by the state practice reviewed. The functional justification doubtless suits the U.S. interest, and it may well be that its rejection by other states also reflects a calculus of self-interest. No state has a monopoly on self-interest.

Finally we must admit that it is extremely difficult to draw neat conceptual lines between the many legal and factual categories which come together in the analysis of the extraterritorial application of export controls. The definition of extraterritorial measures is open to argument. The existence of a general rule or of specific categories of justification for their application to specific contexts is hotly debated. The nature of national security and the extent to which high technology goes to the security of a state is also much debated. The great debate continues between the proponents of security based on arms and the proponents of security based on peaceful trading relationships. The extent to which the rule of refusal to enforce foreign public law is still relevant to modern conditions and theories of law is also open to dispute, as is the relevance of the distinction between prescription and enforcement. But the complexity of the problem should not lead to abandonment of the attempt to analyse or to distinguish basic principles. The law and practice reviewed reveal, in the final analysis, the existence of fundamental principles which place limitations on the extraterritorial prescription of export controls and even more severe limitations on their extraterritorial enforcement and related adjudication.

3. The Rule Today

The conclusions of this book may not be entirely satisfying for any reader. The functionalist view which would justify the existing policies of the U.S. is not borne out by the state practice reviewed. Even in the U.S., the *Third Restatement* has deprived this position of some, but not all, of its legitimacy. At the other end of the spectrum the strict territorialist view is shown to be built upon shifting sands. The orthodoxy of a number of European states is subject to several exceptions and the E.C., the voice of the modern *Europa Economica*, is displaying distressing tendencies in favour of extraterritoriality with respect to competition policy. Even the Canadian reader, ever ready to defend national sovereignty, may be distressed to find that principle and tolerance live in sometimes uneasy coexistence. Wherever we turn there is some form of compromise, for it should not be forgotten that even the U.S. is often forced to compromise.

The closest approximation to a new international rule is found in the work of the Organization for Economic Cooperation and Development which proposes that in the face of conflicting national requirements, states act with moderation and restraint. This is a principle upon which more specific new rules could be built. It is unfortunate that in order to reconcile conflicting views of participating delegations much of this work has remained confidential to participants.

But in the final analysis there is a rule and it is a relatively simple one. In theory states are free to adopt extraterritorial export controls, but the moment these controls enter into conflict with the laws of a foreign state they cannot be enforced. Deference to the territorial sovereign is still the basic principle.

Notes

1. H.C. Debates, 1985, vol.II, July 10, 1958, p. 2090. See *supra*, Chapter V, Section C.1.
2. *Ibid.*
3. See *supra*, Chapter V, notes 435 and 522.
4. *Supra*, Chapter 5, note 505.
5. *Supra*, Note No. 591, November 21, 1977, cited in Chapter V, note 339.
6. See *supra*, Chapter V, notes 223 and 224.
7. See *supra*, Chapter V, note 546.
8. See *supra*, Chapter V, note 338.
9. Such as the Diefenbaker-Eisenhower joint-communiqué of 1958, see *supra*, Chapter V, note 405.
10. S.C. 1984, c.49.
11. See *supra*, Chapter V, Section A, 1, (a).
12. See *supra*, Chapter V, Section A, 1, (b).
13. Reviewed in Chapter III, *supra*, n.131 and Chapter IV, *supra*, note 113.
14. See *supra*, Chapter V, note 251.
15. See *supra*, Chapter V, note 342.
16. See *supra*, Chapter IV, note 130.
17. See *supra*, Chapter IV, note 136.
18. See *supra*, Chapter IV, note 144.
19. See *supra*, Chapter V, Section 2 (a) (ii).
20. UN Doc. TD/RBP/Conf./10 (1980).

INDEX